Java 17 Recipes

A Problem-Solution Approach

Fourth Edition

Josh Juneau
Luciano Manelli

Apress®

Java 17 Recipes: A Problem-Solution Approach

Josh Juneau
Hinckley, IL, USA

Luciano Manelli
TARANTO, Taranto, Italy

ISBN-13 (pbk): 978-1-4842-7962-5
https://doi.org/10.1007/978-1-4842-7963-2

ISBN-13 (electronic): 978-1-4842-7963-2

Managing Director, Apress Media LLC: Welmoed Spahr
Acquisitions Editor: Steve Anglin
Development Editor: James Markham
Coordinating Editor: Mark Powers
Copyeditor: Kim Burton

Cover designed by eStudioCalamar

Cover image by Sama Hosseini on Unsplash (www.unsplash.com)

Distributed to the book trade worldwide by Apress Media, LLC, 1 New York Plaza, New York, NY 10004, U.S.A. Phone 1-800-SPRINGER, fax (201) 348-4505, e-mail orders-ny@springer-sbm.com, or visit www. springeronline.com. Apress Media, LLC is a California LLC and the sole member (owner) is Springer Science + Business Media Finance Inc (SSBM Finance Inc). SSBM Finance Inc is a **Delaware** corporation.

For information on translations, please e-mail booktranslations@springernature.com; for reprint, paperback, or audio rights, please e-mail bookpermissions@springernature.com.

Apress titles may be purchased in bulk for academic, corporate, or promotional use. eBook versions and licenses are also available for most titles. For more information, reference our Print and eBook Bulk Sales web page at http://www.apress.com/bulk-sales.

Any source code or other supplementary material referenced by the author in this book is available to readers on GitHub (https://github.com/Apress). For more detailed information, please visit http://www.apress.com/source-code.

Printed on acid-free paper

This book is dedicated to my wife and children.
—Josh Juneau

To my daughter, Sara
To my son, Marco
To my mum, Anna
Everyone must always follow their dreams and fight for them.
—Luciano Manelli

Table of Contents

About the Authors

 **Josh Juneau** has been developing software and enterprise applications since the early days of Java EE. Application development and database development have been his focus since the start of his career. He became an Oracle database administrator and adopted the PL/SQL language for performing administrative tasks and developing applications for the Oracle database. In an effort to build more complex solutions, he began to incorporate Java into his PL/SQL applications and later developed stand-alone and web applications with Java. Josh wrote his early Java web applications utilizing JDBC and servlets or JSP to work with back-end databases. Later, he incorporated frameworks into his enterprise solutions, such as Java EE and JBoss Seam. Today, he primarily develops enterprise web solutions utilizing Java EE and other technologies. He also includes alternative languages, such as Jython and Groovy, for some of his projects.

Over the years, Josh has dabbled in many different programming languages, including alternative languages for Java Virtual Machine (JVM), in particular. In 2006, Josh began devoting time to the Jython Project as editor and publisher of the *Jython Monthly* newsletter. In late 2008, he began a podcast dedicated to the Jython programming language. Josh was the lead author of *The Definitive Guide to Jython* (Apress, 2010), *Oracle PL/SQL Recipes* (Apress, 2010), and *Java 7 Recipes* (Apress, 2011), and the solo author of *Java EE 7 Recipes* (Apress, 2013), and *Introducing Java EE 7* (Apress, 2013). He works as an application developer and system analyst at Fermi National Accelerator Laboratory, and he also writes technical articles for Oracle and OTN. He was a member of the JSR 372 and JSR 378 expert groups and is an active member of the Java Community, helping to lead the Chicago Java User Group's Adopt-a-JSR effort.

When not coding or writing, Josh enjoys spending time with his wonderful wife and five children, especially swimming, fishing, playing ball, and watching movies. To hear more from Josh, follow his blog at `http://jj-blogger.blogspot.com`. You can also follow him on Twitter at `@javajuneau`.

ABOUT THE AUTHORS

 **Luciano Manelli** was born in Taranto, Italy, where he currently resides with his family. He graduated with a degree in electronic engineering from the Polytechnic of Bari, and then he served as an officer in the Italian Navy. In 2012, he earned a PhD in computer science from the University of Bari Aldo Moro. His PhD focused on grid computing and formal methods, and he published the results in international publications. He is a professionally certified engineer and an innovation manager. In 2014, he began working for the Port Network Authority of the Ionian Sea—Port of Taranto, after working for 13 years for InfoCamere SCpA as a software developer. He has worked mainly in the design, analysis, and development of large software systems, research and development, testing, and production with roles of increasing responsibility in several areas over the years. Luciano has developed a great capability to make decisions in a technical and business context and is mainly interested in project management and business process management. He deals with port community systems and digital innovation in his current position.

Additionally, he has written several IT books and is a contract professor at the Polytechnic of Bari. You can find out more on his LinkedIn page at `it.linkedin.com/in/lucianomanelli`.

About the Technical Reviewer

Manuel Jordan Elera is an autodidactic developer and researcher who enjoys learning new technologies for his own experiments and creating new integrations. Manuel won the Springy Award 2013 Community Champion and Spring Champion. In his little free time, he reads the Bible and composes music on his guitar. Manuel is known as dr_pompeii. He has tech-reviewed numerous books, including *Pro Spring MVC with Webflux* (Apress, 2020), *Pro Spring Boot 2* (Apress, 2019), *Rapid Java Persistence and Microservices* (Apress, 2019), *Java Language Features* (Apress, 2018), *Spring Boot 2 Recipes* (Apress, 2018), and *Java APIs, Extensions and Libraries* (Apress, 2018). You can read his detailed tutorials on Spring technologies and contact him through his blog at www.manueljordanelera.blogspot.com. You can follow Manuel on his Twitter account, @dr_pompeii.

Introduction

This book teaches you many features of the Java programming language, from those introduced in Java 1.0 to those that made their way to Java 17. Released in September 2021, the Java Development Kit (JDK) 17 is a long-term support (LTS) release (i.e., a stable release supported for several years). Java is backward compatible. Even if a new Java version is released every six months, you do not need to learn a specific version. Rather, you need to get a good foundation in all language features to use them in your applications. Since the last edition of this book, many enhancements have occurred. This book includes new recipes covering features from Java 9 to Java 17. The recipes you implement always use open source tools, such as OpenJDK and Eclipse.

This book covers the fundamentals of Java development, such as installing the JDK, writing classes, and running applications. It delves into essential topics such as the development of object-oriented constructs, exception handling, unit testing, and localization. This book can be used as a guide for solving problems that ordinary Java developers may encounter at some point, as a starting point for anyone beginning the study of Java for the first time, or for developers who have used the Java language for some time to refine Java development skills. It will also be useful to help advanced Java application developers to learn a thing or two regarding the language's new features and perhaps even stumble upon some techniques that were not used in the past. This book discusses a broad range of topics, and the solutions to the problems covered are concise. Whatever your skill level, this book is good to have close at hand as a reference for solutions to those problems that you encounter in your daily programming.

The Java programming language was introduced in 1995 by Sun Microsystems. Derived from languages such as C and C++, Java was designed to be more intuitive and easier to use than older languages, specifically due to its simplistic object model and automated facilities such as memory management. At the time, Java drew the interest of developers because of its object-oriented, concurrent architecture, excellent security and scalability, and applications developed in the Java language could run on any operating system that contained a JVM. Since its inception, Java has been described as a language that allows developers to "write once, run everywhere" as code is compiled into class files that contain bytecode. The resulting class files can run on any compliant

JVM. This concept made Java an immediate success for desktop development, which later branched off into different technological solutions over the years, such as web-based applications. Today, Java is deployed on a broad range of devices, including mobile phones, printers, medical devices, and so on.

The Java platform consists of a hierarchy of components, starting with the JDK, which is composed of the Java Runtime Environment (JRE), the Java programming language, and platform tools that are necessary to develop and run Java applications. The JRE contains the JVM, plus the Java application programming interfaces (APIs) and libraries that assist in developing Java applications. The JVM is the base upon which compiled Java class files run and is responsible for interpreting compiled Java classes and executing the code. Every operating system capable of running Java code has its own version of the JVM. To that end, the JRE must be installed on any system running local Java desktop or stand-alone Java applications. But there is no problem because JRE implementations are provided for most major operating systems. Each operating system can have its own flavor of the JRE. For instance, mobile devices can run a scaled-down version of the full JRE optimized to run Java Mobile Edition (ME) and Java SE embedded applications. The Java platform APIs and libraries are a collection of predefined classes used by all Java applications. Any application that runs on the JVM makes uses the Java platform APIs and libraries. This allows applications to use the predefined and loaded functionality into the JVM and leaves developers with more time to worry about the details of their specific application. The classes that comprise the Java platform APIs and libraries allow Java applications to use one set of classes to communicate with the underlying operating system. As such, the Java platform takes care of interpreting the set of instructions provided by a Java application into operating system commands that are required for the machine on which the application is being executed. This creates a facade for Java developers to write code against to develop applications that can be written once and run on every machine that contains a relevant JVM.

The JVM and the Java platform APIs and libraries play key roles in the life cycle of every Java application. Entire books have been written to explore the platform and JVM. This book focuses on the Java language, which is used to develop Java applications, although the JVM and Java platform APIs and libraries are referenced as needed. The Java language is a robust, secure, and modern object-oriented language that can develop applications to run on the JVM. The Java programming language has been refined over several iterations, and it becomes more powerful, secure, and modern with each new release.

This book's official reference is OpenJDK, an open source implementation of Java Platform, Standard Edition (Java SE). For the recipes, you use Eclipse, an open source Java integrated development environment (IDE) for developing software applications with various plug-ins for C/C++, JavaScript, PHP, HTML5, Python and Java programming languages.

We hope that you enjoy reading this book.

Who This Book Is For

This book is intended for anyone interested in learning the Java programming language and/or who already knows the language, but would like some information regarding Java features even if they have no experience with algorithms. Those who have not yet programmed in the Java language can read this book, and will allow them to get up and running quickly. Intermediate and advanced Java developers looking to update their arsenal with the latest features that Java makes available to them can also read the book to update and refresh their skill set. There is, of course, a myriad of other essential topics that will be useful to Java developers of any type.

How This Book Is Structured

This book is structured such that it does not have to be read from cover to cover. It is structured so that developers can choose which topics they wish to read about and jump right to them. Each recipe contains a problem to solve, one or more solutions to solve that problem, and an explanation of how the solution works. The book is designed to allow developers to quickly get a solution up and running so that they can be home in time for dinner.

Source Code

You can access the source code for this book at `github.com/apress/java17-recipes`.

CHAPTER 1

Getting Started with Java 17

This chapter presents a handful of recipes to help programmers who are new to the Java language and those with experience in other languages become accustomed to Java 17. You learn to install Java and configure an integrated development environment (IDE) from which you develop applications and experiment with the solutions provided in this book. For security reasons, we don't recommend installing something unless absolutely necessary. With no alternative, it is easier and safer to download a compressed version and run the relevant scripts for the respective operating system. You should be able to adapt our instructions to install in the future any latest versions and releases of all the packages mentioned in the book without any problem. You learn the basics of Java, such as creating a class and accepting keyboard input. Documentation is often overlooked, but you also quickly learn how to create great documentation for your Java code in this chapter.

Note   *Java 17 Recipes* is not intended as a complete tutorial. Rather, it covers key concepts of the Java language. If you are truly new to Java, you may want to pick up *Java 17 for Absolute Beginners* by Iuliana Cosmina (Apress, 2022).

1-1. Installing Java

Problem

You want to install Java and experiment with the language.

© Josh Juneau, Luciano Manelli 2022
J. Juneau and L. Manelli, *Java 17 Recipes*, https://doi.org/10.1007/978-1-4842-7963-2_1

Solution

Install Java Development Kit 17 (JDK), which provides the language and a compiler.

Nothing runs without Java. The runtime environment (JRE) lets you execute Java. The JDK lets you compile Java sources into executable classes. There are two main distributions: Oracle JDK and OpenJDK. We chose the second one under the GNU General Public License because the Oracle JDK license changed for releases starting in April 2019, permitting only certain uses at no cost. However, you can download the commercial builds of JDK from Oracle under a non-open-source license at the Oracle Technology Network.

Download the OpenJDK release for your platform from `https://jdk.java.net/17/`, shown in Figure 1-1 and extract the archive file on your PC.

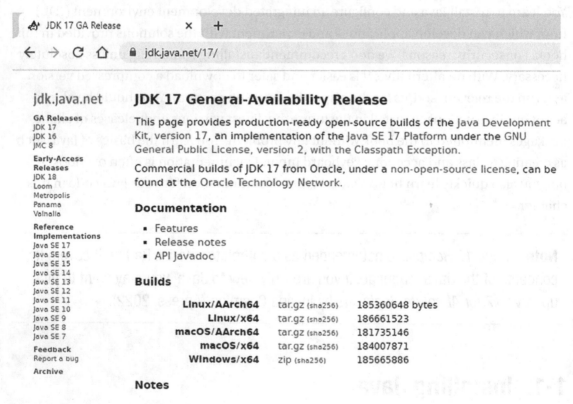

Figure 1-1. *OpenJDK 17 home page*

How It Works

Java is a trademark owned by the Oracle Corporation. The language itself is open source, and its evolution is controlled by the Java Community Process (JCP). You can read about it at www.jcp.org/en/home/index. While Oracle Corporation does not own the language, its core development tends to be steered by that company. It is Oracle Corporation that runs the JCP and owns the jcp.org domain.

The Java home folder has the bin subfolder that help you to develop and execute programs in Java language (with tools and utilities) and that supports the execution of programs written in the Java programming language (with an implementation of the Java Runtime Environment (JRE), class libraries, and other files). Since Java 11, Oracle and the OpenJDK team decided to distribute only the JDK and stop duplicating some of the things in JDK in the JRE folder.

There are many editions of Java, such as the Mobile Edition (ME) (www.oracle.com/java/technologies/javameoverview.html) and the Enterprise Edition (EE) (www.oracle.com/it/java/technologies/java-ee-glance.html). Java SE is the Standard Edition and represents the heart of the language. We built the recipes in this book for Java SE programmers. Those interested in developing embedded applications for devices may be interested in learning more about Java ME. Similarly, those interested in developing web applications and working with enterprise solutions may be interested in learning more about Java EE.

OpenJDK and Oracle JDK binaries are compatible and close to each other, but there are some differences.

- Oracle JDK source code includes the following text: "ORACLE PROPRIETARY/CONFIDENTIAL. Use is subject to license terms." The OpenJDK refers to the GPL license terms.

- The output of Java the version in Oracle JDK includes the Oracle-specific identifier. OpenJDK does not include the Oracle-specific identifier.

- Oracle JDK uses the Java Cryptography Extension (JCE) Code Signing Certificate. OpenJDK allows unsigned third-party crypto providers.

- OpenJDK is offered only as a compressed archive. Oracle JDK offers installers.

Go to www.oracle.com/java/technologies/javase/17-relnote-issues.html for more information on the Oracle JDK.

1-2. Configuring the PATH
Problem

You want to test the Java installation and compile Java from the command line.

Solution

Add the JDK path to the PATH environment variable. You should have the jdk-17 folder at the root of your OS drive or a custom location.

In Windows, search and for select the control panel. Click the Advanced System settings and then Environment Variables. In the System Variables section, find the PATH environment variable and select it. In the Edit System Variable field or the New System Variable field, insert the text **C:\jdk-17\bin;** in the field "Variable value". You can also set the JAVA_HOME with the value of C:\jdk-17 and, then, set in the Path the value %JAVA_HOME%\bin). The semicolon at the end of the text is essential because it separates the new path from the existing ones. Do not insert additional spaces before or after.

In Unix and Linux systems, you edit the environment file and modify the PATH variable. In this case, you execute a command such as the following.

```
export PATH=/usr/local/jdk-17/ /bin
```

At last, to find out if the path is properly set, open a command-line window, go to the command prompt, and type the following command.

java -version.

If you see a screen like the one shown in Figure 1-2, the correct Java version is installed.

Note   A *terminal* (or command prompt in Windows) is a command-line interface that allows you to control your operating system by using a command prompt.

```
C:\>java -version
openjdk version "17" 2021-09-14
OpenJDK Runtime Environment (build 17+35-2724)
OpenJDK 64-Bit Server VM (build 17+35-2724, mixed mode, sharing)
```

Figure 1-2. *Testing Java version*

How It Works

To compile and execute a Java program, you must add the JDK path to the PATH environment variable (a string of paths separated by semicolons in Windows and colons in Unix OS). All operating systems use the PATH environment variable to determine where executable files are located on your system to execute any stored or downloaded file on your personal computer. This variable tells the operating systems where the to-run programs reside when a user executes a file. The environment variables can also be stored information used by applications or operating systems.

PATH contains a string of directories separated by semicolons in Windows and colons in Unix OS. PATH is used because any executable file in the directories listed in PATH can be executed without specifying the full path to the file. This allows you to run those executables with only the file name from the command line or for other applications to run those executables without knowledge of their directory path.

So, when you execute a file, you need to specify the full path to that file, but if the command does not include the path, the OS uses the executable file that matches your file in the PATH.

1-3. Testing Java

Problem

You want to compile Java from the command line.

Solution

Use the little application shown in Listing 1-1. You can use a smart editor like Notepad++ or a different text editor in this example.

To create the source code for your first Java program, you must do the following.

1. Declare a class named Hello.

2. Declare public static void main(String args[]) or String... args as the main method.

3. Enter the System.out.println("Hello World") command to display "Hello World" in the command prompt window.

Listing 1-1. Hello.java

```
public class Hello {
    public static void main(String args[]){
        System.out.println("Hello World");
    }
}
```

Now, save the file as Hello.java in your working folder. Open the command window. After changing to your work directory, enter the following to compile the application.

```
javac Hello.java
```

It should return the prompt without saying anything. It also means that you have correctly updated the Path system variable. If you want to know more about what the javac compiler is doing, type -verbose between javac and the name of the file (javac -verbose Hello.java). You see a file named Hello.class in your work directory.

Enter the following in the command prompt to run the application (see Figure 1-3).

```
java Hello
```

```
C:\Users\lucky\OneDrive\Desktop>javac Hello.java

C:\Users\lucky\OneDrive\Desktop>java Hello
Hello World
```

Figure 1-3. *Testing a Java class*

Note   All the code described in this book is available for download from `github .com/apress/java17-recipes`. In this case, you can simply type the code; in others, you don't need to retype it. It is important that you improve your programming skills using the Eclipse Environment, which is a famous free and open source Java IDE, containing a workspace for developing applications, that you can download at `www.eclipse.org`. You can find the examples in folders with the same names as the corresponding chapters.

How It Works

Java is an object-oriented programming language based on classes and objects with attributes and methods. A class is necessary for creating objects. To create a Java program (i.e., a .class file), you must create a .java file. A .java file is a readable text file, while a .class file is a binary file, which is a file containing Java bytecode that can be executed on the Java Virtual Machine (JVM), and that is produced by a Java compiler from the .java file.

Tip   You must compile source code. Source code is kept in files with a `.java` suffix, so your operating system's file and directory path notation are appropriate. One executes a class. A class is an abstract concept in the language, so its dot-notation becomes appropriate (i.e., it is necessary to write a dot (.) after the name of the instance of a class followed by the method to be used). Keep this distinction in mind to help yourself remember when to use which notation.

The Main Program

The incantation `public static void main(...)` is used from within a public class to denote the entry point of a Java program. That declaration begins an executable method named `main`. You must specify one parameter that is an array of strings, and typically that parameter is defined as `String[] args`. When you execute the currently selected class, the JVM transfers control to the `main()` method, which makes a call to `System.out .println()` to show the Hello World message displayed in the command window.

1-4. Installing Eclipse

Problem

You want to install a reasonable IDE to use with it.

Solution

Install the Eclipse IDE to provide a more productive working environment.

First, you need to download the package. Go to www.eclipse.org/downloads/packages/ and click **Eclipse IDE for Java Developers**, as shown in Figure 1-4.

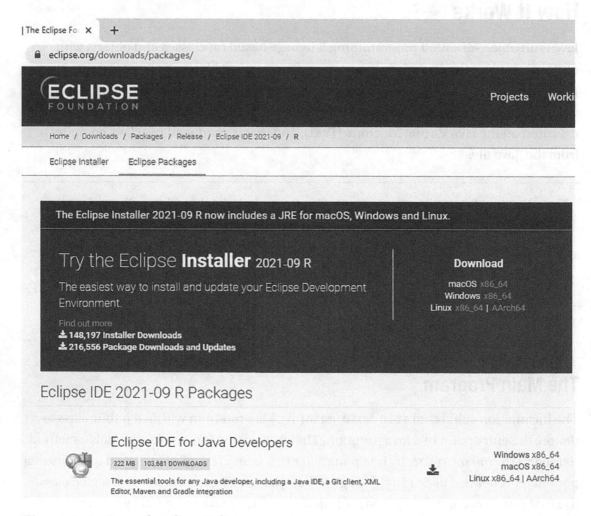

Figure 1-4. *Downloading Eclipse*

The website suggests a mirror site for the download. The installation of Eclipse is very easy: expand the downloaded file in the root of your personal computer. When you execute Eclipse, it asks you to select a workspace. The workspace is the folder where Eclipse stores your development projects. Therefore, it makes sense to place it on a drive or in a directory that you back up regularly. Before clicking the OK button, select the **Use this as the default and do not ask again** check box. It makes your life easier. You can choose the root and use the `eclipse-workspace` default folder, which is the user's home directory. The first time it executes, Eclipse displays a Welcome screen. To enter the screen where you do development, click the Workbench icon, as shown in Figure 1-5.

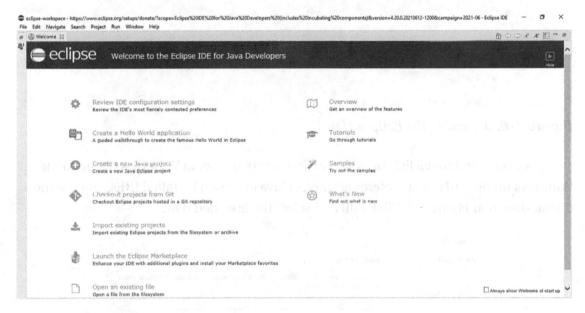

Figure 1-5. *Eclipse–the Welcome screen*

The IDE is ready. You should see a workspace resembling the one in Figure 1-6.

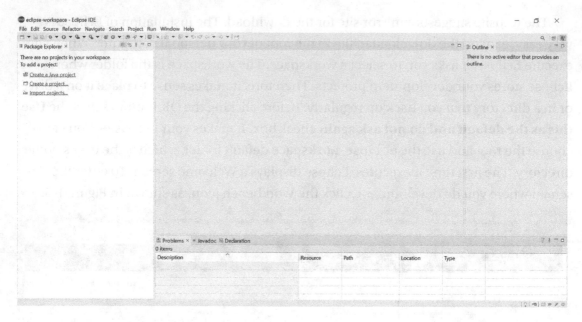

Figure 1-6. *Opening the Eclipse IDE*

Next, you need to tell Eclipse what version of JDK to use. In Windows OS, go to the Windows menu and select Preferences. Select Java and then Installed JREs. You see the dialog shown in Figure 1-7. Click Edit and select the installed JDK.

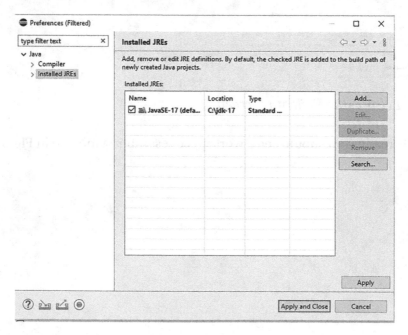

Figure 1-7. *Eclipse–JDK configuration*

You can verify that Eclipse uses the correct JDK. Go to Help ➤ About Eclipse IDE and click the Installation Detail button. You can see the path and the name of the installed and used JDK, as shown in Figure 1-8.

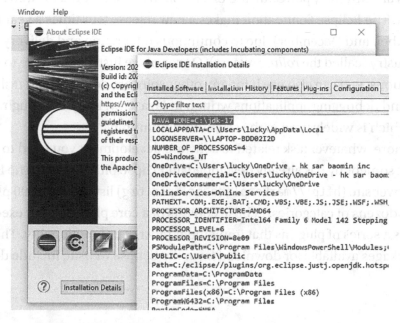

Figure 1-8. *Eclipse installation details*

How It Works

Although it's possible to build web applications by compiling Java modules from the command line, it's more efficient to use an IDE. This way, you can concentrate on the more creative part of developing software rather than fix inconsistency and fiddle with folder hierarchies.

An IDE integrates all the applications that you need to develop software—from a source editor and a compiler to tools to automate the application building process and a debugger—into a single application. When developing in Java or another object-oriented language, an IDE also includes tools to visualize class and object structure and inheritance and containment. Another advantage of using an IDE is that it propagates changes you make to individual modules. For example, if you rename a class, the IDE can automatically update its occurrences throughout your project files.

As the applications you develop become more complex, it makes more and more sense to use an IDE. That's why, before continuing to the next project, let's discuss how to install and configure Eclipse.

Eclipse is an extremely powerful and extensible IDE, well suited for web application development. The Eclipse Foundation makes a new release four times a year (in March, June, September, and December) due to continuous integration and delivery in the software industry (called the *rolling release*). Once you've installed Eclipse to develop your applications, you can also use it for any other software development task, such as developing and debugging applications written in Java, C++, Python through a plug-in, or Fortran, which is widely used in the scientific community.

Furthermore, whatever task related to software development you need to perform, it's likely that somebody has already developed an Eclipse plug-in for it. The Eclipse Marketplace website (`http://marketplace.eclipse.org`) lists about 2,000 plug-ins organized in dozens of categories. Eclipse consists of a core platform that executes plug-ins, plus a series of plug-ins that implement most of its functionality. Therefore, the standard packages available for download from the Eclipse website include dozens of plug-ins.

1-5. Getting to "Hello, World"
Problem

You've installed Java SE 17 and the Eclipse IDE. Now you want to run a simple Java program to verify that your installation is working properly.

Solution

Begin by opening the Eclipse IDE. You may see some projects in the left pane if you've already been working on projects within the IDE.

Go to the File menu and select New ➤ Java Project, as shown in Figure 1-9.

Figure 1-9. *Selecting Java project*

The dialog is shown in Figure 1-10.

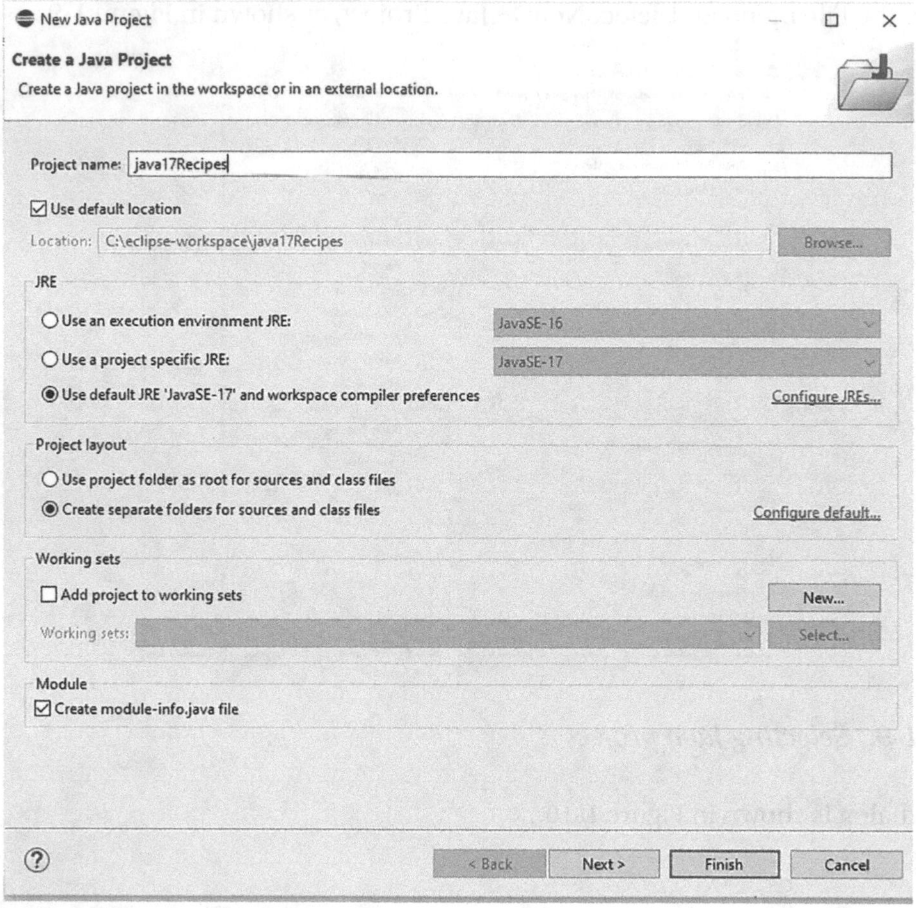

Figure 1-10. *Creating a new Java project*

Name your project **java17Recipes**. Enter the project name in the text box at the top of the dialog, as shown in Figure 1-10.

In the JRE section, select the installed JDK (i.e., the JavaSE-17 that you just configured). Press Finish to complete the wizard and create a skeleton project.

Tip   Java is case-sensitive. Moreover, by convention, project names should start with a lowercase letter.

Now, create a new package. Go to the File menu and select New ➤ Package, as shown in Figure 1-11.

Figure 1-11. *Creating a new package in Eclipse IDE*

Name the package org.java17recipes.chapter01.recipe01_05 as shown in Figure 1-12.

New Java Package	—	□	×

Java Package

Create a new Java package.

Creates folders corresponding to packages.

Source folder:	java17Recipes/src	Browse...
Name:	org.java17recipes.chapter01.recipe01_05	

☐ Create package-info.java

    ☐ Generate comments (configure templates and default value here)

(?)   **Finish**   Cancel

Figure 1-12. *Naming the package in Eclipse IDE*

Tip   By convention, package names usually start with a lowercase letter.

Next, create a new class. Go to the File menu, select New ➤ Class, and name the class HelloWorld, as shown in Figure 1-13.

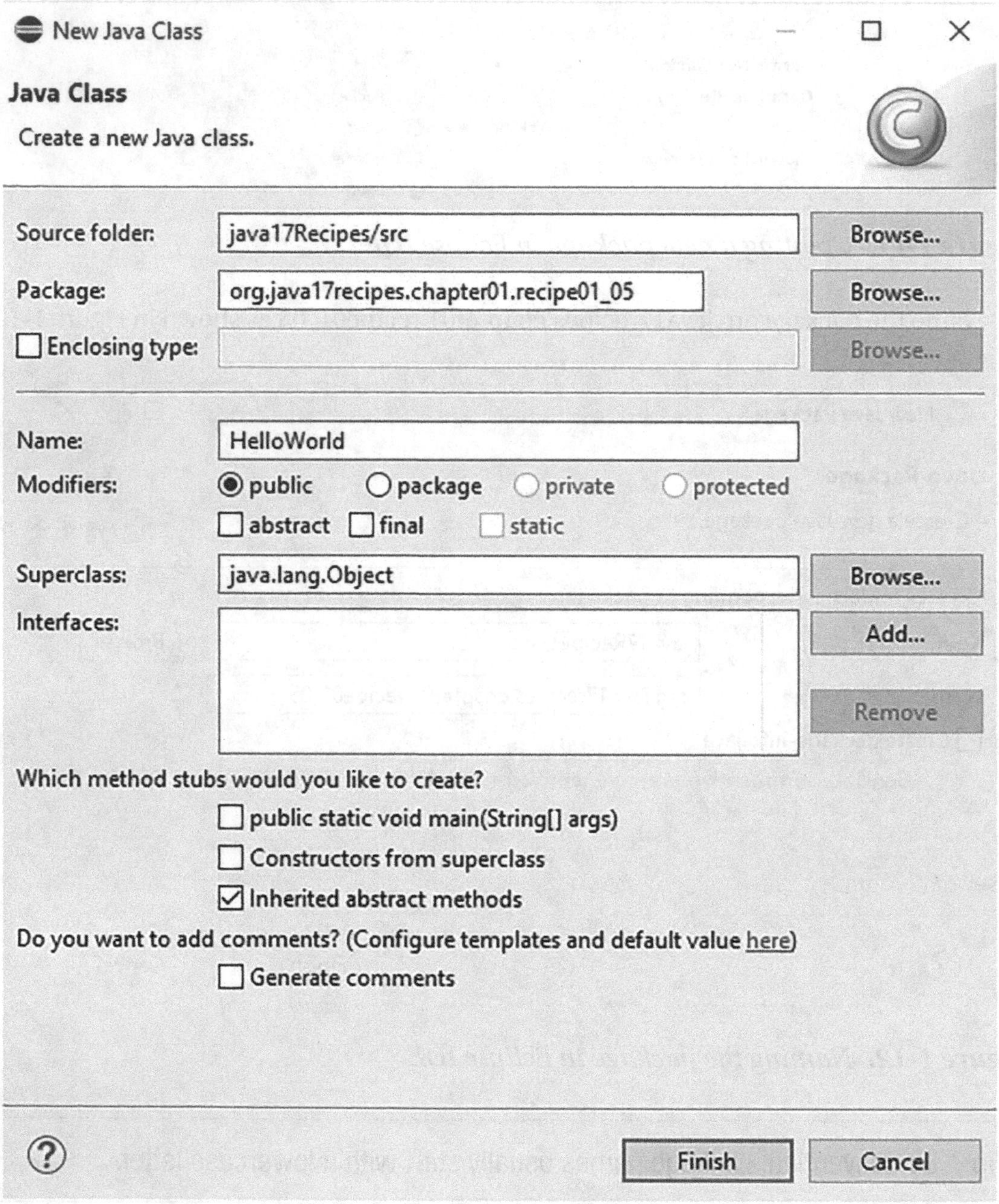

Figure 1-13. *Creating and naming a new class in Eclipse IDE*

Tip   You can create package and class in the same configuration window by simply creating a new class and typing package and class name in the Name field. Moreover, by convention, class names usually start with an uppercase letter.

Make sure that you enter the project name, the package name, and the class name exactly as we provide them here because the code to follow depends on your doing so. Make sure the project name is java17Recipes. Make sure the package is org.java17recipes.chapter01.recipe01_05. Make sure the class is HelloWorld.

Next, you should look at a Java source file. Skeleton code is generated for you, and your Eclipse IDE window should resemble the one shown in Figure 1-14.

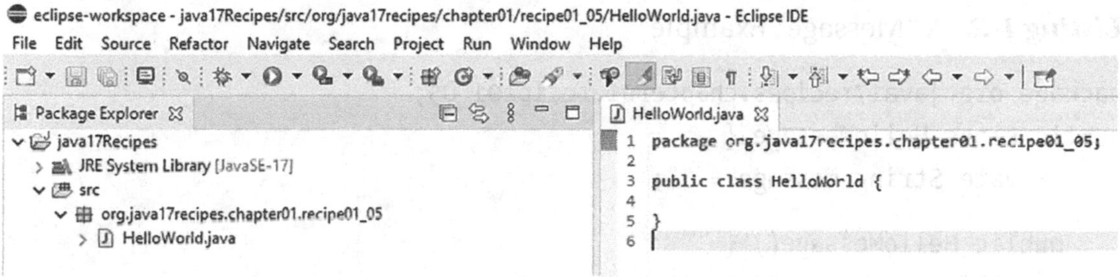

Figure 1-14. *Viewing the skeleton code generated by Eclipse*

Place your cursor anywhere in the source code pane. Press Ctrl+A to select all the skeleton code. Then press Delete to get rid of it. Replace the deleted code with that from Listing 1-2. Then, create another class, name it HelloMessage, and copy the code from Listing 1-3.

You can find the code in Listing 1-2 and Listing 1-3 as part of our example download for the book. There are two files named HelloMessage.java and HelloWorld.java, which reside in a Java package named org.java17recipes.chapter01.recipe01_05. Note that all recipe solutions of substance throughout this book are in that example download.

The class is named HelloWorld, and it initiates the program.

Listing 1-2. A "Hello, World" Example

```
package org.java17recipes.chapter01.recipe01_05;
public class HelloWorld {
    /* The main method begins in this class */
    public static void main(String[] args) {
```

```
        HelloMessage hm;
        hm = new HelloMessage();

        System.out.println(hm.getMessage());

        hm.setMessage("Hello, World");

        System.out.println(hm.getMessage());
    }
}
```

The second class, HelloMessage, is a container class that holds a string-based message.

Listing 1-3. A "Message" Example

```
package org.java17recipes.chapter01.recipe01_05;
public class HelloMessage {
    private String message = "";

    public HelloMessage() {
        this.message = "Default Message";
    }

    public void setMessage (String m) {
        this.message = m;
    }

    public String getMessage () {
        //it changes the message to uppercase
        return message.toUpperCase();
    }
}
```

Make sure you have pasted (or typed) the code. Compile and run the program. Right-click in the project and select Run As ➤ Java Application, as shown in Figure 1-15.

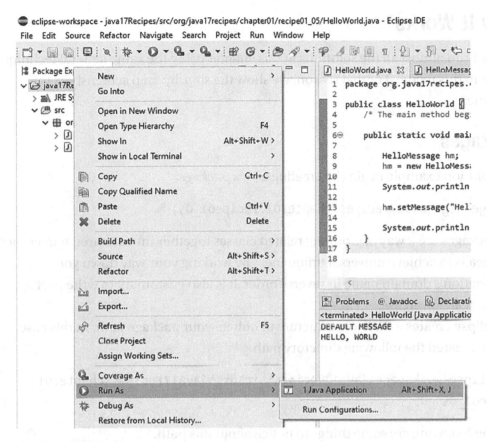

Figure 1-15. *Running a project in Eclipse IDE*

Now you should see the following output.

```
DEFAULT MESSAGE
HELLO, WORLD
```

This output appears in a new view named Console, which Eclipse opens at the bottom of the IDE window, as shown in Figure 1-16.

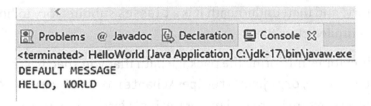

Figure 1-16. *Console view in Eclipse IDE*

How It Works

You can run almost all the solutions in this chapter using the same general technique shown in this recipe. For that reason, we show the step-by-step screenshots this one time.

Packages

The solution example begins by creating a Java *package*.

```
package org.java17recipes.chapter01.recipe01_05;
```

Packages are a way of grouping related classes together into a shared namespace. The idea is to achieve universal uniqueness by working your way down your organization's domain name in reverse order. It is also customary to write package names in all lowercase.

Eclipse creates a directory structure to imitate your package path. In this case, Eclipse created the following directory path.

```
C:\eclipse-workspace\java17Recipes\src\org\java17recipes\chapter01\
recipe01_05
```

The following are some things to notice about this path.

- The front part is C:\eclipse-workspace. Eclipse creates all projects under a workspace directory that you can change. Developers specify different paths.

- Next is the first occurrence of java17Recipes. This corresponds to the project name (see Figure 1-10).

- Any source files you create go into the src directory. Eclipse creates other directories at this level. For example, Eclipse creates a bin directory, and then underneath it is a classes subdirectory to hold your compiled class files.

- The directories mirroring the package path that you specify are last, in this case, org\java17recipes\chapter01\recipe01_05. An identical structure is created under the bin\classes directory when you compile your code. Note that if using another IDE, you may see differences in the directories that are created.

You need to explicitly create a package. Organization and a judiciously chosen naming convention are important when developing any significant application.

JavaBeans-style Classes

Next in the solution example is a class definition following the JavaBeans pattern. The definition of `HelloMessage` follows a pattern that you often encounter in Java programming, and we include it for that reason. The class is simple, capable of holding a single string field named `message`.

Three methods are defined in the class.

- `HelloMessage()`. This method, also known as the constructor, is named the same as the class. In this case, it takes no arguments. It's automatically invoked whenever you create a new object of the class. Note that this is known as a no-arg or *no-argument* constructor because it is typed out within the class and takes no arguments. If you do not supply a constructor, the JVM supply a default constructor (also takes no arguments) automatically.

- `setMessage(String)`. This accessor method begins with the word `set`. It takes one parameter. It specifies the message to be returned by the corresponding get method.

- `getMessage()`. This accessor method returns the currently defined message. In this example, we chose to make the message uppercase.

Note   Accessor methods are used in JavaBeans classes to access any privately declared class members. In this case, the private variable identified as `message` can be accessed using these methods. Accessor methods are more commonly referred to as getters and setters.

Methods beginning with `set` and `get` are the *setter* and *getter* methods. The IDE generates these methods. The `message` variable is private to the class, which means you have no direct access to `message` from outside the class.

You see the `this` keyword used in the class. It is a special keyword in Java that references the current object. Its use is redundant but would be needed if any of the methods happened to create variables of their own that were also named `message`: the setter is mandatory due to the parameter name. It is common practice to use the this keyword to reference the class members from within the getter and setter methods, mostly for the latter.

It is common in Java to mediate access to class variables through setter and getter methods like in our example. Those methods represent a contract of sorts with other classes and your main program: public methods let the class state to be read or written, but the external code is unaware of the mapping. Their benefit is that you can change the storage implementation of HelloMessage however you like. It has its fields and state information saved and restored independently from the type of storage. The other code that depends on HelloMessage continues to work properly so long as you maintain the external behavior of setMessage() and getMessage().

The Main Program

When you execute the currently selected class, Eclipse compiles the code to a set of binary files and then transfers control to the main() method. Eclipse can also be configured to recompile on save, which would then cause the transfer of control to the main() method. That method, in turn, does the following.

1. Executes HelloMessage to create a variable named hm that can hold an instance of the HelloMessage class. The hm variable is null at this point.

2. Invokes new HelloMessage() to create an object of the class by that name. The no-argument constructor is executed, and "Default Message" is now set as the greeting text. The new object is now stored in the hm variable.

3. Makes a call to System.out.println() to show that the object's no-argument constructor has indeed executed as expected. The getter changes to uppercase the text and returns the value. The "DEFAULT MESSAGE" greeting is displayed in the Console pane.

4. Sets the message to be the traditional "Hello, World" text.

5. Makes another call to System.out.println() to output the new message that was just set. Now you see the greeting "HELLO, WORLD" added to the Console pane has become uppercase.

The pattern in the solution is common in Java programming. The main() method is where execution begins. Variables are defined, and objects are created using the new operator. Object variables are often set and retrieved using setter and getter methods.

1-6. Configuring the CLASSPATH

Problem

You want to execute a Java program or include an external Java library in the application you are executing.

Solution

Set the CLASSPATH variable equal to the directory location of the user-defined Java classes or Java Archive (JAR) files you need to have access to to execute your application. Let's say that you have a directory named JAVA_DEV located at the root of your OS drive, and all the files your applications need to access are located in this directory. If this is the case, you would execute a command such as the following.

```
set CLASSPATH=C:\JAVA_DEV\some-jar.jar
```

Use the following in Unix and Linux systems.

```
export CLASSPATH=/JAVA_DEV/some-jar.jar
```

Alternately, the javac command provides an option for specifying the location of resources to be loaded for an application. On all platforms, setting the CLASSPATH using this technique can be done via the -classpath option as follows.

```
javac -classpath /JAVA_DEV/some-jar.jar...
```

Of course, the file path uses the backslash (\) on Microsoft Windows machines.

Note   The javac -cp option may be used, rather than specifying the -classpath option.

How It Works

Java implements the concept of a *classpath*. This is a directory search path that you can specify system-wide using the CLASSPATH environment variable. You can also specify the classpath for a specific invocation of the JVM via the `java` command's `-classpath` option.

When executing Java programs, the JVM finds and loads classes as needed using the following search order.

1.   The classes that are fundamental to the Java platform and are contained in the Java installation directory

2.   Any packages or JAR files that are located within the extension directory of the JDK

3.   Packages, classes, JAR files, and libraries that are loaded somewhere on the specified classpath

You may need to access more than one directory or JAR file for an application. This could be the case if your dependencies are located in more than one location. To do so, simply use the delimiter for your operating system (a `;` for Windows and a `:` for Unix OS) as a separator between the locations specified by the CLASSPATH variable. The following is an example of specifying multiple JAR files in the CLASSPATH environment variable on Unix and Linux systems.

```
export CLASSPATH=/JAVA_DEV/some-jar.jar:/JAVA_LIB/myjar.jar
```

Alternatively, you can specify the classpath via a command-line option.

```
javac –classpath /JAVA_DEV/some-jar.jar:/JAVA_LIB/myjar.jar...
```

When loading the resources for a Java application, the JVM loads all the classes and packages specified in the first location, followed by the second, and so on. This is important because the order of loading may make a difference in some instances to avoid interfering with one another.

Note   JAR files package applications and Java libraries into a distributable format. If you have not packaged your application in that manner, you may simply specify the directory or directories in which your `.class` files reside.

Sometimes you want to include all JAR files within a specified directory. Do that by specifying the wildcard character (*) after the directory containing the files. The following is an example.

```
javac -classpath /JAVA_DEV/*:/JAVA_LIB/myjar.jar...
```

Specifying a wildcard tells the JVM that it should only load JAR files. It does not load class files located in a directory specified with the wildcard character. You need to specify a separate path entry for the same directory if you also want the class files. The following is an example.

```
javac -classpath /JAVA_DEV/*:/JAVA_DEV
```

Subdirectories within the classpath are not searched. To load files contained within subdirectories, those subdirectories and/or files must be explicitly listed in the classpath. However, Java packages that are equivalent to the subdirectory structure *are* loaded. Therefore, any Java classes that reside within a Java package that is equivalent to the subdirectory structure are loaded.

Note   It is a good idea to organize your code; it is also good to organize where you place your code on the computer. A good practice is to place all your Java projects within the same directory; it can become your workspace. Place all the Java libraries that are contained in JAR files into the same directory for easier management. You can also use tools like Maven and Gradle to organize your project.

1-7. Organizing Code with Packages

Problem

Your application consists of Java classes, interfaces, and other types. You want to organize these source files to make them easier to maintain and avoid potential class-naming conflicts.

Solution

Create Java packages and place source files within them. Java packages can organize logical groups of source files within an application. Packages can help organize code, reduce naming conflicts among different classes and other Java-type files, and provide access control. To create a package, simply create a directory within the root of your application source folder and name it. Packages are usually nested within each other and conform to a standard naming convention. For this recipe, assume that the organization is named JavaBook and makes widgets. To organize all the code for the widget application, create a group of nested packages conforming to the following directory structure.

```
/org/javabook
```

Any source files placed within a package must contain the package statement as the first line in the source. The package statement lists the name of the package in which the source file is contained. For instance, suppose that the main class for the widget application is named JavaBookWidgets.java. To place this class into a package named org.javabook, physically move the source file into a directory named javabook, which resides within the org directory, which resides within the root of the source folder for the application. The directory structure should look like the following.

```
/org/javabook/JavaBookWidgets.java
```

The source for JavaBookWidgets.java is as follows.

```java
package org.javabook;
/**
* The main class for the JavaBook Widgets application.
* @author
*/
public class JavaBookWidgets {
    public static void main(String[] args){
        System.out println("Welcome to my app!");
    }
}
```

The first line in the source contains the package statement, which lists the name of the package that the source file is located within. The entire package path is listed in the statement, and dots separate the names in the path.

Note   A package statement must be the first statement listed within the Java source. However, a comment or JavaDoc comment may be written before the package statement.

An application can consist of any number of packages. If the widget application contains a few classes representing widget objects, they could be placed within the org.javabook.widget package. The application may have interfaces that interact with the widget objects. In this case, a package named org.javabook.interfaces may also contain any such interfaces.

How It Works

Java packages are useful for organizing source files, controlling access to different classes, and ensuring that there are no naming conflicts. Packages are represented by a series of physical directories on a file system, and they can contain any number of Java source files. Each source file must contain a package statement before any other statements in the file. This package statement lists the name of the package in which the source file resides. The source included the following package statement in the solution to this recipe.

```
package org.javabook;
```

This package statement indicates that the source file resides within a directory named javabook, which resides within a directory named org. Package naming conventions can vary by company or organization. However, words must be in all lowercase so that they do not conflict with any Java class file names. Many companies or organizations use the reverse of their domain name for package naming. However, underscores should be used if a domain name includes hyphens.

Note   When a class resides within a Java package, it is no longer referenced by only the class name; instead, the package name is prepended to the class name, known as the *fully qualified* name. For instance, the class that resides within the file `JavaBookWidgets.java` is contained within the `org.javabook` package. The class is referenced using `org.javabook.JavaBookWidgets`, not simply `JavaBookWidgets`. An identically named class can reside within a different package (e.g., `org.java17recipes.JavaBookWidgets`).

Packages are very useful for establishing levels of security as well as organization. By default, different classes that reside within the same package have access to each other. If a source file resides within a package different from another file it needs to use, an `import` statement must be declared at the top of the source file (underneath the package statement) to import that other file. And the source file must declare the class/interface/ enum element type as **public**; otherwise, the fully qualified `package.class` name must be used within the code. Classes may be imported separately, as demonstrated in the following `import` statement.

```
import org.javabook.JavaBookWidgets;
```

However, it is often likely that all classes and type files that reside within a package need to be used. A single `import` statement utilizing a wildcard character (*) can import all files within a named package as follows.

```
import org.javabook.*;
```

Although it is possible to import all files, it is not recommended unless necessary. It is considered a poor programming practice to include many `import` statements that use the wildcard. Instead, classes and type files should be imported individually.

Organizing classes within packages can prove to be very helpful. Suppose that the widget application described in the solution to this recipe includes different Java classes for each widget object. Each widget class could be grouped into a single package named `org.javabook.widgets`. Similarly, each of the widgets could extend some Java type or interface. All such interfaces could be organized into a package named `org.javabook. interfaces`.

Any substantial Java application includes packages. Any Java library or application programming interface (API) that you use includes packages. When you import classes or types from those libraries and APIs, you are really importing packages.

1-8. Declaring Variables and Access Modifiers

Problem

You want to create some variables and manipulate data within your program. Furthermore, you wish to make some of the variables available to only the current class, whereas others should be available to all classes or only the other classes within the current package.

Solution

Java implements eight primitive data types. There is also special support for the `String` class type. Listing 1-4 shows an example declaration of each. Draw from the example to declare the variables needed in your own application.

Listing 1-4. Declarations for Primitive and String Types

```
package org.java17recipes.chapter01.recipe01_08;
public class DeclarationsExample {
    public static void main (String[] args) {
        boolean booleanVal = true;   /* Default is false */

        char charval = 'G';          /* Unicode UTF-16 */
        charval = '\u0490';          /* Ukrainian letter Ghe(Г) */

        byte byteval;       /*  8 bits, -127 to 127 */
        short shortval;     /* 16 bits, -32,768 to 32,768 */
        int intval;         /* 32 bits, -2147483648 to 2147483647 */
        long longval;       /* 64 bits, -(2^64) to 2^64 - 1 */

        float   floatval = 10.123456F;          /* 32-bit IEEE 754 */
        double doubleval = 10.12345678987654; /* 64-bit IEEE 754 */
```

```
        String message = "Darken the corner where you are!";
        message = message.replace("Darken", "Brighten");
    }
}
```

Note   If you're curious about the Ukrainian letter in Listing 1-4, it is the Cyrillic letter *Ghe with upturn*. You can read about its history at `http://en.wikipedia.org/wiki/Ghe_with_upturn`. You can find its code point value in the chart at `www.unicode.org/charts/PDF/U0400.pdf`. And the URL `www.unicode.org/charts/` is a good place to start whenever you need to find the code point corresponding to a given character.

Variables are subject to the concept of *visibility*. Those created in Listing 1-5 are visible from the main() method after being created, and they are deallocated when the main() method ends. They have no "life" beyond the main() method and are not accessible from outside of main().

Variables created at the class level are a different story. Such variables can be termed as *class fields or class members*, as in *fields or members of the class*. The use of a member can be restricted to objects of the class in which it is declared or to the package in which it is declared, or it can be accessed from any class in any package.

Listing 1-5. Visibility and the Concept of Fields

```
package org.java17recipes.chapter01.recipe01_08;

class TestClass {
    private long visibleOnlyInThisClass;
    double visibleFromEntirePackage;
    void setLong (long val) {
        visibleOnlyInThisClass = val;
    }
    long getLong () {
        return visibleOnlyInThisClass;
    }
}
```

```
public class VisibilityExample {
    public static void main(String[] args) {
        TestClass tc = new TestClass();
        tc.setLong(32768);
        tc.visibleFromEntirePackage = 3.1415926535;
        System.out.println(tc.getLong());
        System.out.println(tc.visibleFromEntirePackage);
    }
}
```

The following is the output.

```
32768
3.1415926535
```

Members are typically bound to an object of a class. Each class object contains an instance of each member in the class. However, you can also define *static* fields that occur only once and with a single value that is shared by all instances of the given class. Listing 1-6 illustrates the difference.

Listing 1-6. Static Fields

```
package org.java17recipes.chapter01.recipe01_08;
class StaticDemo {
    public static boolean oneValueForAllObjects = false;
}
public class StaticFieldsExample {
    public static void main (String[] args) {
        StaticDemo sd1 = new StaticDemo();
        StaticDemo sd2 = new StaticDemo();
        System.out.println(sd1.oneValueForAllObjects);
        System.out.println(sd2.oneValueForAllObjects);
        sd1.oneValueForAllObjects = true;
        System.out.println(sd1.oneValueForAllObjects);
        System.out.println(sd2.oneValueForAllObjects);
    }
}
```

Listing 1-6 produces the following output.

```
false
false
true
true
```

The field oneValueForAllObjects was set to true only for the class instance named sd1. Yet it is true, for instance, sd2 also. This is because of the keyword static used in declaring that field. Static fields occur one time for all objects of their class. Moreover, the compiler in the IDE raises a warning about that. In fact, it should be used through StaticDemo.oneValueForAllObjects.

How It Works

Listing 1-6 illustrates the basic format of a variable declaration.

```
type variable;
```

It's common to initialize variables when declaring them, so you often see the following.

```
type variable = initialValue;
```

Modifiers can precede field declarations. The following is an example.

```
public static variable = initialValue;
protected variable;
private variable;
```

It's common to put the visibility modifier—public, protected, or private—first, but you are free to list the modifiers in any order you like. By default, if no modifier has been specified, the class or member is made package-private, meaning that only other classes within the package have access to the member.

Note   If a class member is specified as protected, then it is also package-private, except that any subclass of its class in another package also has access.

The String type is special in Java. It's a class type, but syntactically you can treat it as a primitive type. Java automatically creates a String object whenever you enclose a string of characters within double quotes ("..."). You aren't required to invoke a constructor or specify the new keyword. Yet String is a class, and there are methods in that class that are available to you. One such method is the replace() method shown at the end of Listing 1-4.

Strings are composed of characters. Java's char type is a two-byte construct for storing a single character in Unicode's UTF-16 encoding. You can generate literals of the char type in two ways.

- If a character is easy to type, enclose it within single quotes (e.g., 'G').

- Otherwise, specify the four-digit UTF-16 *code point* value prefaced by \u (e.g., '\u0490').

Some Unicode code points require five digits. These cannot be represented in a single char value. See Chapter 12 if you need more information on Unicode and internationalization.

Avoid using any of the primitive types for monetary values. Especially avoid either of the floating-point types for that purpose. Refer instead to Chapter 12 and its recipe on using the Java Money API to calculate monetary amounts (Recipe 12-10). BigDecimal can also be useful anytime you need accurate, fixed-decimal arithmetic.

If you are new to Java, you may be unfamiliar with the String[] array notation, as demonstrated in the examples. Please see Chapter 7 for more information on arrays. It covers enumerations, arrays, and generic data types. Also in that chapter are examples showing how to write iterative code to work with collections of values such as an array.

1-9. Converting to and from a String

Problem

You have a value stored within a primitive data type, and you want to represent that value as a human-readable string. Or, you want to go in the other direction by converting a human-readable string into a primitive data type.

Solution

Follow one of the patterns from Listing 1-7. The listing shows the conversion from a string to a double-precision floating-point value and shows two methods for getting back to a string again.

Listing 1-7. General Pattern for String Conversions

```
package org.java17recipes.chapter01.recipe01_09;

public class StringConversion {

    public static void main (String[] args) {
        double pi;
        String strval;

        pi = Double.parseDouble("3.14");
        System.out.println(strval = String.valueOf(pi));
        System.out.println(Double.toString(pi));
    }
}
```
The output is 3.14.

How It Works

The solution illustrates some conversion patterns that work for all the primitive types. First, there is converting a floating-point number from its human-readable representation into the IEEE 754 format used by the Java language for floating-point arithmetic.

```
pi = Double.parseDouble("3.14");
```

Notice the pattern. You can replace Double with Float or Long, or whatever other type your target data type is. Each primitive type has a corresponding wrapper class by the same name but the initial letter is uppercase. The primitive type here is a double, and the corresponding wrapper is Double. The wrapper classes implement helper methods such as Double.parseDouble(), Long.parseLong(), Boolean.parseBoolean(), and so forth. These parse methods convert human-readable representations into values of the respective types.

Going the other way, it is often easiest to invoke `String.valueOf()`. The `String` class implements this method, which is overloaded for each of the primitive data types. Alternatively, the wrapper classes also implement `toString()` methods that you can invoke to convert values of the underlying type into their human-readable forms. It's your preference as to which approach to take.

Conversions targeting the numeric types require some exception handling to be practical. You generally need to gracefully accommodate a case in which a character-string value is expected to be a valid numeric representation, but it's not. Chapter 9 covers exception handling in detail, and the upcoming Recipe 1-10 provides a simple example to get you started.

Caution   Literals for the Boolean type are "`true`" and "`false`". They are case-sensitive. Any value other than these two is silently interpreted as false when converting from a string using the `Boolean parseBoolean()` conversion method.

1-10. Passing Arguments via Command-Line Execution

Problem

You want to pass values into a Java application invoked via the `java` utility command line.

Solution

Run the application using the `java` utility, and specify the arguments that you want to pass into it after the application name. If you're passing more than one argument, each should be separated by a space. For example, suppose you want to pass the arguments to the class created in Listing 1-8.

Listing 1-8. Example of Accessing Command-Line Arguments

```java
public class PassingArguments {
    public static void main(String[] args){
        if(args.length > 0){
            System.out.println("Arguments that were passed to the program: ");
            for (String arg:args){
                System.out.println(arg);
            }
        } else {
            System.out.println("No arguments passed to the program.");
        }
    }
}
```

First, make sure to compile the program so that you have a `.class` file to execute. You can do that via the `javac` utility at the command line or terminal.

Therefore, open a command prompt or a terminal window for compiling and executing your Java class. Now issue a `java` command to execute the class and type some arguments on the command line following the class name. The following example passes two arguments.

```
java PassingArguments Luciano Manelli
```

You should see the following output.

```
Luciano
Manelli
```

Spaces separate arguments. Enclose strings in double quotes when you want to pass an argument containing spaces or other special characters. The following is an example.

```
C:\Users\lucky\OneDrive\Desktop>java PassingArguments "Luciano Manelli"
```

The output now shows just one argument.

```
Arguments that were passed to the program:
Luciano Manelli
```

The double quotes translate the "Luciano Manelli" string into a single argument.

How It Works

All Java classes that are executable from the command line or terminal contain a `main()` method. If you look at the signature for the `main()` method, you can see that it accepts a `String[]` argument. In other words, you can pass an array of `String` objects into the `main()` method. Command-line interpreters such as the Windows command prompt and the various Linux and Unix shells build an array of strings out of your command-line arguments and pass that array to the `main()` method on your behalf.

The `main()` method in the example displays each passed argument. First, the length of the array named `args` is tested to see whether it is greater than zero. If it is, the method loop through each of the arguments in the array executes a `for` loop, displaying each argument along the way. If there are no arguments passed, the length of the `args` array is zero, and a message indicating this is printed; otherwise, you see a different message followed by a list of arguments.

Command-line interpreters recognize spaces and sometimes other characters as delimiters. It's generally safe to pass numeric values as arguments delimited by spaces without bothering to enclose each value within quotes. However, as shown in the final solution example, you should get into the habit of enclosing character-string arguments in double quotes. Do that to eliminate any ambiguity over where each argument begins and ends.

Note   Java sees all arguments as character strings. If you pass numeric values as parameters, they enter Java as character strings in human-readable form. You can convert them into their appropriate numeric types using the conversion methods shown in Recipe 1-9.

1-11. Accepting Input from the Keyboard
Problem

You are interested in writing a command-line or terminal application that accept user input from the keyboard.

Solution

Use the `java.io.BufferedReader` and `java.io.InputStreamReader` classes to read keyboard entry and store it into local variables. Listing 1-9 shows a program that keeps prompting for input until you enter some characters representing a valid value of type long.

Listing 1-9. Keyboard Input and Exception Handling

```
package org.java17recipes.chapter01.recipe01_11;
import java.io.*;
public class AcceptingInput {
    public static void main(String[] args){
        BufferedReader readIn = new BufferedReader(
                new InputStreamReader(System.in)
        );
        String numberAsString = "";
        long numberAsLong = 0;
        boolean numberIsValid = false;
        do {
            /* Ask the user for a number. */
            System.out.println("Please enter a number: ");
            try {
                numberAsString = readIn.readLine();
                System.out.println("You entered " + numberAsString);
            } catch (IOException ex){
                System.out.println(ex);
            }
            /* Convert the number into binary form. */
            try {
                numberAsLong = Long.parseLong(numberAsString);
                numberIsValid = true;
            } catch (NumberFormatException nfe) {
                System.out.println ("Not a number!");
            }
        } while (numberIsValid == false);
    }
}
```

The following is an example run of this program.

```
Please enter a number:
No
You entered No
Not a number!
Please enter a number:
Yes
You entered Yes
Not a number!
Please enter a number:
75
You entered 75
```

The first two inputs did not represent valid values in the long data type. The third value was valid, and the run ended.

How It Works

Quite often, our applications need to accept user input of some kind. Granted, most applications are not used from the command line or terminal nowadays, but having the ability to create an application that reads input from the command line or terminal helps lay a good foundation and may be useful in some applications or scripts. Terminal input can also be useful in developing administrative applications that you or a system administrator may use.

Two helper classes were used in the solution to this recipe. They are java.io.BufferedReader and java.io.InputStreamReader. The early portion of the code that uses those classes is especially important.

```
BufferedReader readIn = new BufferedReader(
        new InputStreamReader(System.in)
);
```

The innermost object in this statement is System.in. It represents the keyboard. You do not need to declare System.in. Java's runtime environment creates the object for you. It is simply available to be used.

System.in provides access to raw bytes of data from the input device, which is the keyboard in our example. The InputStreamReader class's job is to take those bytes and convert them into characters in your current character set. System.in is passed to the InputStreamReader() constructor to create an InputStreamReader object.

InputStreamReader knows about characters but not about lines. The BufferedReader class's job is to detect line breaks in the input stream and enable you to conveniently read a line at a time. BufferedReader also aids efficiency by allowing physical reads from the input device to be done in different-size chunks than when your application consumes the data. This aspect can make a difference when the input stream is a large file rather than the keyboard.

The following shows how the program in Listing 1-9 uses an instance (named readIn) of the BufferedReader class to read a line of input from the keyboard.

```
numberAsString = readIn.readLine();
```

Executing this statement triggers the following sequence.

1. System.in returns a sequence of bytes.

2. InputStreamReader converts those bytes into characters.

3. BufferedReader breaks the character stream into lines of input.

4. readLine() returns one line of input to the application.

I/O calls must be wrapped in try-catch blocks. These blocks catch any exceptions that may occur. The try part in the example fails if a conversion is unsuccessful. A failure prevents the numberIsValid flag from being set to true, which causes the do loop to make another iteration so that the user can try again at entering a valid value. To learn more about catching exceptions, please see Chapter 9.

The following statement at the top of Listing 1-9 deserves some attention.

```
import java.io.*;
```

This statement makes available the classes and methods defined in the java.io package. These include InputStreamReader and BufferedReader. Also included is the IOException class used in the first try-catch block. NumberFormatException (used in the second try-catch block) belongs to the java.lang package.

1-12. Documenting Your Code

Problem

You want to document some of your Java classes to assist in future maintenance.

Solution

Use JavaDoc to place comments before any package, class, method, or field that you want to document. To begin such a comment, write the characters /**. Then begin each subsequent line with an asterisk (*). Lastly, close the comment with the characters */ on a line by themselves at the end. Listing 1-10 shows a method commented with JavaDoc.

Listing 1-10. Comments Made in JavaDoc Form

```
package org.java17recipes.chapter01.recipe01_12;
import java.math.BigInteger;
public class JavadocExample {
    /**
     * Accepts an unlimited number of values and
     * returns the sum.
     *
     * @param nums Must be an array of BigInteger values.
     * @return Sum of all numbers in the array.
     */
    public static BigInteger addNumbers(BigInteger[] nums) {
        BigInteger result = new BigInteger("0");
        for (BigInteger num:nums){
            result = result.add(num);
        }
        return result;
    }
    /**
     * Test the addNumbers method.
     * @param args not used
     */
```

```
public static void main (String[] args) {
    BigInteger[] someValues = {BigInteger.TEN, BigInteger.ONE};
    System.out.println(addNumbers(someValues));
}
}
```

Comments can be added to the beginning of the package, classes, and fields in the same way. The comments are helpful to you and other programmers maintaining the code, and their specific format enables the easy generation of an HTML reference to your code.

Generate the HTML reference by invoking the JavaDoc tool. This command-line tool parses a named Java source file and formulates HTML documentation based on the defined class elements and JavaDoc comments. The following is an example.

```
javadoc JavadocExample.java
```

This command produces several HTML files containing the documentation for the package, class, methods, and fields. If no JavaDoc comments exist within the source, some default documentation is still produced. To view the documentation, load the following file into your browser.

```
index.html
```

The file is in the same directory as the class or package you are documenting. There is also an `index-all.html` file giving a strict alphabetical listing of documented entities.

Keep in mind that the same rules apply when using the JavaDoc tool as when using `javac`. You must reside within the same directory as the source file or prepend the file's name with the path to where the file is located.

The output is shown in Figure 1-17.

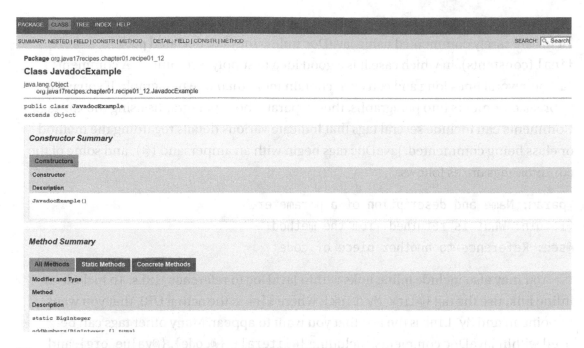

Figure 1-17. *JavaDoc example in Eclipse IDE*

How It Works

Generating documentation for applications from scratch can be quite tedious. Maintaining documentation can be even more troublesome. The JDK comes packaged with an extensive system for documentation known as JavaDoc. Placing special comments throughout your code source and running a simple command-line tool makes it easy to generate useful documentation and keep it current. Even if some of the classes, methods, or fields in an application are not specifically commented on by the JavaDoc utility, default documentation is produced for these elements.

Formatting the Documentation

To create a JavaDoc comment, begin with the characters /**. Although optional since Java 1.4, a common practice is to include an asterisk as the first character of every subsequent line within the comment. Another good practice is to indent the comment to align with the code that is being documented. Lastly, close the comment with the characters */.

JavaDoc comments should begin with a short description of the class or method. Fields are rarely commented using JavaDoc unless they are declared `public static final` (constants), in which case it is a good idea to supply a comment. A comment can be several lines long and can even contain more than one paragraph. If you want to break comments into paragraphs, then separate those paragraphs using the `<p>` tag. Comments can include several tags that indicate various details regarding the method or class being commented. JavaDoc tags begin with an ampersand (@), and some of the common tags are as follows.

```
@param: Name and description of a parameter
@return: What is returned from the method
@see: Reference to another piece of code
```

You may also include inline links within JavaDoc to reference URLs. To include an inline link, use the tag {@link My Link}, where `link` is the actual URL that you want to point at, and `My Link` is the text that you want to appear. Many other tags can be used within JavaDoc comments, including {@literal}, {@code}, {@value org}, and many others.

Executing the Tool

The JavaDoc tool can be run against entire packages or sources. Simply pass a package name to the JavaDoc tool rather than individual source file names. For instance, if an application includes a package named `org.luciano.beans`, all source files within that package can be documented by running the tool, as follows.

```
javadoc org.luciano.beans
```

By default, the JavaDoc tool generates HTML and places it into the same package as documented code. That result can become a cluttered nightmare if you like to have source files separate from the documentation. Instead, you can set up a destination for the generated documentation by passing the –d flag to the JavaDoc tool.

1-13. Reading Environment Variables

Problem

The application you are developing needs to make use of some environment variables. You want to read the values that have been set from the operating-system level.

Solution

Use the Java System class to retrieve any environment variable values. The System class has a method called getenv() that accepts a String argument corresponding to the name of a system environment variable. The method then returns the value of the given variable. If no matching environment variable exists, a NULL value is returned. Listing 1-11 is an example. The ReadOneEnvVariable class accepts an environment variable name as a parameter and displays the variable's value that has been set at the operating-system level.

Listing 1-11. Reading an Environment Variable's Value

```
package org.java17recipes.chapter1.recipe1_13;
public class ReadOneEnvVariable {
    public static void main(String[] args) {
        if (args.length > 0) {
            String value = System.getenv(args[0]);
            if (value != null) {
                System.out.println(args[0].toUpperCase() + " = " + value);
            } else {
                System.out.println("No such environment variable exists");
            }
        } else {
            System.out.println("No arguments passed");
        }
    }
}
```

If you are interested in retrieving the entire list of environment variables defined on a system, do not pass any arguments to the System.getenv() method. You receive an object of type Map having all the values. You can iterate through them, as shown in Listing 1-12.

Listing 1-12. Iterating Through a Map of Environment Variables

```
package org.java17recipes.chapter1.recipe1_13;
import java.util.Map;
public class ReadAllEnvVariables {
    public static void main(String[] args){
        if(args.length > 0){
            String value = System.getenv(args[0]);
        if (value != null) {
            System.out.println(args[0].toUpperCase() + " = " + value);
        } else {
            System.out.println("No such environment variable exists");
        }
        } else {
            Map<String, String> vars = System.getenv();
            for(String var : vars.keySet()){
                System.out.println(var + " = " + vars.get(var));
            }
        }
    }
}
```

How It Works

The System class contains many different utilities that can aid in application development. One of those is the getenv() method, which returns a value for a given system environment variable.

You can also return the values from all environment variables in which case those values are stored in a *map*. A map is a collection of name/value pairs. Chapter 7 provides additional information about maps.

Note the method invoked to obtain environment variable values in Listings 1-11 and 1-12. It's been overloaded to handle both cases shown in the solution. Pass the name of a variable as a string if you want to obtain that variable's value. Pass no argument at all to get back the names and values of all variables that are currently set.

1-14. Summary

This chapter includes recipes that allow you to quickly start working with Java. It covered the installation of the OpenJDK to the configuration and use of the Eclipse IDE. The chapter also covered basics such as declaring variables, compiling code, and documentation. The rest of this book dives deeper into each of the different areas of the Java language, covering a variety of topics from beginner to expert. Refer to this chapter for configuration specifics as you work through the examples in the rest of the book.

CHAPTER 2

Enhancements from Java 9 Through Java 17

Since Java 9, newer versions of Java follow every six months, but this is a long-term support (LTS). It receives support for at least eight years and surely until the next LTS version in 2023. Each release of the JDK brings new enhancements and capabilities to the Java platform. Since the last version of this book, many enhancements have occurred. This book includes several recipes covering the new features from Java 9 to Java 17. Each release also carries backward compatibility with previous releases. This chapter showcases a few of the top enhancements to whet your appetite. By no means is this chapter a complete listing of all Java enhancements. Rather, it is a jump start to get you going on some of the hot new features of Java up to the last version.

2-1. Introduction to the var Keyword

Problem

You want to use a keyword detecting the data type of a variable based on the surrounding context.

Solution

Use the local variable type inference introduced in Java 10. Listing 2-1 is an example.

Listing 2-1. Declarations Local Variable Type Inference Package

```
org.java17recipes.chapter01.recipe02_01;
public class KeywordVar {
    public static void main (String[] args) {
```

© Josh Juneau, Luciano Manelli 2022
J. Juneau and L. Manelli, *Java 17 Recipes*, https://doi.org/10.1007/978-1-4842-7963-2_2

```
var num = 1;
var city = "Taranto";
System.out.println(num);
System.out.println(city);
}
}
```

Now you should see the following output.

```
1
Taranto
```

How It Works

Prior to Java 10, you declared in the following way.

```
String city = "Taranto";
```

Next, you can declare the following.

```
var city = "Taranto"
```

It allows programmers to declare the type of the local variable instead of the actual type and increases code readability. The compiler decides the type based on the value assigned to the variable. In Java 11, the usage of var uniform was extended to lambda parameters, as explained in Chapter 6.

The local variable type inference cannot be used as a global variable. In fact, if you use the following, the IDE raises a compilation error.

```
// instance variable
  var x = 50;
  public static void main(String[] args)
  {
      System.out.println(x);
  }
```

The output is an error.

```
'var' is not allowed here
```

For more information on the var keyword, see the documentation at
`http://openjdk.java.net/jeps/286`.

Note   The JEP–JDK Enhancement Proposal collects proposals for enhancements to the JDK and allows OpenJDK to develop more informally changes. It does not replace JCP, however, which is required to approve changes in Java API.

2-2. Reading the Contents of Files
Problem

You want to read the contents of a file.

Solution

Use the `java.nio.file.Files` class, which provides static methods operating on files and directories (see Listing 2-2).

Listing 2-2. Reading Content of File

```java
import java.nio.file.Path;
import java.nio.file.Paths;
import java.nio.file.Files;
import java.io.IOException;

class ReadContentsFile
{
    public static void main(String[] args)
    {
        Path filePathHello = Paths.get("C:/hello.txt");

        try
        {
            String contents = Files.readString(filePath filePathHello);
            System.out.println(contents);
        }
```

```
        catch (IOException err)
        {
            err.printStackTrace();
        }
    }
}
```

The following is the output.

```
Ciao da
Luciano Manelli
Taranto
ITALY
```

This is the content of a text file on the author's computer.

How It Works

Java 11 included some new `Files` class methods to read content from a file.
The `Files.readString(Path)` method reads characters from a file, accepts the file's
path, and returns a string with the file's contents. It throws an IOException if an error
occurs. The used charset for the decoding is the UTF-8.

You can also use the `Files.readString(Path, Charset)` method. It is used for
using a specific charset to decode bytes to characters. It reads from the file and throws
an IOException. The `Files.readString(Path)` method is equal to `readString(path,
StandardCharsets.UTF_8)`.

Listing 2-3 is an example.

Listing 2-3. Reading the File Content with charset

```
import java.nio.file.Path;
import java.nio.file.Paths;
import java.nio.file.Files;
import java.io.IOException;
import java.nio.charset.StandardCharsets;
```

```
public class Main
{
    public static void main(String[] args)
    {
        Path filePathHello = Paths.get("C:/hello.txt");

        try
        {
            String contents = Files.readString(filePath filePathHello,
            StandardCharsets.UTF_8);
            System.out.println(contents);
        }
        catch (IOException err)
        {
            err.printStackTrace();
        }
    }
}
```

2-3. Writing a Text Block

Problem

You want to write a string in multiple lines in a smart way.

Solution

A smart form for writing a multiline string in a simple text block was introduced in Java 15 (JEP 378), though first proposed in Java 13.

The following is an example.

```
public class MultipleLineStringEx {
    public static void main (String[] args) {
        String writeTextStandard = "<html>\n" +
            "       <p>Ciao, hello</p>\n" +
            "</html>\n";
```

```
                String writeTextSmart = """
                    <html>
                        <p>Ciao, hello</p>
                    </html>
                    """;
                System.out.println(writeTextStandard);
                System.out.println(writeTextSmart);
        }
}
```

The output is the same.

How It Works

Java 13 introduced an enhancement to make multiline strings more readable. So, text block efficiently eliminates the concatenation of multiple strings together. The need was to choose a way to visually text blocks and string literals: the delimiter """ was chosen. Moreover, indentation was removed and replaced with whitespace characters.

For more information on text blocks, see the documentation at `https://openjdk` `.java.net/jeps/378`.

2-4. The Enhancement of NullPointerException

Problem

You want to know which variable is null when a NullPointerException occurs.

Solution

Java 14 improved the NullPointerException functionalities generated when an error occurs.

The following is an example.

```
Line 1:package org.java17recipes.chapter02.recipe02_04;
Line 2:
Line 3:public class NullPointerExample {
```

```
Line 4:        public static void main (String[] args) {
Line 5:            String professor= null;
Line 6:            System.out.println(professor.length());
Line 7:        }
Line 8:}
```

The following is the output.

```
Exception in thread "main" java.lang.NullPointerException:
    Cannot invoke "String.length()" because "professor" is null
    at org.java17recipes.chapter02.recipe02_04.NullPointExample.
    main(NullPointerExample.java:6)
```

How It Works

In Java 14, the Java Virtual Machine describes exactly which variable is null. The exception message is on the line of the exception type: in a previous version, there is the lack of the sentence: "Cannot invoke "String.length()" because "professor" is null." On the other hand, this enhancement can naturally create overhead to producing a stack trace. For more information on NullPointerException, see the documentation at https://openjdk.java.net/jeps/358.

2-5. Pattern Matching for instanceof
Problem

You want to simplify the conditional extraction of components from objects.

Solution

Java 14 improves the function, making the cast simpler.

In the following example, the first lines represent the old version of the functionality.

```
public class InstanceOfExample {
        public static void main (String[] args) {
                Object selectedObject="I love Taranto";
```

55

```
        if (selectedObject instanceof String) {
            String selectedString = (String) selectedObject;
            System.out.println(selectedString.length());
        }

        if (selectedObject instanceof String selectedString) {
            System.out.println(selectedString.length());
        }
    }
}
```

How It Works

This enhancement was proposed in Java 14 and in production in Java 16 (JEP 394). It is a readable and concise form that improves pattern matching for the instanceof operator.

The new version improves the readability of the code, and it avoids repeating the type name more times and the probability of generating errors

For more information on pattern matching for the instanceof operator, see the documentation at https://openjdk.java.net/jeps/394.

2-6. Using Record

Problem

You want to declare classes with simple management of the main and standard methods.

Solution

Use Record classes, which efficiently model classes. In the following, there is a standard code for an entity class.

```
public class Professor {
    private Integer id;
    private String name;
    private String surname;
```

```
    public Professor () {
    }

    public Integer getId() {
        return id;
    }

    public void setId(Integer id) {
        this.id = id;
    }

    public String getName() {
        return name;
    }

    public void setName(String name) {
        this.name = name;
    }

    public String getSurname() {
        return surname;
    }

    public void setSurname(String surname) {
        this.surname = surname;
    }
}
```

Since Java 14, this lengthy class can be defined as follows.

```
record Professor (Integer id, String name, String surname) {}
```

So, you can simply create a new prof.

```
Professor prof = new Professor (1, "Luciano", "Manelli");
```

And not in a standard old way.

```
Professor prof = new Professor ();
            prof.setId(1);
            prof.setName("Luciano");
            prof.setSurname("Manelli");
```

The following is the main class.

```java
public class Main {
        public static void main (String[] args) {
                Professor prof = new Professor ();
                prof.setId(1);
                prof.setName("Luciano");
                prof.setSurname("Manelli");
                System.out.println("Prof "+prof.getId()+":"+prof.getName()+
                " "+prof.getSurname());

                record ProfessorRecord (Integer id, String name,
                String surname) {};
                ProfessorRecord profRecord = new ProfessorRecord
                (1, "Luciano", "Manelli");
                System.out.println("Prof using Record "+profRecord.id()+
                ":"+profRecord.name()+" "+profRecord.surname());
        }
}
```

How It Works

This enhancement was proposed in Java 14 and became a standard feature in Java 16 (JEP 394). It helps developers by providing a compact syntax for declaring classes, avoiding the well-known verbosity of the Java language.

In some cases, it is useful to preserve the immutability of data creating equals, hashCode, and toString methods. The first method verifies the equality for objects when all fields match the same class. The second method returns a unique integer value when all fields match. The third method gives a string derived from the name of the class and the names and values of each component.

For more information on the Record class, see the documentation at https:// openjdk.java.net/jeps/395.

2-7. Restore Always-Strict Floating-Point Semantics

Problem

You want to ensure the same precision and result on every platform for floating points.

Solution

Java 17 restores the default always-strict function, making the floating-point operations uniformly strict. So, you can ensure platform-independent floating-point computations; for example, the following is the old version.

```
strictfp class  AppliedClass{}//strict floating point applied on class
strictfp interface AppliedInterface{}// strict floating point applied on
interface
```

And simply, the new version is as follows.

```
class AppliedClass{}//strictfp applied on class
interface AppliedInterface{}//strictfp applied on interface
```

The following is an example.

```
public strictfp class SumFPnumbersStrict {
    public double sumNumbers(double fpOne, double fpTwo) {
        return fpOne + fpTwo;
    }
```

It becomes the following.

```
public class sumFPnumbers {
    public double SumNumbers(double fpOne, double fpTwo) {
        return fpOne + fpTwo;
    }
}
```

The following is an example of the main class.

```
public class Main {
        public static void main (String[] args) {
                SumFPnumbers sn = new SumFPnumbers ();
                System.out.println("SUM :   "+sn.sumNumbers(1.2,3.4));
```

```
                SumFPnumbersStrict sns = new SumFPnumbersStrict();
                System.out.println("SUM :    "+sns.sumNumbers(1.2,3.4));
        }
}
```

How It Works

Since Java 17, floating-point computations were platform-dependent (i.e., depends on the hardware). This enhancement helps avoid strictfp behavior and not make all floating-point operations uniformly strict. Existing Java code using strictfp could be used without the modifier.

For more information on floating points, see the documentation at `https://openjdk.java.net/jeps/306`.

2-8. Pseudorandom Number Generators
Problem

You want to create random numbers.

Solution

Java 17 improves the functionality by providing new interface types and implementations for pseudorandom number generators (PRNGs) and preserving previous behavior of the `java.util.Random` class.

An example is the creation of a pseudorandom integer number.

```
import java.util.random.RandomGenerator;
import java.util.Random;
public class UseNewPRNGs implements RandomGenerator {
        static UseNewPRNGs testGen = new UseNewPRNGs();
        public static void main(String[] args){

                for (int i = 0; i < 5; i++) {
                        System.out.println(testGen.nextBoolean());
                        System.out.println(testGen.nextDouble());
```

```
            System.out.println(testGen.nextInt());
            System.out.println(testGen.nextLong());
        }
    }
    @Override
    public long nextLong() {
            //Returns a pseudorandomly chosen long value.
            Random r= new Random();
            return r.nextLong();
    }
}
```

The following is the output.

```
false
0.4134883035327678
1576006117
7534183938614386691
true
0.37651481128199904
682788707
-6435840544183136500
true
0.8508900370304876
833362345
45614195681877909
true
0.10116382711133465
-663894214
-3718926050146429223
false
0.01988848947697064
1224659827
-2167276196617947918
```

How It Works

Java 17 provides a new interface, RandomGenerator, which supplies a uniform API for all existing and new PRNGs. It has default methods, and in the previous code was only overridden the `nextLong` method. It provides a common protocol for objects that generate random or pseudorandom sequences of numbers or Boolean values. This enhancement mainly aims to use various PRNG algorithms interchangeably in applications and preserve the existing behavior of the `java.util.Random` class.

For more information on PRNGs, see the documentation at `https://openjdk.java .net/jeps/356`.

2-9. Sealed Classes

Problem

You want to create a class or interface and decide which modifier should be used simply.

Solution

Java 17 finalizes the sealed scope modifier for classes and interfaces.

In the following example, the LineShape class permits exactly and only three subclasses: Rectangle, Triangle, and Square.

```
public sealed class LineShape permits Rectangle, Triangle, Square {}
```

In the following example, the Rectangle class is declared as final. Thus no other classes can extend this class.

```
public final class Rectangle extends LineShape {}
```

In the following example, the Triangle class is declared non-sealed, opening an extension for unknown classes.

```
public non-sealed class Triangle extends LineShape {}
```

Finally,

```
public sealed class Square extends LineShape permits ColorSquare {}
```
where the Square class permits exactly and only ColorSquare:
```
public final class ColorSquare extends Square {}
```

How It Works

This enhancement was proposed in Java 15 and finalized in Java 17 (JEP 409) with no changes from the last version. The sealed scope modifier allows controlling the permitted subtypes for classes and interfaces. A class can also be non-sealed (i.e., it can be extended by any unknown subclasses).

A sealed class sets three constraints on its permitted subclasses (i.e., the Rectangle and Triangle subclasses) must belong to the same module as the sealed class, they must extend the sealed class (Rectangle extends LineShape and public non-sealed class Triangle extends LineShape). The subclass must define a modifier: final, sealed, or non-sealed.

To compile LineShape.java, the compiler must access all the permitted classes of Shape: Triangle.java, Square.java, and Rectangle.java. In addition, because Square is a sealed class, the compiler also needs access to ColorSquare.java. Moreover, if an "invalid" class tries to extend LineShape, as shown in the following example, the compiler gives a warning: "The type Rhombus extending a sealed class LineShape should be a permitted subtype of LineShape."

```
public final class Rhombus extends LineShape {}
```

This feature introduces three new keywords in the Java language: sealed, permits, and non-sealed.

For more information on sealed classes, see the documentation at `https://openjdk.java.net/jeps/409`.

2-10. The Vector API

Problem

You want a portable API for expressing vector computations.

Solution

Java 17 introduces an API for vector computations achieving performance superior to equivalent scalar computations. The following is standard code for summing two arrays.

```
static void nonVectorSumInt(int[] arrayOne, int[] arrayTwo, int[] s) {
            for (int i = 0; i < arrayOne.length; i++) {
                    s[i] = (arrayOne[i]  +  arrayTwo[i]) ;
            }
    }
```

The following is the code using vector.

```
static final VectorSpecies<Integer> SPECIES = IntVector.SPECIES_PREFERRED;
static void vectorSumInt(int[] arrayOne, int[] arrayTwo, int[] s) {
            int i = 0;
            int upperBound = SPECIES.loopBound(arrayOne.length);
            for (; i < upperBound; i += SPECIES.length()) {
                    var vIntaOne = IntVector.fromArray(SPECIES,
                    arrayOne, i);
                    var vIntaTwo = IntVector.fromArray(SPECIES,
                    arrayTwo, i);
                    var vs = vIntaOne.add(vIntaTwo);
                    vs.intoArray(s, i);
            }
            for (; i < arrayOne.length; i++) {
                    s[i] = (arrayOne[i]  + arrayTwo[i] );
            }
    }
```

For testing the provious code, create the main class.

```
    public static void main(String[] args) {
    int[] a = new int[]{1, 3, 2, 4};
    int[] b = {5, 6, 7, 8};
    int[] c = {0, 0, 0, 0};
    VectorExample.nonVectorSumInt(a, b, c);
            System.out.println("nonVectorSumInt");
    for (int i = 0; i < c.length; i++) {
            System.out.println(c[i]);
    }
```

```
        VectorExample.vectorSumInt(a, b, c);
                System.out.println("vectorSumInt");
        for (int i = 0; i < c.length; i++) {
                        System.out.println(c[i]);
        }
}
```

A *preferred* species is a species of maximal bit size for the platform (i.e., the preferred length of vectors supported by the platform). Open a terminal window for compiling and executing command lines.

The following is the output.

```
nonVectorSumInt
6
9
9
12
vectorSumInt
6
9
9
12
```

How It Works

You can compile and execute from the terminal window. Use the following command to add the jdk.incubator.vector module to the class.

--add-modules jdk.incubator.vector

So, you must write the following.

```
javac --add-modules jdk.incubator.vector  VectorExample.java
```

After compiling the class, you can run it with the following command.

```
java --add-modules jdk.incubator.vector  VectorExample
```

This enhancement was proposed in Java 16 (JEP 338) to increase the number of computations performed by vector instructions on supported CPU architectures. In the preceding example, the aim is to add two vectors, each containing two integer values: in this case, vector hardware performs two additions in a single CPU cycle while an ordinary operation is allowed.

For more information on vectors, see the documentation at https://openjdk.java .net/jeps/414.

2-11. Avoiding Redundancy in Interface Code

Problem

You want to implement two or more default methods within an interface with very similar code. Rather than copying code into each of the different default methods and maintaining each default method separately, you'd like to encapsulate the similar code into its own method for reuse.

Solution

Use a private method in an interface to alleviate this issue. Java 9 provides the ability to include private methods within an interface. A private method is only available within that interface, and it cannot be used by any class that implements the interface. However, each default method implementation that is part of the interface can use the private method.

The following interface includes two default methods and one private method. The private method encapsulates functionality that can be used in each of the default method implementations.

```java
public interface Pool {
    /**
     * Calculate volume (gal) for a fixed depth square or rectangular pool.
     */
    public default double squareOrRectConstantDepth(double length, double
    width, double depth){
        return volumeCalc(length, width, depth);
    } .
```

```
    /**
     * Calculate volume (gal) for a variable depth square or rectangular pool.
     */
    public default double squareOrRectVariableDepth(double length,
                            double width, double shallowDepth,
                            double middleDepth, double deepDepth){
        double avgDepth = (shallowDepth + middleDepth + deepDepth) / 3;
        return volumeCalc(length, width, avgDepth);
    }
    /**
     * Standard square or rectangular volume calculation.
     */
    private double volumeCalc(double length, double width, double depth){
        return length * width * depth * 7.5;
    }
}
```

For testing the previous code, create the main class.

```
public class PoolExample implements Pool {
                public static void main(String args[]) {
                    PoolExample pe = new PoolExample();
                    System.out.println(pe.squareOrRectConstantDepth(
                    10,10,10));
                }
}
```

The following is the output.

```
7500.0
```

How It Works

Before Java 8, it was impossible to include code implementation within a Java interface. An interface is a reference type in Java, similar to a class. However, its original intent only allowed abstract methods, constants, static methods, and nested types. Therefore, classes that implemented an interface must implement each abstract method. In Java 8, that restriction was lifted, and it became possible to include method implementations in the form of default methods. A default method can contain an implementation in the interface, or an implementing class could override its implementation to do a complete override or add an extension. Hence, the term *default method*, meaning that the default method implementation resides in the interface if the implementation class does not provide one. Private methods were not allowed in interfaces.

Situations have arisen by which multiple default methods within an interface may contain similar code. This code can now be encapsulated within a private method implementation within the interface. The private method implementation cannot be used outside of the interface. In the solution to this recipe, the volumeCalc() method returns the calculated volume of a square or rectangular swimming pool using a standard formula. Each of the default methods within the interface can utilize the volumeCalc() method to find the volume. However, the volumeCalc() method is not available outside the interface.

This seems controversial, as interfaces were originally intended for field and method declarations only. It can also be argued that copying the same code throughout several default method implementations would be a bad practice. Take it as you will, this feature makes it easier to reuse code within an interface, thereby reducing the chance for errors and making maintenance much easier.

2-12. Easily Retrieving Information on OS Processes

Problem

You want the ability to find information regarding operating system processes.

Solution

Use the updated Process API. The new ProcessHandle interface lets you easily obtain information on operating system processes. In the following code, all operating system processes are listed and printed to the terminal window.

```
public static void listProcesses(){
    ProcessHandle.allProcesses()
```

```
        .forEach(System.out::println);
}
```

However, this is not very helpful, as it simply lists the process number of each operating system, which is not very useful. To obtain more detail on the process, we need to obtain the ProcessHandle and call on its helper methods, which is quite easy. The following code print much more information regarding each process, as it prints the ProcessHandle.Info itself.

```
public static void detailListProcesses(){
    ProcessHandle.allProcesses()
            .forEach(h->System.out.println(formattedProcess(h)));
}
public static String formattedProcess(ProcessHandle handle){
        long pid = handle.pid();
        boolean alive = handle.isAlive();
        Optional<Duration> cpuDuration = handle.info().totalCpuDuration();
        Optional<String> handleName = handle.info().command();
        return pid + " " + alive + " " + handleName + ":"+ cpuDuration;
    }
```

The following is the main class.

```
        public static void main (String[] args){
            listProcesses();
            detailListProcesses();
            detailListProcessUsers();
        }
```

Sample output may look as follows.

```
3216 true Optional[C:\Program Files
(x86)\Google\Chrome\Application\chrome.exe]:Optional[PT0.15625S]
2588 false Optional.empty:Optional.empty
6636 false Optional.empty:Optional.empty
10140 false Optional.empty:Optional.empty
8776 true Optional[C:\Program Files
(x86)\Notepad++\notepad++.exe]:Optional[PT2.859375S]
```

```
11128 true Optional[C:\Program Files
(x86)\Google\Chrome\Application\chrome.exe]:Optional[PT0.0625S]
14184 true Optional[C:\Program Files
(x86)\Google\Chrome\Application\chrome.exe]:Optional[PT0.109375S]
14316 true Optional[C:\Windows\System32\SearchProtocolHost.exe]:
Optional[PT0.0625S]
11356 false Optional.empty:Optional.empty
1468 true Optional[C:\jdk-17\bin\javaw.exe]:Optional[PT0.25S]
```

If you wish to retrieve information pertaining to the user that is running the process, that is easy to do as well.

```
public static void detailListProcessUsers(){
    ProcessHandle.allProcesses()
            .forEach(h->System.out.println(listOsUser(h)));
}
public static String listOsUser(ProcessHandle handle){
    ProcessHandle.Info procInfo = handle.info();
    return handle.pid() + ": " +procInfo.user();
}
```

Sample output using this technique may look as follows.

```
412: Optional.empty
14444: Optional[LAPTOP-BDD02I2D\lucky]
11648: Optional[LAPTOP-BDD02I2D\lucky]
7012: Optional[LAPTOP-BDD02I2D\lucky]
12908: Optional[LAPTOP-BDD02I2D\lucky]
10408: Optional[LAPTOP-BDD02I2D\lucky]
7984: Optional[LAPTOP-BDD02I2D\lucky]
1528: Optional[LAPTOP-BDD02I2D\lucky]
```

How It Works

The ProcessHandle interface is introduced in Java 9, making the retrieval of operating system process information a first-class citizen of the JDK.

2-13. Handling try-with-resources Construct

Problem

You'd like to easily manage the closing of effectively final variables.

Solution

The try-with-resources construct was introduced in Java 7, allowing easy resources management. It became even easier in the Java 9 version because there is no need to effectively create a new variable for the sake of the construct. In the following code, the writeFile() method takes a BufferedWriter as an argument, and since it is passed into the method and ready to use, it is effectively final. This means it can simply be listed in the try-with-resources rather than creating a new variable.

```
public static void main(String[] args) {
    try {
        writeFile(new BufferedWriter(
                new FileWriter("Easy TryWithResources")),
                "This is easy since Java 9");
    } catch (IOException ioe) {
        System.out.println(ioe);
    }
}

public static void writeFile(BufferedWriter writer, String text) {
    try (writer) {
        writer.write(text);
    } catch (IOException ioe) {
        System.out.println(ioe);
    }
}
```

This code creates a new file named EasyTryWithResources. It adds the "This is easy in Java 9" text.

How It Works

The `try-with-resources` construct has become even easier with Java 9 and allows one to handle the opening and closing of resources very easily. If we have a resource, such as a database connection or a `BufferedStream`, it is good to manage wisely. In other words, open the resource, then use it accordingly, and finally close the resource when finished to ensure no resource leaks. The `try-with-resources` construct allows one to open a resource within the try block and have it automatically cleaned up once it completes.

The solution was shown in Java 9. It is possible to simply begin using a resource within a `try-with-resources` construct if it is passed into a method as an argument or a final field. While this is not a major language change, it certainly makes handling resources a bit easier, making the `try-with-resources` block even easier to understand.

2-14. Filtering Data Before and After a Condition with Streams

Problem

You wish to utilize streams for effective manipulation of your collections. While doing so, you wish to filter those streams before and/or after a specified condition occurs. In the end, you want to retrieve all data within the collection before a given predicate condition is met. You also wish to retrieve all data within the collection after a given predicate condition is met.

Solution

Utilize the new Java `takeWhile()` and `dropWhile()` constructs with your stream. Suppose we have the following collection of data, and we wish to retrieve all the elements before the element containing the word *Java*.

```
List<String> myLangs = Arrays.asList("Jython is great","Groovy is awesome",
"Scala is functional", "JRuby is productive","Java is
streamlined","","Kotlin is interesting");
```

To retrieve all elements prior to the element containing the "Java" string, we could use the `takeWhile()` construct, as follows.

```
Stream.of("Jython is great","Groovy is awesome","Scala is functional",
        "JRuby is productive","Java is streamlined","","Kotlin is
        interesting")
    .takeWhile(s -> !s.contains("Java"))
    .forEach(System.out::println);
```

Let's suppose that we wish to retrieve all elements that occur after the element containing the "Java" string. We could use the dropWhile() construct, as follows.

```
Stream.of("Jython is great","Groovy is awesome","Scala is functional",
        "JRuby is productive","Java is streamlined","","Kotlin is
        interesting")
    .dropWhile(s -> !s.contains("Java"))
    .forEach(System.out::println);
```

The following is the main class.

```
public static void main(String[] args){
    List<String> myLangs = Arrays.asList("Jython is great","Groovy
    is awesome","Scala is functional","JRuby is productive","Java is
    streamlined","","Kotlin is interesting");
    System.out.println("Collection Data: " + myLangs);
    takeWhileExample();
    dropWhileExample();
}
```

The following is the output.

```
Collection Data: [Jython is great, Groovy is awesome, Scala is functional,
JRuby is productive, Java is streamlined, , Kotlin is interesting]
takeWhileExample:
Jython is great
Groovy is awesome
Scala is functional
JRuby is productive
dropWhileExample:
Java is streamlined

Kotlin is interesting
```

How It Works

Streams changed how we develop code and handle data collections in Java. The original set of filters available for use with streams was fairly generous. However, from Java 8, more options have been added, making it even easier to refine data with streams. The `takeWhile()` and `dropWhile()` constructs allow streams to be parsed. On one side they return a new stream that contains all elements before the first one that fails the specified predicate condition. On the other side they return a new stream containing all elements including and after the first element that fails a specified predicate, respectively.

The solution to this recipe parses the list of strings and prints each element to the terminal window for the first pass. The `takeWhile()` construct is then applied to the same stream of strings, and the elements from the stream before the element that fails the specified condition are printed to the terminal window. The `takeWhile()` accepts a predicate condition, which it then applies to each element in the stream. Then only those elements that are iterated before the predicate condition that is not matched is returned. All elements that reside in the stream at and after the position where the condition is not met are not returned.

The opposite result occurs when using the `dropWhile()` construct. In the solution, all stream elements are ignored until the first element upon which the specified condition that is no longer met is returned. Each subsequent element in the stream is also returned.

The `takeWhile` and `dropWhile` constructs are very similar to the filter, except that only one failed condition causes the remaining elements to be ignored or returned, respectively.

2-15. Utilizing Factory Methods to Create Immutable Collections

Problem

You wish to generate an immutable collection (its state does not change after it is constructed) of values.

Solution

Utilize the Collection.of() construct to generate an immutable collection. In the following example, two collections are created. The first is an immutable List<String>, and the second is an immutable Map<Integer, String>.

```
public static void main(String[] args){
        List<String> jvmLanguages = List.of("Java", "Scala", "JRuby",
        "Groovy", "Jython", "Kotlin");
        System.out.println(jvmLanguages);
        try {
            jvmLanguages.add("Exception");
        } catch (UnsupportedOperationException uoe){
        System.out.println(uoe);
        }
        Map <Integer, String> players = Map.of(1, "Josh Juneau", 2,
        "Jonathan Gennick", 3, "Freddy Guime", 4, "Carl Dea", 5, "Luciano
        Manelli");
        System.out.println(players.values());
         System.out.println("Player 5: " + players.get(5));
        try {
                players.put(6,"Exception");
        } catch (UnsupportedOperationException uoe){
            System.out.println(uoe);
        }
}
```

The output looks like the following. Note that the example includes a try-catch block to catch the UnsupportedOperationException thrown when there is an attempt to modify the list and the map.

```
[Java, Scala, JRuby, Groovy, Jython, Kotlin]
java.lang.UnsupportedOperationException
[Josh Juneau, Jonathan Gennick, Freddy Guime, Carl Dea, Luciano Manelli]
Player 5: Luciano Manelli
java.lang.UnsupportedOperationException
```

How It Works

Java has historically been a verbose language for performing small tasks. In the past, constructing a populated collection of data took a few lines of code. On the first line, the collection must be initialized, followed by a line of code for each item that was added to it. Java adds the convenient API for quickly producing an unmodifiable collection of data, whereby one can now initialize and populate the construct in one line of code.

Factory methods have been added to List<E>, Set <E>, and Map<K,V> interfaces for creating such unmodifiable collections of data. The factory methods consist of the of() method, which accepts up to ten values, quickly creating an immutable collection. The Map<K,V> factory method accepts ten key/value pairs. Furthermore, no null values can populate as elements, keys, or values.

2-16. Pattern Matching for switch (Preview)

Problem

You want to efficiently test the same variable against a different number of values.

Solution

The switch command will not support this feature until Java 17, and as a preview. For now, you use a chain of if-else tests. The following is an example.

```
public static void main(String[] args){
Object inputObject  = 500L;
String formattedObject ="input object is not formatted corretly!";
      if (inputObject instanceof Integer i) {
        formattedObject = String.format("Integer %d", i);
    } else if (inputObject instanceof String s) {
        formattedObject = String.format("String %s", s);
    } else if (inputObject instanceof Long l) {
        formattedObject = String.format("Long %d", l);
    } else if (inputObject instanceof Double d) {
        formattedObject = String.format("Double %f", d);
    }
```

The code can be rewritten smartly and reliably in Java 17, as follows.

```
Object inputObject   = 500L;
String formattedObject = switch (inputObject ) {
    case Integer i -> String.format("int %d", i);
    case Long l    -> String.format("long %d", l);
    case Double d  -> String.format("double %f", d);
    case String s  -> String.format("String %s", s);
    default        -> inputObject .toString();
};
```

Open a terminal window for compiling and executing command lines. The following is the output.

```
long 500
```

How It Works

Java 17 introduces the pattern matching for the switch command because the if...else code is complex and not optimizable, while switch is good for pattern matching. In fact, a case label matches the selector expression if the value matches the pattern.

The written patterns in switch statements are a preview feature and are disabled by default. You can compile ad execute from the terminal window. Use the following command to enable the patterns preview feature in switch statements.

```
--enable-preview
```

Use the following command to compile the specified Java 17 SE release.

```
-release 17
```

```
javac --enable-preview --release 17 PattSwitchEx.java
```

If you also use the -Xlint command for details, the compiler warns about the preview feature patterns because they may be removed in a future release.

When you execute the compiled class, you can simply write the following.

```
java --enable-preview PattSwitchEx
```

For more information on pattern matching for switch, see the documentation at https://openjdk.java.net/jeps/406.

2-17. Summary

This chapter covered a handful of the new features and enhancements through Java 17. While certainly not a complete listing of new features, this chapter delved into a few of the most anticipated features, including vectors and pattern matching for switch. The entire book should be read to gain a more complete knowledge of new features. However, this chapter gave you a taste of what is to come.

CHAPTER 3

Strings

This chapter focuses on some of the most common String methods and techniques for working with String objects. In fact, they are one of the most used data types in any programming language. They can be used to obtain text from a keyboard, print messages to a command line, and much more. Given that strings are used so often, there have been many features added to the String object over time to make them easier to work with. After all, a string is an object in Java, so it contains methods that can manipulate the contents of the string.

3-1. Compact Strings

Since the Java language was introduced, strings have been stored into an array of type UTF-16 char. The char array contains two bytes for each character, which eventually produces a large memory heap since strings are often used in our applications. In Java 9, strings are stored in an array of type byte, and stored characters are encoded either as ISO-8859-1/Latin-1 (one byte per character) or as UTF-16 (two bytes per character). There is also an encoding flag on the char array, indicating which type of encoding is used for the string. These changes are otherwise known as *compact strings*.

3-2. Obtaining a Subsection of a String

Problem

You want to retrieve a portion of a string.

© Josh Juneau, Luciano Manelli 2022
J. Juneau and L. Manelli, *Java 17 Recipes*, https://doi.org/10.1007/978-1-4842-7963-2_3

Solution

Use the substring() method to obtain a portion of the string between two different positions. In the following solution, a string is created, and then various portions of the string are printed out using the substring() method.

```
public static void substringExample(){
    String originalString = "This is the original String";
        System.out.println(originalString.substring(0,
        originalString.length()));
        System.out.println(originalString.substring(5, 20));
        System.out.println(originalString.substring(12));
    }
```

Running this method would yield the following results.

```
This is the original String
is the original
original String
```

How It Works

The String object contains many helper methods. One such method is substring(), which can return portions of the string. There are two variations of the substring() method. One of them accepts a single argument, that being the starting index. The other accepts two arguments: startingindex and endingindex. Having two variations of the substring() method makes it seem as though the second argument is optional; if it is not specified, the length of the calling string is used in its place. It should be noted that indices begin with 0, so the first position in a string has an index of 0, and so on.

As you can see from the solution to this recipe, the first use of substring() prints out the entire contents of the string. This is because the first argument passed to the substring() method is 0, and the second argument passed is the length of the original string. In the second example of substring(), an index of 5 is used as the first argument, and an index of 20 is used as the second argument. This effectively causes only a portion of the string to be returned, beginning with the character in the string that is located in the sixth position, or index 5 because the first position has an index of 0; and ending with the character in the string that is located in the twentieth position, the index of 19. The third example specifies only one argument; therefore, the original string begins with the position specified by that argument.

Note   The substring() method only accepts positive integer values. If you attempt to pass a negative value, a java.lang.StringIndexOutOfBoundsException is thrown.

3-3. Comparing Strings
Problem

An application that you are writing needs to have the ability to compare two or more string values.

Solution

Use the built-in equals(), equalsIgnoreCase(), compareTo(), and compareToIgnoreCase() methods to compare the values contained within the strings. The following is a series of tests using different string-comparison operations.

As you can see, various if statements are used to print messages if the comparisons are equal.

```
String one = "one";
String two = "two";

String var1 = "one";
String var2 = "Two";

String pieceone = "o";
String piecetwo = "ne";

// Comparison is equal
if (one.equals(var1)){
    System.out.println ("String one equals var1 using equals");
}
```

```java
// Comparison is NOT equal
if (one.equals(two)){
    System.out.println ("String one equals two using equals");
}

// Comparison is NOT equal
if (two.equals(var2)){
    System.out.println ("String two equals var2 using equals");
}

// Comparison is equal, but is not directly comparing String values
using ==
if (one == var1){
    System.out.println ("String one equals var1 using ==");
}

// Comparison is equal
if (two.equalsIgnoreCase(var2)){
    System.out.println ("String two equals var2 using equalsIgnoreCase");
}

String piecedTogether = pieceone + piecetwo;
// Comparison is equal
if (one.equals(piecedTogether)){
    System.out.println("The strings contain the same value using equals");
}

// Comparison is NOT equal using ==
if (one == piecedTogether) {
    System.out.println("The string contain the same value using == ");
}

// Comparison is equal
if (one.compareTo(var1) == 0){
    System.out.println("One is equal to var1 using compareTo()");
}
if (one.compareToIgnoreCase(var1) == 0){
  System.out.println("One is equal to var1 using compareToIgnoreCase()");
}
```

Results in the following output.

```
String one equals var1 using equals
String one equals var1 using ==
String two equals var2 using equalsIgnoreCase
The Strings contain the same value using equals
One is equal to var1 using compareTo()
One is equal to var1 using compareToIgnoreCase()
```

How It Works

One of the trickier parts of using a programming language can come when comparing two or more values, particularly string values. In the Java language, comparing strings can be fairly straightforward, keeping in mind that you should *not* use the == for string comparison. This is because the comparison operator (==) compares references, not values of strings. One of the most tempting things to do when programming with strings in Java is to use the comparison operator, but you must not because the results can vary.

Note   Java uses interning of strings to speed up performance. This means that the JVM contains a table of interned strings, and each time the `intern()` method is called on a string, a lookup is performed on that table to find a match. The interning returns a canonical representation of the string. If no matching string resides within the table, the string is added, and a reference is returned. If the string already resides within the table, the reference is returned. Java automatically interns string literals, which can cause variations when using the == comparison operator.

In the solution to this recipe, you can see various techniques for comparing string values. The `equals()` method is a part of every Java object. The Java string `equals()` method has been overridden to compare the values contained within the string rather than the object itself. As you can see from the following examples that have been extracted from the solution to this recipe, the `equals()` method is a safe way to compare strings.

```
// Comparison is equal
if (one.equals(var1)){
    System.out.println ("String one equals var1 using equals");
}
// Comparison is NOT equal
if (one.equals(two)){
    System.out.println ("String one equals two using equals");
}
```

The equals() method first checks whether the strings reference the same object using the == operator; it returns true if they do. If they do not reference the same object, equals() compare each string character by character to determine whether the strings being compared to each other contain the same values. What if one of the strings has a different case setting than another? Do they still compare equal to each other using equals()? The answer is no, and that is why the equalsIgnoreCase() method was created. Comparing two values using equalsIgnoreCase() causes each of the characters to be compared without paying attention to the case. The following examples have been extracted from the solution to this recipe.

```
// Comparison is NOT equal
if (two.equals(var2)){
    System.out.println ("String two equals var2 using equals");
}
// Comparison is equal
if (two.equalsIgnoreCase(var2)){
    System.out.println ("String two equals var2 using equalsIgnoreCase");
}
```

The compareTo() and compareToIgnoreCase() methods perform a lexicographical comparison of the strings. This comparison is based on the Unicode value of each character contained within the strings. The result is a negative integer if the string lexicographically precedes the argument string. The result is a positive integer if the string lexicographically follows the argument string. The result is zero if both strings are lexicographically equal. The following excerpt from the solution to this recipe demonstrates the compareTo() method.

```
// Comparison is equal
if (one.compareTo(var1) == 0){
    System.out.println("One is equal to var1 using compareTo()");
}
```

Inevitably, many applications contain code that must compare strings at some level. The next time you have an application requiring string comparison, consider the information discussed in this recipe before writing the code.

3-4. Trimming Whitespace
Problem

One of the strings you are working with contains some whitespace on either end. You want to get rid of that whitespace.

Solution

Use the string trim() method to eliminate the whitespace. In the following example, a sentence is printed, including whitespace on either side. The same sentence is then printed again using the trim() method to remove the whitespace so that the changes can be seen.

```
String myString = " This is a String that contains whitespace.    ";
System.out.println(myString);
System.out.println(myString.trim());
```

The output print as follows.

```
This is a String that contains whitespace.
This is a String that contains whitespace.
```

How It Works

Regardless of how careful we are, whitespace can always become an issue when working with strings of text. This is especially the case when comparing strings against matching values. If a string contains an unexpected whitespace character, that could be disastrous for a pattern-searching program. Luckily, the Java String object contains the trim() method that can automatically remove whitespace from each end of any given string.

85

The trim() method is very easy to use. As you can see from the solution to this recipe, all that is required to use the trim() method is a call against any given string. String objects contain many helper methods, making them very easy to work with. After all, strings are one of the most commonly used data types in any programming language, so they'd better be easy to use! The trim() method returns a copy of the original string with all leading and trailing whitespace removed. If, however, there is no whitespace to be removed, the trim() method returns the original string instance. It does not get much easier than that!

3-5. Discovering Blank Strings

Problem

You want to know if the string is empty or contains whitespace.

Solution

Use the java.lang.String.isBlank() method that returns a Boolean variable.

```
boolean blank = string.isBlank();
```

In the following examples, the method returns true only when the strings are empty or have only whitespace characters.

The following is an example.

```
System.out.println("".isBlank());
prints True in the Console pane, while:
System.out.println(" ".isBlank());
prints True in the Console pane:
but:
System.out.println("Luciano Manelli".isBlank());
prints False in the Console pane.
```

How It Works

Before Java 11, there was only the java.lang.String.isEmpty() method, which checks if this string is empty. It returns true if the length is 0; otherwise, it is false.

The following is an example.

```
System.out.println("".isEmpty());
prints True in the Console pane, while:
System.out.println(" ".isEmpty());
prints False in the Console pane.
In Java 11 the new isBlank() method is equal to trim().isEmpty().
```

3-6. Stripping Whitespace
Problem

You want to remove whitespace.

Solution

Use the java.lang.String.strip() method, which deletes whitespaces, as shown in Listing 3-1.

Listing 3-1. Using the strip Method

```
class StripClassExample
{
    public static void main(String[] args)
    {
        String nameString = "  Ciao Sara!   ";
        System.out.println( nameString.strip() );
        System.out.println( nameString.stripLeading() );
        System.out.println( nameString.stripTrailing() );
    }
}
```

It returns the following output.

```
//"Ciao Sara!"
//"Ciao Sara!   "
//"  Ciao Sara!"
```

How It Works

The strip method was introduced in Java 11 to remove the whitespace from both, beginning and the end of the string. It produces the same result of trim(), while stripLeading() removes the whitespace from the beginning and stripTrailing() removes the whitespace from the end.

3-7. Breaking String Lines
Problem

You want to break the string into lines.

Solution

Use the java.lang.String.lines() method that allows the division in lines, as shown in Listing 3-2.

Listing 3-2.   Using the lines Method

```java
import java.util.stream.Stream;
class LineTerminators {
        public static void main(String[] args) {
                String nameString = "Luciano \nManelli \nTaranto";
                Stream<String> stringStream = nameString.lines();
                stringStream.forEach(System.out::println);
        }
}
```

It returns the following output.

```
Luciano
Manelli
Taranto
```

How It Works

A new method was included in the `String` class in Java 11. It read contents of files processing each line separately and returns a stream of lines extracted from the string based on line terminators, such as a line feed character (\n), a carriage return character (\r), or a carriage return immediately followed by a line feed (\r\n).

3-8. Repeating Strings

Problem

You want to repeat strings.

Solution

Use the `java.lang.String.repeat(int)` method as follows.

```
String nameString = "luciano";
String repeatString = nameString.repeat(3);
```

It returns the following output.

```
lucianolucianoluciano
```

How It Works

Java 11 introduced the repeat method, which returns the concatenation of a string repeated as many times as provided by the int (count) parameter.

3-9. Changing the Case of a String

Problem

A portion of your application contains case-sensitive string values. You want to change all the strings to uppercase or lowercase before they are processed to avoid any case sensitivity issues down the road.

Solution

Use the toUpperCase() and toLowerCase() methods. The String object provides these two helper methods to change the case of all the characters in a given string.

For example, given the string in the following code, each of the two methods is called.

```
String str = "This String will change case.";
System.out.println(str.toUpperCase());
System.out.println(str.toLowerCase());
```

The following output is produced.

```
THIS STRING WILL CHANGE CASE.
this String will change case.
```

How It Works

To ensure that the case of every character within a given string is either upper or lowercase, use the toUpperCase() and toLowerCase() methods, respectively. There are a couple of items to note when using these methods. First, if a given string contains an uppercase letter, and the toUpperCase() method is called against it, the uppercase letter is ignored. The same concept applies to calling the toLowerCase() method. Any punctuation or numbers contained within the given string are also ignored.

There are two variations for each of these methods. One of the variations does not accept any arguments, while the other accepts an argument pertaining to the locale you wish to use. Calling these methods without arguments results in a case conversion using the default locale. If you want to use a different locale, you can pass the desired locale as an argument, using the variation of the method that accepts an argument. For instance, if you want to use an Italian or French locale, you use the following code.

```
System.out.println(str.toUpperCase(Locale.ITALIAN));
System.out.println(str.toUpperCase(new Locale("it","US")));
System.out.println(str.toLowerCase(new Locale("fr", "CA")));
```

The following is the output is.

```
THIS STRING WILL CHANGE CASE.
THIS STRING WILL CHANGE CASE.
this string will change case.
```

Converting strings to uppercase or lowercase using these methods can make life easy. They are also very useful for comparing strings that are taken as input from an application. Consider the case in which a user is prompted to enter a username, and the result is saved into a string. Later in the program, that string is compared against all the usernames stored within a database to ensure that the username is valid. What happens if the person who entered the username types it with an uppercase first character? What happens if the username is stored within the database in all uppercase? The comparison will never be equal. In such a case, a developer can use the `toUpperCase()` method to alleviate the problem. Calling this method against the strings that are being compared will result in a comparison in which the case is the same in both.

3-10. Concatenating Strings

Problem

There are various strings that you want to combine into one.

Solution 1

If you want to concatenate strings onto the end of each other, use the `concat()` method. The following example demonstrates the use of the `concat()` method.

```
String one = "Hello";
String two = "Java17";
String result = one.concat(" ".concat(two));
```

The following is the result.

```
Hello Java
```

Solution 2

Use the concatenation operator to combine the strings using shorthand. In the following example, a space character is placed between the two strings.

```
String one = "Hello";
String two = "Java17";
String result = one + " " + two;
```

The following is the result.

```
Hello Java17
```

Solution 3

Use `StringBuilder` or `StringBuffer` to combine the strings. The following example demonstrates the use of `StringBuffer` to concatenate two strings.

```
String one = "Hello";
String two = "Java17";
StringBuffer buffer = new StringBuffer();
buffer.append(one).append(" ").append(two);
String result = buffer.toString();
System.out.println(result);
```

The following is the result.

```
Hello Java17
```

How It Works

The Java language provides a couple of different options for concatenating strings of text. Although none is better than the others, you may find one to work better in different situations. The `concat()` method is a built-in string helper method. It provides the ability to append one string onto the end of another, as demonstrated by solution 1 to this recipe. The `concat()` method accepts any string value; therefore, you can explicitly type a string value to pass as an argument if you want. As demonstrated in solution 1, simply passing one string as an argument to this method append it to the end of the string, which the method is called upon. However, if you wanted to add a space character between the two strings, you could do so by passing a space character and the string you want to append as follows.

```
String result = one.concat(" ".concat(two));
```

As you can see, having the ability to pass any string or combination of strings to the `concat()` method makes it very useful. Because all the helper methods return copies of the original string with the helper method functionality applied, you can pass strings calling other helper methods to concat() (or any other string helper method). Consider that you want to display the text "Hello Java" rather than "Hello Java17". The following combination of string helper methods would allow you to do just that.

```
String one = "Hello";
String two = "Java17";
String result = one.concat(" ".concat(two.substring(0, two.length()-2)));
```

The concatenation operator (+) can combine any two strings. It is almost thought of as a shorthand form of the concat() method. The last technique demonstrated in solution 3 to this example is the use of StringBuffer, a mutable sequence of characters, much like a string, except that it can be modified through method calls. The StringBuffer class contains several helper methods for building and manipulating character sequences. In the solution, the append() method append two string values. The append() method places the string that is passed as an argument at the end of the StringBuffer.

3-11. Converting Strings to Numeric Values

Problem

You want to have the ability to convert any numeric values that are stored as strings into integers.

Solution 1

Use the Integer.valueOf() helper method to convert strings to int data types. The following is an example.

```
String one = "1";
String two = "2";
int result = Integer.valueOf(one) + Integer.valueOf(two);
```

As you can see, both string variables are converted into integer values. After that, they perform an addition calculation and then stored into an int.

The final result is 3.

Note   A technique known as *autoboxing* is used in this example. Autoboxing is a feature of the Java language that automates converting primitive values to their appropriate wrapper classes. For instance, this occurs when you assign an int value to an integer. Similarly, *unboxing* automatically occurs when you convert in the opposite direction, from a wrapper class to a primitive.

Solution 2

Use the `Integer.parseInt()` helper method to convert strings to int data types. The following is an example.

```
String one = "1";
String two = "2";
int result = Integer.parseInt(one) + Integer.parseInt(two);
System.out.println(result);
```

The final result is 3.

How It Works

The `Integer` class contains the `valueOf()` and `parseInt()` methods, which convert strings or int types into integers. There are two different forms of the `Integer` class's `valueOf()` type that can convert strings into integer values. Each of them differs by the number of arguments that they accept. The first `valueOf()` method accepts only a string argument. This string is then parsed as an integer value if possible, and then an integer holding the value of that string is returned. If the string does not convert into an integer correctly, then the method throws `NumberFormatException`.

The second version of the `valueOf()` method accepts two arguments: a string argument parsed as an integer and an int representing the radix used for the conversion.

Note   Many Java-type classes contain `valueOf()` methods that can be used to convert different types into that class's type. Such is the case with the `String` class because it contains many different `valueOf()` methods that can be used for conversion.

There are also two different forms of the Integer class's parseInt() method. One of them accepts one argument: the string you want to convert into an integer. The other form accepts two arguments: the string that you want to convert to an integer and the radix. The first format is the most widely used, and it parses the string argument as a signed decimal integer. A NumberFormatException is thrown if a parsable unsigned integer is not contained within the string. The second format, which is less widely used, returns an Integer object holding the value represented by the string argument in the given radix, given a parsable unsigned integer is contained within that string.

Note   One of the biggest differences between parseInt() and valueOf() is that parseInt() returns an int and valueOf() returns an integer from the cache.

3-12. Iterating Over the Characters of a String

Problem

You want to iterate the characters in a string of text so that you can manipulate them at the character level.

Solution

Use a combination of string helper methods to access the string at a character level. If you use a string helper method within the context of a loop, you can easily traverse a string by character. In the following example, the string named str is broken down using the toCharArray() method.

```
String str = "Break down into chars";
System.out.println(str);
for (char chr : str.toCharArray()){
    System.out.println(chr);
}
```

The same strategy could be used with the traditional `for` loop. An index could be created to allow access to each character of the string using the `charAt()` method.

```
for (int x = 0; x <= str.length()-1; x++){
System.out.println(str.charAt(x));
}
```

Both solutions yield the following result.

```
B
r
e
a
k

d
o
w
n

i
n
t
o

c
h
a
r
s
```

Note   The first example using `toCharArray()` generates a new character array. Therefore, the second example, using the traditional `for` loop, might perform faster.

How It Works

String objects contain methods that can be used for performing various tasks. The solution to this recipe demonstrates a number of different String methods. The toCharArray() method can be called against a string in order to break it into characters and then store those characters in an array. This method is very powerful, and it can save a bit of time when performing this task is required. The result of calling the toCharArray() method is a char[], which can then be traversed using an index. Such is the case in the solution to this recipe. An enhanced for loop iterates through the contents of the char[] and print out each of its elements.

The length() method finds the number of characters contained within a string. The result is an int value that can be very useful in the context of a for loop, as demonstrated in the solution to this recipe. In the second example, the length() method finds the number of characters in the string so that they can be iterated using the charAt() method. The charAt() method accepts an int index value as an argument and returns the character that resides at the given index in the string.

Often the combination of two or more String methods can obtain various results. In this case, using the length() and charAt() methods within the same code block provided the ability to break down a string into characters.

3-13. Finding Text Matches
Problem

You want to search a body of text for a particular sequence of characters.

Solution 1

Use regular expressions and the matches() helper method to determine how many matches exist. To do this, simply pass a string representing a regular expression to the matches() method against any string you are trying to match. In doing so, the string is compared with one that matches() is being called upon. Once evaluated, the matches() method yields a Boolean result, indicating whether it is a match. The following code excerpt contains a series of examples using this technique. The comments contained within the code explain each of the matching tests.

```
String str = "Here is a long String...let's find a match!";
// This will result in a "true" since it is an exact match
boolean result = str.matches("Here is a long String...let's find a
match!");
System.out.println(result);
// This will result iin "false" since the entire String does not match
result = str.matches("Here is a long String...");

System.out.println(result);


str = "true";
// This will test against both upper & lower case "T"...this will be TRUE
result = str.matches("[Tt]rue");
System.out.println(result);

// This will test for one or the other
result = str.matches("[Tt]rue|[Ff]alse]");
System.out.println(result);

// This will test to see if any numbers are present, in this case the
// person writing this String would be able to like any Java release!
str = "I love Java 8!";
result = str.matches("I love Java [0-9]!");
System.out.println(result);

// This will test TRUE as well...
str = "I love Java 7!";
result = str.matches("I love Java [0-9]!");
System.out.println(result);

// The following will test TRUE for any language that contains
// only one word for a name. This is because it tests for
// any alphanumeric combination. Notice the space character
// between the numeric sequence...
result = str.matches("I love .*[ 0-9]!");
System.out.println(result);
```

```
// The following String also matches.
str = "I love Jython 2.5.4!";
result = str.matches("I love .*[ 0-9]!");
System.out.println(result);
```

Each of the results printed out in the example is true, except the second example because it does not match.

Solution 2

Use the regular expression Pattern and Matcher classes for a better-performing and more versatile matching solution than the matches() method. Although the matches() method gets the job done most of the time, there are some occasions in which you require a more flexible way of matching. Using this solution is a three-step process.

1. Compile a pattern into a Pattern object.

2. Construct a Matcher object using the matcher() method on the Pattern object.

3. Call the matches() method on the Matcher object.

The Pattern object and Matcher object techniques are demonstrated in the following example code.

```
String str = "I love Java 17!";
boolean result = false;
Pattern pattern = Pattern.compile("I love .*[ 0-9]!");
Matcher matcher = pattern.matcher(str);
result = matcher.matches();
System.out.println(result);
```

The previous example yields a TRUE value, just like its variant, which was demonstrated in solution 1.

How It Works

Regular expressions are a great way to find matches because they allow patterns to be defined so that an application does not have to explicitly find an exact string match. They can be very useful for finding matches against some text that a user may be typing into your program. However, they could be overkill if you are trying to match strings against a string constant you have defined in your program because the String class provides many methods that could be used for such tasks. Nevertheless, there certainly comes a time in almost every developer's life when regular expressions can come in handy. They can be found in just about every programming language used today. Java makes them easy to use and understand.

Note   Although regular expressions are used in many different languages today, the expression syntax for each language varies.

The easiest way to use regular expressions is to call the matches() method on the String object. Passing a regular expression to the matches() method yield a Boolean result that indicates whether the string matches the given regular expression pattern or not. At this point, it is useful to know what a regular expression is and how it works.

A *regular expression* is a string pattern that can be matched against other strings to determine its contents. Regular expressions can contain several different patterns that enable them to be dynamic in that they can have the ability to match many different strings that contain the same format. For instance, in the solution to this recipe, the following code can match several different strings.

```
result = str.matches("I love Java [0-9]!");
```

The regular expression string in this example is "I love Java [0-9]!", and it contains the pattern [0-9], which represents any number between 0 and 9. Therefore, any string that reads "I love Java" followed by the numbers 0 through 9 and an exclamation point matches the regular expression string. To see a listing of all the different patterns used in a regular expression, see the online documentation available at the URL in the previous note.

A combination of Pattern and Matcher objects can also achieve similar results as the string matcher() method. The Pattern object can compile a string into a regular expression pattern. A compiled pattern can provide performance gains to an application if the pattern is used multiple times. You can pass the same string-based regular expressions to the Pattern.compile() method as you would pass to the string matches() method. The result is a compiled Pattern object that can be matched against a string for comparison. A Matcher object can be obtained by calling the Pattern object's matcher() method against a given string. Once a Matcher object is obtained, it can match a given string against a pattern using any of the following three methods, which each return a Boolean value indicating a match. The following three lines of solution 2 could be used as an alternate solution to using the `Pattern.matches()` method, minus the reusability of the compiled pattern.

```
Pattern pattern = Pattern.compile("I love .*[ 0-9]!");
Matcher matcher = pattern.matcher(str);
result = matcher.matches();
```

- The `Matcher` object's `matches()` method attempts to match the entire input string with the pattern.

- The `Matcher` object's `lookingAt()` method attempts to match the input string to the pattern starting at the beginning.

- The `Matcher` object's `find()` method scans the input sequence looking for the next matching sequence in the string.

In the solution to this recipe, the `matches()` method is called against the `Matcher` object to match the entire string. Regular expressions can be very useful for matching strings against patterns in any event. The technique used for working with the regular expressions can vary in different situations, using whichever method works best.

3-14. Replacing All Text Matches
Problem

You have searched a body of text for a particular sequence of characters, and you are interested in replacing all matches with another string value.

Solution

Use a regular expression pattern to obtain a `Matcher` object; then use the `Matcher` object's `replaceAll()` method to replace all matches with another string value. The following example demonstrates this technique.

```
String str = "I love Java 8!  It is my favorite language.  Java 8
 is the " + "8th version of this great programming language.";
```

```
Pattern pattern = Pattern.compile("[0-9]");
Matcher matcher = pattern.matcher(str);
System.out.println("Original: " + str);
System.out.println(matcher.matches());
System.out.println("Replacement: " + matcher.replaceAll("17"));
```

This example yield the following results.

```
Original: I love Java 8! It is my favorite language. Java 8 is the 8th
version of this great programming language.
Replacement: I love Java 17! It is my favorite language. Java 17 is the
17th version of this great programming language.
```

How It Works

The replaceAll() method of the Matcher object makes it easy to find and replace a string or a portion of the string contained within a body of text. To use the replaceAll() method of the Matcher object, you must first compile a Pattern object by passing a regular expression string pattern to the Pattern.compile() method. Use the resulting Pattern object to obtain a Matcher object by calling its matcher() method. The following lines of code show how this is done.

```
Pattern pattern = Pattern.compile("[0-9]");
Matcher matcher = pattern.matcher(str);
```

Once you have obtained a Matcher object, call its replaceAll() method by passing a string that you want to use to replace all the text matched by the compiled pattern. In the solution to this recipe, the string "17" is passed to the replaceAll() method, so it replaces all the areas in the string that match the "[0-9]" pattern.

3-15. Determining Whether a File Suffix Matches a Given String

Problem

You are reading a file from the server, and you need to determine what type of file it is to read it properly.

Solution

Determine the suffix of the file by using the endsWith() method on a given file name. In the following example, assume that the filename variable contains the name of a given file. The code uses the endsWith() method to determine whether the filename variable ends with a particular string.

```
if(filename.endsWith(".txt")){
    System.out.println("Text file");
} else if (filename.endsWith(".doc")){
    System.out.println("Document file");
} else if (filename.endsWith(".xls")){
    System.out.println("Excel file");
} else if (filename.endsWith(".java")){
System.out.println("Java source file");
} else {
    System.out.println("Other type of file");
}
```

Given that a file name and its suffix are included in the filename variable, this block of code reads its suffix and determines what type of file the given variable represents.

How It Works

As mentioned, the String object contains many helper methods that can perform tasks. The String object's endsWith() method accepts a character sequence and returns a Boolean value representing whether the original string ends with the given sequence. In the case of the solution to this recipe, the endsWith() method is used in an if block. A series of file suffixes are passed to the endsWith() method to determine what type of file is represented by the filename variable. If any of the file name suffixes match, a line prints, stating which type of file it is.

3-16. Making a String That Can Contain Dynamic Information

Problem

You want to generate a string that can contain a dynamic placeholder such that the string can change depending on application data variations.

Solution 1

Utilize the built-in `format()` method for generating a string containing placeholders for dynamic data. The following example demonstrates a string that contains a dynamic placeholder that allows different data to be inserted into the same string. As the temperature variable changes, the string is dynamically altered.

```
public static void main(String[] args){
    double temperature = 37.1;
    String temperatureString = "The current temperature is %.1f degrees
    Celsius.";

    System.out.println(String.format(temperatureString, temperature));

    temperature = 38.4;

    System.out.println(String.format(temperatureString, temperature));
}
```

It returns the following output.

```
The current temperature is 37.1 degrees Celsius.
The current temperature is 38.4 degrees Celsius.
```

Solution 2

If you wish to print the contents of the string out, rather than store them for later use, the `System.out.printf()` method can position dynamic values within a string. The following example demonstrates the same concept as that in solution 1, except this time, rather than using the `String.format()` method, a string is simply printed out, and the placeholders passed to the `System.out.printf()` method are replaced with the dynamic content at runtime.

```
public static void main(String[] args){
    double temperature = 37.1;
    System.out.printf("The current temperature is %.1f degrees Celsius.\n",
    temperature);

    temperature = 38.4;

    System.out.printf("The current temperature is %.1f degrees Celsius.",
    temperature);
}
```

It returns the following output.

```
The current temperature is 37.1 degrees Celsius.
The current temperature is 38.4 degrees Celsius.
```

How It Works

When you require dynamic string content, the `format()` utility can come in handy. The built-in `format()` method allows one to position a placeholder within a string, such that the placeholder is replaced with dynamic content at runtime. The format method accepts a string and a series of variables that displaces the placeholders within the string with dynamic content at runtime. The placeholders must be designated specifically for the type of content with which they are displaced. Each placeholder must begin with a % character to denote a placeholder within the string. The placeholder can also contain flags, width, and precision indicators to help format the dynamic value. The following format should build each placeholder.

`%[flags][width][.precision]conversion_indicator`

The second solution demonstrates how to utilize the `System.out.printf()` method, which accepts the same arguments as the `System.format()` method. The main difference is that the `System.out.printf()` method is handy for printing formatted content. If your application requires storing a formatted value, you are more likely to use the `String.format()` method.

3-17. Summary

This chapter covered the basics of working with strings. Although a string may look like a simple string of characters, it is an object that contains many methods that can be useful for obtaining the required results. Although strings are immutable objects, many methods within the String class contain a copy of the string, modified to suit the request. The chapter also covered a handful of these methods, demonstrating features such as concatenation, obtaining portions of strings, trimming whitespace, and replacing portions of a string.

CHAPTER 4

Numbers and Dates

This chapter helps you understand how to perform some of the most basic operations with numbers and dates that play a significant role in many applications. You learn to work with date, time, and time zone data. Moreover, the chapter provides examples that work with different kinds of numbers and format them to fit most situations. It also provides insight on performing advanced tasks such as working with currency.

4-1. Rounding Float and Double Values to Integers

Problem

You need to round floating-point numbers or doubles in your application to integer values.

Solution

Use one of the `java.lang.Math round()` methods to round the number into the format you require. The `Math` class has two methods that can be used for rounding floating-point numbers or double values. The following code demonstrates how to use each of these methods.

```java
public static int roundFloatToInt(float myFloat){
    return Math.round(myFloat);
}
public static long roundDoubleToLong(double myDouble){
    return Math.round(myDouble);
}
```

© Josh Juneau, Luciano Manelli 2022
J. Juneau and L. Manelli, *Java 17 Recipes*, https://doi.org/10.1007/978-1-4842-7963-2_4

The first method, roundFloatToInt(), accepts a floating-point number and uses the java.lang.Math class to round that number to an int. The second method, roundDoubleToLong(), accepts a double value and uses the java.lang.Math class to round that double value to a long value.

The following is the main class.

```java
public static void main(String[] args){
        Float floatValue =  7.82f;
        Double doubleValue = 9.9d;
        System.out.println(roundFloatToInt(floatValue));
        System.out.println(roundDoubleToLong(doubleValue));
    }
```

The result is:
8
10

How It Works

The java.lang.Math class contains plenty of helper methods to make our lives easier when working with numbers. The round() methods are no exception since they can easily round floating-point or double values. One version of the java.lang.Math round() method accepts a float as an argument. It rounds the float to the closest int value, with ties rounding up. If the argument is *not a number* (NaN), a zero is returned. When arguments that are positive or negative infinity are passed into a round() method, a result equal to the value of Integer.MAX_VALUE or Integer.MIN_VALUE, respectively, is returned. The second version of the java.lang.Math round() method accepts a double value, which is rounded to the closest long value, with ties rounding up. Like the other round() method, if the argument is NaN, a zero is returned. Similarly, when positive or negative infinity arguments are passed into a round() method, a result is equal to a Long.MAX_VALUE or Long.MIN_VALUE value is returned.

Note   NaN, POSITIVE_INFINITY, and NEGATIVE_INFINITY are constant values defined within the Float and Double classes. NaN (Not a Number) is an undefined or unrepresentable value. For example, a NaN value can be produced by dividing 0.0f by 0.0f. The values represented by POSITIVE_INFINITY and NEGATIVE_INFINITY refer to values produced by operations that generate such extremely large or negative values of a particular type (floating-point or double) that they cannot be represented normally: the output is Infinity or –Infinity. For instance, 1.0/0.0 or –1.0/0.0 would produce such values. In fact, Java uses some special numeric values to handle the floating-point arithmetic results of such an operation due to its specification of the division operations. On the other hand, an ArithmeticException error is thrown for the integer. Test the following code.

```java
public static void main(String[] args){
        Float floatValue1 =  1.0f;
        Float floatValue1n =  -1.0f;
        Float floatValue0 =  0.0f;
        System.out.println(floatValue1/floatValue0);
        System.out.println(floatValue0/floatValue0);
        System.out.println(floatValue1n/floatValue0);
        Double doubleValue1 =  1.0d;
        Double doubleValue1n =  -1.0d;
        Double doubleValue0 =  0.0d;
        System.out.println(doubleValue1/doubleValue0);
        System.out.println(doubleValue0/doubleValue0);
        System.out.println(doubleValue1n/doubleValue0);
    }
```

The following is the output.

```
Infinity
NaN
-Infinity
Infinity
NaN
-Infinity
```

4-2. Formatting Double and Long Decimal Values

Problem

You need to format double and long numbers in your application.

Solution

Use the DecimalFormat class to format and round the value to the precision your application requires. In the following method, a double value is accepted and a formatted string value is printed.

```
public static void formatDouble(double myDouble){
    NumberFormat numberFormatter = new DecimalFormat("##.000");
    String result = numberFormatter.format(myDouble);
    System.out.println(result);
}
```

The main class is:

```
public static void main(String[] args) {
        formatDouble(Double.valueOf("345.9372"));
}
```

For instance, if the double value passed into the formatDouble() method is 345.9372, the result is 345.937. Similarly, if .7697 is passed to the method, the result is .770.

Each of the results is formatted using the specified pattern and then rounded accordingly.

How It Works

The DecimalFormat class can be used along with the NumberFormat class to round and/or format double or long values. NumberFormat is an abstract class that provides the interface for formatting and parsing numbers. This class provides the ability to format and parse numbers for each locale and obtain formats for currency, percentage, integers, and numbers. By itself, the NumberFormat class can be very useful as it contains factory methods that obtain formatted numbers. In fact, little work needs to be done to obtain a formatted string. For example, the following code demonstrates calling some factory methods on the NumberFormat class.

```java
// Obtains an instance of NumberFormat class
NumberFormat format = NumberFormat.getInstance();
// Format a double value for the current locale
String result = format.format(83.404);
System.out.println(result);
// Format a double value for an Italian locale
result = format.getInstance(Locale.ITALIAN).format(83.404);
System.out.println(result);
// Parse a String into a Number
try {
    Number num = format.parse("75.736");
    System.out.println(num);
} catch (java.text.ParseException ex){
    System.out.println(ex);
}
```

The output is:

```
Current Locale: 83,404
Italian Locale: 83,404
Now a number: 75736
```

To format using a pattern, the DecimalFormat class can be used along with NumberFormat. In the solution to this recipe, you saw that creating a new DecimalFormat instance by passing a pattern to its constructor would return a NumberFormat type. This is because DecimalFormat extends the NumberFormat class. Because the NumberFormat class is abstract, DecimalFormat contains all the functionality of NumberFormat, plus added functionality for working with patterns. Therefore, it can work with different formats from the locales, just as you have seen in the previous demonstration. This provides the ultimate flexibility when working with double or long formatting.

As mentioned previously, the DecimalFormat class can take a string-based pattern in its constructor. You can also use the applyPattern() method to apply a pattern to the Format object after the fact. Each pattern contains a prefix, numeric part, and suffix, allowing you to format a particular decimal value to the required precision and include leading digits and commas. Each of the patterns also contains a positive and negative subpattern. A semicolon separates these two subpatterns (;), and the negative subpattern is optional. If there is no negative subpattern present, the localized minus sign is used. For instance, a complete pattern example would be ###,##0.00;(###,##0.00).

> **Note**   The constructor Double(string), Float(float), Integer(int), Long(long), Character(char), Short(short), Byte(byte) and Boolean(boolean) have been deprecated since version 9 and marked for removal. It is possible to use to use
>
> ```
> Float floatValue = 7.82f;
> Float floatValue = Float.valueOf("7.82");
> ```
> instead of
>
> ```
> new Double("345.9372");
> ```

4-3. Formatting Compact Number

Problem

You want to represent a number in a short or human-readable form.

Solution

Use the CompactNumberInstance method introduced in Java 12.

```
For example:
        public static void main (String[] args) {
        NumberFormat numberFormat = NumberFormat.
        getCompactNumberInstance(Locale.US, NumberFormat.Style.SHORT);
        String result = numberFormat.format(1000);
}
```

The following is the output.

```
1k
```

How It Works

Java 12 introduced support for formatting a number in its compact form with the method. In the previous example, 1000 is formatted as "1K" in the en_US locale. The form depends on the style specified by NumberFormat.Style.

4-4. Comparing int Values

Problem

You need to compare two or more int values.

Solution 1

Use the comparison operators to compare integer values against one another. In the following example, three int values are compared against each other, demonstrating various comparison operators.

```
public static void compareIntegers(){
        int int1 = 1;
        int int2 = 10;
        int int3 = -5;
        System.out.println(int1 == int2);  // Result:  false
        System.out.println(int3 == int1);  // Result:  false
        System.out.println(int1 == int1);  // Result:  true
        System.out.println(int1 > int3);   // Result:  true
        System.out.println(int2 < int3);   // Result:  false
}
The main class is:
    public static void main(String[] args){
        compareIntegers();
    }
```

As you can see, comparison operators generate a boolean result.

Solution 2

Use the Integer.compare(int,int) method to compare two int values numerically. The following lines could compare the same int values declared in the first solution.

```
System.out.println("Compare method -> int3 and int1:
" + Integer.compare(int3, int1));
// Result -1
```

```
System.out.println("Compare method -> int2 and int1:
" + Integer.compare(int2, int1));
// Result 1
```

How It Works

Perhaps the most used numeric comparisons are against two or more int values. The Java language makes it easy to compare an int using the comparison operators (see Table 4-1).

Table 4-1. *Comparison Operators*

Operator	Function
==	Equal to
!=	Not equal to
>	Greater than
<	Less than
>=	Greater than or equal to
<=	Less than or equal to

The second solution to this recipe demonstrates the integer compare() method added in Java 7. This static method accepts two int values and compares them, returning a 1 if the first int is greater than the second, a 0 if the two int values are equal, and a –1 if the first int value is less than the second. To use the Integer.compare() method, pass two int values as demonstrated in the following code.

```
Integer.compare(int3, int1));
Integer.compare(int2, int1));
```

Just like in your math lessons at school, these comparison operators determine whether the first integer is equal to, greater than, or less than the second integer. Straightforward and easy to use, these comparison operators are most often seen within the context of an if statement.

4-5. Comparing Floating-Point Numbers

Problem

You need to compare two or more floating-point values in an application.

Solution 1

Use the Float object's compareTo() method to compare one float against another. The following example shows the compareTo() method in action.

```
public static void compareFloat(){
        Float float1 = Float.valueOf ("9.675");
        Float float2 = Float.valueOf ("7.3826");
        Float float3 = Float.valueOf ("23467.373");

        System.out.println(float1.compareTo(float3));  // Result: -1
        System.out.println(float2.compareTo(float3));  // Result: -1
        System.out.println(float1.compareTo(float1));  // Result: 0
        System.out.println(float3.compareTo(float2));  // Result: 1
}
The main class is:
    public static void main(String[] args){
        compareFloat();
    }
```

The result of calling the compareTo() method is an integer value. A negative result indicates that the first float is less than the float being compared against. A zero indicates that the two float values are equal. Lastly, a positive result indicates that the first float is greater than the float being compared against.

Solution 2

Use the Float class compare() method to perform the comparison. The following example demonstrates the Float.compare(float, float) method.

```
System.out.println(Float.compare(float1, float3)); // Result: -1
System.out.println(Float.compare(float2, float3)); // Result: -1
System.out.println(Float.compare(float1, float1)); // Result: 0
System.out.println(Float.compare(float3, float2)); // Result: 1
```

How It Works

The most useful way to compare two float objects is to use the compareTo() method. This method perform a numeric comparison against the given float objects. The result is an integer value indicating whether the first float is numerically greater than, equal to, or less than the float it is compared against. If a float value is NaN, it is considered equal to other NaN values or greater than all other float values. Also, a float value of 0.0f is greater than a float value of –0.0f.

An alternative to using compareTo() is the compare() method, which is also native to the Float class. The compare() method was introduced in Java 1.4, and it is a static method that compares two float values in the same manner as compareTo(). It only makes the code read a bit differently. The format for the compare() method is as follows.

```
Float.compare(primitiveFloat1, primitiveFloat2)
```

The compare() method shown make the following call using compareTo().

```
new Float(float1).compareTo(new Float(float2));
```

In the end, the same results is returned using either compareTo() or compare().

4-6. Randomly Generating Values

Problem

An application that you are developing requires the use of randomly generated numbers.

Solution 1

Use the java.util.Random class to help generate the random numbers. The Random class was developed to generate random numbers for a handful of the Java numeric data types. This code demonstrates the use of Random class to generate such numbers.

```java
public static void randomExamples() {
            // Create a new instance of the Random class
            Random random = new Random();
            System.out.println("Random: " + random);

            // Generates a random Integer
            int myInt = random.nextInt();
            System.out.println("Random int: " + myInt);
            // Generates a random Double value
            double myDouble = random.nextDouble();
            System.out.println("Random double: " + myDouble);

            // Generates a random float
            float myFloat = random.nextFloat();
            System.out.println("Random float: " + myFloat);

            // Generates a random Gaussian double
            // mean 0.0 and standard deviation 1.0
            // from this random number generator's sequence.
            double gausDouble = random.nextGaussian();
            System.out.println("Random Gaussian double:
            " + gausDouble);
            // Generates a random Long
            long myLong = random.nextLong();
            System.out.println("Random long: " + myLong);
            // Generates a random boolean
            boolean myBoolean = random.nextBoolean();
            System.out.println("Random boolean: " + myBoolean);

}
```

The main class is:

```
public static void main(String[] args){
        randomExamples();
}
```

An output is:

```
Random: java.util.Random@17f052a3
Random int: 626546817
Random double: 0.3717917526454104
Random float: 0.23121738
Random Gaussian double: -0.4810858819406O814
Random long: 686366349321458218
Random boolean: false
```

Solution 2

Use the Math.random() method. This produces a double value greater than 0.0, but less than 1.0. The following code demonstrates the use of this method.

```
double rand = Math.random();
```

How It Works

The java.util.Random class uses a 48-bit seed to generate a series of pseudorandom values. As you can see from the example in the solution to this recipe, the Random class can generate many different types of random number values based on the given seed. By default, the seed is generated based on a calculation derived from the number of milliseconds that the machine has been active. However, the seed can be set manually using the Random setSeed() method. If two Random objects have the same seed, they produce the same results.

It should be noted that there are cases in which the Random class might not be the best choice for generating random values. For instance, if you are attempting to use a thread-safe instance of java.util.Random, you might run into performance issues if you're working with many threads. In such a case, you might consider using the ThreadLocalRandom class instead. Similarly, if you require the use of a cryptographically secure Random object, consider using SecureRandom.

The java.util.Random class comes in very handy when you need to generate a type-specified random value. Not only is it easy to use, but it also provides a wide range of options for the return type. Another easy technique is to use the Math.random() method, which produces a double value within the range of 0.0 to 1.0, as demonstrated in solution 2. Both techniques provide a good means of generating random values. However, if you need to generate random numbers of a specific type, java.util.Random is the best choice.

4-7. Obtaining the Current Date Without Time

Problem

You are developing an application for which you want to obtain the current date, not including the time, to display on a form.

Solution

Use the Date-Time API to obtain the current date. The LocalDate class represents an ISO calendar in the year-month-day format. The following lines of code capture the current date and display it.

```
public static void newDate() {
        LocalDate date = LocalDate.now();
        System.out.println("Current Date:" + date);
}
The output is:
Current Date: 2021-11-30
```

How It Works

The Date-Time API makes it easy to obtain the current date, without including other information. To do so, import the java.time.LocalTime class and call on its now() method. The LocalTime class cannot be instantiated, as it is immutable and thread-safe. A call to the now() method returns another LocalDate object, containing the current date in the year-month-day format.

Another version of the now() method accepts a java.time.Clock object as a parameter and returns the date based on that clock. For instance, the following lines of code demonstrate how to obtain a Clock object that represents the system time.

```
public static void newDateFromClock() {
        Clock clock = Clock.systemUTC();
        LocalDate date = LocalDat.now(clock);
        System.out.println("Date from clock: " + date);
}
The output is:
Date from clock: 2021-11-30

The main class is:
        public static void main(String[] args) {
                newDate();
                newDateFromClock();
        }
```

There were other ways to obtain the current date in previous releases, but usually, the time came with the date, and then formatting had to be done to remove the unneeded time digits. The new java.time.LocalDate class makes it possible to work with dates separate from times.

4-8. Obtaining a Date Object Given Date Criteria

Problem

You want to obtain a Date object, given a year-month-day specification.

Solution

Invoke the LocalDate.of() method for the year, month, and day you want to obtain the object. For example, suppose that you want to obtain a Date object for a specified date in November of 2021. You could pass the date criteria to the LocalDate.of() method, as demonstrated in the following lines of code.

```
public static void newSpecifiedDate() {
        LocalDate date = LocalDate.of(2021, Month.NOVEMBER, 12);
        System.out.println("Date from specified date: " + date);
}
```
The main is:
```
public static void main(String[] args) {
        newSpecifiedDate();
}
```

Here's the result.

```
Date from specified date: 2021-11-12
```

How It Works

The LocalDate.of() method accepts three values as parameters. Those parameters represent the year, month, and day. The year parameter is always treated as an int value. The month parameter can be presented as an int value, corresponding to an enum representing the month. The Month enum returns an int value for each month, with JANUARY returning a 1 and DECEMBER returning a 12. Therefore, Month.NOVEMBER returns an 11. A Month object could also be passed as the second parameter instead of an int value. Lastly, the day of the month is specified by passing an int value as the third parameter to the of() method.

4-9. Obtaining a Year-Month-Day Date Combination

Problem

You want to obtain a specified date's year, year-month, or month.

Solution 1

To obtain the year-month of a specified date, use the java.time.YearMonth class. This class represents the month of a specific year. In the following lines of code, the YearMonth object obtains the year and month of the current date and another specified date.

```
public static void obtainYearMonth() {
        YearMonth yearMo = YearMonth.now();
        System.out.println("Current Year and month:" + yearMo);
        YearMonth specifiedDate = YearMonth.of(2021, Month.NOVEMBER);
        System.out.println("Specified Year-Month: " + specifiedDate);
}
```

Here is the result.

```
Current Year and month:2021-10
Specified Year-Month: 2021-11
```

Solution 2

To obtain the month-day for the current date or a specified date, simply use the java.
time.MonthDay class. The following lines of code demonstrate how to obtain a month-day combination.

```
public static void obtainMonthDay(){
        MonthDay monthDay = MonthDay.now();
        System.out.println("Current month and day: " + monthDay);
        MonthDay specifiedDate = MonthDay.of(Month.NOVEMBER, 12);
        System.out.println("Specified Month-Day: " + specifiedDate);
}
```

Here's the result.

```
Current month and day: --10-24
Specified Month-Day: --11-12
The main is:
        public static void main(String[] args) {
                obtainYearMonth();
                obtainMonthDay();
        }
```

Note that by default, MonthDay does not return a very useful format.

How It Works

The Date-Time API includes classes that make it easy to obtain the date information that your application requires. Two of those are the YearMonth and MonthDay classes. The YearMonth class obtains the date in year-month format. It contains a few methods that obtain the year-month combination. As demonstrated in the solution, you can call the now() method to obtain the current year-month combination. Like the LocalDate class, YearMonth also contains an of() method that accepts a year in int format and a number that represents the month of the year. In the solution, Month enum obtains the month value.

Like the YearMonth class, MonthDay obtains the date in a month-day format. It also contains a few different methods for obtaining the month-day combination. Solution 2 demonstrates two such techniques. Obtaining the current month-day combination by calling the now() method and using the of() method to obtain a month-day combination for a specified date. The of() method accepts an int value for the month of the year as its first parameter, and for the second parameter it accepts an int value indicating the day of the month.

4-10. Obtaining and Calculating Times Based on the Current Time

Problem

You want to obtain the current time to stamp a given record. You would also like to perform calculations based on that time.

Solution

Use the LocalTime class, which is part of the new Date-Time API, to obtain and display the current time. In the following lines of code, the LocalTime class is demonstrated.

```
public static void currentTime(){
        LocalTime time = LocalTime.now();
        System.out.println("Current Time: " + time);
}
```

Once the time has been obtained, methods can be called against the LocalTime instance to achieve the desired result. In the following lines of code, there are some examples of using the LocalTime methods.

```
// atDate(LocalDate): obtain the local date and time
LocalDateTime ldt = time.atDate(LocalDate.of(2021,Month.NOVEMBER,12));
System.out.println("Local Date Time object: " + ldt);
// of(int hours, int min): obtain a specific time
LocalTime pastTime = LocalTime.of(1, 10);
// compareTo(LocalTime): compare two times.  Positive
// return value returned if greater
System.out.println("Comparing times: " + time.compareTo(pastTime));
// getHour(): return hour in int value (24-hour format)
int hour = time.getHour();
System.out.println("Hour: " + hour);
// isAfter(LocalTime): return Boolean comparison
System.out.println("Is local time after pastTime? " + time.
isAfter(pastTime));
// minusHours(int): Subtract Hours from LocalTime
LocalTime minusHrs = time.minusHours(5);
System.out.println("Time minus 5 hours: " + minusHrs);
// plusMinutes(int): Add minutes to LocalTime
LocalTime plusMins = time.plusMinutes(30);
System.out.println("Time plus 30 mins: " + plusMins);
```

Here are the results.

```
Current Time: 12:43:58.048247
Local Date Time object: 2021-11-12T12:43:58.048247
Comparing times: 1Hour: 12
Is local time after pastTime? true
Time minus 5 hours: 07:43:58.048247
Time plus 30 mins: 13:13:58.048247
```

The main is:

```
    public static void main(String[] args){
        currentTime();
    }
```

How It Works

Sometimes it is necessary to obtain the current system time. The LocalTime class obtains the current time by calling its now() method. Similar to the LocalDate class, the LocalTime.now() method can be called to return a LocalTime object that is equal to the current time. The LocalTime class also contains several methods that can be utilized to manipulate the time. The examples contained in the solution provide a brief overview of the available methods.

Let's look at a handful of examples to provide some context for how the LocalTime methods are invoked. To obtain a LocalTime object set to a specific time, invoke the LocalTime.of(int, int) method, passing int parameters representing the hour and minute.

```
// of(int hours, int min): obtain a specific time
LocalTime pastTime = LocalTime.of(1, 10);
```

The atDate(LocalDate) instance method applies a LocalDate object to a LocalTime instance, returning a LocalDateTime object.

```
LocalDateTime ldt = time.atDate(LocalDate.of(2021,Month.NOVEMBER,12));
```

There are several methods that can obtain portions of the time. For instance, the getHour(), getMinute(), getNano(), and getSecond() methods return those specified portions of the LocalTime object.

```
int hour = time.getHour();
int min  = time.getMinute();
int nano = time.getNano();
int sec  = time.getSecond();
```

Several comparison methods are also available for use. For example, the compareTo(LocalTime) method compares one LocalTime object to another. isAfter(LocalTime) determines if the time is after another, and isBefore(LocalTime) specifies the opposite.

125

4-11. Obtaining and Using the Date and Time Together

Problem

In your application, you want to display the current date and the current time.

Solution 1

Use the LocalDateTime class, which is part of the new Date-Time API, to capture and display the current date and time. The LocalDateTime class contains a method named now(), which obtains the current date and time. The following lines of code demonstrate how to do so.

```
LocalDateTime ldt = LocalDateTime.now();
System.out.println("Local Date and Time: " + ldt);
```

The resulting LocalDateTime object contains both the date and time but no time zone information. The LocalDateTime class also contains additional methods that provide options for working with date-time data. For instance, to return a LocalDateTime object with a specified date and time, pass parameters of int type to the LocalDateTime.of() method, as follows.

```
// Obtain the LocalDateTime object of the date 11/11/2021 at 12:00
LocalDateTime ldt2 = LocalDateTime.of(2021, Month.NOVEMBER, 11, 12, 00);
```

The following examples demonstrate a handful of the methods that are available in a LocalDateTime object.

```
public static void obtainDatesWithTime(){
        LocalDateTime ldt = LocalDateTime.now();
        System.out.println("Local Date and Time: " + ldt);

        // Obtain the LocalDateTime object of the date 11/11/2021 at 12:00
        LocalDateTime ldt2 = LocalDateTime.of(2021, Month.NOVEMBER, 11,
        12, 00);
        System.out.println("Specified Date and Time: " + ldt2);
        // Obtain the month from LocalDateTime object
```

```
        Month month = ldt.getMonth();
        int monthValue = ldt.getMonthValue();
        System.out.println("Month: " + month);
        System.out.println("Month Value: " + monthValue);

        // Obtain day of Month, Week, and Year
        int day = ldt.getDayOfMonth();
        DayOfWeek dayWeek = ldt.getDayOfWeek();
        int dayOfYr = ldt.getDayOfYear();
        System.out.println("Day: " + day);
        System.out.println("Day Of Week: " + dayWeek);
        System.out.println("Day of Year: " + dayOfYr);

        // Obtain year
        int year = ldt.getYear();
        System.out.println("Date: " + monthValue + "/" + day + "/" + year);

        int hour = ldt.getHour();
        int minute = ldt.getMinute();
        int second = ldt.getSecond();
        System.out.println("Current Time: " + hour + ":" + minute +
        ":" + second);

        // Calculation of Months, etc.
        LocalDateTime currMinusMonths = ldt.minusMonths(12);
        LocalDateTime currMinusHours = ldt.minusHours(10);
        LocalDateTime currPlusDays = ldt.plusDays(30);
        System.out.println("Current Date and Time Minus 12 Months:
        " + currMinusMonths);
        System.out.println("Current Date and Time MInus 10 Hours:
        " + currMinusHours);
        System.out.println("Current Date and Time Plus 30 Days:"
        + currPlusDays);
    }
```

Here's the result.

```
Local Date and Time: 2021-12-06T19:37:53.422560400
Specified Date and Time: 2021-11-11T12:00
Month: DECEMBER
Month Value: 12
Day: 6
Day Of Week: MONDAY
Day of Year: 340
Date: 12/6/2021
Current Time: 19:37:53
Current Date and Time Minus 12 Months: 2020-12-06T19:37:53.422560400
Current Date and Time MInus 10 Hours: 2021-12-06T09:37:53.422560400
Current Date and Time Plus 30 Days:2022-01-05T19:37:53.422560400
```

The main is:

```java
    public static void main(String[] args){
            obtainDatesWithTime();
    }
```

Solution 2

If you only need to obtain the current date without going into calendar details, use the java.util.Date class to generate a new Date object. Doing so generates a new Date object that is equal to the current system date. In the following code, you can see how easy it is to create a new Date object and obtain the current date.

```java
Date date = new Date();
System.out.println("Using java.util.Date(): " + date);
System.out.println("Getting time from java.util.Date():
" + date.getTime());
```

The result is a Date object that contains the current date and time taken from the system that the code is run on, including the time zone information, as shown in the following example. The time is the number of milliseconds since January 1, 1970, 00:00:00 GMT.

```
Using java.util.Date(): Mon Dec 06 19:37:53 CET 2021
Getting time from java.util.Date(): 1638815873430
```

Solution 3

If you need to be more precise regarding the calendar, use the java.util.Calendar class. Although working with the Calendar class makes your code longer, the results are more granular than using java.util.Date. The following code demonstrates just a handful of the capabilities of using this class to obtain the current date.

```
Calendar gCal = Calendar.getInstance();

// Month is based upon a zero index, January is equal to 0,
// so we need to add one to the month for it to be in
// a standard format
int month = gCal.get(Calendar.MONTH) + 1;int day = gCal.get(Calendar.DATE);
int yr = gCal.get(Calendar.YEAR);

String dateStr = month + "/" + day + "/" + yr;
System.out.println(dateStr);

int dayOfWeek = gCal.get(Calendar.DAY_OF_WEEK);

// Print out the integer value for the day of the week
System.out.println(dayOfWeek);

int hour = gCal.get(Calendar.HOUR);
int min  = gCal.get(Calendar.MINUTE);
int sec = gCal.get(Calendar.SECOND);

// Print out the time
System.out.println(hour + ":" + min + ":" + sec);

// Create new DateFormatSymbols instance to obtain the String
// value for dates
DateFormatSymbols symbols = new DateFormatSymbols();
String[] days = symbols.getWeekdays();
System.out.println(days[dayOfWeek]);

// Get crazy with the date!
int dayOfYear = gCal.get(Calendar.DAY_OF_YEAR);
System.out.println(dayOfYear);
```

```
// Print the number of days left in the year
System.out.println("Days left in " + yr + ": " + (365-dayOfYear));

int week = gCal.get(Calendar.WEEK_OF_YEAR);
// Print the week of the year
System.out.println(week);
```

This code demonstrates that it is possible to obtain more detailed information regarding the current date when using the Calendar class. The results of running the code look like the following.

```
12/6/2021
2
7:37:53
lunedì
340
Days left in 2021: 25
49
```

How It Works

Many applications require the use of the current calendar date. It is often also necessary to obtain the current time. There are different ways to do that, and the solution to this recipe demonstrates three of them. The Date-Time API includes a LocalDateTime class that enables you to capture the current date and time by invoking its now() method. A specified date and time can be obtained by specifying the corresponding int and month type parameters when calling LocalDateTime.of(). There are also a multitude of methods available for use via a LocalDateTime instance, such as getHours(), getMinutes(), getNanos(), and getSeconds(), which allow for finer-grained control of the date and time. An instance of LocalDateTime also contains methods for performing calculations, conversions, comparisons, and more. Solution 1 to this recipe demonstrates the use of the LocalDateTime, showcasing how to perform calculations and obtain portions of the date and time for further use.

By default, the java.util.Date class can be instantiated with no arguments to return the current date and time. The Date class can also return the current time via the getTime() method. As mentioned in the solution, the getTime() method returns the number of milliseconds since January 1, 1970, 00:00:00 GMT, represented by the

Date object that is in use. Several other methods can be called against a Date object with regard to breaking down the current date and time into more granular intervals. For instance, the Date class has the getHours(), getMinutes(), getSeconds(), getMonth(), getDay(), getTimezoneOffset(), and getYear() methods. However, it is not advisable to use any of these methods, except getTime(), because each has been deprecated using java.time.LocalDateTime and the java.util.Calendar get() methods. When a method or class is deprecated, it should no longer be used because it might be removed in some future release of the Java language. However, a few of the methods contained within the Date class have not been tagged as deprecated, so the Date class most likely be included in future releases of Java. The methods that were left intact include the after(), before(), compareTo(), setTime(), and equals() comparison methods. Solution 2 to this recipe demonstrates instantiating a Date object and printing out the current date and time.

As mentioned previously, the Date class has many methods that have become deprecated and should no longer be used. In solution 3 of this recipe, the java.util. Calendar class is demonstrated as one successor for obtaining much of this information. The Calendar class was introduced in JDK 1.1, at which time many of the Date methods were deprecated. As you can see from solution 3, the Calendar class contains all the same functionality included in the Date class, except the Calendar class is much more flexible. The Calendar class contains methods used for converting between a specific time and date and manipulating the calendar in various ways. The Calendar class gained a few new methods in Java 8. One new method was java.util.

For some applications, the Date class works fine. For instance, the Date class can be useful when working with timestamps. However, if the application requires detailed manipulation of dates and times, then it is advisable to use a LocalDateTime or the Calendar class, which both include all the functionality of the Date class and more features as well. All solutions to this recipe are technically sound; choose the one that best suits the needs of your application.

4-12. Obtaining a Machine Timestamp

Problem

You need to obtain a machine-based timestamp from the system.

Solution

Utilize an Instant class, which represents the start of a nanosecond on the timeline based on machine time. In the following example, an Instant class obtains the system timestamp. The Instant class is also utilized in other scenarios, such as when calculating different dates based on the Instant.

```
public static void instants(){
        Instant timestamp = Instant.now();
        System.out.println("The current timestamp: " + timestamp);

        //Now minus three days
        Instant minusThree = timestamp.minus(3, ChronoUnit.DAYS);
        System.out.println("Now minus three days:" + minusThree);

        ZonedDateTime atZone = timestamp.atZone(ZoneId.of("GMT"));
        System.out.println(atZone);

        Instant yesterday = Instant.now().minus(24, ChronoUnit.HOURS);
        System.out.println("Yesterday: " + yesterday);
    }
```

Here is the result.

```
The current timestamp: 2021-10-13T21:06:50.203477900Z
Now minus three days:2021-10-10T21:06:50.203477900Z
2021-10-13T21:06:50.203477900Z[GMT]
Yesterday: 2021-10-12T21:06:50.221430600Z
```

How It Works

The Date-Time API introduces a new class named Instant, which represents the start of a nanosecond on the timeline in machine-based time. Based on machine time, the value in an Instant class counts from EPOCH (January 1, 1970 00:00:00Z). Any values prior to the EPOCH are negative, and after the EPOCH the values are positive. The Instant class is perfect for obtaining a machine timestamp, as it includes all pertinent date and time information to the nanosecond.

An Instant class is static and immutable, so the now() method can be called to obtain the current timestamp. Doing so returns a copy of the current Instant. The Instant class also includes conversion and calculation methods. Each returns copies of the Instant class or other types. In the solution, the now() method returns the current timestamp, and then a couple of examples follow, showing how to perform calculations and obtain information on the Instant.

The Instant class is an important new feature in Java 8 because it makes it easy to work with the current time and date data. The other date and time classes, such as LocalDateTime, are also useful. However, the Instant class is the most accurate timestamp because it's based on nanosecond accuracy.

4-13. Converting Dates and Times Based on he Time Zone

Problem

The application you are developing has the potential to be utilized throughout the world. In some areas of the application, static dates and times need to be displayed, rather than the system date and time. In such cases, those static dates and times need to be converted to suit the particular time zone in which the application user is currently residing.

Solution

The Date-Time API provides the proper utilities for working with time zone data via the Time Zone and Offset classes. In the following scenario, suppose that the application works with reservations for rental vehicles. You could rent a vehicle in one time zone and return it in another. The following lines of code demonstrate how to print out an individual's reservation in such a scenario. The following method, named scheduleReport, accepts LocalDateTime objects representing check-in and check-out date/time, along with ZoneIds for each. An airline could use this method to print time zone information for a particular flight.

```
public static void scheduleReport(LocalDateTime checkOut, ZoneId checkOutZone,
                    LocalDateTime checkIn, ZoneId checkInZone){
```

133

```
ZonedDateTime beginTrip = ZonedDateTime.of(checkOut, checkOutZone);
System.out.println("Trip Begins: " + beginTrip);

// Get the rules of the check out time zone
ZoneRules checkOutZoneRules = checkOutZone.getRules();
System.out.println("Checkout Time Zone Rules: " + checkOutZoneRules);

//If the trip took 4 days
ZonedDateTime beginPlus = beginTrip.plusDays(4);
System.out.println("Four Days Later: " + beginPlus);

// End of trip in starting time zone
ZonedDateTime endTripOriginalZone = ZonedDateTime.of(checkIn,
checkOutZone);
ZonedDateTime endTrip = ZonedDateTime.of(checkIn, checkInZone);
int diff = endTripOriginalZone.compareTo(endTrip);
String diffStr = (diff >= 0) ? "NO":"YES";
System.out.println("End trip date/time in original zone: " +
endTripOriginalZone);
System.out.println("End trip date/time in check-in zone: " + endTrip );
System.out.println("Original Zone Time is less than new zone time? " +
        diffStr );
ZoneId checkOutZoneId = beginTrip.getZone();
ZoneOffset checkOutOffset = beginTrip.getOffset();
ZoneId checkInZoneId = endTrip.getZone();
ZoneOffset checkInOffset = endTrip.getOffset();

System.out.println("Check out zone and offset: " + checkOutZoneId +
checkOutOffset);
System.out.println("Check in zone and offset: " + checkInZoneId
+ checkInOffset);
}
```

Here is the result.

```
Trip Begins: 2021-12-13T13:00-05:00[US/Eastern]
Checkout Time Zone Rules: ZoneRules[currentStandardOffset=-05:00]
Four Days Later: 2021-12-17T13:00-05:00[US/Eastern]
```

End trip date/time in original zone: 2021-12-18T10:00-05:00[US/Eastern]
End trip date/time in check-in zone: 2021-12-18T10:00-07:00[US/Mountain]
Original Zone Time is less than new zone time? YES
Check out zone and offset: US/Eastern-05:00
Check in zone and offset: US/Mountain-07:00

How It Works

Time zones add yet another challenge for developers, and the Java Date-Time API
provides an easy facet for working with them. The Date-Time API includes a java.time
.zone package, which contains several classes that can assist in working with time zone
data. These classes support time zone rules, data, and resulting gaps and overlaps in the
local timeline that are typically the result of daylight savings conversions. The classes
that make up the zone package are outlined in Table 4-2.

Table 4-2. *Time Zone Classes*

Class Name	Description
ZoneId	Specifies zone identifier and is used for conversions
ZoneOffset	Specifies a time zone offset from Greenwich/UTC time
ZonedDateTime	A date-time object that also handles the time zone data with time zone offset from Greenwich/UTC time
ZoneRules	Rules defining how a zone offset varies for a specified time zone
ZoneRulesProvider	Provider of time zone rules to a particular system
ZoneOffsetTransition	Transition between two offsets by a discontinuity in the local timeline
ZoneOffsetTransitionRule	Rules expressing how to create a transition

Starting with the most fundamental time zone class, ZoneId, each time zone contains
a particular time zone identifier. This identifier can be useful for assigning a particular
time zone to a date-time. In the solution, the ZoneId class calculates any differences
between two time zones. It identifies the rules that should be used for converting, based
on a particular offset, either fixed or geographical region-based.

ZonedDateTime is an immutable class that works with date-time and time zone data together. This class represents an object, much like LocalDateTime, which includes ZoneId. It expresses all facets of a date, including year, month, day, hours, minutes, seconds, nanoseconds, and time zone. The class contains a bevy of useful methods for performing calculations, conversions, and so on.

ZoneOffset specifies a time zone offset from Greenwich/UTC time. You can find the offset for a particular time zone by invoking the ZonedDateTime.getOffset() method. The ZoneOffset class includes methods that make it easy to break down an offset into different time units. For instance, the getTotalSeconds() method returns the total hours, minutes, and seconds fields as a single offset that can be added to a time.

Many rules can be defined for determining how zone offset varies for a single time zone. The ZoneRules class defines these rules for a zone. For instance, ZoneRules can be called on to specify or determine if daylight savings time is a factor. An Instant or LocalDateTime can also be passed to ZoneRules methods such as getOffset() and getTransition() to return ZoneOffset or ZoneOffsetTransition.

Another time zone class that is used often is ZoneOffsetTransition. This class models the transition between the spring and autumn offsets due to daylight savings time. It determines if there is a gap between transitions, obtaining the duration of a transition, and so on.

ZoneRulesProvider, ZoneOffsetTransitionRule, and other classes are typically not utilized as often as others for working with dates and time zones. These classes are useful for managing the configuration of time zone rules and transitions.

Note   The classes within the java.time.zone package are significant, in that there are a multitude of methods that can be invoked on each class. This recipe provides a primer for getting started, with only the basics of time zone usage. For more detailed information, see the online documentation.

4-14. Comparing Two Dates
Problem

You want to determine whether one date is greater than another.

Solution

Utilize one of the compareTo() methods that are part of the Date-Time API classes. In the following solution, two LocalDate objects are compared and an appropriate message is displayed.

```
public static void compareDates(LocalDate ldt1,
            LocalDate ldt2) {
        int comparison = ldt1.compareTo(ldt2);
        if (comparison > 0) {
            System.out.println(ldt1 + " is larger than " + ldt2);
        } else if (comparison < 0) {
            System.out.println(ldt1 + " is smaller than " + ldt2);
        } else {
            System.out.println(ldt1 + " is equal to " + ldt2);
        }
    }
```

Similarly, there are convenience methods for use when performing date comparison. Specifically, the isAfter(), isBefore(), and isEqual() methods can compare in the same manner as compareTo(), as seen in the following example.

```
public static void compareDates2(LocalDate ldt1, LocalDate ldt2){
    if(ldt1.isAfter(ldt2)){
        System.out.println(ldt1 + " is after " + ldt2);
    } else if (ldt1.isBefore(ldt2)){
        System.out.println(ldt1 + " is before " + ldt2);
    } else if (ldt1.isEqual(ldt2)){
        System.out.println(ldt1 + " is equal to " + ldt2);
    }
}
```

The main is:

```
        public static void main(String[] args) {
                LocalDate anniversary = LocalDate.of(2000,
                Month.NOVEMBER, 11);
                LocalDate today = LocalDate.now();
                compareDates(anniversary, today);
```

```
            compareDates2(anniversary, anniversary);
    }
```
The output is:

```
2000-11-11 is before 2021-11-30
2000-11-11 is equal to 2000-11-11
```

How It Works

Many of the Date-Time API classes contain a method that compares two different date-time objects. In the solution to this example, the LocalDate.compareTo() method determines if one LocalDate object is greater than another. The compareTo() method returns a negative int value if the first LocalDate object is greater than the second, a zero if they are equal, and a positive number if the second LocalDate object is greater than the first. Each of the date-time classes that contain compareTo() has the same outcome. An int value is returned indicating if the first object is greater than, less than, or equal to the second.

As seen in the second example, the isAfter(), isBefore(), and isEqual() methods can also be used for comparison purposes. These methods return a boolean to indicate the comparison results. While the outcome of these methods can perform date comparison in much the same way as compareTo(), they can make code a bit easier to read.

4-15. Finding the Interval Between Dates and Times

Problem

You need to determine how many hours, days, weeks, months, or years have elapsed between two dates or times.

Solution 1

Utilize the Date-Time API to determine the difference between two dates. Specifically, use the Period class to determine the period of time, in days, between two dates. The following example demonstrates how to obtain the interval of days, months, and years between two dates.

> **Note**   This example shows the difference in days, months, and years, but not the cumulative days or months between two dates. To determine the total cumulative days, months, and years between two dates, read on for solutions #2 and #3.

```
public static void intervals(){
        LocalDate anniversary = LocalDate.of(2015, Month.NOVEMBER, 11);
        LocalDate today = LocalDate.now();
        Period period = Period.between(anniversary, today);
        System.out.println("Number of Days Difference:
        " + period.getDays());
        System.out.println("Number of Months Difference:
        " + period.getMonths());
        System.out.println("Number of Years Difference:
        " + period.getYears());
}
```

Here is the difference result for today's date (**2021-12-06**).

```
Number of Days Difference: 25
Number of Months Difference: 0
Number of Years Difference: 6
```

Solution 2

Use `java.util.concurrent.TimeUnit` enum to perform calculations between given dates. Using this enum, you can obtain the integer values for days, hours, microseconds, milliseconds, minutes, nanoseconds, and seconds. Doing so allow you to perform the necessary calculations.

```
public static void compareDatesCalendar() {
        // Obtain two instances of the Calendar class
        Calendar cal1 = Calendar.getInstance();
        Calendar cal2 = Calendar.getInstance();

        // Set the date to 01/01/2010:12:00
        cal2.set(2010,0,1,12,0,0);
```

```
        Date date1 = cal2.getTime();
        System.out.println(date1);
        System.out.println(cal1.getTime());

        long mill = Math.abs(cal1.getTimeInMillis() - date1.getTime());
        // Convert to hours
        long hours = TimeUnit.MILLISECONDS.toHours(mill);
        // Convert to days
        Long days = TimeUnit.HOURS.toDays(hours);
        String diff = String.format("%d hour(s) %d min(s)", hours,
        TimeUnit.MILLISECONDS.toMinutes(mill) -
        TimeUnit.HOURS.toMinutes(hours));
        System.out.println(diff);

        diff = String.format("%d days", days);
        System.out.println(diff);

        // Divide the number of days by seven for the weeks
        int weeks = days.intValue()/7;
        diff = String.format("%d weeks", weeks);
        System.out.println(diff);
}
```

Here is the result for today's date (**2021-12-06 19:42**).

```
Fri Jan 01 12:00:00 CET 2010
Mon Dec 06 19:42:17 CET 2021
104575 hour(s) 42 min(s)
4357 days
622 weeks
Years between dates: 6
Days between dates:2216
```

The output of this code is formatted to display strings of text that indicate the differences between the current date and the Date object that is created.

The following is the main class.

```
public static void main(String[] args){
        intervals();
        compareDatesCalendar();
}
```

How It Works

As with most programmatic techniques, Java has more than one way to perform date calculations. The Date-Time API introduced in Java 8 includes new techniques for determining time intervals. The `Period` class determines the difference period between two units for specified objects. To obtain a period between two date-time objects, call the `Period.between()` method, passing the two date-time objects for which you'd like to obtain the period. The `Period` class has several methods to break down the intervals into different units. For instance, the number of days in the two date-time objects can be obtained using the `getDays()` method. Similarly, the `getMonths()` and `getYears()` methods can be called to return the number of months or years in the period.

One of the most useful techniques is to perform calculations based on the given date's time in milliseconds. This provides the most accurate calculation because it works at a very small interval: milliseconds. The current time in milliseconds can be obtained from a `Calendar` object by calling the `getTimeInMillis()` method against it. Likewise, a `Date` object returns its value represented in milliseconds by calling the `getTime()` method. As you can see from the solution to this recipe, the first calculation finds the difference between the given dates in milliseconds. Obtaining that value and then taking its absolute value provides the base needed to perform the date calculations.

4-16. Obtaining Date-Time from a Specified String

Problem

You want to parse a string into a date-time object.

Solution

Utilize the parse() method of a temporal date-time class to parse a string using a predefined or custom format. The following lines of code demonstrate how to parse a string into a date or date-time object using variations of the parse() method.

```
public static void parseDateTime(){
        // Parse a string to form a Date-Time object
        LocalDate ld = LocalDate.parse("2019-12-28");
        LocalDateTime ldt = LocalDateTime.parse("2019-12-28T08:44:00");
        System.out.println("Parsed Date: " + ld);
        System.out.println("Parsed Date-Time: " + ldt);

        // Using a different Parser
        LocalDate ld2 = LocalDate.parse("2019-12-28",
        DateTimeFormatter.ISO_DATE);
        System.out.println("Different Parser: " + ld2);

        // Custom Parser
        String input = "12/28/2019";
        try {
            DateTimeFormatter formatter = DateTimeFormatter.ofPattern
            ("MM/dd/yyyy");
            LocalDate ld3 = LocalDate.parse(input, formatter);
            System.out.println("Custom Parsed Date: " + ld3);
        } catch (DateTimeParseException ex){
            System.out.println("Not parsable: " + ex);
        }
}
```

Here is the result.

```
Parsed Date: 2019-12-28
Parsed Date-Time: 2019-12-28T08:44
Different Parser: 2019-12-28
Custom Parsed Date: 2019-12-28
```

The main is:

```
    public static void main(String[] args) {
        parseDateTime();
    }
```

How It Works

The temporal classes of the Date-Time API include a `parse()` method, which parses a given input string using a specified format. By default, the `parse()` method format is based on the target object's default `DateTimeFormatter`. For example, to parse the string "2019-01-01", the default `LocalDate.parse()` method can be called.

```
LocalDate date = LocalDate.parse("2019-01-01");
```

However, another `DateTimeFormatter` can be specified as a second argument to the `parse()` method. `DateTimeFormatter` is a final class used for formatting and printing dates and times. It contains several built-in formatters that can be specified to coerce strings into date-time objects. Often, it is necessary to parse strings of text into date-time objects. Such tasks are made easy with the `parse()` method built into many core date-time classes.

4-17. Formatting Dates for Display
Problem

Dates need to be displayed by your application using a specific format. You want to define that format once and apply it to all dates that need to be displayed.

Solution 1

Utilize the `DateTimeFormatter` class, part of the Date-Time API, to format dates and times according to the pattern you want to use. The `DateTimeFormatter` class includes an `ofPattern()` method, which accepts a string pattern argument to designate the desired pattern. Each of the temporal date-time classes includes a `format()` method, which accepts a `DateTimeFormatter` and returns the string-based format of the target date-time object. In the following lines of code, the `DateTimeFormatter` is demonstrated.

```
    public static void formatting() {
        try {
        DateTimeFormatter dateFormatter = DateTimeFormatter.ofPattern
        ("MMMM dd yyyy");

        LocalDateTime now = LocalDateTime.now();
        String output = now.format(dateFormatter);
        System.out.println(output);

        DateTimeFormatter dateFormatter2 = DateTimeFormatter.ofPattern
        ("MM/dd/YY HH:mm:ss");
        String output2 = now.format(dateFormatter2);
        System.out.println(output2);

        DateTimeFormatter dateFormatter3 = DateTimeFormatter.ofPattern
        ("hh 'o''clock' a, zzzz");
        ZonedDateTime zdt = ZonedDateTime.now();
        String output3 = zdt.format(dateFormatter3);
        System.out.println(output3);
    } catch (DateTimeException ex) {
            System.out.println("Cannot be formatted: " + ex);
        }
}
```

Here is the result.

```
ottobre 13 2021
10/13/21 22:44:00
10 o'clock PM, Ora legale dell'Europa centrale
```

Solution 2

Use the java.util.Calendar class to obtain the date that you require and then format
that date using the java.text.SimpleDateFormat class. The following example
demonstrates the use of the SimpleDateFormat class.

```
public static void formatExamplesCalendar() {
        // Create new calendar
```

```
Calendar cal = Calendar.getInstance();

// Create instance of SimpleDateFormat class using pattern
SimpleDateFormat dateFormatter1 = new SimpleDateFormat
("MMMMM dd yyyy");
String result = null;

result = dateFormatter1.format(cal.getTime());
System.out.println(result);

dateFormatter1.applyPattern("MM/dd/YY hh:mm:ss");
result = dateFormatter1.format(cal.getTime());
System.out.println(result);

dateFormatter1.applyPattern("hh 'o''clock' a, zzzz");
result = dateFormatter1.format(cal.getTime());
System.out.println(result);
}
```

Running this example would yield the following result.

```
ottobre 13 2021
10/13/21 10:44:01
10 o'clock PM, Ora legale dell'Europa centrale
```

The main is:

```
public static void main(String[] args) {
    formatting();
    formatExamplesCalendar();
}
```

As you can see from the results, the DateTimeFormatter and SimpleDateFormat classes make it easy to convert a date into just about any format.

How It Works

Date formatting is a common concern when it comes to any program. People like to see their dates in a certain format for different situations. The Java language contains a couple of handy utilities for properly formatting date-time data. Specifically, the newer API includes the `DateTimeFormatter` class, and previous editions of Java SE include the `SimpleDateFormat` class, each of which can come in handy for performing formatting processes.

The `DateTimeFormatter` class is a final class with the primary purpose of printing and formatting date-time objects. To obtain a `DateTimeFormatter` that can be applied to objects, call the `DateTimeFormatter.ofPattern()` method, passing the string-based pattern representing the desired output. The `SimpleDateFormat` class was created in previous editions of Java, so you don't have to perform manual translations for a given date.

Note   Different date formats are used within different locales, and the `SimpleDateFormat` class facilitates locale-specific formatting.

To use the class, an instance must be instantiated either by passing a string-based pattern as an argument to the constructor or by passing no argument to the constructor at all. The string-based pattern provides a template that should be applied to the given date, and then a string representing the date in the given pattern style is returned. A pattern consists of many different characters strung together.

Any pattern characters can be placed together in a string and then passed to the `SimpleDateFormat` class. If the class is instantiated without passing a pattern, the pattern can be applied later using the class's `applyPattern()` method. The `applyPattern()` method also comes in handy when you want to change the pattern of an instantiated `SimpleDateFormat` object, as seen in the solution to this recipe. The following excerpts of code demonstrate the application of a pattern.

```
SimpleDateFormat dateFormatter1 = new SimpleDateFormat("MMMMM dd yyyy");
dateFormatter1.applyPattern("MM/dd/YY hh:mm:ss");
```

Once a pattern has been applied to a `SimpleDateFormat` object, a long value representing time can be passed to the `SimpleDateFormat` object's `format()` method. The `format()` method returns the given date\time formatted using the applied pattern. The string-based result can then be used however your application requires.

4-18. Writing Readable Numeric Literals
Problem

Some of the numeric literals in your application are rather long and you want to make it easier to tell how large a number is at a glance.

Solution

Use underscores in place of commas or decimals in larger numbers to make them more readable. The following code shows some examples of making your numeric literals more readable by using underscores in place of commas.

```
public static void main(String[] args) {
    int million = 1_000_000;
    int billion = 1_000_000_000;
    float ten_pct = 1_0f;
    double exp = 1_234_56.78_9e2;
    System.out.println(million);
    System.out.println(billion);
    System.out.println(ten_pct);
    System.out.println(exp);
}
```
The output is:

1000000

1000000000

10.0

1.23456789E7

Note   Decimal point values automatically default to a double value unless a trailing "f" indicates that the value is a float.

How It Works

Sometimes working with large numbers can become cumbersome and difficult to read. Since Java 7, underscores can be used with numeric literals to make code a bit easier to read. The underscores can appear anywhere between digits in a numeric literal. This allows underscores in place of commas or spaces to separate the digits and make them easier to read.

Note   Underscores cannot be placed at the beginning or the end of a number, adjacent to a decimal point or floating-point literal, before an *F* or *L* suffix, or in positions where a string of digits is expected.

4-19. Declaring Binary Literals

Problem

You are working on an application that requires the declaration of binary numbers.

Solution

Use binary literals to make your code readable. The following code segment demonstrates the use of binary literals.

```
public static void main(String[] args) {
    int bin1 = 0b1100;
    short bin2 = 0B010101;
    short bin3 = (short) 0b1001100110011001;

    System.out.println(bin1);
    System.out.println(bin2);
    System.out.println(bin3);

}
```

This result in the following output.

```
12
21
-26215
```

How It Works

Binary literals became part of the Java language starting in Java 7. The byte, short, int, and long types can be expressed using the binary number system. This feature can help to make binary numbers easier to recognize in code. To use the binary format, simply prefix the number with 0b or 0B.

4-20. Period of Day

Problem

You want to express the periods of a day not as a.m. or p.m. but as "in the morning" or "in the afternoon" or "at night".

Solution

Java 16 addresses that goal with a new formatter pattern, called B. In the following example, the period of the day is translated into text according to the time of the day.

```java
public static void main(String[] args) {
        final String whatPeriodOfTheDay
        = DateTimeFormatter.ofPattern("B").format(LocalTime.now());
        System.out.println("Pattern B: " + whatPeriodOfTheDay);
}
```

The following is the output in Italian.

```
Pattern B: del pomeriggio (in the afternoon)
```

How It Works

In Java 16, the period of the day was added to java.time formats.

4-21. Summary

Numbers and dates play an integral role in most applications. This chapter reviewed some techniques that can be used for rounding and formatting numbers and generating random values. It also provided a brief overview of some commonly used date-time features.

CHAPTER 5

Object-Oriented Java

Object-oriented programs consist of many different pieces of code that all work together in unison. Rather than write a program that contains a long list of statements and commands, an object-oriented philosophy is to break functionality into separate organized objects. Each of the objects contains functionality that pertains to it, and as the objects are pieced together, they can be used to develop sophisticated solutions. In this chapter, we touch on some of the key object-oriented features of the Java language. From the basic recipes covering access modifiers to the advanced recipes that deal with inner classes, this chapter contains recipes that help you understand Java's object-oriented methodologies.

5-1. Controlling Access to Members of a Class
Problem

You want to create members of a class that are not accessible from any other class.

Solution

Create `private` instance members rather than making them available to other classes (`public` or `protected`). For instance, suppose you are creating an application to manage a team of players for a sport. You create a class named `Player` that represents a player on the team. You do not want the fields for that class to be accessible from any other class. The following code demonstrates the declaration of some instance members, making them accessible only from within the class in which they were defined.

```
private String firstName;
private String lastName;
```

151

© Josh Juneau, Luciano Manelli 2022
J. Juneau and L. Manelli, *Java 17 Recipes*, https://doi.org/10.1007/978-1-4842-7963-2_5

```java
private String position;
private int status = -1;
```

How It Works

To designate a class member as `private`, prefix its declaration or signature using the `private` keyword. The `private` access modifier hides members of a class so that outside classes cannot access them. Any members of a class marked as `private` are available only to other members of the same class. Any outside class cannot access fields or methods designated as private, and an IDE that uses code completion cannot see them.

As mentioned in the solution to this recipe, three different access modifiers can be used when declaring members of a class. Those modifiers are `public`, `protected`, and `private`. Members that are declared as `public` are available for any other class. Those declared as `protected` are available for any other class within the same package and subclasses. It is best to declare `public` or `protected` only those class members that need to be directly accessed from another class. Hiding members of a class using the `private` access modifier helps to enforce better object-orientation. Moreover, a default scope is accessible from the package and the class— that occurs when it is not assigned scope to a class element.

5-2. Making Private Fields Accessible to Other Classes

Problem

You want to create `private` instance members so that outside classes cannot access them directly. However, you would also like to make those `private` members accessible in a controlled manner.

Solution

Encapsulate the `private` fields by making getters and setters to access them. The following code demonstrates the declaration of a `private` field, followed by accessor (getter) and mutator (setter) methods that obtain or set the value of that field from an outside class.

```java
private String firstName;
/**
 * @return the firstName
 */
public String getFirstName() {
 return firstName;
}
/**
 * @param firstName the firstName to set
 */
public void setFirstName(String firstName) {
    this.firstName = firstName;
}
```

The getFirstName() method can be used by an outside class to obtain the value of the firstName field. Likewise, an outside class can use the setFirstName(String firstName) method to set the value of the firstName field.

How It Works

Often when fields are marked as private within a class, they still need to be made accessible to outside classes to set or retrieve their value. Why not just work with the fields directly and make them public then? It is not good programming practice to work directly with fields of other classes because access can be granted in a controlled fashion by using accessors (getters) and mutators (setters). By not coding directly against members of another class, you also help decouple the code, which helps to ensure that if an object changes, others that depend on it are not adversely affected. As you can see from the example in the solution to this recipe, hiding fields and working with public methods to access those fields is fairly easy. Simply create two methods; one to obtain the value of the private field, the *getter* or accessor method. And the other to set the value of the private field, the *setter* or mutator method. In the solution to this recipe, the getter returns the unaltered value contained within the private field. Similarly, the setter sets the value of the private field by accepting an argument of the same data type as the private field and then setting the value of the private field to the value of the argument.

The class using the getters or setters for access to the fields does not know any details behind the methods. For instance, a getter or setter method could contain more functionality if required. Furthermore, the details of these methods can be changed without altering any code that accesses them.

Note   Using getters and setters does not completely decouple code. In fact, many people argue that using getters and setters is not a good programming practice. Objects that use the accessor methods still need to know the type of instance field they are working against. That said, getters and setters are standard techniques for providing external access to `private` instance fields of an object. To make the use of accessor methods in a more object-oriented manner, declare them within interfaces and code against the interface rather than the object itself.

5-3. Creating a Class with a Single Instance

Problem

You want to create a class for which only one instance can exist in the entire application so that all application users interact with the same instance of that class.

Solution 1

Create the class using the singleton pattern. A class implementing the singleton pattern allows for only one instance of the class and provides a single point of access to the instance. Suppose that you wanted to create a `Statistics` class that would calculate the statistics for each team and player within an organized sport. It does not make sense to have multiple instances of this class within the application, so you want to create the `Statistics` class as a singleton to prevent multiple instances from being generated. The following class represents the singleton pattern.

```
package org.java17recipes.chapter05.recipe05_03;

import java.util.ArrayList;
import java.util.List;
```

```java
import java.io.Serializable;

public class Statistics implements Serializable {

private static final long serialVersionUID = 1L;

// Definition for the class instance
private static final Statistics INSTANCE = new Statistics();
private List<String> teams = new ArrayList ();

/**
 * Constructor has been made private so that outside classes do not have
 * access to instantiate more instances of Statistics.
 */
private Statistics(){
}

/**
 * Accessor for the statistics class.  Only allows for one instance of the
 * class to be created.
 * @return
 */
public static Statistics getInstance(){
    return INSTANCE ;
}
/**
 * @return the teams
 */
public List<String> getTeams() {
    return teams;
}
/**
 * @param teams the teams to set
 */
public void setTeams(List<String> teams) {
    this.teams = teams;
}
}
```

If another class attempts to create an instance of this class, it uses the getInstance() accessor method to obtain the singleton instance. It is important to note that the solution code demonstrates eager instantiation, which means that the instance is instantiated when the singleton is loaded. For lazy instantiation, which is instantiated on the first request, you must take care to synchronize the getInstance() method to make it thread-safe. The following code demonstrates an example of lazy instantiation.

```java
public static Statistics getInstance(){
    synchronized(Statistics.class){
        if (instance == null){
            instance = new Statistics();
        }
    }
    return instance;
}
```

Solution 2

First, create an enum and declare a single element named INSTANCE within it. Next, declare other fields within the enum that you can use to store the values that are required for use by your application. The following enum represents a singleton with the same abilities as solution 1.

```java
import java.util.ArrayList;
import java.util.List;

public enum StatisticsSingleton {
    INSTANCE;
    private List<String> teams = new ArrayList ();
    /**
     * @return the teams
     */
    public List<String> getTeams() {
        return teams;
    }
```

```
    /**
     * @param teams the teams to set
     */
    public void setTeams(List<String> teams) {
        this.teams = teams;
    }
}
```

The main class is:

```
public static void main(String[] args){
        StatisticsSingleton stats = StatisticsSingleton.INSTANCE;

        System.out.println("Adding objects to the list using stats object");

        List<String> mylist = stats.getTeams();
        mylist.add("One");
        mylist.add("Two");

        System.out.println("Reading objects from the list using stats2
        object");
        StatisticsSingleton stats2 = StatisticsSingleton.INSTANCE;
        List<String> mylist2 = stats2.getTeams();
        for(Object name : mylist2){
            System.out.println(name.toString());
        }
```

The output is:

```
Adding objects to the list using stats object
Reading objects from the list using stats2 object
One
Two
```

Note There is a test class within the recipe05_03 package that you can use to work with the enum singleton solution.

How It Works

The singleton pattern creates classes that cannot be instantiated by any other class. This can be useful when you only want one instance of a class to be used for the entire application. The singleton pattern can be applied to a class by following three steps. First, make the constructor of the class `private` so that no outside class can instantiate it. Next, define a `private static volatile` field representing an instance of the class. The `volatile` keyword guarantees each thread uses the same instance. Create an instance of the class and assign it to the field. In the solution to this recipe, the class name is `Statistics`, and the field definition is as follows.

```
private static volatile Statistics instance = new Statistics();
```

Lastly, implement an accessor method called `getInstance()` that simply returns the instance field. The following code demonstrates such an accessor method.

```
public static Statistics getInstance(){
    return instance;
}
```

To use the singleton from another class, call the singleton's `getInstance()` method. This returns an instance of the class. The following code shows an example of another class obtaining an instance to the `Statistics` singleton defined in solution 1 to this recipe.

```
Statistics statistics = Statistics.getInstance();
List<String> teams = statistics.getTeams();
```

Any class that calls the `getInstance()` method obtains the same instance. Therefore, the fields contained within the singleton have the same value for every call to `getInstance()` within the entire application.

What happens if the singleton is serialized and then deserialized? This situation may cause another object instance to be returned on deserialization. To prevent this issue from occurring, be sure to implement the `readResolve()` method, as demonstrated in solution 1. This method is called when the object is deserialized, and simply returning the instance ensures that another instance is not generated.

Solution 2 demonstrates a different way to create a singleton, using a Java enum rather than a class. Using this approach can be beneficial because an enum provides serialization, prohibits multiple instantiations, and allows you to work with code more concisely to implement the enum singleton, create an enum and declare an INSTANCE element. This is a static constant that returns an instance of the enum to classes that reference it. You can then add elements to the enum that can be used by other classes within the application to store values.

As with any programming solution, there is more than one way to do things. Some believe that the standard singleton pattern demonstrated in solution 1 is not the most desirable solution. Others do not like the enum solution for different reasons. Although you may find that one works better than the other in certain circumstances, both work.

5-4. Generating Instances of a Class
Problem

In one of your applications, you want to provide the ability to generate instances of an object on the fly. Each instance of the object should be ready to use, and the object creator should not need to know about the details of the object creation.

Solution

Use the factory method pattern to instantiate instances of the class while abstracting the creation process from the object creator. Creating a factory enables new instances of a class to be returned on invocation. The following class represents a simple factory that returns a new instance of a Player subclass each time its createPlayer(String) method is called. The subclass of Player that is returned depends on what string value is passed to the createPlayer method.

```java
public class PlayerFactory {
    public static Player createPlayer(String playerType){
        Player returnType;
        switch(playerType){
        case "GOALIE":
            returnType = new Goalie();
            break;
        case "LEFT":
            returnType = new LeftWing();
            break;
```

```java
        case "RIGHT":
            returnType = new RightWing();
            break;
        case "CENTER":
            returnType = new Center();
            break;
        case "DEFENSE":
            returnType = new Defense();
            break;
        default:
            returnType = new AllPlayer();
        }
        return returnType;
    }
}
```

If a class wants to use the factory, it simply calls the static createPlayer method, passing a string value representing a new instance of Player. The following code represents one of the Player subclasses; the others could be very similar.

```java
public class Goalie extends Player {
    private int totalSaves;
    public Goalie(){
        this.setPosition("GOALIE");
    }
    /**
     * @return the totalSaves
     */
    public int getTotalSaves() {
        return totalSaves;
    }
    /**
     * @param totalSaves the totalSaves to set
     */
```

```java
    public void setTotalSaves(int totalSaves) {
        this.totalSaves = totalSaves;
    }
}
```

The Player class is:

```java
package org.java17recipes.chapter05.recipe05_04;

public abstract class Player implements PlayerType {

    private String firstName;
    private String lastName;
    private String position;
    private int status = -1;

    public Player(){

    }

    public Player (String position, int status){
        this.position = position;
        this.status = status;
    }

    protected String playerStatus(){
        String returnValue = null;

        switch(getStatus()){
                case 0:
                        returnValue = "ACTIVE";
                case 1:
                        returnValue = "INACTIVE";
                case 2:
                        returnValue = "INJURY";
                default:
                        returnValue = "ON_BENCH";
        }

        return returnValue;
    }
```

```java
public String playerString(){
    return getFirstName() + " " + getLastName() + " -
    " + getPosition();
}

/**
 * @return the firstName
 */
public String getFirstName() {
    return firstName;
}

/**
 * @param firstName the firstName to set
 */
public void setFirstName(String firstName) {
    if (firstName.length() > 30){
        this.firstName = firstName.substring(0, 29);
    } else {
        this.firstName = firstName;
    }
}

/**
 * @return the lastName
 */
public String getLastName() {
    return lastName;
}

/**
 * @param lastName the lastName to set
 */
public void setLastName(String lastName) {
    this.lastName = lastName;
}
```

```java
    /**
     * @return the position
     */
  @Override
    public String getPosition() {
        return position;
    }

    /**
     * @param position the position to set
     */
    public void setPosition(String position) {
        this.position = position;
    }

    /**
     * @return the status
     */
    public int getStatus() {
        return status;
    }

    /**
     * @param status the status to set
     */
    public void setStatus(int status) {
        this.status = status;
    }
}
```

The PlayerType interface is:

```java
public interface PlayerType {
    public String position="";
    public String getPosition();
}
```

Each of the other `Player` subclasses is very similar to the `Goalie` class. The most important code to note is the factory method, `createPlayer`, which can create new instances of the `Player` class.

Note   To take this example one step further, you can limit the methods that can be accessed. You do this by returning objects of type `PlayerType`, and only declaring the accessible methods within that interface.

How It Works

Factories are generate objects. They are generally used to abstract the creation of an object from its creators. This can come in very handy when the creator does not need to know about the actual implementation details of generating the new object. The factory pattern can also be useful when controlled access to the creation of an object is required. To implement a factory, create a class containing at least one method used for returning a newly created object.

In the solution to this recipe, the `PlayerFactory` class contains a `createPlayer(String)` method that returns a newly created `Player` object. This method doesn't do anything special behind the scenes; it simply instantiates a new `Player` instance depending on the string value passed to the method. Another object with access to the `PlayerFactory` class can use `createPlayer` to return new `Player` objects without knowing how the object is created. While this does not hide much in the case of the `createPlayer` method, the `PlayerFactory` abstracts the details of which class is being instantiated so that the developer only has to worry about obtaining a new `Player` object.

The factory pattern effectively controls how objects are created and makes it easier to create objects of a certain type. Imagine if a constructor for an object took more than just a handful of arguments; creating new objects that require more than just a couple of arguments can become a hassle. Generating a factory to create those objects so that you do not have to hard-code all the arguments with each instantiation can make you much more productive!

5-5. Creating Reusable Objects

Problem

You want to generate an object that could represent something within your application. Furthermore, you want to reuse the object to represent multiple instances. For instance, suppose that you create an application that generates statistics and league information for different sports teams. In this case, you want to create an object representing a team.

Solution

Create a JavaBean that represents the object that you want to create. JavaBean objects provide the capability for object fields to be declared as private, and they also allow the attributes to be read and updated so that an object can be passed around and used within an application. This recipe demonstrates the creation of a JavaBean named Team. The Team object contains a few different fields that can contain information.

```java
public class Team implements TeamType {
    private List<Player> players;
    private String name;
    private String city;

    /**
     * @return the players
     */
    public List<Player> getPlayers() {
        return players;
    }
    /**
     * @param players the players to set
     */
@Override
    public void setPlayers(List<Player> players) {
        this.players = players;
    }
    /**
     * @return the name
```

```
    */
    public String getName() {
        return name;
    }
    /**
     * @param name the name to set
     */
@Override
    public void setName(String name) {
        this.name = name;
    }
    /**
     * @return the city
     */
    public String getCity() {
        return city;
    }
    /**
     * @param city the city to set
     */
@Override
    public void setCity(String city) {
        this.city = city;
    }
}
```

The PlayerType interface is:

```
public interface TeamType {
    void setPlayers(List<Player> players);
    void setName(String name);
    void setCity(String city);
}
```

As you can see, the object in this solution contains three fields, and each of those fields is declared as private. However, each field has two accessor methods—getters and setters—that allow the fields to be indirectly accessible.

How It Works

The JavaBean is an object that holds information so that it can be passed around and used within an application. One of the most important aspects of a JavaBean is that its fields are declared as `private`. This prohibits other classes from accessing the fields directly. Instead, each field should be encapsulated by methods defined to make them accessible to other classes. These methods must adhere to the following naming conventions.

- Methods used for accessing the field data should be named using a get prefix, followed by the field name.

- Methods used for setting the field data should be named using a set prefix, followed by the field name.

For instance, in the solution to this recipe, the `Team` object contains a field with players' names. To access that field, a `getPlayers` method should be declared. It should return the data that is contained within the `players` field. Likewise, a `setPlayers` method should be declared to populate the `players` field. It should accept an argument of the same type as the `players` field, and it should set the value of the `players` field equal to the argument. This can be seen in the following code.

```java
public List<Player> getPlayers() {
    return players;
}

void setPlayers(List<Player> players) {
    this.players = players;
}
```

JavaBeans can populate lists of data written to a database record or for a myriad of other functions. Using JavaBeans makes code easier to read and maintain. It also helps to increase the likelihood of future code enhancements because very little code implementation is required. Another benefit of using JavaBeans is that most major IDEs autocomplete the encapsulation of the fields for you.

5-6. Defining an Interface for a Class

Problem

You want to create a set of method signatures and fields that can be used as a common template to expose the methods and fields that a class implements.

Solution

Generate a Java interface to declare each field and method that a class must implement. Such an interface can then be implemented by a class and represent an object type. The following code is an interface that declares the methods that the Team object must implement.

```java
public interface TeamType {
    void setPlayers(List<Player> players);
    void setName(String name);
    void setCity(String city);
    String getFullName();
}
```

All the methods in the interface are implicitly abstract. That is, only a method signature is provided. It is also possible to include static final field declarations in an interface.

How It Works

A Java interface is a construct that defines the structures, be it fields or methods that a class must implement. In most cases, interfaces do not include method implementations; rather, they only include method signatures. Interfaces can include variables that are implicitly `static` and `final`.

The interface does not include any constant field declarations in the solution to this recipe. However, it includes four method signatures. All the method signatures have no access modifier specified because all declarations within an interface are implicitly `public`. Interfaces expose a set of functionalities; therefore, all methods exposed within an interface must be implicitly `public`. Any class that implements an interface must implement any method signatures declared in the interface, except default methods and abstract classes, in which case an interface may leave the implementation for one of its subclasses.

While the Java language does not allow multiple inheritance, a Java class can implement multiple interfaces, allowing for a controlled form of multiple inheritance. Abstract classes can also implement interfaces. The following code demonstrates a class implementing an interface: the Team object declaration implements the TeamType interface.

```java
public class Team implements TeamType {

    private List<Player> players;
    private String name;
    private String city;

    /**
     * @return the players
     */
    public List<Player> getPlayers() {
        return players;
    }
    /**
     * @param players the players to set
     */
@Override
    public void setPlayers(List<Player> players) {
        this.players = players;
    }
    /**
     * @return the name
     */
    public String getName() {
        return name;
    }
    /**
     * @param name the name to set
```

```java
        */
@Override
    public void setName(String name) {
        this.name = name;
    }
    /**
     * @return the city
     */
    public String getCity() {
        return city;
    }
    /**
     * @param city the city to set
     */
@Override
    public void setCity(String city) {
        this.city = city;
    }
public String getFullName() {
        return this.name + " - " + this.city;
    }
}
```

Interfaces can declare a type for an object. Any object declared to have an interface type must adhere to all the implementations declared in the interface unless a default implementation exists. For instance, the following field declaration defines an object containing all the properties declared within the TeamType interface.

```java
TeamType team;
```

Interfaces can also extend other interfaces (thus the same type of theory provided by multiple inheritance). However, because no method implementation is present in an interface, it is much safer to implement multiple interfaces in a Java class than extending multiple classes in C++.

Interfaces are some of the single most important constructs of the Java language. They provide the interfaces between the user and the class implementations. Although it is possible to create entire applications without using interfaces, they help promote object orientation and hide method implementations from other classes.

5-7. Modifying Interfaces Without Breaking Existing Code

Problem

You've got a utility class that implements an interface, and many different classes within the utility library implement that interface. Suppose that you want to add a new method to the utility class and make it available for other classes via its interface. However, changing the interface likely breaks some existing classes that already implement that interface.

Solution

Add the new method and its implementation to the utility class interface as a default method. By doing so, each class that implements the interface automatically uses the new method and is not forced to implement it since a default implementation exists. The following class interface contains a default method, which can be used by any class that implements the interface.

```
public interface TeamType {

    List<Player> getPlayers();

    void setPlayers(List<Player> players);

    void setName(String name);

    void setCity(String city);

    String getFullName();

    default void listPlayers() {
        getPlayers().stream().forEach((player) -> {
```

```
            System.out.println(player.getFirstName() + " " + player
            .getLastName());
        });
    }
}
```

The interface TeamType contains a default method named listPlayers(). This method does not need to be implemented by any classes implementing TeamType since there is a default implementation within the interface.

How It Works

In previous releases of Java, interfaces could only contain method signatures and constant variables. It was not possible to define a method implementation within an interface. This works well in most cases, as interfaces are a construct that is meant to enforce type safety and abstract implementation details. However, it is beneficial to allow interfaces to contain a default method implementation in some circumstances. For instance, if many classes implement an existing interface, lots of code can be broken if that interface were to be changed. This would create a situation where backward compatibility would not be possible. In such a case, it would make sense to place a default method implementation into an interface rather than forcing all classes to implement a new method that is placed within the interface. This is why default methods became a necessity and were included in the Java 8 release.

To create a default method (a.k.a. a *defender method*) within an interface, use the keyword default within the method signature, and include a method implementation. An interface can contain zero or more default methods. In the solution to this recipe, the listPlayers() method is a default method within the TeamType interface, and any class implementing TeamType automatically inherits the default implementation. Theoretically, any classes that implement TeamType would be completely unaffected by the addition of the listPlayers() default method. This enables you to alter an interface without breaking backward compatibility, which can be of great value.

5-8. Constructing Instances of the Same Class with Different Values

Problem

Your application requires the ability to construct instances of the same object, but each instance must contain different values, thereby creating different types of the same object.

Solution

Use the builder pattern to build different types of the same object following a step-by-step procedure. For instance, suppose that you are interested in creating different teams for a sports league. Each team must contain the same attributes, but the values for those attributes vary by team. So you create many objects of the same type, but each of the objects is unique. The following code demonstrates the builder pattern, which creates the required teams.

First, you need to define a set of attributes that each team needs to contain. To do this, a Java interface should be created, containing the different attributes that need to be applied to each Team object. The following is an example of such an interface.

```java
public interface TeamType {
    public void setPlayers(List<Player> players);
    public void setName(String name);
    public void setCity(String city);
    public String getFullName();
}
```

Next, define a class to represent a team. This class needs to implement the TeamType interface that was just created so that it adheres to the format that is required to build a team.

```java
public class Team implements TeamType {

    private List<Player> players;
    private String name;
    private String city ;
    private int wins
```

```java
    private int losses
    private int ties
    /**
     * @return the players
     */
    public List<Player> getPlayers() {
        return players;
    }
    /**
     * @param players the players to set
     */
@Override
    public void setPlayers(List<Player> players) {
        this.players = players;
    }
    /**
     * @return the name
     */
    public String getName() {
        return name;
    }
    /**
     * @param name the name to set
     */
@Override
    public void setName(String name) {
        this.name = name;
    }
    /**
     * @return the city
     */
    public String getCity() {
        return city;
    }
    /**
```

```
     * @param city the city to set
     */
@Override
    public void setCity(String city) {
        this.city = city;
    }
    public String getFullName(){
        return this.name + "  -  "  + this.city;
    }
}
```

Now that the Team class has been defined, a builder needs to be created. The purpose of the builder object is to allow the step-by-step creation of a Team object. A builder class interface should be created to abstract the details of building an object. The interface should define any of the methods that build the object and a method that return a fully built object. In this case, the interface defines each of the methods needed to build a new Team object, and then the builder implementation implements this interface.

```
public interface TeamBuilder {
    public void buildPlayerList();
    public void buildNewTeam(String teamName);
    public void designateTeamCity(String city);
    public Team getTeam();
}
```

The following code demonstrates a builder class implementation. Although the following code would not create a custom player list, it contains all the features required to implement the builder pattern. The details of creating a more customized player list can be worked out later, probably by allowing the user to create players via a keyboard entry. Furthermore, the TeamBuilder interface could implement teams for different sports. The following class is named HockeyTeamBuilder, but a similar class implementing TeamBuilder could be named FootballTeamBuilder, and so forth.

```
public class HockeyTeamBuilder implements TeamBuilder {

    private Team team;

    public HockeyTeamBuilder(){
```

```
        this.team = new Team();
    }

    @Override
    public void buildPlayerList() {
        List players = new ArrayList();
        for(int x = 0; x <= 10; x++){
            players.add(PlayerFactory.getPlayer());
        }
        team.setPlayers(players);
    }

    @Override
    public void buildNewTeam(String teamName) {
        team.setName(teamName);
    }

    @Override
    public void designateTeamCity(String city){
        team.setCity(city);
    }

    @Override
    public Team getTeam(){
        return this.team;
    }
}
```

Last, use the builder by calling on the methods defined in its interface to create teams. The following code demonstrates how this builder could create one team. You can use the Roster class within the sources for this recipe to test this code.

```
public Team createTeam(String teamName, String city){
    TeamBuilder builder = new HockeyTeamBuilder();
    builder.buildNewTeam(teamName);
    builder.designateTeamCity(city);
    builder.buildPlayerList();
    return builder.getTeam();
}
```

Although this demonstration of the builder pattern is relatively short, it demonstrates how to hide implementation details of an object, thereby making objects easier to build. You do not need to know what the methods within the builder do; you only need to call on them.

How It Works

The builder pattern provides a way to generate new instances of an object in a procedural fashion. It abstracts away the details of object creation, so the creator does not need to do any specific work to generate new instances. By breaking the work down into a series of steps, the builder pattern allows objects to implement its builder methods in different ways. Because the object creator only has access to the builder methods, it makes creating different object types much easier.

A few classes and interfaces are necessary for using the builder pattern. First, you need to define a class and its different attributes. As the solution to this recipe demonstrates, the class may follow the JavaBean pattern. You can populate the object by using its setters and getters by creating a JavaBean. Next, you should create an interface that can be used to access the setters of the object you created. Each setter method should be defined in the interface, and then the object itself should implement that interface. As seen in the solution, the Team object contains the following setters, and each of them is defined in the TeamType interface.

```
public void setPlayers(List<Player> players);
public void setName(String name);
public void setCity(String city);
```

In real life, a team probably contains more attributes. For instance, you'd probably want to set up a mascot and a home stadium name and address. The code in this example can be thought of as abbreviated because it demonstrates the creation of a generic "team object" rather than showing you all the code for creating a team that is true to life. Because the Team class implements these setters that are defined within the TeamType interface, the interface methods can be called on to interact with the actual methods of the Team class.

After the object and its interface have been coded, the actual builder needs to be created. The builder consists of an interface and its implementation class. To start, you must define the methods you want other classes to call on when building your object.

For instance, in the solution to this recipe, the buildNewTeam(), designateTeamCity(), and buildPlayerList() methods are defined within the builder interface named TeamBuilder. When a class wants to build one of these objects later, it only needs to call these defined methods. Next, define a builder class implementation. The implementation class implements the methods defined within the builder interface, hiding all the details of those implementations from the object creator. The builder class, HockeyTeamBuilder, implements the TeamBuilder interface in the solution to this recipe. When a class wants to create a new Team object, it simply instantiates a new builder class.

```
TeamBuilder builder = new HockeyTeamBuilder();
```

To populate the newly created class object, the builder methods are called upon it.

```
builder.buildNewTeam(teamName);
builder.designateTeamCity(city);
builder.buildPlayerList();
```

Using this technique provides a step-by-step creation for an object. The implementation details for building that object are hidden from the object creator. It would be easy for a different builder implementation to use the same TeamBuilder interface to build Team objects for different types. For instance, a builder implementation could be written for generating Team objects for soccer, and another one could be defined for generating Team objects for baseball. Each of the Team object implementations would be different. However, both could implement the same interface—TeamBuilder—and the creator could simply call on the builder methods without caring about the details.

5-9. Interacting with a Class via Interfaces
Problem

You have created a class that implements an interface or class type. You want to interact with the methods of that class by calling on methods declared within the interface rather than working directly with the class.

Solution

Declare a field of the same type as an interface. You can then assign classes that implement the interface to the field you had declared and call upon the methods declared in the interface to perform work. In the following example, a field is declared to be of type TeamType. Using the same classes from Recipe 5-8, you can see that the class Team implements the TeamType interface. The field that is created in the following example holds a reference to a new Team object.

Because the Team class implements the TeamType interface, the methods that are exposed in the interface can be used.

```java
public class InterfaceTester {
    static TeamType team = new Team();
    public static void main(String[] args){
        team.setCity("SomeCity");
        team.setName("SomeName");
        team.setPlayers(null);
        System.out.println(team.getFullName());
    }
}
```

Where the interface is

```java
public interface TeamType {

    void setPlayers(List<Player> players);
    void setName(String name);
    void setCity(String city);
    String getFullName();

}
```

The resulting output is as follows.

```
SomeName - SomeCity
```

How It Works

Interfaces are useful for many reasons. Two of the most important use cases for interfaces are conformity and abstraction. Interfaces define a model, and any class that implements the interface must conform to that model. Therefore, if a constant is defined within the interface, it is automatically available for use in the class. If there is a method defined within the interface, the class must implement that method unless a default implementation has been defined. Interfaces provide a nice way to allow classes to conform to a standard.

Interfaces hide unnecessary information from any class that does not need to see it. Any method defined within the interface is made `public` and accessible to any class. As demonstrated in the solution to this recipe, an object was created and declared the type of an interface. The interface in the example, `TeamType`, only includes a small subset of available methods within the `Team` object. Therefore, the only methods that are accessible to any class working against an object declared to be of `TeamType` are the ones defined within the interface. The class using this interface type does not have access to any of the other methods or constants, nor does it need to. Interfaces are a great way for hiding logic that does not need to be used by other classes. Another great side effect: A class that implements an interface can be changed and recompiled without affecting code that works against the interface. However, if an interface is changed, there could be an effect on any classes that implement it. Therefore, if the `getFullName()` method implementation changes, any class coded against the `TeamType` interface is not affected because the interface is unchanged. The implementation changes behind the scenes, and any class working against the interface begins to use the new implementation without needing to know.

Lastly, interfaces help to promote security. They hide implementation details of methods declared in an interface from any class that may call upon that method using the interface. As mentioned in the previous paragraph, if a class calls the `getFullName()` method against the `TeamType` interface, it does not need to know the implementation details of that method as long as a result is returned as expected.

The older Enterprise JavaBean (EJB) model used interfaces for interacting with methods that performed database work. This model worked very well for hiding the details and logic that were not essential for use from other classes. Other frameworks use similar models, exposing functionality through Java interfaces. Interface use has proven to be a smart way to code software because it promotes reusability, flexibility, and security.

5-10. Making a Class Cloneable

Problem

You want to enable a class to be cloned or copied by another class.

Solution

Implement the Cloneable interface within the class that you want to clone; then call that object's clone method to make a copy of it. The following code demonstrates how to make the Team class cloneable.

```java
public class Team implements TeamType, Cloneable, Serializable {
    private String name;
    private String city;

    /**
     * @return the name
     */
    public String getName() {
        return name;
    }
    /**
     * @param name the name to set
     */
@Override
    public void setName(String name) {
        this.name = name;
    }
    /**
     * @return the city
     */
    public String getCity() {
        return city;
    }
```

```java
    /**
     * @param city the city to set
     */
@Override
    public void setCity(String city) {
        this.city = city;
    }
    public String getFullName() {
        return this.name + " - " + this.city;
    }
    /**
     * Overrides Object's clone method to create a deep copy
     *
     * @return
     */
    @Override
    public Team clone() {
        Team obj = null;
        try {
            ByteArrayOutputStream baos = new ByteArrayOutputStream();
            ObjectOutputStream oos = new ObjectOutputStream(baos);
            oos.writeObject(this);
            oos.close();
            ByteArrayInputStream bais = new ByteArrayInputStream
            (baos.toByteArray());
            ObjectInputStream ois = new ObjectInputStream(bais);
            obj = (Team) ois.readObject();
            ois.close();
        } catch (IOException e) {
            e.printStackTrace();
        } catch (ClassNotFoundException cnfe) {
            cnfe.printStackTrace();
        }
        return obj;
    }
```

```java
/**
 * Overrides Object's clone method to create a shallow copy
 *
 * @return
 */
public Team shallowCopyClone() {
    try {
        return (Team) super.clone();
    } catch (CloneNotSupportedException ex) {
        return null;
    }
}

@Override
public boolean equals(Object obj) {
    if (this == obj) {
        return true;
    }
    if (obj instanceof Team) {
        Team other = (Team) obj;
        return other.getName().equals(this.getName())
                && other.getCity().equals(this.getCity());
    } else {
        return false;
    }
}
}
```

To make a deep copy of a Team object, the clone() method needs to be called against that object. To make a shallow copy of the object, the shallowCopyClone() method must be called. The following code demonstrates these techniques.

```java
public static void main(String[] args){
    Team team1 = new Team();
    Team team2 = new Team();

    team1.setCity("Boston");
```

```
    team1.setName("Bandits");

    team2.setCity("Chicago");
    team2.setName("Wildcats");

    Team team3 = team1;
    Team team4 = team2.clone();

    Team team5 = team1.shallowCopyClone();

    System.out.println("Team 3:");
    System.out.println(team3.getCity());
    System.out.println(team3.getName());
    System.out.println("Team 4:");
    System.out.println(team4.getCity());
    System.out.println(team4.getName());

    // Teams move to different cities
    team1.setCity("St. Louis");
    team2.setCity("Orlando");

    System.out.println("Team 3:");
    System.out.println(team3.getCity());
    System.out.println(team3.getName());
    System.out.println("Team 4:");
    System.out.println(team4.getCity());
    System.out.println(team4.getName());
    System.out.println("Team 5:");
    System.out.println(team5.getCity());
    System.out.println(team5.getName());

    if (team1 == team3){
        System.out.println("team1 and team3 are equal");
    } else {
        System.out.println("team1 and team3 are NOT equal");
    }

    if (team1 == team5){
        System.out.println("team1 and team5 are equal");
```

```
    } else {
        System.out.println("team1 and team5 are NOT equal");
    }
}
```

This code demonstrates how to make a clone of an object. The resulting output would be as follows.

```
Team 3:
Boston
Bandits
Team 4:
Chicago
Wildcats
Team 3:
St. Louis
Bandits
Team 4:
Chicago
Wildcats
Team 5:
Boston
Bandits
team1 and team3 are equal
team1 and team5 are NOT equal
```

How It Works

There are two different strategies to copy an object: shallow and deep copies. A *shallow copy* can be made to copy the object without any of its contents or data. Rather, all the variables are passed by reference into the copied object. After a shallow copy of an object has been created, the objects within the original and copy objects refer to the same data and memory. Thus, modifying the original object's contents also modifies the copied object. By default, calling the super.clone() method against an object performs a shallow copy. The shallowCopyClone() method in the solution to this recipe demonstrates this technique.

The second type of copy that can be made is a *deep copy*, which copies the object, including all the contents. Therefore, each object refers to a different space in memory, and modifying one object does not affect the other. The difference between a deep and a shallow copy is demonstrated in the solution to this recipe. First, team1 and team2 objects are created. Next, they are populated with some values. The team3 object is then set equal to the team1 object, and the team4 object is made a clone of the team2 object. When the values are changed within the team1 object, they are also changed in the team3 object because both objects' contents refer to the same space in memory. This is an example of a shallow copy of an object. When the values are changed within the team2 object, they remain unchanged in the team4 object because each object has its own variables that refer to different spaces in memory. This is an example of a deep copy.

To make an exact copy of an object (deep copy), you must serialize the object so that it can be written to disk. The base Object class implements the clone() method. By default, the Object class's clone() method is protected. To make an object cloneable, it must implement the Cloneable interface and override the default clone() method. You can make a deep copy of an object by serializing it through a series of steps, such as writing the object to an output stream and then reading it back via an input stream. The steps shown in the clone() method of the solution to this recipe do just that. The object is written to a ByteArrayOutputStream and then read using a ByteArrayInputStream. Once that has occurred, the object has been serialized, which creates the deep copy. The clone() method in the solution to this recipe has been overridden to create a deep copy.

Once these steps have been followed and an object implements Cloneable and overrides the default object clone() method, it is possible to clone the object. To make a deep copy of an object, simply call that object's overridden clone() method as seen in the solution. If you were to simply return the object from the clone() method, there would need to be a typecast, as shown in the following.

```
Team team4 = (Team) team2.clone();
```

Cloning objects is not very difficult, but understanding the differences that can vary with object copies is important.

5-11. Comparing Objects

Problem

Your application requires comparing two or more objects to see whether they are the same.

Solution 1

To determine whether the two object references point to the same object, use the == and != operators. The following solution demonstrates the comparison of two object references to determine whether they refer to the same object.

```
public static void main(String[] args){
        // Compare if two objects contain the same values
        Team team1 = new Team();
        Team team2 = new Team();

        team1.setName("Jokers");
        team1.setCity("Crazyville");

        team2.setName("Jokers");
        team2.setCity("Crazyville");

        if (team1 == team2){
            System.out.println("These object references refer to the same
            object.");
        } else {
            System.out.println("These object references do NOT refer to the
            same object.");
        }
        // Compare two objects to see if they refer to the same object
        Team team3 = team1;
        Team team4 = team1;
        if (team3 == team4){
            System.out.println("These object references refer to the same
            object.");
```

```
        } else {
            System.out.println("These object references do NOT refer to the
            same object.");
        }
}
```

The following are the results of running the code.

```
These object references do NOT refer to the same object.
These object references refer to the same object.
```

Solution 2

To determine whether the two objects contain the same values, use the equals()
method. The object being compared must implement equals() and hashCode()for this
solution to work properly. The following is the code for the Team class that overrides
these two methods.

```
public class Team implements TeamType, Cloneable {
    private List<Player> players;
    private String name;
    private String city;
    // Used by the hashCode method for performance reasons
    private volatile int cachedHashCode = 0;

    /**
     * @return the players
     */
    public List<Player> getPlayers() {
        return players;
    }
    /**
     * @param players the players to set
     */
    public void setPlayers(List<Player> players) {
        this.players = players;
    }
```

```java
    /**
     * @return the name
     */
    public String getName() {
        return name;
    }
    /**
     * @param name the name to set
     */
@Override
    public void setName(String name) {
        this.name = name;
    }
    /**
     * @return the city
     */
    public String getCity() {
        return city;
    }
    /**
     * @param city the city to set
     */
@Override
    public void setCity(String city) {
        this.city = city;
    }
    public String getFullName() {
        return this.name + " - " + this.city;
    }
    /**
     * Overrides Object's clone method
     *
     * @return
     */
    public Object clone() {
```

```java
        try {
            return super.clone();
        } catch (CloneNotSupportedException ex) {
            return null;
        }
    }
    @Override
    public boolean equals(Object obj) {
        if (this == obj) {
            return true;
        }
        if (obj instanceof Team) {
            Team other = (Team) obj;
            return other.getName().equals(this.getName())
&& other.getCity().equals(this.getCity())
&& other.getPlayers().equals(this.getPlayers());
        } else {
            return false;
        }
    }
@Override
    public int hashCode() {
        int hashCode = cachedHashCode;
        if (hashCode == 0) {
            String concatStrings = name + city;
            if (players.size() > 0) {
                for (Player player : players) {
                    concatStrings = concatStrings
                            + player.getFirstName()
                            + player.getLastName()
                            + player.getPosition()
                            + String.valueOf(player.getStatus());
                }
            }
```

```
        hashCode = concatStrings.hashCode();
    }
    return hashCode;
  }
}
```

The following solution demonstrates the comparison of two objects that contain the same values.

```
public static void main(String[] args){
    // Compare if two objects contain the same values
    Team team1 = new Team();
    Team team2 = new Team();

    // Build Player List
    Player newPlayer = new Player("Josh", "Juneau");
    playerList.add(0, newPlayer);
    newPlayer = new Player("Jonathan", "Gennick");
    playerList.add(1, newPlayer);
    newPlayer = new Player("Joe", "Blow");
    playerList.add(1, newPlayer);
    newPlayer = new Player("John", "Smith");
    playerList.add(1, newPlayer);
    newPlayer = new Player("Paul", "Bunyan");
    playerList.add(1, newPlayer);

    team1.setName("Jokers");
    team1.setCity("Crazyville");
    team1.setPlayers(playerList);

    team2.setName("Jokers");
    team2.setCity("Crazyville");
    team2.setPlayers(playerList);

    if (team1.equals(team2)){
        System.out.println("These object references contain the same
        values.");
    } else {
```

```
            System.out.println("These object references do NOT contain the
            same values.");
        }
}
```

The following are the results of running this code.

```
These object references do NOT refer to the same object.
These object references contain the same values.
These object references refer to the same object.
```

How It Works

The comparison operator (==) can determine the equality of two objects. This equality does not pertain to the object values but rather to the object references. Often an application is more concerned with the values of objects; in such cases, the equals() method is the preferred choice because it compares the values contained within the objects rather than the object references.

The comparison operator looks at the object reference and determines whether it points to the same object as the object reference that it is being compared against. A Boolean true result is returned if the two objects are equal; otherwise, a Boolean false result is returned. In solution 1, the first comparison between the team1 object reference and the team2 object reference returns a false value because those two objects are separate in memory, even though they contain the same values. The second comparison in solution 1 between the team3 object reference and the team4 object reference returns a true value because both of those references refer to the team1 object.

The equals() method tests whether two objects contain the same values. To use the equals() method for comparison, the object that is being compared should override the Object class equals() and hashCode() methods. The equals() method should implement a comparison against the values contained within the object that would yield a true comparison result. The following code is an example of an overridden equals() method that has been placed into the Team object.

```
@Override
public boolean equals(Object obj) {
    if (this == obj) {
        return true;
```

```
    }
    if (obj instanceof Team) {
        Team other = (Team) obj;
        return other.getName().equals(this.getName())
&& other.getCity().equals(this.getCity())
&& other.getPlayers().equals(this.getPlayers());
    } else {
        return false;
    }
}
```

As you can see, the overridden equals() method first checks whether the object that is passed as an argument is referencing the same object as the one it is being compared against. If so, a true result is returned. If both objects are not referencing the same object in memory, the equals() method checks whether the fields are equal. In this case, any two Team objects that contain the same values within the name and city fields would be considered equal. Once the equals() method has been overridden, the comparison of the two objects can be performed, as demonstrated in solution 2 to this recipe.

The hashCode() method returns an int value that consistently returns the same integer. There are many ways in which to calculate the hashCode of an object. Perform a web search on the topic, and you find various techniques. One of the most basic ways to implement the hashCode() method is to concatenate all the object's variables into string format and return the resulting string's hashCode(). It is a good idea to cache the value of the hashCode for later use because the initial calculation may take some time. The hashCode() method in solution 2 demonstrates this tactic.

Comparing Java objects can become confusing, considering that there are multiple ways to do it. If the comparison you want to perform is against the object identity, use the comparison (==) operator. However, if you want to compare the values within the objects, or the state of the objects, then the equals() method is the way to go.

5-12. Extending the Functionality of a Class

Problem

One of your applications contains a class that you want to use as a base for another class. You want your new class to contain the same functionality as this base class but also include additional functionality.

Solution

Extend the functionality of the base class by using the extends keyword followed by the name of the class that you want to extend. The following example shows two classes. The first class, named HockeyStick, represents a hockey stick object. It is extended by the second class named WoodenStick. By doing so, the WoodenStick class inherits all the properties and functionality within the HockeyStick class, except private variables and those with the default access level. The WoodenStick class becomes a subclass of HockeyStick. First, let's take a look at the HockeyStick class, which contains the basic properties of a standard hockey stick.

```java
public class HockeyStick {

    private int length;
    private boolean curved;
    private String material;

    public HockeyStick(int length, boolean curved, String material){
        this.length = length;
        this.curved = curved;
        this.material = material;
    }

     /**
     * @return the length
     */
    public int getLength() {
        return length;
    }
}
```

```java
    /**
     * @param length the length to set
     */
    public void setLength(int length) {
        this.length = length;
    }
    /**
     * @return the curved
     */
    public boolean isCurved() {
        return curved;
    }
    /**
     * @param curved the curved to set
     */
    public void setCurved(boolean curved) {
        this.curved = curved;
    }
    /**
     * @return the material
     */
    public String getMaterial() {
        return material;
    }
    /**
     * @param material the material to set
     */
    public void setMaterial(String material) {
        this.material = material;
    }
}
```

Next, look at the subclass of HockeyStick, a class named WoodenStick.

```java
public class WoodenStick extends HockeyStick {
    private static final String material = "WOOD";
```

```java
    private int lie;
    private int flex;

    public WoodenStick(int length, boolean isCurved){
        super(length, isCurved, material);
    }

    public WoodenStick(int length, boolean isCurved, int lie, int flex){
        super(length, isCurved, material);
        this.lie = lie;
        this.flex = flex;
    }
    /**
     * @return the lie
     */
    public int getLie() {
        return lie;
    }
    /**
     * @param lie the lie to set
     */
    public void setLie(int lie) {
        this.lie = lie;
    }
    /**
     * @return the flex
     */
    public int getFlex() {
        return flex;
    }
    /**
     * @param flex the flex to set
     */
    public void setFlex(int flex) {
        this.flex = flex;
    }
}
```

Note   In this example, we assume that there may be more than one type of HockeyStick. In this case, we extend HockeyStick to create a WoodenStick, but we may also extend HockeyStick to create other types of HockeyStick, such as AluminumStick or GraphiteStick.

How It Works

Object inheritance is a fundamental technique in any object-oriented language. Inheriting from a base class adds value because it allows code to become reusable in multiple places. This helps to make code management much easier. If a change is made in the base class, it automatically inherits the child. On the other hand, if you had duplicate functionality scattered throughout your application, one minor change could mean that you would have to change code in many places. Object inheritance also makes it easy to designate a base class to one or more subclasses so that each class can contain similar fields and functionality.

The Java language allows a class to extend only one other class. This differs in concept from other languages such as C++, which contain multiple inheritance. Although some look at single class inheritance as a hindrance to the language, it was designed to add safety and ease of use to the language. When a subclass contains multiple superclasses, confusion can ensue.

5-13. Defining a Template for Classes to Extend

Problem

You want to define a template that generates objects containing similar functionality.

Solution

Define an abstract class that contains fields and functionality that can be used in other classes. The abstract class can also include unimplemented methods, known as *abstract methods*, which need to be implemented by a subclass of the abstract class. The following example demonstrates the concept of an abstract class.

The abstract class in the example represents a team schedule, and it includes some basic field declarations and functionality that every team's schedule needs to use. The Schedule class is then extended by the TeamSchedule class, which implements specific functionality for each team. First, let's take a look at the abstract Schedule class.

```java
public abstract class Schedule {
    public String scheduleYear;
    public String teamName;

    public List<Team> teams;

    public Map<Team, LocalDate> gameMap;

    public Schedule(){}

    public Schedule(String teamName){
        this.teamName = teamName;
    }

    abstract void calculateDaysPlayed(int month);
}
```

Next, the TeamSchedule extends the functionality of the abstract class.

```java
public class TeamSchedule extends Schedule {
    public TeamSchedule(String teamName) {
        super(teamName);
    }
    @Override
    void calculateDaysPlayed(int month) {
        int totalGamesPlayedInMonth = 0;
        for (Map.Entry<Team, LocalDate> entry : gameMap.entrySet()) {
            if (entry.getKey().equals(teamName)
                    && entry.getValue().getMonth().equals(month)) {
                totalGamesPlayedInMonth++;
            }
        }
```

```
      System.out.println("Games played in specified month: " +
      totalGamesPlayedInMonth);
   }
}
```

As you can see, the TeamSchedule class can use all the fields and methods contained within the abstract Schedule class. It also implements the abstract method that is contained within the Schedule class.

How It Works

Abstract classes are labeled as such, and they contain field declarations and methods that can be used within subclasses. What makes them different from a regular class is that they contain abstract methods, which are method declarations with no implementation. The solution to this recipe contains an abstract method named calculateDaysPlayed(). Abstract classes may or may not contain abstract methods. They can contain fields and fully implemented methods as well. Abstract classes cannot be instantiated; other classes can only extend them. When a class extends an abstract class, it gains all the fields and functionality of the abstract class. However, any abstract methods declared within the abstract class must be implemented by the subclass.

You may wonder why the abstract class wouldn't just contain the implementation of the method so that it was available for all its subclasses to use. If you think about the concept, it makes perfect sense. One type of object may perform a task differently from another. Using an abstract method forces the class extending the abstract class to implement it, but it allows the ability to customize how it is implemented.

5-14. Increasing Class Encapsulation
Problem

One of your classes requires the use of another class's functionality. However, no other class requires the use of that same functionality. Rather than creating a separate class that includes this additional functionality, you'd like to generate an implementation that can only be used by the class that needs it while placing the code in a logical location.

Solution

Create an *inner class* within the class that requires its functionality.

```java
import java.util.ArrayList;
import java.util.List;
/**
 * Inner class example. This example demonstrates how a team object
   could be
 * built using an inner class object.
 *
 * @author juneau
 */
public class TeamInner {

    private Player player;
    private List<Player> playerList;
    private int size = 4;
    /**
     * Inner class representing a Player object
     */
    class Player {

        private String firstName ;
        private String lastName ;
        private String position ;
        private int status = -1;

        public Player() {
        }

        public Player(String position, int status) {
            this.position = position;
            this.status = status;
        }

        protected String playerStatus() {
            String returnValue = null;
            switch (getStatus()) {
```

```java
        case 0:
            returnValue = "ACTIVE";
            break;
        case 1:
            returnValue = "INACTIVE";
            break;
        case 2:
            returnValue = "INJURY";
            break;
        default:
            returnValue = "ON_BENCH";
            break;
    }
    return returnValue;
}
public String playerString() {
    return getFirstName() + " " + getLastName() + " - " +
    getPosition();
}
/**
 * @return the firstName
 */
public String getFirstName() {
    return firstName;
}
/**
 * @param firstName the firstName to set
 */
public void setFirstName(String firstName) {
    this.firstName = firstName;
}
/**
 * @return the lastName
 */
```

```java
public String getLastName() {
    return lastName;
}
/**
 * @param lastName the lastName to set
 */
public void setLastName(String lastName) {
    this.lastName = lastName;
}
/**
 * @return the position
 */
public String getPosition() {
    return position;
}
/**
 * @param position the position to set
 */
public void setPosition(String position) {
    this.position = position;
}
/**
 * @return the status
 */
public int getStatus() {
    return status;
}
/**
 * @param status the status to set
 */
public void setStatus(int status) {
    this.status = status;
}
@Override
public String toString(){
```

```
            return this.firstName + " " + this.lastName + " - "+
                this.position + ": " + this.playerStatus();
        }
    }

public TeamInner() {
    final int ACTIVE = 0;
    // In reality, this would probably read records from a
    database using
    // a loop...but for this example we will manually enter the
    player data.
    playerList = new ArrayList();
    playerList.add(constructPlayer("Josh", "Juneau", "Right Wing",
    ACTIVE));
    playerList.add(constructPlayer("Joe", "Blow", "Left Wing",
    ACTIVE));
    playerList.add(constructPlayer("John", "Smith", "Center", ACTIVE));
    playerList.add(constructPlayer("Bob","Coder", "Defense", ACTIVE));
    playerList.add(constructPlayer("Jonathan", "Gennick", "Goalie",
    ACTIVE));
}
public Player constructPlayer(String first, String last, String
position, int status){
        Player player = new Player();
        player.firstName = first;
        player.lastName = last;
        player.position = position;
        player.status = status;
        return player;
}
public List<Player> getPlayerList() {
    return this.playerList;
}
```

```
    public static void main(String[] args) {
TeamInner inner = new TeamInner();
        System.out.println("Team Roster");
        System.out.println("===========");
for(Player player:inner.getPlayerList()){
            System.out.println(player.playerString());
        }
    }
}
```

The result of running this code lists the players on the team.

```
Team Roster
===========
Josh Juneau - Right Wing
Joe Blow - Left Wing
John Smith - Center
Bob Coder - Defense
Jonathan Gennick - Goalie
```

How It Works

Sometimes it is important to encapsulate functionality within a single class. It does not make sense to include a separate class for functionality that is only used within one other class. Imagine that you are developing a GUI, and you need to use a class to support functionality for one button. If there is no reusable code within that button class, it does not make sense to create a separate class and expose that functionality for other classes to use. Instead, it makes sense to encapsulate that class inside the class that requires the functionality. This philosophy is a use case for inner classes (also known as *nested classes*).

An inner class is a class that is contained within another class. The inner class can be made public, private, or protected like any other class. It can contain the same functionality as a normal class; the only difference is that the inner class is contained within an enclosing class, otherwise referred to as an *outer class*. The solution to this recipe demonstrates this technique. The TeamInner class contains one inner class named Player. The Player class is a JavaBean class that represents a Player object.

The Player object can inherit functionality from its containing class, including its private fields. This is because inner classes contain an implicit reference to the outer class. It can also be accessed by containing the TeamInner class, as demonstrated within the constructPlayer() method.

```java
public Player constructPlayer(String first, String last, String position,
int status){
        Player player = new Player();
        player.firstName = first;
        player.lastName = last;
        player.position = position;
        player.status = status;
        return player;
    }
```

Outer classes can instantiate an inner class as many times as needed. In the example, the constructPlayer() method could be called any number of times, instantiating a new inner class instance. However, when the outer class is instantiated, no inner class instances are instantiated. Similarly, when the outer class is no longer in use, all inner class instances are destroyed.

Inner classes can reference outer class methods by referring to the outer class and the method(s) it wants to call. The following line of code demonstrates such a reference using the same objects represented in the solution to this recipe. Suppose that the Player class needed to obtain the player list from the outer class; you would write something similar to the following.

```java
TeamInner.this.getPlayerList();
```

Although not very often used, classes other than the outside class can obtain access to a public inner class by using the following syntax.

```java
TeamInner outerClass = new TeamInner();
outerClass.player = outerClass.new Player();
```

Static inner classes are a bit different in that they cannot directly reference any instance variables or methods of its enclosing class. The following is an example of a static inner class.

```java
public class StaticInnerExample {

    static String hello = "Hello";

    public static void sayHello(){
        System.out.println(hello);
    }

    static class InnerExample {
        String goodBye = "Good Bye";

        public void sayGoodBye(){
            System.out.println(this.goodBye);
        }
    }

    public static void main (String[] args){
        StaticInnerExample.sayHello();
        StaticInnerExample.InnerExample inner =
                new StaticInnerExample.InnerExample();
        inner.sayGoodBye();
    }
}
```

Inner classes help to provide encapsulation of logic. Furthermore, they allow inheritance of `private` fields, which is not possible using a standard class.

5-15. Summary

Java is an object-oriented language. To harness the capabilities of the language, you must learn how to become proficient with object-orientation. This chapter covered basics such as class creation and access modifiers. It also covered encapsulation, interfaces, and recipes to help developers take advantage of the power of object-orientation.

CHAPTER 6

Lambda Expressions

A convenient way to create anonymous functions is using the *lambda expressions* using an expression or series of statements. Lambda expressions are built on functional interfaces, which contain a single abstract method, and that method has no implementation.

They can be applied in many contexts, ranging from simple anonymous functions to sorting and filtering collections. Moreover, lambda expressions can be assigned to variables and then passed into other objects.

In this chapter, you learn how to create lambda expressions, and you'll see many examples of how they can be applied in common scenarios. You'll also learn how to generate the building blocks for lambda expressions so that you can construct applications to facilitate their use. After reading this chapter, you can see the impact of lambda expressions on the Java language. They modernize the language by allowing developers to be more productive and opening new possibilities in many areas. Lambda expressions turned the page on Java, bringing the language into a new light, with the likes of other languages that have had similar constructs for some time. Those languages helped pave the way for lambda expressions in the Java language. There is no doubt that lambda expressions continue to pave the way for many elegant solutions.

Note   The functional interface was introduced in Java 8. It is an Interface that contains exactly one abstract method (i.e., any interface with one abstract method is a functional interface). Moreover, it's recommended that a functional interface has an informative @FunctionalInterface annotation.

© Josh Juneau, Luciano Manelli 2022
J. Juneau and L. Manelli, *Java 17 Recipes*, https://doi.org/10.1007/978-1-4842-7963-2_6

6-1. Writing a Simple Lambda Expression

Problem

You want to encapsulate functionality that prints a simple message.

Solution

Write a lambda expression that accepts a single parameter that contains the message you want to print, and implement the printing functionality within the lambda. In the following example, a functional interface, HelloType, is implemented via a lambda expression and assigned to the helloLambda variable. Lastly, the lambda is invoked, printing the message.

```java
public class HelloLambda {
    /**
     * Functional Interface
     */
    @FunctionalInterface
    public interface HelloType {
        /**
         * Function that will be implemented within the lambda
         * @param text
         */
        void hello(String text);
    }

    public static void main(String[] args){
        // Create the lambda, passing a parameter named "text" to the
        // hello() method, returning the string.  The lambda is assigned
        // to the helloLambda variable.
        HelloType helloLambda =
                (String text) -> {System.out.println("Hello " + text);};
        // Invoke the method call
        helloLambda.hello("Lambda");
    }
}
```

The following is the result.

```
Hello Lambda
```

How It Works

A lambda expression is an anonymous block of code that encapsulates an expression or a series of statements and returns a result. Lambda expressions are also known as *closures* in some other languages. They can accept zero or more parameters, which can be passed with or without type specification since the type can be automatically derived from the context.

The syntax of a lambda expression includes an argument list, a new character to the language known as the "arrow token" (->), and a body. The following model represents the structure of a lambda expression.

```
(argument list) -> { body }
```

The argument list for a lambda expression can include zero or more arguments. If there are no arguments, then an empty set of parentheses can be used. If there is only one argument, then no parentheses are required. Each argument on the list can include an optional type specification. If the type of the argument is left off, then the type is derived from the current context.

In the solution for this recipe, curly braces surround the body of a block, which contains more than a single expression. The curly braces are not necessary if the body consists of a single expression. The curly braces in the solution could have been left off, but they've been included for ease of readability. The body is simply evaluated and then returned. If the body of the lambda is an expression and not a statement, a `return` is implicit. On the contrary, if the body includes more than one statement, a `return` must be specified, and it marks a return of control back to the caller.

The following code demonstrates a lambda expression that does not contain any arguments.

```
StringReturn msg = () ->  "This is a test";
```

The `StringReturn` interface, which is used by the lambda, is also known as a functional interface.

```
/**
 * Functional interface returning a string
 */
@FunctionalInterface
public interface StringReturn {
    String returnMessage();
}
```

Let's take a look at how this lambda expression works. In the previous listing, an object of type StringReturn is returned from the lambda expression. The empty set of parentheses denotes that there are no arguments being passed to the expression. The return is implicit, and the string "This is a test" is returned from the lambda expression to the invoker. The expression in the example is assigned to a variable identified by msg. Assume that the functional interface, StringReturn, contains an abstract method identified as returnMessage(), as seen in the code. In this case, the msg.returnMessage() method can be invoked to return the string.

The body of a lambda expression can contain any Java construct that an ordinary method may contain. For instance, suppose a string was passed as an argument to a lambda expression, and you wanted to return some value that is dependent on the string argument. The following lambda expression body contains a block of code, which returns an int, based on the string value of the argument passed into the expression.

```
ActionCode code = (codestr) -> {
    switch(codestr){
        case "ACTIVE": return 0;
        case "INACTIVE": return 1;
        default:
            return -1;
    }
};
```

In this example, the ActionCode functional interface infers the return type of the lambda expression. For clarification, let's see what the interface looks like.

```
@FunctionalInterface
public interface ActionCode{
    int returnCode(String codestr);
}
```

The code implies that the lambda expression implements the `returnCode` method, which is defined within the `ActionCode` interface. This method accepts a string argument (`codestr`), which is passed to the lambda expression, returning an int. Therefore, from this example, you can see that a lambda can encapsulate the functionality of a method body.

While it is possible for code written in the Java language to move forward without the use of lambda expressions, they are an important addition that greatly improves overall maintainability, readability, and developer productivity. Lambda expressions are an evolutionary change to the Java language, as they are another step toward modernization of the language and help keep it in sync with other languages.

Note A lambda expression can contain any statement that an ordinary Java method contains. However, the `continue` and `break` keywords are not legal within the body of a lambda expression.

6-2. Enabling the Use of Lambda Expressions

Problem

You are interested in authoring code that enables the use of lambda expressions.

Solution 1

Write custom functional interfaces that can be implemented via lambda expressions. All lambda expressions implement a functional interface (i.e., a single abstract method declaration). The following lines of code demonstrate a functional interface that contains a single method declaration.

```java
@FunctionalInterface
public interface ReverseType {
    String reverse(String text);
}
```

The functional interface contains a single abstract method declaration, identified as String reverse(String text). The following code, which contains a lambda expression, demonstrates how to implement ReverseType.

```
ReverseType newText = (testText) -> {
    String tempStr = "";
    for (String part : testText.split(" ")) {
        tempStr += new StringBuilder(part).reverse().toString() + " ";
    }
    return tempStr;
};
```

The following code could invoke the lambda expression.

```
System.out.println(newText.reverse("HELLO WORLD"));
```

This is the result.

```
OLLEH DLROW
```

Solution 2

Use a functional interface that is contained within the java.util.function package to implement a lambda expression to suit the application's needs. The following example uses Function<T,R> (where T is the input type and R is the result type) interface to perform the same task as the one demonstrated in solution 1. This example accepts a string argument and returns a string result.

```
Function<String,String> newText2 = (testText) -> {
    String tempStr = "";
    for (String part : testText.split(" ")) {
        tempStr += new StringBuilder(part).reverse().toString() + " ";
    }
    return tempStr;
};
```

This lambda expression is assigned to the `newText2` variable, which is of type `Function<String,String>`. Therefore, a string is passed as an argument, and a string is returned from the lambda expression. The functional interface of `Function<T,R>` contains an abstract method declaration of `apply()`. To invoke this lambda expression, use the following syntax.

```
System.out.println(newText2.apply("HELLO WORLD"));
```

The following is the result.

```
OLLEH DLROW
```

How It Works

A basic building block of a lambda expression is the functional interface. This standard Java interface contains a single abstract method declaration and provides a target type for lambda expressions and method references. A functional interface may contain default method implementations, but only one abstract declaration. The abstract method is then implicitly implemented by the lambda expression. As a result, the lambda expression can be assigned to a variable of the same type as the functional interface. The method can be called on from the assigned variable later, thus invoking the lambda expression. Following this pattern, lambda expressions are method implementations that can be invoked by name. They can also be passed as arguments to other methods.

At this point, you may be wondering if you are required to develop a functional interface for each situation that may be suitable for use with a lambda expression. This is not the case since many functional interfaces are already available for use. Some examples include `java.lang.Runnable`, `javafx.event.EventHandler<T extends Event>`, and `java.util.Comparator<T>`. See some of the other recipes in this chapter for examples using lambda expressions that implement these interfaces. However, many more functional interfaces are less specific, enabling them to be tailored to suit the needs of a particular requirement. The `java.util.function` package contains several functional interfaces that can be useful when implementing lambda expressions. The functional interfaces contained within the package are utilized throughout the JDK and can also be utilized in developer applications. Utilizing functional interfaces contained within the `java.util.function` package can greatly reduce the amount of code you need to write. The functional interfaces are geared toward tasks performed a high percentage of the time. They are also written using generics, which can be applied in many different contexts. Solution 2 demonstrates such an example, whereby the Function<T,R> interface implements a lambda expression that accepts a string argument and returns a string result.

6-3. Invoking Existing Methods by Name
Problem

You are developing a lambda expression that merely invokes a method that already exists in the object being passed to the lambda. Rather than write out the entire ceremony to invoke the method, you'd like to utilize a minimal amount of code.

Solution

Rather than writing a lambda expression, use a method reference to call an existing method. In the following scenario, the Player object contains a static method named compareByGoal(), which takes two Player objects and compares the number of goals each contains. It then returns an integer representing the outcome. The compareByGoal() method is the same as Comparator<T>.

```
public class Player {
    private String firstName ;
    private String lastName ;
    private String position ;
    private int status = -1;
    private int goals;
    public Player(){
    }
    public Player(String position, int status){
        this.position = position;
        this.status = status;
    }
    public String findPlayerStatus(int status){
        String returnValue = null;
        switch(status){
```

214

```
        case 0:
                returnValue = "ACTIVE";
        case 1:
                returnValue = "INACTIVE";
        case 2:
                returnValue = "INJURY";
        default:
                returnValue = "ON_BENCH";
    }
    return returnValue;
}
public String playerString(){
    return getFirstName() + " " + getLastName() + " - " +
    getPosition();
}
// ** getters and setters removed for brevity **
/**
 * Returns a positive integer if Player A has more goals than Player B
 * Returns a negative integer if Player A has fewer goals than Player B
 * Returns a zero if both Player A and Player B have the same number
   of goals
 */
public static int compareByGoal(Player a, Player b){
    int eval;
    if(a.getGoals() > b.getGoals()){
        eval = 1;
    } else if (a.getGoals() < b.getGoals()){
        eval = -1;
    } else {
        eval = 0;
    }
    return eval;
}
}
```

The `Player.compareByGoal()` method could sort an array of `Player` objects. To do so, pass an array of `Player` objects (`Player[]`) to the `Arrays.sort()` method as the first argument, and pass a method reference `Player::compareByGoal` as the second argument. The result is a sorted list (in ascending order) of `Player` objects by the number of goals. The following line of code shows how to accomplish this task.

```
Arrays.sort(teamArray, Player::compareByGoal);
```

How It Works

Consider that your lambda expression will invoke a single method by name, perhaps returning a result. If a lambda expression fits this scenario, it is a prime candidate for use with a method reference. A method reference is a simplified form of a lambda expression, which specifies the class name or instance name, followed by the method to be called in the following format.

```
<class or instance name>::<methodName>
```

The double colon (`::`) operator specifies a method reference. Since a method reference is a simplified lambda method, it must implement a functional interface. The abstract method within the interface must have the same argument list and return type as the method being referenced. Any arguments are subsequently derived from the context of the method reference. For instance, consider the same scenario as the solution, whereby you wanted to sort an array of `Player` objects by calling on the `Player.compareByGoal()` method to perform goal comparisons. The following code could enable this functionality via a lambda expression.

```
Arrays.sort(teamArray, (p1, p2) -> Player.compareByGoal(p1,p2));
```

In this code, the array is passed as the first argument to `Arrays.sort()`. The second argument is a lambda expression that passes two `Player` objects to the `Player.compareByGoal()` method. The lambda expression uses the functional interface `Comparator<Player>.compare`, which utilizes the (`Player, Player`) parameter list. The `compareByGoal()` method contains that same parameter list. Likewise, the return type of `compareByGoal()` matches the return type within the functional interface. Therefore, the parameter list does not need to be specified in the listing. It can be inferred from the context of the `Player::compareByGoal` method reference instead.

There are four different types of method references. Table 6-1 lists each of them.

Table 6-1. *Method Reference Types*

Type	Description
Static Reference	Uses a static method of an object
Instance Reference	Uses an instance method of an object
Arbitrary Object Method	Used on an arbitrary object of a particular type, rather than a particular object
Constructor Reference	Generates a new object by invoking a constructor with the new keyword

In the solution, the static method reference type is demonstrated since compareByGoal() is a static method within the Player class. It is possible to invoke a method of an object instance using an instance reference. Consider the following class, which contains a nonstatic method for comparing goals within Player objects.

```
public class PlayerUtility {
    public int compareByGoal(Player a, Player b){
        int eval;
        if(a.getGoals() > b.getGoals()){
            eval = 1;
        } else if (a.getGoals() < b.getGoals()){
            eval = -1;
        } else {
            eval = 0;
        }
        return eval;
    }
}
```

This class can be instantiated, and the new instance references the compareByGoals() method, similar to the technique used in the solution to this recipe.

```
Player[] teamArray2 = team.toArray(new Player[team.size()]);
PlayerUtility utility = new PlayerUtility();
Arrays.sort(teamArray2, utility::compareByGoal);
```

Suppose that your application contained a list of an arbitrary type, and you want to apply a method to each of the objects in that list. Method references can be used in this scenario, given the object contains methods that are candidates for use via reference. In the following example, the `Arrays.sort()` method is applied to a list of int values. A method reference applies the `Integer compare()` method to the elements within the list. Thus, the resulting list is sorted, and the method reference automatically passes the int arguments and returns the int comparison.

```
Integer[] ints = {3,5,7,8,51,33,1};
Arrays.sort(ints, Integer::compare);
```

The last type of method reference can be utilized for referencing the constructor of an object. This type of method reference can be especially useful when creating new objects via a factory. Let's take a look at an example. Suppose that the `Player` object contained the following constructor.

```
public Player(String position, int status, String first, String last){
    this.position = position;
    this.status = status;
    this.firstName = first;
    this.lastName = last;
}
```

You want to generate `Player` objects on the fly using a factory pattern. The following code demonstrates an example of a functional interface containing a single abstract method named `createPlayer()`, which accepts the same argument list as the constructor for the `Player` object.

```
@FunctionalInterface
public interface PlayerFactory {
    Player createPlayer(String position,
                        int status,
                        String firstName,
                        String lastName);
}
```

The factory can now be created from a lambda expression and then created new objects. The following lines of code demonstrate.

```
PlayerFactory player1 = Player::new;
Player newPlayer = player1.createPlayer("CENTER", 0, "Constructor",
"Referenceson");
```

The double colon operator (::), introduced in Java 8, simplifies to create a new instance. Method references were perhaps one of the most significant new features introduced in Java 8, although lambda expressions have more use cases. They provide an easy-to-read, simplified technique for generating lambda expressions, and they'll work in most cases where lambda is merely invoking a single method by name.

6-4. Sorting with Fewer Lines of Code

Problem

Your application contains a list of Player objects for a hockey team. You want to sort that list of players by those who scored the most goals, and you want to do so using terse yet easy-to-follow code.

Solution 1

Create a comparator using an accessor method contained within the Player object for the field you want to sort. In this case, you want to sort by the number of goals, so the comparator should be based on the value returned from getGoals(). The following line of code shows how to create such a comparator using the Comparator interface and a method reference.

```
public static void main(String[] args) {
        loadTeam();
        Comparator<Player> byGoals =
        Comparator.comparing(Player::getGoals);
```

Next, utilize a mixture of lambda expressions and streams (see Chapter 7 for more information on streams), along with the forEach() method, to apply the specified sort on the list of Player objects. In the following line of code, a stream is obtained from the list, which allows you to apply functional-style operations on the elements.

```
team.stream().sorted(byGoals)
            .map(p -> p.getFirstName() + " " + p.getLastName() + " - "
                + p.getGoals())
            .forEach(element -> System.out.println(element));
```

Assuming that the list referenced by team is loaded with Player objects, the previous line of code first sorts that list by the player goals and then prints information on each object.

The following are the results of the sort.

```
== Sort by Number of Goals ==
Jonathan Gennick - 1
Josh Juneau - 5
Steve Adams - 7
Duke Java - 15
Bob Smith - 18
```

Solution 2

Utilize the Collections.sort() method, passing the list to sort along with a lambda expression that performs the comparisons on the list elements. The following code demonstrates how to accomplish this task using the Collections.sort() technique.

```
public static void main(String[] args) {
    loadTeam();
    Collections.sort(team, (p1, p2)
            -> p1.getLastName().compareTo(p2.getLastName()));
    team.stream().forEach((p) -> {
        System.out.println(p.getLastName());
    });
}
```

The following is the result.

```
== Sort by Last Name ==
Adams
Gennick
Java
Juneau
Smith
```

Where the function loadTeam is:

```java
public class Sorter {
  static List<Player> team;

    private static void loadTeam() {
        System.out.println("Loading team...");
        team = new ArrayList();
        Player player1 = new Player();
        player1.setFirstName("Josh");
        player1.setLastName("Juneau");
        player1.setGoals(5);
        Player player2 = new Player();
        player2.setFirstName("Duke");
        player2.setLastName("Java");
        player2.setGoals(15);
        Player player3 = new Player();
        player3.setFirstName("Jonathan");
        player3.setLastName("Gennick");
        player3.setGoals(1);
        Player player4 = new Player();
        player4.setFirstName("Bob");
        player4.setLastName("Smith");
        player4.setGoals(18);
        Player player5 = new Player();
        player5.setFirstName("Steve");
        player5.setLastName("Adams");
        player5.setGoals(7);

        team.add(player1);
        team.add(player2);
        team.add(player3);
        team.add(player4);
        team.add(player5);

    }
...
}
```

How It Works

Java 8 introduced new features that greatly increase developer productivity for sorting collections. Three features are demonstrated in the solution to this recipe: lambda expressions, method references, and streams. We look into streams in more detail within other recipes in this book, but we also briefly describe them here to help you understand this recipe. Streams can be applied to data collections, and they allow enhanced functional-style operations to be applied to the elements within the collections. Streams do not store any data; rather, they enable more functionality on the collections obtained from them.

In solution 1, a comparator is generated, by which the `Player` objects are evaluated for the number of goals scored (`getGoals`). A stream is then generated from a `List<Player>` that is referenced as a team. The stream provides the `sorted()` function, which accepts a comparator to perform a sort on a stream of data. The comparator that was initially generated is passed to the `sorted()` function, and then the `map()` function is called on the result. The `map()` function can apply an expression to each element within the stream. Therefore, within the map, this solution utilizes a lambda expression to create a string that contains each `Player` object's `firstName`, `lastName`, and `goals` fields. Lastly, since `List<Player>` is iterable, it contains the `forEach()` method. The `forEach()` method enables an expression or group of statements to be applied to each element within the list. In this case, each element in the list is printed to the command line. Since the `map()` function was applied to the stream, each element in the list is subsequently printed per the algorithm applied within `map()`. The result is that the players' first and last names and the number of goals each has scored are printed on the command line.

Solution 2 uses a different technique to accomplish a similar task. The `Collections .sort()` method is invoked on the list. The first argument to `Collections.sort()` is the list itself, and the second argument is the comparison implementation in the form of a lambda expression. The lambda expression, in this case, has two parameters passed to it, both `Player` objects, and it compares the last name of the first player to the last name of the second player. Therefore, the sort is performed on the `lastName` field of the `Player` object, in ascending order. To finish solution 2, the sorted list is printed out. To do this, a stream is generated from the sorted list, and the `forEach()` method is then invoked on the stream of data, printing out each player's last name.

6-5. Filtering a Collection of Data

Problem

You have a list of data to which you'd like to apply some filtering so that you can extract objects meeting the specified criteria.

Solution

Create a stream from the list of data and apply a filter, passing the desired predicate, otherwise known as a *conditional expression*. Finally, add each object matching the specified filter criteria to a new list. In the following example, a list of Player objects is being filtered to capture only those players who have scored ten or more goals.

```
public static void main(String[] args){
        loadTeam();
        // Create Array to store the matching reaults
        List<Player> gteTenGoals = new ArrayList<Player>();

team.stream().filter(
    p -> p.getGoals() >= 10
    && p.getStatus() == 0)
    .forEach(element -> gteTenGoals.add(element));
System.out.println("Number of Players Matching Criteria: " + gteTenGoals.
size());
```

Where the function loadTeam is:
```
public class Filter {
    static List<Player> team;

    private static void loadTeam() {
        System.out.println("Loading team...");
        team = new ArrayList();
        Player player1 = new Player();
        player1.setFirstName("Josh");
        player1.setLastName("Juneau");
        player1.setGoals(5);
        player1.setStatus(0);
```

```
        Player player2 = new Player();
        player2.setFirstName("Duke");
        player2.setLastName("Java");
        player2.setGoals(15);
        player2.setStatus(0);
        Player player3 = new Player();
        player3.setFirstName("Jonathan");
        player3.setLastName("Gennick");
        player3.setGoals(1);
        player3.setStatus(0);
        Player player4 = new Player();
        player4.setFirstName("Bob");
        player4.setLastName("Smith");
        player4.setGoals(18);
        player4.setStatus(0);
        Player player5 = new Player();
        player5.setFirstName("Steve");
        player5.setLastName("Adams");
        player5.setGoals(7);
        player5.setStatus(1);
        team.add(player1);
        team.add(player2);
        team.add(player3);
        team.add(player4);
        team.add(player5);

    }
```

How It Works

The solution to this recipe makes use of a data stream since it contains an easy-to-use filter function. The collection of data, team, generates a stream, and then the filter function is called on it, accepting a predicate to filter the data within the collection. The predicate is written as a lambda expression that contains two such filtering criteria. The lambda expression passes a Player object as an argument and then filters the data based on the number of goals greater than or equal to ten and an active status.

Once the data has been filtered, the forEach() method adds each element that meets the filtering criteria to a list. This is also done using a lambda expression. The element added to the list is passed to the lambda expression as an argument and subsequently added to the list within the body of the expression.

Lambda expressions are very well suited for working within stream functions. Not only do they enable easier development of business logic, but they also make collections filtering easier to read and maintain.

6-6. Implementing Runnable
Problem

You want to create a runnable piece of code in a terse manner.

Solution

Utilize a lambda expression to implement the java.util.Runnable interface. The java.util.Runnable interface is a perfect match for lambda expressions since it contains only a single abstract method, run(). This solution compares the legacy technique, creating a new Runnable interface, and the new technique using a lambda expression.

The following lines of code demonstrate how to implement a new Runnable piece of code using the legacy technique.

```
public static void main(String[] args) {

    Runnable oldRunnable = new Runnable() {
        @Override
        public void run() {
            int x = 5 * 3;
            System.out.println("The variable using the old way
            equals: " + x);
        }
    };
    Runnable lambdaRunnable = () -> {
        int x = 5 * 3;
```

```
            System.out.println("The variable using the lambda
            equals: " + x);
    };
    // Calling the runnables
    oldRunnable.run();
    lambdaRunnable.run();
}
```

The following is the output.

```
The variable using the old way equals: 15
The variable using the lambda equals: 15
```

Now take a look at how this can be written using a lambda expression instead.

```
Runnable lambdaRunnable = () -> {
    int x = 5 * 3;
    System.out.println("The variable using the lambda equals: " + x);
};
```

As you can see, the legacy procedure for implementing a Runnable takes a few more lines of code than implementing Runnable with a lambda expression. The lambda expression also makes the Runnable implementation easier to read and maintain.

How It Works

Since java.util.Runnable is a functional interface, the boilerplate of implementing the run() method can be abstracted away using a lambda expression. The following is the general format for implementing a Runnable with a lambda expression.

```
Runnable assignment = () -> {expression or statements};
```

A Runnable interface can be implemented using a zero-argument lambda expression containing an expression or a series of statements within the lambda body. The key is that the implementation takes zero arguments and returns nothing.

6-7. Accessing Class Variables from a Lambda Expression

Problem

The class you are writing contains instance variables, and you want to make them available for use via a lambda expression within the class.

Solution

Use instance variables contained in enclosing classes, as needed, from within lambda expressions. In the following class, the lambda expression contained within the VariableAccessInner.InnerClass.lambdaInMethod() method can access all enclosing class instance variables. Thus, it can print the VariableAccessInner CLASSA variable, if needed.

```
public class VariableAccessInner {
    public String CLASSA = "Class-level A";
    class InnerClass {
        public String CLASSA = "Class-level B";
        void lambdaInMethod(String passedIn) {
            String METHODA = "Method-level A";
            Consumer<String> l1 = x -> {
                System.out.println(x);
                System.out.println("CLASSA Value: " + CLASSA);
                System.out.println("METHODA Value: " + METHODA);
            };
            l1.accept(CLASSA);
            l1.accept(passedIn);
        }
    }
}
```

Now, let's execute lambdaInMethod using the following code.

```
VariableAccessInner vai = new VariableAccessInner();
VariableAccessInner.InnerClass inner = vai.new InnerClass();
inner.lambdaInMethod("Hello");
```

The main class is as follows.

```
public class MainClass {
    public static void main(String[] args){
        System.out.println("==VariableAccessInner==");
        VariableAccessInner vai = new VariableAccessInner();
        VariableAccessInner.InnerClass inner = vai.new InnerClass();
        inner.lambdaInMethod("Hello");

    }
}
```

The following is the result.

```
==VariableAccessInner==
Class-level B
CLASSA Value: Class-level B
METHODA Value: Method-level A
Hello
CLASSA Value: Class-level B
METHODA Value: Method-level A
```

Note   The CLASSA variable is overridden by a variable using the same identifier within the InnerClass class. Therefore, the CLASSA instance variable that belongs to VariableAccessInner is not printed within the lambda expression.

How It Works

Lambda expressions have access to the variables located within the enclosing class. Thus, a lambda expression contained within a class method can access any instance variables of the enclosing class. No additional scope is added to a lambda expression, so it can access fields, methods, and local variables of the enclosing scope. In the solution, the lambda expression contained within the lambdaInMethod() method can access all of the fields that are declared within either class. This is because both the inner and outer classes enclose the lambda. One thing to note is that if an inner class contains an instance variable of the same name as a variable that has been declared in the outer class, then the lambda uses the variable of its enclosing class. Therefore, in the solution, the InnerClass CLASSA field is accessed from within the lambda expression rather than the outer class reference.

Local variables referenced from within a lambda expression must be either final or effectively final. An error occurs when a lambda expression attempts to access a variable that was changed within the context of an enclosing method. For instance, suppose that the method in the solution was changed to the following.

```
void lambdaInMethod(String passedIn) {
    String METHODA = "Method-level A";
    passedIn = "test";
    Consumer<String> l1 = x -> {
        System.out.println(x);
        System.out.println("CLASSA Value: " + CLASSA);
        System.out.println("METHODA Value: " + METHODA);
        System.out.println(passedIn);
    };
    l1.accept(CLASSA);
    l1.accept(passedIn);
}
```

Note that the string passed into lambdaInMethod() is assigned a new value just before the lambda expression is invoked. Therefore, the passedIn variable is no longer effectively final, and lambda expressions cannot introduce a new scope level. Consequently, the lambda expression does not have access to the passedIn variable from within the context of the expression.

6-8. Passing Lambda Expressions to Methods

Problem

A lambda expression has been created to encapsulate some functionality. You want to take that functionality and pass it into a method as an argument so that the method implementation can take advantage of the expression.

Solution

Create portable functions using lambda expressions by implementing a functional interface and assigning the lambda expression to a variable of the same type as the interface. The variable can be passed to other objects as an argument.

The following class, `PassingLambdaFunctions`, contains a `calculate()` method, which performs calculations of any type given an array of values. Note that the `calculate()` method accepts a `Function<List<Double>,Double>` and an array of `Double` values as arguments.

```
public class PassingLambdaFunctions {
    /**
     * Calculates a value based upon the calculation function that
       is passed
     * in.
     * @param f1 Double input value
     * @param args  Double input value
     * @return
     */
    public Double calculate(Function<List<Double>, Double> f1,
                                    Double [] args){
        Double returnVal;
        List<Double> varList = new ArrayList();
        int idx = 0;
        while (idx < args.length){
          varList.add(args[idx]);
          idx++;
        }
```

```
        returnVal=f1.apply(varList);
        return returnVal;
    }
}
```

To use the calculate method, a lambda expression that implements
Function<List<Double>,Double> must be passed as the first argument to the
calculate() method, along with an array of Double arguments that contains the value
to be used within the calculation. In the following class, a function for calculating
volume is generated using a lambda expression. It is assigned to a variable identified
as volumeCalc of type Function<List<Double>,Double>. Another lambda expression
creates a function for calculating area, and it is assigned to a variable of the same
type, identified as areaCalc. In separate calls, these variables are then passed to the
PassingLambdaFunctions.calculate() method, along with an array of values, resulting
in the calculated answer.

```
public class MainClass {
    public static void main(String[] args){
        double x = 16.0;
        double y = 30.0;
        double z = 4.0;

        // Create volume calculation function using a lambda.
           The calculator checks to ensure that the array contains the
           three necessary elements for the calculation.
        Function<List<Double>, Double> volumeCalc = list -> {
            if(list.size() == 3){
                return list.get(0) * list.get(1) * list.get(2);
            } else {
                return Double.valueOf("-1");
            }
        };
        Double[] argList = new Double[3];
        argList[0] = x;
        argList[1] = y;
        argList[2] = z;
```

```
    // Create area calculation function using a lambda.
       This particular calculator checks to ensure that the array only
       contains two elements.
    Function<List<Double>, Double> areaCalc = list -> {
        if(list.size() == 2){
            return list.get(0) * list.get(1);
        } else {
            return Double.valueOf("-1");
        }
    };
    Double[] argList2 = new Double[2];
    argList2[0] = x;
    argList2[1] = y;

    PassingLambdaFunctions p1 = new PassingLambdaFunctions();

    // Pass the lambda expressions to the calculate() method, along
       with the argument lists.
    System.out.println("The volume is: " + p1.calculate(volumeCalc,
    argList));
    System.out.println("The area is: " + p1.calculate(areaCalc,
    argList2));
    }
}
```

The following is the result.

```
The volume is: 1920.0
The area is: 480.0
```

How It Works

Lambda expressions can be assigned to variables of the same type as the implemented functional interface. Such expressions can contain a single-line expression or a multistatement body. Since the lambda expression can accept arguments, there are use cases for assigning such expressions to variables and then passing those variables into other objects to modify functionality. This pattern is useful for creating solutions containing more than one implementation. The solution to this recipe demonstrates this concept.

In the solution, the `PassingLambdaFunctions` class contains a `calculate()` method, which performs calculations on `Double` values passed into it as arguments. However, the `calculate()` method contains no calculation functionality at all. Rather, the calculation functionality is passed as an argument of type `Function<List<Double>,Double>` via a lambda expression. This type is one of the standard functional interfaces within the `java.util.function` package and the interface can be implemented by lambda expressions and then invoked later by calling its solo `apply()` method. Looking at the code in the `calculate()` method, the arguments contained within the `Double[]` are first added to a list. Next, lambda expression's `apply()` method is invoked, passing the new list of values and returning a result into `returnVal`. Finally, `returnVal` is returned to the method invoker.

```
returnVal=f1.apply(varList);
return returnVal;
```

To implement the calculation functionality within the solution, lambda expressions are created in a separate class named `MainClass`. Each expression accepts a list of arguments and then calculates the values in the list, returning a result. For instance, the first lambda generated in `MainClass` calculates volume by multiplying together all of the values in the argument list and returning the result. This functionality is then assigned to a variable of type `Function<List<Double>,Double>`, and then it is passed into the `PassingLambdaFunctions.calculate()` method later on.

Any functionality can be implemented within a lambda expression and then passed around to different objects for use. This is an excellent way to promote code reuse and high maintainability.

6-9. Local Variable

Problem

You want to skip the parameter types and use the var local variable.

Solution

You can skip the parameter types and rewrite the lambda from this form

```
(String str1, String str2) -> s1 + s2
```

to the following form.

```
(var str1, var str2) -> str1 + str2
```

You can rewrite Recipe 6-1 using var in the following form.

```
public static void main(String[] args){
    // Create the lambda, passing a parameter named "text" to the
    // hello() method, returning the string.  The lambda is assigned
    // to the helloLambda variable.
    HelloType helloLambda =
            (var text) -> {System.out.println("Hello " + text);};
    // Invoke the method call
    helloLambda.hello("Lambda");
}
```

The following is the output.

```
Hello Lambda
```

In this case, the type of the variable text is inferred from context by the compiler, and the output is the same. It does not create warnings or errors.

How It Works

Java 11 introduced the local variable syntax for lambda parameters to align the syntax of a parameter declaration in an implicitly typed lambda expression with the syntax of a local variable declaration. It surely makes our code *more* readable. For more information on the var keyword, see the documentation at https://openjdk.java.net/jeps/323.

6-10. Switch Expressions
Problem

You want to efficiently use a switch expression issues without the break.

Solution

Simply you can use a lambda-style syntax for your expressions. So, you can rewrite the lambda from this form.

```
switch(input_variable) {
  case one:
    returnValue = 12
    break;
  case two:
    returnValue = 75
    break;
  default:
    // code of default block
}
```

To that form:

```
int numLetters = switch (input_variable) {
    case one -> 12;
    case two -> 75;
    default -> {// code of default block }
};
```

You can rewrite Recipe 6-4 using lambda-style syntax for switch expression from

```
switch(status){
        case 0:
                returnValue = "ACTIVE";
        case 1:
                returnValue = "INACTIVE";
        case 2:
                returnValue = "INJURY";
        default:
                returnValue = "ON_BENCH";
}
```

to the following form.

```
returnValue =switch(status){
        case 0  -> "ACTIVE";
        case 1  -> "INACTIVE";
        case 2  -> "INJURY";
        default -> "ON_BENCH";
};
```

The output is the same.

How It Works

This enhancement was proposed in Java 12 and in production in Java 14 (JEP 361). This functionality introduces a new form of switch label, where only the code to the right of the label (->) is to be executed if the label is matched.

For information on the var keyword, see the documentation at https://openjdk .java.net/jeps/361.

6-11. Summary

Lambda expressions brought new life to the Java language with their introduction in Java 8, providing capabilities unavailable to Java developers in the past. Developers of desktop, mobile, and enterprise applications alike can now take advantage of the lambda expression to create more robust and sophisticated solutions. Lambda expressions are a revolutionary change to the language, and they have a significant impact on development across the platform.

CHAPTER 7

Data Sources and Collections

Applications use data structures to store data that can be utilized throughout the lifetime of an application instance. The Java language contains several data structures known as collection types, and they can be utilized for this purpose. These data structures implement the `java.util.Collection<E>` interface, which provides a variety of methods that are useful for adding, removing, and performing tasks against the data that is used with the collection. This chapter introduces some of the data structures that can be utilized within a Java application for the storage of user data. It discusses some of the data structures in detail and introduces operations performed on the data. The concepts of pipelines and streams are introduced in this chapter, and it provides recipes that demonstrate their usage.

7-1. Defining a Fixed Set of Related Constants

Problem

You need a type that can represent a fixed set of related constants.

Solution

Use an enum type. The following example defines an enum type, called `FieldType`, to represent various form fields you might find on the GUI of an application.

```
public enum FieldType { PASSWORD, EMAIL_ADDRESS, PHONE_NUMBER,
SOCIAL_SECURITY_NUMBER }
```

© Josh Juneau, Luciano Manelli 2022
J. Juneau and L. Manelli, *Java 17 Recipes*, https://doi.org/10.1007/978-1-4842-7963-2_7

This is the simplest form of an enum type, which often suffice when needed is a related set of named constants. In the following code, a `field` variable of type `FieldType` is declared and initialized to the `FieldType.EMAIL_ADDRESS` enum constant. Next, the code prints the results from calling various methods that are defined for all enum types.

```
public static void main(String[] args) {
    FieldType field = FieldType.EMAIL_ADDRESS;

    System.out.println("field.name(): " + field.name());
    System.out.println("field.ordinal(): " + field.ordinal());
    System.out.println("field.toString(): " + field.toString());

    System.out.println("field.isEqual(EMAIL_ADDRESS): " +
                    field.equals(FieldType.EMAIL_ADDRESS));
    System.out.println("field.isEqual(\"EMAIL_ADDRESS\"'): " +
                    field.equals("EMAIL_ADDRESS"));

    System.out.println("field == EMAIL_ADDRESS: " + (field ==
                    FieldType.EMAIL_ADDRESS));
    // Won't compile - illustrates type safety of enum
    // System.out.println("field == \"EMAIL_ADDRESS\": " + (field ==
                    "EMAIL_ADDRESS"));

    System.out.println("field.compareTo(EMAIL_ADDRESS): " +
                    field.compareTo(FieldType.EMAIL_ADDRESS));

    System.out.println("field.compareTo(PASSWORD): " +
                    field.compareTo(FieldType.PASSWORD));

    System.out.println("field.valueOf(\"EMAIL_ADDRESS\"): " +
                    field.valueOf("EMAIL_ADDRESS"));
    try {
        System.out.print("field.valueOf(\"email_address\"): ");
        System.out.println(FieldType.valueOf("email_address"));
    } catch (IllegalArgumentException e) {
        System.out.println(e.toString());
    }
    System.out.println("FieldType.values(): " + Arrays.toString
                    (FieldType.values()));
}
```

Running this code result in the following output.

```
field.name(): EMAIL_ADDRESS
field.ordinal(): 1
field.toString(): EMAIL_ADDRESS
field.isEqual(EMAIL_ADDRESS): true
field.isEqual("EMAIL_ADDRESS"'): false
field == EMAIL_ADDRESS: true
field.compareTo(EMAIL_ADDRESS): 0
field.compareTo(PASSWORD): 1
field.valueOf("EMAIL_ADDRESS"): EMAIL_ADDRESS
field.valueOf("email_address"): java.lang.IllegalArgumentException:
No enum constant org.java17recipes.chapter07.recipe07_01.BasicEnumExample
.FieldType.email_address
FieldType.values(): [PASSWORD, EMAIL_ADDRESS, PHONE_NUMBER, SSN]
```

How It Works

A common pattern for representing a fixed set of related constants is defining each constant as an int, string, or other data type. Often, these constants are defined in a class or interface whose sole purpose is to encapsulate constants. In any case, constants are sometimes defined with the static and final modifiers, as follows.

```
// Input field constants
public static final int PASSWORD = 0;
public static final int EMAIL_ADDRESS = 1;
public static final int PHONE_NUMBER = 2;
public static final int SOCIAL_SECURITY_NUMBER = 3;
```

There are multiple problems with this pattern, the primary issue being the lack of type safety. By defining these constants as ints, it is possible to assign an invalid value to a variable that is supposed to be allowed to hold only one of the constant values.

```
int inputField = PHONE_NUMBER;  // OK
inputField = 4;  // Bad - no input field constant with value 4;
                 compiles without error
```

As you can see, there is no compiler error or warning produced to inform you of this invalid value assignment. Chances are, you discover this at runtime when your application tries to use inputField, and an incorrect value is assigned to it. In contrast, Java enum types provide compile-time type safety. That is, if one attempts to assign a value of the wrong type to an enum variable, it results in a compiler error. In the solution for this recipe, the FieldType.EMAIL_ADDRESS enum constant is assigned to the field variable. Attempting to assign a value that isn't of type FieldType naturally results in a compiler error.

```
FieldType field = FieldType.EMAIL_ADDRESS;  // OK
field = "EMAIL_ADDRESS"; // Wrong type - compiler error
```

An enum is simply a special type of class. Under the covers, Java implements an enum type as a subclass of the abstract and final java.lang.Enum class. Thus, an enum type cannot be instantiated directly (outside of the enum type) or extended. The constants defined by an enum type are instances of it. The java.lang.Enum class defines several final methods that all enum types inherit. In addition, all enum types have two implicitly declared static methods: values() and valueOf(String). The solution code demonstrates these static methods and some of the more often used instance methods.

Most of these methods are self-explanatory, but you should keep the following in mind.

- Each enum constant has an ordinal value representing its relative position in the enum declaration. The first constant in the declaration is assigned an ordinal value of zero. The ordinal() method can retrieve an enum constant's ordinal value; however, it is not recommended that applications be written to depend on this value for maintainability reasons.

- The name() method and the default implementation of the toString() method both return a string representation of the enum constant (toString() actually calls name()). It is common for toString() to be overridden to provide a more user-friendly string representation of the enum constant. For this reason, and for maintainability reasons, it is recommended that toString() be used in preference to name().

- When testing for equality, note that both the `equals()` method and == perform reference comparison. They can be used interchangeably. However, it is recommended that == take advantage of compile-time type safety. This is illustrated in the solution code. Performing `equals()` comparison with a string parameter, for example, may allow the error to go unnoticed; it compiles, but it always returns false. Conversely, comparing an enum with a string using the == comparison would result in an error at compile time. When you choose to catch errors sooner (at compile time) rather than later (at runtime), choose the former.

- The implicitly declared `values()` and `valueOf(String)` static methods do not appear in the Java documentation or the source code for the `java.lang.Enum` class. However, the Java Language Specification does detail their required implementations. To summarize these methods, `values()` returns an array containing the constants of the enum in the order they are declared. The `valueOf(String)` method returns the enum constant whose name matches (including case) the value of the string argument or throws `IllegalArgumentException` if there is no enum constant with the specified name.

Refer to Java documentation (`https://docs.oracle.com/en/java/javase/17/docs/api/java.base/java/lang/Enum.html`) for more information on `java.lang.Enum` and each of its methods. As the next recipe demonstrates, enum types, as full-fledged Java classes, can build more intelligent constants.

7-2. Designing Intelligent Constants
Problem

You need a type that can represent a fixed set of related constants, and you want to build some state and behavior (logic) around your constants in an object-oriented fashion.

Solution

Use an enum type and take advantage of type safety because enum types are full-fledged
Java classes. An enum type can have state and behavior just like any other class, and the
enum constants, themselves being instances of the enum type, inherit this state and
behavior. An example best illustrates this. Let's expand on the example from the previous
recipe. Imagine that you need to process and validate all the fields from an HTML form
submitted. Each form field has a unique set of rules for validating its content, based on
the field type. For each form field, you have the field's "name" and the value entered in
that form field. The FieldType enum can be expanded to handle this very easily.

```java
public enum FieldType {

    PASSWORD(FieldType.passwordFieldName) {
        // A password must contain one or more digits, one or more
        // lowercase letters, one or more uppercase letters, and be a
        // minimum of 6 characters in length.
        public boolean validate(String fieldValue) {
            return Pattern.matches("((?=.*\\d)(?=.*[a-z])
            (?=.*[A-Z]).{6,})", fieldValue);
        }
    },
    EMAIL_ADDRESS(FieldType.emailFieldName) {
        // An email address begins with a combination of alphanumeric
        // Characters, periods, and hyphens, followed by a mandatory
        // Ampersand ('@') character, followed by a combination of
        // Alphanumeric characters (hyphens allowed), followed by a
        // Ane or more periods (to separate domains and subdomains),
        // And ending in 2-4 lphabetic characters representing
        // A the domain.
        public boolean validate(String fieldValue) {
            return Pattern.matches("^[\\w\\.-]+@([\\w\\-]+\\.)+[A-Z|a-z]
                                    {2,4}$", fieldValue);
        }
    },
```

```
PHONE_NUMBER(FieldType.phoneFieldName) {
    // A phone number must contain a minium of 7 digits.
    // Three optional digits representing the area code may appear in
    // Front of the main 7 digits. The area code may, optionally,
    // Be surrounded by parenthesis. If an area code is included,
    // The number may optionally be prefixed by a '1' for
    // Long distance numbers. Optional hypens my appear after
    // The country code ('1'), the area code, and the
    // first 3 digits of the 7 digit number.
    public boolean validate(String fieldValue) {
        return Pattern.matches("^1?[- ]?\\(?(?(\\d{3})\\)?[- ]?(\\d{3})
                                [- ]?(\\d{4})$", fieldValue);
    }
},
SOCIAL_SECURITY_NUMBER(FieldType.ssnFieldName) {
    // A social security number must contain 9 digits with optional
    // Hyphens after the third and fifth digits.
    public boolean validate(String fieldValue) {
        return Pattern.matches("^\\d{3}[- ]?\\d{2}[- ]?\\d{4}$",
                                fieldValue);
    }
};  // End of enum constants definition
// Instance members
//
private String fieldName;
// Define static constants to increase type safety
static final String passwordFieldName = "password";
static final String emailFieldName = "email";
static final String phoneFieldName = "phone";
static final String ssnFieldName = "ssn";
private FieldType(String fieldName) {
    this.fieldName = fieldName;
}
public String getFieldName() {
    return this.fieldName;
}
```

```java
    abstract boolean validate(String fieldValue);
    // Static class members
    //
    private static final Map<String, FieldType> nameToFieldTypeMap =
    new HashMap<>();
    static {
        for (FieldType field : FieldType.values()) {
            nameToFieldTypeMap.put(field.getFieldName(), field);
        }
    }
    public static FieldType lookup(String fieldName) {
        return nameToFieldTypeMap.get(fieldName.toLowerCase());
    }
    private static void printValid(FieldType field, String fieldValue,
    boolean valid) {
      System.out.println(field.getFieldName() +
                          "(\"" + fieldValue + "\") valid: " + valid);
    }
    public static void main(String... args) {
        String fieldName = FieldType.passwordFieldName;
        String fieldValue = "1Cxy9";  // invalid - must be at least 6
                                      characters
        FieldType field = lookup(fieldName);
        printValid(field, fieldValue, field.validate(fieldValue));
        fieldName = FieldType.phoneFieldName;
        fieldValue = "1-800-555-1234";  // valid
        field = lookup(fieldName);
        printValid(field, fieldValue, field.validate(fieldValue));
        fieldName = FieldType.emailFieldName;
        fieldValue = "john@doe";  // invalid - missing .<tld>
        field = lookup(fieldName);
        printValid(field, fieldValue, field.validate(fieldValue));
        fieldName = FieldType.ssnFieldName;
        fieldValue = "111-11-1111";  // valid
```

```
        field = lookup(fieldName);
        printValid(field, fieldValue, field.validate(fieldValue));
    }
}
```

Running the preceding code results in the following output.

```
password("1Cxy9") valid: false
phone("1-800-555-1234") valid: true
email("john@doe") valid: false
ssn("111-11-1111") valid: true
```

How It Works

Notice that the enhanced FieldType enum defines a fieldName instance variable and a constructor with a fieldName string argument for initializing the instance variable. Each enum constant (each constant being an instance of FieldType) must be instantiated with a fieldName. FieldType also defines an abstract validate(String) method that each enum constant must implement to perform the field validation. Here, each FieldType's validate() method applies a regular expression match against the field value and returns the Boolean result of the match. Imagine the following form input fields corresponding to our FieldType instances.

```
<input type="password" name="password" value=""/>
<input type="tel" name="phone" value=""/>
<input type="email" name="email" value=""/>
<input type="text" name="ssn" value=""/>
```

The value of the input field's name attribute identifies FieldType; you used this same name when you instantiated each FieldType enum constant. When a form is submitted, you have access to each input field's name and the value entered in the field. You need to map the field's name to a field type and call the validate() method with the input value. The class variable, nameToFieldTypeMap, is declared and initialized for this purpose. For each FieldType enum constant, nameToFieldTypeMap stores an entry with the field name as the key and the field type as the value. The lookup(String) class method uses this map to look up the field type from the field name. The code to validate an email input field with an input value of john@doe.com is quite concise.

```java
// <input type="email" name="email" value="john@doe.com"/>
String fieldName = FieldType.emailFieldName;
String fieldValue = "john@doe.com";
boolean valid = FieldType.lookup(fieldName).validate(fieldValue);
```

The `main()` method shows an example validation for each of the `FieldType`s. The `printValid()` method prints the field name, field value, and the field's validation result.

This recipe has demonstrated a lot more potential in the enum type than the ability to define a set of named constants. Enum types have all the power of a normal class, plus additional features that allow you to create well-encapsulated and intelligent constants.

7-3. Executing Code Based on a Specified Value

Problem

You want to execute different blocks of code based on the value of a singular expression.

Solution

Consider using a `switch` statement if your variable or expression result is one of the allowed `switch` types and you want to test for equality against a type-compatible constant. These examples show various ways to use the `switch` statement, including a new feature that became available in Java 7: the ability to switch on strings. First, let's play the rock-paper-scissors game! The `RockPaperScissors` class shows two different `switch` statements: an int as the switch expression type and an enum type.

```java
public class RockPaperScissors {

    enum Hand { ROCK, PAPER, SCISSORS, INVALID };

    private static void getHand(int handVal) {
        Hand hand;
        try {
            hand = Hand.values()[handVal - 1];
        }
        catch (ArrayIndexOutOfBoundsException ex) {
            hand = Hand.INVALID;
```

```
    }
    switch (hand) {
        case ROCK:
            System.out.println("Rock");
            break;
        case PAPER:
            System.out.println("Paper");
            break;
        case SCISSORS:
            System.out.println("Scissors");
            break;
        default:
            System.out.println("Invalid");
    }
}

private static void playHands(int yourHand, int myHand) {
    // Rock = 1
    // Paper = 2
    // Scissors = 3
    // Hand combinations:
    // 1,1; 2,2; 3,3 => Draw
    // 1,2 => sum = 3 => Paper
    // 1,3 => sum = 4 => Rock
    // 2,3 => sum = 5 => Scissors
    //
    switch ((yourHand == myHand) ? 0 : (yourHand + myHand)) {
        case 0:
            System.out.println("Draw!");
            break;
        case 3:
            System.out.print("Paper beats Rock. ");
            printWinner(yourHand, 2);
            break;
```

```java
            case 4:
                System.out.print("Rock beats Scissors. ");
                printWinner(yourHand, 1);
                break;
            case 5:
                System.out.print("Scissors beats Paper. ");
                printWinner(yourHand, 3);
                break;
            default:
                System.out.print("You cheated! ");
                printWinner(yourHand, myHand);
        }
    }
    private static void printWinner(int yourHand, int winningHand) {
        if (yourHand == winningHand) {
            System.out.println("You win!");
        }
        else {
            System.out.println("I win!");
        }
    }

    public static void main(String[] args) {

        Scanner input = new Scanner(System.in);
        System.out.println("Let's Play Rock, Paper, Scissors");
        System.out.println("  Enter 1 (Rock)");
        System.out.println("  Enter 2 (Paper)");
        System.out.println("  Enter 3 (Scissors)");
        System.out.print("> ");

        int playerHand = input.hasNextInt() ? input.nextInt() : -99;
        int computerHand = (int)(3*Math.random()) + 1;
        System.out.print("Your hand: (" + playerHand + ") ");
        getHand(playerHand);
        System.out.print("My hand: (" + computerHand + ") ");
```

```
        getHand(computerHand);
        playHands(playerHand, computerHand);
    }
}
```

When the RockPaperScissors class is executed, an interactive game begins, allowing users to type input at the keyboard. The users can type the number corresponding to the entry they'd like to choose, and the computer utilizes random number calculations to beat the users' choices.

Java 7 added the capability to switch on strings. The SwitchTypeChecker class demonstrates a string as the switch expression type. The isValidSwitchType() method takes a Class object and determines whether the corresponding type is a valid type used in a switch expression. So, SwitchTypeChecker is using a switch statement to simultaneously demonstrate switching on strings and to show the valid types for use in a switch expression:

```
public class SwitchTypeChecker {
    public static Class varTypeClass(Object o) { return o.getClass(); };
    public static Class varTypeClass(Enum e) { return e.getClass()
    .getSuperclass(); };
    public static Class varTypeClass(char c) { return char.class; };
    public static Class varTypeClass(byte b) { return byte.class; };
    public static Class varTypeClass(short s) { return short.class; };
    public static Class varTypeClass(int i) { return int.class; };
    public static Class varTypeClass(long l) { return long.class; };
    public static Class varTypeClass(float f) { return float.class; };
    public static Class varTypeClass(double d) { return double.class; };
    public static Class varTypeClass(boolean d) { return boolean.class; };
    public void isValidSwitchType(Class typeClass) {
        String switchType = typeClass.getSimpleName();
        boolean valid = true;
        switch (switchType) {
            case "char":
            case "byte":
            case "short":
            case "int":
```

```
                System.out.print("Primitive type " + switchType);
                break;
            case "Character":
            case "Byte":
            case "Short":
            case "Integer":
                System.out.print("Boxed primitive type " + switchType);
                break;
            case "String":
            case "Enum":
                System.out.print(switchType);
                break;
            default:  // invalid switch type
                System.out.print(switchType);
                valid = false;
        }
        System.out.println(" is " + (valid ? "" : "not ") +
        "a valid switch type.");
    }

    public static void main(String[] args) {
        SwitchTypeChecker check = new SwitchTypeChecker();
        check.isValidSwitchType(varTypeClass('7'));
        check.isValidSwitchType(varTypeClass(7));
        check.isValidSwitchType(varTypeClass(777.7d));
        check.isValidSwitchType(varTypeClass((short)7));
        check.isValidSwitchType(varTypeClass(new Integer(7)));
        check.isValidSwitchType(varTypeClass("Java 8 Rocks!"));
        check.isValidSwitchType(varTypeClass(new Long(7)));
        check.isValidSwitchType(varTypeClass(true));
        check.isValidSwitchType(varTypeClass(java.nio.file
        .AccessMode.READ));
    }
}
```

Here is the result of executing SwitchTypeChecker.

```
Primitive type char is a valid switch type.
Primitive type int is a valid switch type.
double is not a valid switch type.
Primitive type short is a valid switch type.
Boxed primitive type Integer is a valid switch type.
String is a valid switch type.
Long is not a valid switch type.
boolean is not a valid switch type.
Enum is a valid switch type.
```

How It Works

The switch statement is a control-flow statement that allows you to execute different blocks of code based on the value of a switch expression. It is similar to the if-then-else statement, except that the switch statement can have only a single test expression. The expression type is restricted to one of several different types. When a switch statement executes, it evaluates the expression against constants contained in the switch statement's case labels. These case labels are branch points in the code. If the value of the expression equals the value of a case label constant, control is transferred to the section of code that corresponds to the matching case label. All code statements from that point on are then executed until either the end of the switch statement or a break statement is reached. The break statement causes the switch statement to terminate, with control being transferred to the statement following the switch statement. Optionally, the switch statement can contain a default label, which provides a branch point for the case when there is no case label constant that equates to the switch expression value.

The SwitchTypeChecker isValidSwitchType() method demonstrates the use of a string as the switch test expression. If you closely study the isValidSwitchType() method, you see that it tests whether a Class object represents a type that corresponds to one of the valid switch expression types. The method also demonstrates how case labels can be grouped to implement a logical OR conditional test. If a case label does not have any associated code to execute and no break statement, the flow of execution falls through to the next closest case label containing executable statements, thus allowing common code to be executed if the result of the switch expression matches any one of the grouped case constants.

The RockPaperScissors class implements a command-line rock-paper-scissors game, playing against the computer. There are two methods in this class that demonstrate the switch statement. The getHand() method shows an enum variable in the switch expression. The playHands() method simply intends to show that although often a variable, the switch expression can be any expression whose result is of one of the allowed switch types. In this case, the expression uses a ternary operator that returns an int value.

7-4. Working with Fix-Sized Arrays
Problem

You need a simple data structure that can store a fixed (and possibly large) amount of same-typed data and provide fast sequential access.

Solution

Consider using an array. While Java provides more sophisticated and flexible Collection types, the array type can be a useful data structure for many applications. The following example demonstrates the simplicity of working with arrays. The GradeAnalyzer class provides a means for calculating various grade-related statistics, such as the mean (average) grade, minimum grade, and maximum grade.

```
public class GradeAnalyzer {

    // The internal grades array
    private int[] grades;

    public void setGrades(int[] grades) {
        this.grades = grades;
    }

    // Return cloned grades so the caller cannot modify our internal grades
    public int[] getGrades() {
        return grades != null ? grades.clone() : null;
    }
```

```java
public int meanGrade() {
    int mean = 0;
    if (grades != null&& grades.length > 0) {
        int sum = 0;
        for (int i = 0; i < grades.length; i++) {
            sum += grades[i];
        }
        mean = sum / grades.length;
    }
    return mean;
}
public int minGrade() {
    int min = 0;
    for (int index = 0; index < grades.length; index++) {
        if (grades[index] < min) {
            min = grades[index];
        }
    }
    return min;
}
public int maxGrade() {
    int max = 0;
    for (int index = 0; index < grades.length; index++) {
        if (grades[index] > max) {
            max = grades[index];
        }
    }
    return max;
}
static int[] initGrades1() {
    int[] grades = new int[5];
    grades[0] = 77;
    grades[1] = 48;
    grades[2] = 69;
    grades[3] = 92;
```

```
        grades[4] = 87;
        return grades;
}

    static int[] initGrades2() {
        int[] grades = { 57, 88, 67, 95, 99, 74, 81 };
        return grades;
}

    static int[] initGrades3() {
        return new int[]{ 100, 70, 55, 89, 97, 98, 82 };
    }

    public static void main(String... args) {

        GradeAnalyzer ga = new GradeAnalyzer();
        ga.setGrades(initGrades1());
        System.out.println("Grades 1:");
        System.out.println("Mean of all grades is " + ga.meanGrade());
        System.out.println("Min grade is " + ga.minGrade());
        System.out.println("Max grade is " + ga.maxGrade());
        ga.setGrades(initGrades2());
        System.out.println("Grades 2:");
        System.out.println("Mean of all grades is " + ga.meanGrade());
        System.out.println("Min grade is " + ga.minGrade());
        System.out.println("Max grade is " + ga.maxGrade());
        ga.setGrades(initGrades3());
        System.out.println("Grades 3:");
        System.out.println("Mean of all grades is " + ga.meanGrade());
        System.out.println("Min grade is " + ga.minGrade());
        System.out.println("Max grade is " + ga.maxGrade());

        Object testArray = ga.getGrades();
        Class testClass = testArray.getClass();
        System.out.println("isArray: " + testClass.isArray());
        System.out.println("getClass: " + testClass.getName());
        System.out.println("getSuperclass: " +
        testClass.getSuperclass().getName());
```

```
        System.out.println("getComponentType: " +
        testClass.getComponentType());
        System.out.println("Arrays.toString: " +
        Arrays.toString((int[])testArray));
    }
}
```

Running this code result in the following output.

```
Grades 1:
Mean of all grades is 74
Min grade is 0
Max grade is 92
Grades 2:
Mean of all grades is 80
Min grade is 0
Max grade is 99
Grades 3:
Mean of all grades is 84
Min grade is 0
Max grade is 100
isArray: true
getClass: [I
getSuperclass: class java.lang.Object
getComponentType: int
Arrays.toString: [100, 70, 55, 89, 97, 98, 82]
```

How It Works

The Java array type works differently than Java's ArrayList (part of the Java collections framework). Java arrays hold a fixed amount of data. When an array is created, you must specify how much data it can hold. Once an array has been created, you cannot insert or remove array items or otherwise change the size of the array. However, an array may be a good choice if you have a fixed amount (and especially a very large amount) of data that you need to work on while iterating over it sequentially.

The first thing you need to know about the Java `array` type is that it is an `Object` type. Regardless of the type of data they contain, all arrays have `Object` type as their superclass. The elements of an array may be of any type if all elements are of the same type—either primitive or object reference. Regardless of the array type, the memory for an array is always allocated out of the heap space for the application. The heap is the area of memory used by the JVM for dynamic memory allocation.

Note   It is possible to create an array of `Objects` (`Object[]`) that can hold references to objects of different types; however, this is not recommended. It requires you to check the type of elements and perform explicit type casting when retrieving elements from the array.

There are two steps to completely defining an array object in Java: array variable declaration, which specifies the array element type, and array creation, which allocates the memory for the array. Once an array is declared and the memory is allocated, it can be initialized. There are multiple ways to initialize an array, which are shown in the solution to this recipe. If you know in advance what data you need to store in the array, you can combine array declaration, creation, and initialization in one step using a shortcut syntax you see demonstrated in the solution.

Let's walk through the `GradeAnalyzer` class and examine the various ways to declare, create, initialize, and access arrays. First, notice that the class has one instance variable to hold the grades to be analyzed.

```
private int[] grades;
```

Like all uninitialized `Object` reference instance variables, the `grades` array instance variable is automatically initialized to `null`. Before you can start analyzing grades, you have to set the `grades` instance variable to reference the grades data you want to analyze. This is done using the `setGrades(int[])` method. Once `GradeAnalyzer` has a collection of grades to analyze, the `meanGrade()`, `minGrade()`, and `maxGrade()` methods can be called on to compute their respective statistics. Together, these three methods demonstrate how to iterate the elements of an array, how to access elements of an array, and how to determine the number of elements an array can hold. To determine the number of elements an array can hold, simply access the implicitly defined, final instance variable, `length`, which is available for all arrays.

```
grades.length
```

To iterate the elements of an array, simply use a `for` loop, whose index variable goes through all possible indices of the array. Array indices start at 0, so the last array index is always (`grades.length - 1`). While iterating over the array, you can access the array element at the current index by using the name of the array variable followed by the current index enclosed in brackets (often called an *array subscript*).

```
// From the meanGrade() method:
for (int i = 0; i < grades.length; i++) {
    sum += grades[i];
}
```

Alternatively, the enhanced `for` loop, also known as the `foreach` loop, could iterate the array.

```
for (int grade : grades) {
    sum += grade;
}
```

Notice that to determine the min and max grade, the grades are first sorted in their natural (ascending) order using the utility sort method from the `java.util.Arrays` class. After sorting, the min grade is simply the first element (at index 0) of the array, and the max grade is the last element (at index length –1) of the array.

The three static class methods in the solution—`initGrades1()`, `initGrades2()`, and `initGrades3()`—demonstrate three different ways of creating and initializing the array data you use to "seed" the `GradeAnalyzer` class. The `initGrades1()` method declares and creates an array (using new) that can hold five grades, then manually sets the value at each element index to an integer grade value. The `initGrades2()` method combines array creation and initialization in one line using the special array initializer syntax.

```
int[] grades = { 57, 88, 67, 95, 99, 74, 81 };
```

This syntax creates an array with a length of 7 and initializes the elements from index 0 through index 6 with the integer values shown. Note that this syntax can be used only in an array declaration, so the following is not allowed.

```
int[] grades;
grades = { 57, 88, 67, 95, 99, 74, 81 }; // won't compile
```

The initGrades3() method looks very similar to initGrades2() but is slightly different. This code creates and returns an anonymous (unnamed) array.

```
return new int[]{ 100, 70, 55, 89, 97, 98, 82 };
```

With this syntax, you use the new keyword with the array element type, but the size of the array is not explicitly specified. Similar to the array initializer syntax shown in the initGrades2() method, the number of elements given within the initializer brackets implies the array size. So, again, this code is creating and returning an array with a length of 7.

After computing the grade statistics for the three sets of grades data, the remainder of the GradeAnalyzer class main() method demonstrates various methods to determine array type information and convert an array to a printable string. You see that the code first assigns the array returned from a call to the getGrades() instance method to an Object variable called testArray.

```
Object testArray = ga.getGrades();
```

You can make this assignment because, as stated previously, an array is an Object. You can also see this from the call to testArray.getSuperclass(). The call to testArray.getClass().getName() is also interesting; it returns "I." The left bracket means "I am an array type", and the "I" means "with a component type of integer." This is also backed up by the call to testArray.getComponentType(). Finally, you call the Arrays.toString(int[]) method, which returns a nicely formatted string representation of the array and its contents. Notice that testArray is an Object reference, so it must be cast to an int array for the Arrays.toString(int[]) method. (See the Java documentation for the java.util.Arrays class for other useful utility methods that can be used with arrays).

7-5. Safely Enabling Types or Methods to Operate on Objects of Various Types

Problem

Your application uses many different object types, and there are containers within your class that are available for holding each of these different types. You are interested in ensuring your application remains bug-free, yet you want to dynamically change the type of object a particular container may hold. In other words, you want to define a generic container, but can specify its type each time a new instance of the container is instantiated.

Solution

Use generic types to decouple the type from the container. Generics are a way to abstract over object types, not explicitly declaring the type of an object or container. All collection types are parameterized to allow you to specify, at the time of instantiation, the type of elements the collection can hold. The following example code demonstrates how to use generics in various scenarios. The comments in the code indicate where the generics are utilized.

```
public class MainClass {

    static List<Player> team;

    private static void loadTeam() {
        System.out.println("Loading team...");

        // Use of the diamond operator
        team = new ArrayList<>();
        Player player1 = new Player("Josh", "Juneau", 5);
        Player player2 = new Player("Duke", "Java", 15);
        Player player3 = new Player("Jonathan", "Gennick", 1);
        Player player4 = new Player("Bob", "Smith", 18);
        Player player5 = new Player("Steve", "Adams", 7);

        team.add(player1);
        team.add(player2);
        team.add(player3);
        team.add(player4);
        team.add(player5);
    }

    public static void main(String[] args) {
        loadTeam();
```

```
    // Create a list without specifying a type
    List objectList = new ArrayList();
    Object obj1 = "none";
    objectList.add(obj1);

    // Create a List that can be of type that is any superclass of
    Player (or only Player type itself)
    List<? super Player> myTeam = objectList;
    for (Object p : myTeam) {
        System.out.println("Printing the objects...");
        System.out.println(p.toString());
    }

    // Create a Map of String keys and String values
    Map<String, String> strMap = new HashMap<>();
    strMap.put("first", "Josh");
    strMap.put("last", "Juneau");
    System.out.println(strMap.values());
  }
}
```

Note   When we generally talk about a *collection* or a *collection type*, you can read this as those types that make up the Java collections framework. This includes all the classes and interfaces from the Collection and Map interfaces. Collection types generally refer to types that descend from the Collection interface.

How It Works

The solution code demonstrates some basic use cases for generics. The examples in the GenericsDemo.java file, contained within the recipe sources, go into more detail to demonstrate the use of generics with Java collections versus showing you how to create generic types. Unless you develop a library API, you probably won't be creating your own generic types. However, if you understand how generics are used with the Collection interfaces and classes, you can create your own generic types.

The first thing to understand and remember about Java generics is that they are strictly a compile-time feature that aids the developer in creating more type-safe code. All the type information that you specify when you parameterize a generic type gets "erased" by the compiler when the code is compiled down to byte code. You'll see this described as *type erasure*. Let's look at an example of a generic Collection type: the List. List is an interface defined as follows.

```
public interface List<E> extends Collection<E> { ... };
```

Now that is a strange syntax, especially because there is no object or type identified as E. As it turns out, the E is known as a *type parameter*, which is a placeholder to indicate to the compiler that a type is assigned to the object at runtime. Type parameters are typically uppercased letters that indicate the type of parameter being defined. There are a variety of different type parameters to note, but keep in mind that these are only applicable when defining a generic type. In most cases, generic types are only defined when developing a library or API.

- E – Element

- K – Key

- N- Number

- T – Type

- V – Value

- S, U, V, and so on—second, third, and fourth types

To specify the element type for a List (or any Collection type), simply include the type name in angle brackets when declaring and instantiating objects. When you do this, you are specifying a *parameterized type*. The following code declares a list of integers. A variable, aList, of the parameterized type List<Integer> is declared and then initialized with the reference obtained from the instantiation of the parameterized type, LinkedList<Integer> (also called a *concrete parameterized type*).

```
List<Integer> aList = new LinkedList<Integer>();
```

Now that you've parameterized these types to restrict the element type to Integers, the List add(E e) method becomes

```
boolean add(Integer e);
```

If you try to add anything other than an integer to aList, the compiler generates an error.

```
aList.add(new Integer(121));
aList.add(42);        // 42 is the same as new Integer(42), due to autoboxing.
aList.add("Java");  // won't compile, wrong type
```

It's important to note that it's the reference type checked at compile time, so the following also results in a compiler error.

```
Number aNum = new Integer("7");
aList.add(aNum);  // won't compile, wrong type
```

This is a compile error because aNum could reference any Number object. If the compiler were to allow this, you could end up with a set containing doubles, floats, and so on, which would violate the Integer parameter constraint specified when you created aList. Of course, a simple type cast could get you around the compiler error, but this would surely cause unintended consequences when casting between incompatible Number objects. Generics were designed to reduce the amount of explicit type casting you must do in your code, so if you find yourself using explicit type casting when using methods of parameterized types, this is a clue of potentially dangerous code.

```
aList.add((Integer)aNum);  // compiles, but don't do this.
```

Other things to watch out for when using generic types are compiler warnings. They may indicate that you're doing something that is not recommended and it usually indicates that your code has a potential runtime error looming. An example can help to illustrate this. The following code compile but produce two compiler warnings.

```
List rawList = new LinkedList();
aList = rawList;
```

First, you're creating rawList, which is a *raw type*, a generic type that isn't parameterized. When generics were introduced into the language, the language designers decided that to maintain compatibility with pregenerics code, they would need to use raw types. However, the use of raw types is strongly discouraged for newer (post–Java 5) code, so compilers generate a raw type warning if you use them. Next, rawList is assigned to aList, which was created using parameterized types. Again, the compiler allows this (due to generics type erasure and backward compatibility).

An unchecked conversion warning is generated for the assignment to flag potential runtime type incompatibility. Imagine if `rawList` contained strings. Later, if you tried to retrieve integer elements from `aList`, you would get a runtime error.

Regarding type compatibility, it doesn't apply to generic type parameters. For example, the following is not a valid assignment.

```
List<Number> bList = new LinkedList<Integer>();  // won't compile;
                                                    incompatible types
```

Although integers are numbers (`Integer` is a subtype of `Number`), and `LinkedList` is a subtype of `List`, `LinkedList<Integer>` is not a subtype of `List<Number>`. Fortunately, this won't slip by you if you accidentally write code like this. The compiler generates an "incompatible types" warning.

So you may be wondering whether there is a way to achieve a variant subtyping relationship similar to what we tried to do in the previous line of code. The answer is yes, by using a generics feature called the *wildcard*. A wildcard is denoted by using a question mark (?) within the type parameter angle brackets. Wildcards declare parameterized types that are either bounded or unbounded. The following is an example declaration of a bounded parameterized type.

```
List<? extends Number> cList;
```

An upper bound is established for the type parameter when a wildcard is used with the extends keyword. In this example, `? extends Number` means any type that is either a `Number` or a subtype of a `Number`. Therefore, the following would be valid assignments because both `Integer` and `Double` are subtypes of `Number`.

```
cList = new LinkedList<Number>();
cList = new LinkedList<Integer>();
cList = new LinkedList<Double>();
```

So, `cList` can hold a reference to any `List` instance with an element type compatible with `Number`. `cList` could even reference a raw type. This makes it a challenge for the compiler to enforce type safety to allow elements to be added to cList. Therefore, the compiler does not allow elements (other than a null) to be added to a collection type that is parameterized with ? extends. The following would result in a compiler error.

```
cList.add(new Integer(5));  // add() not allowed; cList could be
                                LinkedList<Double>
```

However, you can get an element from the list without any problem.

```
Number cNum = cList.get(0);
```

The only restriction here is that the reference you get from the list must be treated like a number. Remember, cList could be pointing to a list of integers, a list of doubles, or list of any other subtype of Number.

A wildcard can also be used with the super keyword. In this case, a lower bound is established for the type parameter.

```
List<? super Integer> dList;
```

In this example, ? super Integer means any type that is either Integer or any supertype of it. Therefore, the following would be valid assignments because Number and Object are the only supertypes of Integer.

```
dList = new LinkedList<Integer>();
dList = new LinkedList<Number>();
dList = new LinkedList<Object>();
```

So, you see that Integer is the lower bound. This lower bound now restricts retrieving elements from the list. Because dList can reference any one of the previous parameterized types, the compiler would not be able to enforce type safety if an assumption were made about the type of the element being retrieved. Therefore, the compiler must not allow calls to get() on a collection type that is parameterized with ? super, and the following would result in a compiler error.

```
Integer n = dList.get(0);  // get() not allowed; dList.get(0) could be a
                              Number or Object
```

However, now you can add elements to the list, but the lower bound, Integer, still applies. Only Integers can be added because Integer is compatible with Number and Object.

```
dList.add(new Integer(5));  // OK
Number dNum = new Double(7);
dList.add(dNum);  // won't compile; dList could be LinkedList<Integer>
```

You see the use of the wildcard with both extends and super throughout the collection types. You often see them used in method parameter types, such as the addAll() method, which is defined for all collections. Sometimes you see the collection types using the wildcard (?) alone as a type parameter, which is called an *unbounded wildcard*. The collection removeAll() method is such an example. In most cases, this usage is self-explanatory. You probably won't be (probably shouldn't be) defining your own parameterized types using an unbounded wildcard. If you try to do this, you soon learn there isn't much you can do with it. If you understand concrete parameterized types, wildcard parameterized types, and the concept of bounded and unbounded types, as described in this recipe, you have most of what you need to work with the generic collection types and create your own generic types if you so choose.

Now that we've talked a lot about parameterizing types, we're going to tell you to forget about some of them. When Java 7 was released, a new feature called the *diamond* (sometimes referred to as the diamond operator, although it is not considered an operator in Java) was introduced. The diamond allows the compiler to infer the type argument(s) from the context of the parameterized type usage. A simple example of diamond usage follows.

```
List<Integer> eList = new ArrayList<>();
```

Notice there is no type argument specified between the angle brackets when instantiating the ArrayList. The compiler can easily infer the type to be an integer based on the context of the assignment or initializer. Integer is the only type that would work in this context. In fact, the Java compiler (and most compliant IDEs) warn you if you do not use a diamond where it is possible to use it. Another more complex example shows the benefit even better.

```
Map<Integer, List<String>> aMap = new HashMap<>();  // Nice!
```

The diamond can similarly be used in return statements, as well as in method arguments.

```
// diamond in method return
public static List<String> getEmptyList() {
    return new ArrayList<>();
}
// diamond in method argument
List<List<String>> gList = new ArrayList<>();
gList.set(0, new ArrayList<>(Arrays.asList("a", "b")));
```

Note that using the diamond as shown here is different from using a raw type. The following is not equivalent to the declaration of aMap that uses the diamond; it result in an "unchecked conversion" warning, and possibly a raw type warning, from the compiler.

```
Map<Integer, List<String>> bMap = new HashMap();   // compiler warnings;
                                                   avoid raw types
```

The discussion around why this is different from the diamond example is beyond the scope of this recipe. If you remember to avoid the use of raw types, you shouldn't need to worry about this. Use the diamond whenever possible to save yourself some typing and make your code more robust, readable, and concise.

7-6. Working with Dynamic Arrays
Problem

You need a flexible data structure that can store a variable amount of data and allow for easy insertion and deletion of data.

Solution

Consider using an ArrayList<E>. The following example code is the StockScreener class, which allows you to screen a list of stocks or a single stock based on a specific screen parameter (P/E, Yield, and Beta) and screen value. The class uses an ArrayList<E> for containing stock strings. An example screen might be "Tell me which of the stocks in this list has a P/E (price-to-earnings ratio) of 15 or less." Don't worry if you're not familiar with these stock market terms. Whatever you do, don't use this class to make your stock investment decisions!

```
public class StockScreener {

    enum Screen { PE, YIELD, BETA };

    public static boolean screen(String stock, Screen screen, double
    threshold) {
        double screenVal = 0;
        boolean pass = false;
```

```java
    switch (screen) {
        case PE:
            screenVal = Math.random() * 25;
            pass = screenVal <= threshold;
            break;
        case YIELD:
            screenVal = Math.random() * 10;
            pass = screenVal >= threshold;
            break;
        case BETA:
            screenVal = Math.random() * 2;
            pass = screenVal <= threshold;
            break;
    }
    System.out.println(stock + ": " + screen.toString() + " =
    " + screenVal);
    return pass;
}
/**
 * Parse through stock listing to determine if each stock passes the
 * screen tests. If a particular element does not pass the screen,
   then remove it.
 */
public static void screen(List<String> stocks, Screen screen, double
threshold) {
    Iterator<String> iter = stocks.iterator();
    while (iter.hasNext()) {
        String stock = iter.next();
        if (!screen(stock, screen, threshold)) {
            iter.remove();
        }
    }
}
public static void main(String[] args) {
    List<String> stocks = new ArrayList<>();
    stocks.add("ORCL");
```

```
        stocks.add("AAPL");
        stocks.add("GOOG");
        stocks.add("IBM");
        stocks.add("MCD");
        System.out.println("Screening stocks: " + stocks);
        if (stocks.contains("GOOG") &&
            !screen("GOOG", Screen.BETA, 1.1)) {
            stocks.remove("GOOG");
        }
        System.out.println("First screen: " + stocks);

        StockScreener.screen(stocks, Screen.YIELD, 3.5);
        System.out.println("Second screen: " + stocks);
        StockScreener.screen(stocks, Screen.PE, 22);
        System.out.println("Third screen: " + stocks);

        System.out.println("Buy List: " + stocks);
    }
}
```

The output from running this code varies because it randomly assigns a stock's screen result value. Here is one sample of output from running the class.

```
Screening stocks: [ORCL, AAPL, GOOG, IBM, MCD]
GOOG: BETA = 1.9223516769748348
First screen: [ORCL, AAPL, IBM, MCD]
ORCL: YIELD = 6.140018494585904
AAPL: YIELD = 7.875759429097191
IBM: YIELD = 7.715436753622726
MCD: YIELD = 2.419792753509281
Second screen: [ORCL, AAPL, IBM]
ORCL: PE = 4.396013965331994
AAPL: PE = 14.200385457743778
IBM: PE = 7.6981860501796175
Third screen: [ORCL, AAPL, IBM]
Buy List: [ORCL, AAPL, IBM]
```

How It Works

The ArrayList<E> is one of the most often used classes in the Java collections framework. The ArrayList<E> class implements the List<E> interface, which, in turn, implements the Collection<E> interface. The Collection<E> interface defines the set of common operations for all collection types, and the List<E> interface defines the set of operations that are specific to the list-oriented Collection<E> types. The collections framework makes heavy use of Java generics.

The StockScreener main() method starts by declaring a List<E> of stocks, and specifying with the generic type parameter, that the stocks list elements are of type String. Notice that the actual list type is an ArrayList<E> created using the diamond. The stocks list holds a variable number of stocks, represented by their stock market symbol (a string).

```
List<String> stocks = new ArrayList<>();
```

Now that you've specified that the stocks list can only hold strings, all the List<E> methods, in turn, get parameterized to only allow strings. So, next, the code makes several calls to the ArrayList<E>'s add(String) method to add the stocks to the list. After that, a screen is run on GOOG (Google) based on its beta (a measure of stock risk); if it does not pass the screen, the List remove(String) method is called to remove the stock from the stock list. Two more screens are then run on the entire stock list to get a list of stocks with a P/E of 22.0 or less and a yield of 3.5% or more. The screen() method used for these screens takes a parameter of type List<String>. It has to iterate the list, run the screen for each stock, and remove those stocks that do not pass the screen. Note that to safely remove an element from a Collection<E> while iterating over it, you must use iterate using the Collection<E>'s Iterator<E>, which can be obtained by calling its iterator() method. Here, we show the use of a while loop to iterate the stocks list (a for loop could similarly be used). As long as you're not to the end of the list (iter.hasNext()), you can get the next stock from the list (iter.next()), run the screen, and remove the element from the list (iter.remove()) if the screen didn't pass.

> **Note**   You may find that calling the list's `remove()` method while iterating
> the list seems to work. The problem is that it's not guaranteed to work
> and produce unexpected results. At some point, the code also throws
> `ConcurrentModificationException`, regardless of whether you have multiple
> threads accessing the same list. Remember to always remove elements through
> the iterator when iterating over any `Collection<E>`.

The `ArrayList<E>` is a very useful data structure that should normally be used in
place of the array type. It provides more flexibility than a simple array because elements
can be added and removed dynamically with ease. While it is true that ArrayList<E> uses
an array internally, you benefit from optimized `add()` and `remove()` operations that are
implemented for you. Also, `ArrayList<E>` implements many other very useful methods.

Refer to Java documentation for more information (`https://docs.oracle.com/en/`
`java/javase/17/docs/api/java.base/java/util/ArrayList.html`).

7-7. Making Your Objects Iterable
Problem

You have created a custom collection–based class that wraps (instead of extends) the
underlying collection type. Without exposing the internal implementation details of
your class, you want objects of your class to become iterable, especially with the use of a
`foreach` statement.

Solution

Have your class extend the `Iterable<T>` interface, where `T` is the element type of the
collection to be iterated. Implement the `iterator()` method to return the `Iterator<E>`
object from this collection. The example for this recipe is the `StockPortfolio` class.
Internally, `StockPortfolio` manages a collection of `Stock` objects. We want users of our
class to treat `StockPortfolio` objects as iterable objects using a `foreach` statement. The
`StockPortfolio` class follows.

```java
public class StockPortfolio implements Iterable<Stock> {

    Map<String, Stock> portfolio = new HashMap<>();
    public void add(Stock stock) {
        portfolio.put(stock.getSymbol(), stock);
    }

    public void add(List<Stock> stocks) {
        for (Stock s : stocks) {
            portfolio.put(s.getSymbol(), s);
        }
    }


    @Override
    public Iterator<Stock> iterator() {
        return portfolio.values().iterator();
    }
    public static void main(String[] args) {
        StockPortfolio myPortfolio = new StockPortfolio();
        myPortfolio.add(new Stock("ORCL", "Oracle", 500.0));
        myPortfolio.add(new Stock("AAPL", "Apple", 200.0));
        myPortfolio.add(new Stock("GOOG", "Google", 100.0));
        myPortfolio.add(new Stock("IBM", "IBM", 50.0));
        myPortfolio.add(new Stock("MCD", "McDonalds", 300.0));

        // foreach loop (uses Iterator returned from iterator() method)
        System.out.println("====Print using legacy for-each loop====");
        for (Stock stock : myPortfolio) {
            System.out.println(stock);
        }
        System.out.println("====Print using Java 8 foreach
        implementation====");
        myPortfolio.forEach(s->System.out.println(s));
    }
}
```

The following code is that of the Stock class.

```
public class Stock {
    private String symbol;
    private String name;
    private double shares;
    public Stock(String symbol, String name, double shares) {
        this.symbol = symbol;
        this.name = name;
        this.shares = shares;
    }
    public String getSymbol() {
        return symbol;
    }
    public String getName() {
        return name;
    }
    public double getShares() {
        return shares;
    }
    public String toString() {
        return shares + " shares of " + symbol + " (" + name + ")";
    }
}
```

The main() method creates a StockPortfolio and then calls the add() method to add several stocks to the portfolio. Both variations of the foreach loop (legacy and forEach implementation) then loop over and print all the stocks in the portfolio. Running the StockPortfolio class results in the following output.

```
100.0 shares of GOOG (Google)
200.0 shares of AAPL (Apple)
50.0 shares of IBM (IBM)
500.0 shares of ORCL (Oracle)
300.0 shares of MCD (McDonalds)
```

Note   The order of the lines in the output may differ when you run the StockPortfolio class in your environment because the underlying implementation uses a HashMap <K,V>. A HashMap<K,V> does not guarantee the order of the elements stored in the map, and this extends to its iterators. If you wanted the iterator to return elements sorted by the stock symbol, you could use one of the sorted collections, such as TreeMap<K,V> or TreeSet <E>, instead of HashMap.

How It Works

The Iterable<T> interface was introduced in Java 5 to support the enhanced for loop, which was introduced at the same time. Along with these enhancements to the language, all Collection<E> classes were retrofitted to implement the Iterable interface, thus allowing Collection<E> classes to be iterable using the foreach loop. The Iterable<T> interface is a generic type defined as follows.

```
public interface Iterable<T> {
    Iterator<T> iterator();
}
```

Any class that implements Iterable<T> must implement the iterator() method to return an Iterator<T> object. Typically, the iterator returned is the default iterator of the underlying collection; however, it may also return an instance of a custom Iterator <E>. In the StockPortfolio class, a Map<K,V> represents the stock portfolio. The key for each map entry is the stock symbol, and the value associated with each key is a Stock object. Maps in Java are not iterable; they are not Collection<E> classes. Therefore, they do not implement Iterable <T>. However, both the keys and the values of a map are collections, and therefore are Iterables. We want our implementation of the Iterable<T> iterator() method to return an Iterator<E> over the values (stock references) of the portfolio map; therefore, our Iterable<T> implementation is parameterized by the stock type.

```
public class StockPortfolio implements Iterable<Stock>
```

The Map<K,V> values() method returns the Collection<E> of map values; in this case, a Collection<E> of Stocks. The iterator() method implementation can then simply return the Iterator<E> for this Collection<T>.

```
@Override
public Iterator<Stock> iterator() {
    return portfolio.values().iterator();
}
```

With this implementation of Iterable<Stock>, either the legacy a foreach loop, or the forEach implementation can iterate a StockPortfolio instance and print each stock.

```
myPortfolio.forEach(s->System.out.println(s));
```

The forEach method was new to the Iterable<T> interface with the release of Java 8. The method performs the specified action for each element within the Iterable until all elements have been processed, or the specified action throws an exception. In this solution, the specified action is a lambda expression (see Chapter 6), which prints the value of each element within the myPortfolio iterable.

You notice that StockPortfolio also contains the add(List<Stock>) method, which allows the portfolio to be populated from a List<E>. This method also uses a foreach loop to iterate the input List <T>. Again, this is possible because Lists are Iterables. (Note that this method is never called in the code; it exists only for illustration purposes.)

Note   There's one issue with our implementation of StockPortfolio. We have gone to great lengths not to expose the internal implementation details of our class (the portfolio map). This allows us to change the implementation without affecting the StockPortfolio client code. However, when we implemented Iterable <T>, we effectively exported the underlying portfolio map through the iterator() method. Unfortunately, Java does not provide an UnmodifiableIterator class that could wrap an iterator and prevent modification of the underlying collection. However, it would be simple to implement such a class that forward the hasNext() and next() calls to the wrapped iterator but leaves the remove() method unimplemented (per the iterator Java documentation, UnsupportedOperationException should be thrown). Alternatively, your iterator() method could return the Iterator<E> from an unmodifiable `Collection<E>` obtained through a call to the `Collections.unmodifiableCollection()` class method. You are encouraged to explore these two options. To give you a start, one possible implementation of `UnmodifiableIterator` has been provided in the source code download (see `UnmodifiableIterator.java`).

As you have seen in this recipe, the `Iterable<T>` interface allows you to create iterable objects compatible with a `foreach` implementation. This is very useful when designing a custom collection-based class that encapsulates implementation details. Keep in mind that to enforce the encapsulation and prevent modification of your underlying collection, you should implement one of the solutions mentioned in the preceding note.

7-8. Iterating Collections
Problem

Your application contains Collection<E> types, and you want to iterate the elements within them.

Solution

Generate a stream on any type that extends or implements `java.util.Collection<E>`, and then perform the desired task(s) on each element of the collection. In the following code, an `ArrayList<E>` loaded with `Stock` objects demonstrates the concept of streams.

```
public class StreamExample {
    static List<Stock> myStocks = new ArrayList();
    private static void createStocks(){
        myStocks.add(new Stock("ORCL", "Oracle", 500.0));
        myStocks.add(new Stock("AAPL", "Apple", 200.0));
        myStocks.add(new Stock("GOOG", "Google", 100.0));
        myStocks.add(new Stock("IBM", "IBM", 50.0));
        myStocks.add(new Stock("MCD", "McDonalds", 300.0));
    }
```

```java
public static void main(String[] args){
    createStocks();
    // Iterate over each element and print the stock names
    myStocks.stream()
            .forEach(s->System.out.println(s.getName()));
    boolean allGt = myStocks.stream()
            .allMatch(s->s.getShares() > 100.0);
    System.out.println("All Stocks Greater Than 100.0 Shares? " + allGt);
    // Print out all stocks that have more than 100 shares
    System.out.println("== We have more than 100 shares of the
following:");
    myStocks.stream()
            .filter(s -> s.getShares() > 100.0)
            .forEach(s->System.out.println(s.getName()));
    System.out.println("== The following stocks are sorted by
shares:");
    Comparator<Stock> byShares = Comparator.
comparing(Stock::getShares);
    Stream<Stock> sortedByShares = myStocks.stream()
            .sorted(byShares);
    sortedByShares.forEach(s -> System.out.println("Stock: " +
s.getName() + " - Shares: " + s.getShares()));
    // May or may not return a value
    Optional<Stock> maybe = myStocks.stream()
            .findFirst();
    System.out.println("First Stock: " + maybe.get().getName());
    List newStocks = new ArrayList();
    Optional<Stock> maybeNot = newStocks.stream()
            .findFirst();
    Consumer<Stock> myConsumer = (s) ->
    {
      System.out.println("First Stock (Optional): " + s.getName());
    };
```

```
        maybeNot.ifPresent(myConsumer);
        if(maybeNot.isPresent()){
            System.out.println(maybeNot.get().getName());
        }
        newStocks.add(new Stock("MCD", "McDonalds", 300.0));
        Optional<Stock> maybeNow = newStocks.stream()
                .findFirst();
        maybeNow.ifPresent(myConsumer);
    }
}
```

The output is:

```
Oracle
Apple
Google
IBM
McDonalds
All Stocks Greater Than 100.0 Shares? false
== We have more than 100 shares of the following:
Oracle
Apple
McDonalds
== The following stocks are sorted by shares:
Stock: IBM - Shares: 50.0
Stock: Google - Shares: 100.0
Stock: Apple - Shares: 200.0
Stock: McDonalds - Shares: 300.0
Stock: Oracle - Shares: 500.0
First Stock: Oracle
First Stock (Optional): McDonalds
```

The results of executing this code demonstrate the concept of using streams. External iteration (for loops) is no longer a requirement for iterating over a data collection.

How It Works

Prior to Java 8, iterating over a collection required some kind of looping block. This is known as *external iteration*, a.k.a. *programmatic looping* in sequential order. In most cases, a `for` loop worked through each element within a collection, processing each element according to an application's requirements. While a `for` loop is a reasonable solution for performing iteration, it is both a nonintuitive and verbose strategy. Since the release of Java 8, the boilerplate of iterating over collections was removed, along with the requirement to spell out how the iteration was to be completed. The compiler already knows how to iterate a collection, so why tell it exactly how to do it? Why not simply tell the compiler that you want to iterate the collection and perform a task on each element. The concept of streams enables this hands-off approach to iteration.

Let the compiler take care of the nonintuitive looping, and simply hand the task off to the compiler and tell it what action to perform on each element. This concept is known as *internal iteration*. With internal iteration, your application determines what needs to be iterated, and the JDK decides how to perform the iteration. Internal iteration not only alleviates the requirement to program the looping logic, but it also has other advantages. One such advantage is that internal iteration is not limited to sequential iteration over elements. Therefore, the JDK decides how to iterate, choosing the best algorithm for the task at hand. Internal iteration also can more easily take advantage of parallel computing. This concept involves subdividing tasks into smaller problems, simultaneously solving each, and combining the results.

A stream is a sequence of object references generated on all collection types. The Stream API makes it possible to perform a sequence of aggregate operations on those object references and either return a result or apply the changes to the objects inline. This is also known as a *pipeline*. The pseudocode for generation and use of a stream is as follows.

```
Collection -> (Stream) -> (Zero or More Intermediate Operations) ->
(Terminal Operation)
```

Let's put this pseudocode into a real example. In the solution, a list of `Stock` objects is used for demonstrating stream iteration. Let's suppose you want to print out each stock that contains a number of shares that is over a designated threshold (100 shares in this example). You can use the following code to perform this task.

```
myStocks.stream()
            .filter(s -> s.getShares() > 100.0)
            .forEach(s->System.out.println(s.getName()));
```

In the previous example, an *intermediate* operation known as a `filter()` applies a limitation on the elements, thereby filtering out all elements that do not match the supplied predicate. The predicate is written as a lambda expression; it tests each element and returns a Boolean result. The *terminal* operation in the example uses `forEach()` to print each matching element. A terminal operation is the last operation in a pipeline, and it produces a nonstream result such as a primitive, collection, or no value at all. In the example case, no result is returned.

To generate a stream on a `Collection` type, call the `stream()` method, which returns a `Stream` type. In most cases, the `Stream` type is not the desired result, so the Stream API makes it possible to invoke zero or more intermediate operations on a stream, forming a pipeline of operations. For example, in the solution, the list of `Stock` objects is sorted by the number of shares using the following code. Note that `Comparator byShares` is applied to each object in the stream and `Stream<Stock>` is returned as a result.

```
Stream<Stock> sortedByShares = myStocks.stream()
            .sorted(byShares);
```

A single intermediate operation, `sorted()`, is performed on the stream in the previous example. As mentioned previously, there could be more than one intermediate operation chained to this pipeline, thereby performing the next operation on those objects that meet the criteria of the previous operation. Each of the intermediate operations returns a `Stream` type. Each pipeline can contain a terminal operation, thereby applying the terminal operation to each of the resulting stream objects. As mentioned previously, a terminal operation may or may not return a result. In the previous example, no terminal operation is applied.

Note   The documentation for Stream (`https://docs.oracle.com/en/java/javase/17/docs/api/java.base/java/util/stream/Stream.html`) lists all the intermediate and terminal operations available on a stream.

Streams have been a revolutionary change for the Java programming language. They change how a developer thinks about a program, making the developer more productive and the code more efficient. While legacy iteration techniques such as the for loop are still considered valid procedures, streams are the preferred technique for iteration when you're using Java 8 or beyond.

7-9. Iterating Over a Map
Problem

You use one of the Map classes, such as HashMap or TreeMap, and you need to iterate the keys, values, or both. You also want to remove elements from the map while iterating over it.

Solution

There are multiple ways to iterate a Map class. The method you choose should depend on which portions of the map you need to access and whether you need to remove elements from the map while iterating. The StockPortfolio1 class is a continuation of the StockPorfolio class shown in the previous recipe. It adds three methods—summary(), alertList(), and remove(List<String>)–that demonstrate alternative methods for iterating over the portfolio map: Map<String, Stock> portfolio = new HashMap<>();.

The following is the class.

```
import org.java17recipes.chapter07.recipe07_07.Stock;
import org.java17recipes.chapter07.recipe07_06.StockScreener;
import java.util.ArrayList;
import java.util.HashMap;
import java.util.Iterator;
import java.util.List;
import java.util.Map;
import java.util.stream.Collectors;
```

```java
public class StockPortfolio1 implements Iterable<Stock> {

    Map<String, Stock> portfolio = new HashMap<>();

    public void add(Stock stock) {
        portfolio.put(stock.getSymbol(), stock);
    }

    public void add(List<Stock> stocks) {
        for (Stock s : stocks) {
            portfolio.put(s.getSymbol(), s);
        }
    }

    public void remove(String stock) {
        portfolio.remove(stock);
    }

    public void remove(List<String> sellList) {
        Iterator<String> keyIter = portfolio.keySet().iterator();
        while (keyIter.hasNext()) {
            if (sellList.contains(keyIter.next())) {
                keyIter.remove();
            }
        }
    }

    /**
     * Utilize for-loop to traverse Map keys and apply filter to obtain desired
     * stocks
     * @return
     */
    public List<Stock> alertListLegacy() {
        System.out.println("==Legacy technique for filtering and
        collecting==");
        List<Stock> alertList = new ArrayList<>();
        for (Stock stock : portfolio.values()) {
```

```java
        if (!StockScreener.screen(stock.getSymbol(), StockScreener.
        Screen.PE, 20)) {
            alertList.add(stock);
        }
    }

    return alertList;
}

/**
 * Utilize stream and filters to obtain desired stocks
 * @return
 */
public List<Stock> alertList(){
    return
    portfolio.values().stream()
            .filter(s->!StockScreener.screen(s.getSymbol(),
            StockScreener.Screen.PE, 20))
            .collect(Collectors.toList());

}

public void summary() {
    System.out.println("==Legacy technique for traversing
    Map.Entry==");
    for (Map.Entry<String, Stock> entry : portfolio.entrySet()) {
        System.out.println("Stock = " + entry.getKey() + ", Shares = "
        + entry.getValue().getShares());
    }

    System.out.println("==Utilization of new foreach and lambda
    combination==");
    portfolio.forEach((k,v)->System.out.println("Stock = " + k + ",
    Shares = " + v.getShares()));
}
```

```
    @Override
    public Iterator<Stock> iterator() {
        return portfolio.values().iterator();
    }

    public static void main(String[] args) {

        StockPortfolio1 myPortfolio = new StockPortfolio1();
        myPortfolio.add(new Stock("ORCL", "Oracle", 500.0));
        myPortfolio.add(new Stock("AAPL", "Apple", 200.0));
        myPortfolio.add(new Stock("GOOG", "Google", 100.0));
        myPortfolio.add(new Stock("IBM", "IBM", 50.0));
        myPortfolio.add(new Stock("MCD", "McDonalds", 300.0));

        // foreach loop (uses Iterator returned from iterator() method)
        for (Stock stock : myPortfolio) {
            System.out.println(stock);
        }

        myPortfolio.forEach((stock)->System.out.println(stock));

        List<String> sellList = new ArrayList<>();
        sellList.add("IBM");
        sellList.add("GOOG");

        myPortfolio.remove(sellList);

        System.out.println("Portfolio Summary:");
        myPortfolio.summary();

        System.out.println("Alerts:");
        for (Stock stock : myPortfolio.alertList()) {
            System.out.println("Alert: " + stock.getSymbol());
        }
    }
}
```

The output is:

100.0 shares of GOOG (Google)

200.0 shares of AAPL (Apple)

50.0 shares of IBM (IBM)

500.0 shares of ORCL (Oracle)

300.0 shares of MCD (McDonalds)

100.0 shares of GOOG (Google)

200.0 shares of AAPL (Apple)

50.0 shares of IBM (IBM)

500.0 shares of ORCL (Oracle)

300.0 shares of MCD (McDonalds)

Portfolio Summary:

==Legacy technique for traversing Map.Entry==

Stock = AAPL, Shares = 200.0

Stock = ORCL, Shares = 500.0

Stock = MCD, Shares = 300.0

==Utilization of new foreach and lambda combination==

Stock = AAPL, Shares = 200.0

Stock = ORCL, Shares = 500.0

Stock = MCD, Shares = 300.0

Alerts:

AAPL: PE = 6.152926256441124

ORCL: PE = 13.539727307058891

MCD: PE = 20.073565345827422

Alert: MCD

How It Works

A Map object contains a collection of key/value pairs. Maps can be beneficial when you need to store an index (key) and associate it with a particular value. A Map object must not contain any duplicate keys and each key maps to exactly one value. The source code for the solution (StockPortfolio1.java) demonstrates how to add and remove entries from a map. It also contains the source listed in the solution to this recipe, demonstrating how to iterate map entries using legacy techniques and newer syntax that takes advantage of lambda expressions and streams.

The summary() method uses a foreach loop implementation to iterate the portfolio map's Entry set. To iterate using the legacy code, the Map entrySet() method returns a Set of Map.Entry objects. Within the loop, you then have access to the key and value for the current Map.Entry by calling the respective key() and value() methods on that entry. Use this method of iterating when you need to access both the map keys and values while iterating, and you don't need to remove elements from the map. Looking at the newer syntax, you can see that the same iteration can be performed in a single line of code. The newer syntax utilizes the forEach() method, which was added to the Map interface in Java 8. It applies a lambda expression to each entry within the list. The lambda expression takes both the key and value as arguments and prints them out.

The alertListLegacy() method uses a foreach loop implementation to iterate the values of the portfolio map. The Map values() method returns a collection of the map values; in this case, a collection of stocks. Use this method of iterating when you only need access to the map values, and you don't need to remove elements from the list. Similarly, if you only need access to the map keys (again, without the need to remove elements), you can iterate using the keySet() method.

```
for (String symbol : portfolio.keySet()) {
    ...
}
```

If you also need to access the map value while iterating using the key set, avoid the following, as it is very inefficient. Instead, use the method of iteration shown in the summary() method.

```
for (String symbol : portfolio.keySet()) {
    Stock stock = portfolio.get(symbol);
    ...
}
```

Looking at the alertList() method in the solution, you can see that the same iteration can be performed with much less work using a combination of streams, filters, and collectors. In alertList(), a stream is generated, and then a filter, in the form of a lambda expression, is applied to that stream. Finally, a collector is applied to the filter, creating a List<Stock> to return.

The remove(List<String>) method takes a list of stock symbols representing the stocks to be removed from the portfolio. This method iterates over the portfolio map keys using the keySet() iterator, removing the current map entry if one of the stocks specified for removal. Notice that the map element is removed through the iterator's `remove()` method. This is possible because the map backs the key set, so changes made through the key set's iterator are reflected in the map. You could also iterate the portfolio map using its `values()` iterator.

```
Iterator<Stock> valueIter = portfolio.values().iterator();
while (valueIter.hasNext()) {
    if (sellList.contains(valueIter.next().getSymbol())) {
        valueIter.remove();
    }
}
```

As with the key set, the values collection is backed by the map, so calling `remove()` through the values iterator results in removing the current entry from the portfolio map.

In summary, if you need to remove elements from a map while iterating over the map, iterate using one of the map's collection iterators and remove map elements through the iterator, as shown in the `remove(List<String>)` method. This is the only safe way to remove map elements during iteration. Otherwise, if you don't need to remove map elements, you can use a `foreach` loop and one of the methods of iteration shown in the solution to this recipe.

7-10. Executing Streams in Parallel
Problem
You want to iterate a collection parallel to distribute the work over multiple CPUs.

Solution
Utilize a stream construct on the collection, and invoke `parallelStream()` as the first intermediate operation in order to take advantage of multiple CPU processing. The following class demonstrates multiple uses of the `parallelStream()` operation.

```java
public class StockPortfolio2 {
    static List<Stock> myStocks = new ArrayList();

    private static void createStocks(){
        myStocks.add(new Stock("ORCL", "Oracle", 500.0));
        myStocks.add(new Stock("AAPL", "Apple", 200.0));
        myStocks.add(new Stock("GOOG", "Google", 100.0));
        myStocks.add(new Stock("IBM", "IBM", 50.0));
        myStocks.add(new Stock("MCD", "McDonalds", 300.0));
    }
    public static void main(String[] args){
        createStocks();
        // Iterate over each element and print the stock names
        myStocks.stream()
                .forEach(s->System.out.println(s.getName()));
        boolean allGt = myStocks.parallelStream()
                .allMatch(s->s.getShares() > 100.0);
        System.out.println("All Stocks Greater Than 100.0 Shares? "
        + allGt);
        // Print out all stocks that have more than 100 shares
        System.out.println("== We have more than 100 shares of the
        following:");
        myStocks.parallelStream()
                .filter(s -> s.getShares() > 100.0)
                .forEach(s->System.out.println(s.getName()));
        System.out.println("== The following stocks are sorted by
        shares:");
        Comparator<Stock> byShares =
        Comparator.comparing(Stock::getShares);
        Stream<Stock> sortedByShares = myStocks.parallelStream()
                .sorted(byShares);
        sortedByShares.forEach(s -> System.out.println("Stock: " +
        s.getName() + " - Shares: " + s.getShares()));
```

```java
    // May or may not return a value
    Optional<Stock> maybe = myStocks.parallelStream()
            .findFirst();
    System.out.println("First Stock: " + maybe.get().getName());
    List newStocks = new ArrayList();
    Optional<Stock> maybeNot = newStocks.parallelStream()
            .findFirst();
    Consumer<Stock> myConsumer = (s) ->
    {
      System.out.println("First Stock (Optional): " + s.getName());
    };
    maybeNot.ifPresent(myConsumer);
    if(maybeNot.isPresent()){
        System.out.println(maybeNot.get().getName());
    }
    newStocks.add(new Stock("MCD", "McDonalds", 300.0));
    Optional<Stock> maybeNow = newStocks.stream()
            .findFirst();
    maybeNow.ifPresent(myConsumer);
  }
}
```

How It Works

By default, operations are executed in a serial stream. However, you can specify that the Java runtime splits the operations between multiple subtasks, thus taking advantage of multiple CPUs for performance. When operations are executed in this manner, they are executed in "parallel." The Java runtime can partition streams into multiple substreams by invoking the `parallelStream()` intermediate operation. When this operation is invoked, aggregate operations can process the multiple substreams, and then the results are combined in the end. You can also execute a stream in parallel by invoking the operation `BaseStream.parallel()`. Naturally, parallel streams have higher overhead compared to serial streams, so they are used if there is a performance problem to be addressed.

7-11. Summary

This chapter looked at various data structures and how to work with them. First, you took a look at `Enums` and learned how to utilize them effectively. Next, we covered the basics of `Arrays` and `ArrayList` and learned how to iterate elements within these structures. The chapter also covered Java generics, which allow you to decouple object types from container types, providing more type-safe and efficient code. Lastly, this chapter covered the Streams API, one of the most important updates introduced in Java 8 for working with collections.

CHAPTER 8

Input and Output

The file and network I/O have evolved over the years into a much better framework for handling files, network scalability, and ease of use. Java can monitor folders, access OS-dependent methods, and create scalable asynchronous network sockets. This is in addition to the already robust library for handling input and output streams and serializing (and deserializing) object information.

This chapter covers recipes that demonstrate different input and output processes. You learn about the serialization of files, sending files over the network, file manipulation, and much more. After reading the recipes in this chapter, you are armed to develop applications containing sophisticated input and output tasks.

STREAMS AND THE DECORATOR PATTERN

I/O streams are the foundation of most Java I/O and include a plethora of ready-made streams for just about any occasion, but they are very confusing to use if some context is not provided. A stream (like a river) represents an inflow/outflow of data. Think about it this way. You create a stream of characters that the system receives (input stream) as you type. When the system produces sounds, it sends them to the speaker (output stream). The system could be receiving keystrokes and sending sound all day long, and thus the streams can be either processing data or waiting for more data.

When a stream doesn't receive any data, it waits (nothing else to do, right?). As soon as data comes in, the stream starts processing this data. The stream then stops and waits for the next data item to come. This keeps going until this proverbial river becomes dry (the stream is closed).

Like a river, streams can be connected to each other (this is the decorator pattern). For the content of this chapter, there are mainly two input streams that you care about. One is the file input stream, and the other is the network socket input stream. These two streams are a source of data for your I/O programs. Their corresponding output streams are also file output

© Josh Juneau, Luciano Manelli 2022
J. Juneau and L. Manelli, *Java 17 Recipes*, https://doi.org/10.1007/978-1-4842-7963-2_8

stream and the network socket output streams (creative, isn't it?). Like a plumber, you can hook them together and create something new. For example, you could weld together a file input stream to a network output stream to send the contents of the file through a network socket. Or you could do the opposite and connect a network input stream (data coming in) to a file output stream (data being written to disk). In I/O parlance, the input streams are called *sources*, while the output streams are called *sinks*.

There are other input and output streams that can be glued together. For example, there is a BufferedInputStream, which allows you to read the data in chunks (it's more efficient than reading it byte by byte), and DataOutputStream allows you to write Java primitives to an output stream (instead of just writing bytes). One of the most useful streams is the ObjectInputStream and ObjectOutputStream pair, which allow you to serialize/deserialize objects (there is a recipe for that in this chapter).

The decorator pattern allows you to keep plucking streams together to get many different effects. The beauty of this design is that you can create a stream that takes any input and produce any output and then can be thrown together with every other stream.

8-1. Serializing Java Objects

Problem

You need to serialize a class (save the contents of the class) so that you can restore it at a later time.

Solution

Java implements a built-in serialization mechanism. You access that mechanism via the ObjectOutputStream class. In the following example, the saveSettings() method uses ObjectOutputStream to serialize the settings object to write the object to disk.

```
public class Ch_8_1_SerializeExample {
    public static void main(String[] args) {
        Ch_8_1_SerializeExample example = new Ch_8_1_SerializeExample();
        example.start();
    }
    private void start() {
```

```java
        ProgramSettings settings = new ProgramSettings(new Point(10,10),
                                                new Dimension
                                                (300,200),
                                                Color.blue,
                                               "The title of the
                                                application" );
        saveSettings(settings,"settings.bin");
        ProgramSettings loadedSettings = loadSettings("settings.bin");
        if(loadedSettings != null)
            System.out.println("Are settings are equal? :"+loadedSettings.
            equals(settings));
    }
    private void saveSettings(ProgramSettings settings, String filename) {
        try {
            FileOutputStream fos = new FileOutputStream(filename);
            try (ObjectOutputStream oos = new ObjectOutputStream(fos)) {
                oos.writeObject(settings);
            }
        } catch (IOException e) {
            e.printStackTrace();
        }
    }
    private ProgramSettings loadSettings(String filename) {
        try {
            FileInputStream fis = new FileInputStream(filename);
            ObjectInputStream ois = new ObjectInputStream(fis);
            return (ProgramSettings) ois.readObject();
        } catch (IOException | ClassNotFoundException e) {
            e.printStackTrace();
        }
        return null;
    }
}
```

The following is the ProgramSetting class.

```
package org.java17recipes.chapter08.recipe08_01;

import java.awt.*;
import java.io.Serializable;

public class ProgramSettings implements Serializable {

        private static final long serialVersionUID = 1L;
        private Point locationOnScreen;
        private Dimension frameSize;
        private Color defaultFontColor;
        private String title;

        // Empty constructor

        public ProgramSettings() {

        }

        public ProgramSettings(Point locationOnScreen, Dimension frameSize,
        Color defaultFontColor, String title) {
                this.locationOnScreen = locationOnScreen;
                this.frameSize = frameSize;
                this.defaultFontColor = defaultFontColor;
                this.title = title;
        }

        public Point getLocationOnScreen() {
                return locationOnScreen;
        }

        public void setLocationOnScreen(Point locationOnScreen) {
                this.locationOnScreen = locationOnScreen;
        }

        public Dimension getFrameSize() {
                return frameSize;
        }
```

```java
    public void setFrameSize(Dimension frameSize) {
        this.frameSize = frameSize;
    }

    public Color getDefaultFontColor() {
        return defaultFontColor;
    }

    public void setDefaultFontColor(Color defaultFontColor) {
        this.defaultFontColor = defaultFontColor;
    }

    public String getTitle() {
        return title;
    }

    public void setTitle(String title) {
        this.title = title;
    }

    @Override
    public boolean equals(Object o) {
        if (this == o) return true;
        if (o == null || getClass() != o.getClass()) return false;

        ProgramSettings that = (ProgramSettings) o;

        if (defaultFontColor != null ? !defaultFontColor.
        equals(that.defaultFontColor) : that.defaultFontColor
        != null)
            return false;
        if (frameSize != null ? !frameSize.equals(that.frameSize) :
        that.frameSize != null) return false;
        if (locationOnScreen != null ? !locationOnScreen.
        equals(that.locationOnScreen) : that.locationOnScreen
        != null)
            return false;
```

```
            if (title != null ? !title.equals(that.title) : that.title
            != null) return false;

            return true;
    }

    @Override
    public int hashCode() {
            int result = locationOnScreen != null ? locationOnScreen.
            hashCode() : 0;
            result = 31 * result + (frameSize != null ? frameSize.
            hashCode() : 0);
            result = 31 * result + (defaultFontColor != null ?
            defaultFontColor.hashCode() : 0);
            result = 31 * result + (title != null ? title.
            hashCode() : 0);
            return result;
    }
}
```

How It Works

Java supports *serialization*, which is the capability of taking an object and creating a byte representation that can restore the object later. Using an internal serialization mechanism, most of the setup to serialize objects is taken care of. Java transforms the properties of an object into a byte stream, which can then be saved to a file or transmitted over the wire.

Note   The original Java Serialization framework uses reflection to serialize the objects, so it might be an issue if serializing/deserializing heavily. There are many open source frameworks. Which is best depends on your needs (speed vs. size vs. ease of use). See `https://github.com/eishay/jvm-serializers/wiki/`.

For a class to be serializable, it needs to implement the Serializable interface, which is a *marker interface*. It doesn't have any methods but instead tells the serialization mechanism that allows your class to be serialized. While not evident from the onset, serialization exposes all the internal workings of your class (including protected and private members), so if you want to keep secret the authorization code for a nuclear launch, you might want to make any class that contains such information nonserializable.

It is also necessary that all properties (e.g., members, variables, or fields) of the class are serializable (and/or transient, which we get to in a minute). All primitives—int, long, double, and float (plus their wrapper classes)—and the String class are serializable by design. Other Java classes are serializable on a case-by-case basis. For example, you can't serialize any Swing components (like JButton or JSpinner), and you can't serialize File objects, but you can serialize the Color class (awt.color, to be more precise).

As a design principle, you don't want to serialize your main classes, but instead, you want to create classes containing only the properties you want to serialize. It saves a lot of headaches in debugging because serialization becomes very pervasive. If you mark a major class as serializable (implements Serializable), and this class contains many other properties, you need to declare those classes as serializable as well. If your Java class inherits from another class, the parent class should also be serializable. If the parent class is not serializable, the parent's properties are not serialized.

If you want to mark a property as nonserializable, you may mark it as *transient.* Transient properties tell the Java compiler that you are not interested in saving/loading the property value, so it is ignored. Some properties are good candidates for being transient, like cached calculations or a date formatter that you always instantiate to the same value.

By virtue of the Serialization framework, static properties are not serializable; neither are static classes. The reason is that a static class cannot be instantiated, although a public static inner class can be instantiated. Therefore, if you save and then load the static class at the same time, you have loaded another copy of the static class, throwing the JVM for a loop.

The Java serialization mechanism works behind the scenes to convert and traverse every object within the class that is marked as Serializable. If an application contains objects within objects and even perhaps contains cross-referenced objects, the Serialization framework resolves those objects and stores only one copy of any object. Each property is translated to a byte[] representation. The format of the byte array includes the actual class name (for example, com.somewhere.over.the.rainbow. preferences.UserPreferences), followed by the encoding of the properties (which in turn may encode another object class, with its properties, etc., etc., *ad infinitum*).

For the curious, if you look at the file generated (even in a text editor), you can see the class name as almost the first part of the file.

Note   Serialization is very brittle. By default, the Serialization framework generates a *Stream Unique Identifier (SUID)* that captures information about what fields are presented in the class, what kind they are (public/protected), and what is transient, among other things. Even a perceived slight modification of the class (for example, changing an int to a long property) generates a new SUID. A class that has been saved with a prior SUID cannot be deserialized on the new SUID. This is done to protect the serialization/deserialization mechanism while also protecting the designers.

You can tell the Java class to use a specific SUID. This allows you to serialize classes, modify them, and then deserialize the original classes while implementing some backward compatibility. The danger you run into is that the deserialization must be backward-compatible. Renaming or removing fields generates an exception as the class is being deserialized. If you specify your own serial werializable on your Serializable class, be sure to have some unit tests for backward compatibility every time you change the class.

Due to the nature of serialization, don't expect constructors to be called when an object is deserialized. If you have initialization code in constructors that are required for your object to function properly, you may need to refactor the code out of the constructor to allow proper execution after construction. The reason is that in the deserialization process, the deserialized objects are "restored" internally (not created) and do not invoke constructors.

8-2. Serializing Java Objects More Efficiently

Problem

You want to serialize a class but make the output more efficient or smaller in size than the product generated via the built-in serialization method.

Solution

By making the object implement the Externalizable interface, you instruct the Java Virtual Machine to use a custom serialization/deserialization mechanism, as provided by the readExternal/writeExternal methods in the following example.

```
public class ExternalizableProgramSettings implements Externalizable {
    private Point locationOnScreen;
    private Dimension frameSize;
    private Color defaultFontColor;
    private String title;

    // Empty constructor, required for Externalizable implementors
    public ExternalizableProgramSettings() {
    }

    @Override
    public void writeExternal(ObjectOutput out) throws IOException {
        out.writeInt(locationOnScreen.x);
        out.writeInt(locationOnScreen.y);
        out.writeInt(frameSize.width);
        out.writeInt(frameSize.height);
        out.writeInt(defaultFontColor.getRGB());
        out.writeUTF(title);
    }

    @Override
    public void readExternal(ObjectInput in) throws IOException,
    ClassNotFoundException {
        locationOnScreen = new Point(in.readInt(), in.readInt());
        frameSize = new Dimension(in.readInt(), in.readInt());
        defaultFontColor = new Color(in.readInt());
        title = in.readUTF();
    }
// getters and setters omitted for brevity
}
```

The main class is:

```java
package org.java17recipes.chapter08.recipe08_02;
import java.awt.*;
import java.io.*;

public class Ch_8_2_ExternalizableExample {
    public static void main(String[] args) {
        Ch_8_2_ExternalizableExample example = new Ch_8_2_
        ExternalizableExample();
        example.start();
    }

    private void start() {
        ExternalizableProgramSettings settings = new ExternalizableProgram
        Settings(new Point(10,10),new Dimension(300,200), Color.blue, "The
        title of the application" );
        saveSettings(settings,"settingsExternalizable.bin");
        ExternalizableProgramSettings loadedSettings = loadSettings("setting
        sExternalizable.bin");
        System.out.println("Are settings are equal? :"+loadedSettings.
        equals(settings));

    }

    private void saveSettings(ExternalizableProgramSettings settings, String
    filename) {
        try {
            FileOutputStream fos = new FileOutputStream(filename);
            try (ObjectOutputStream oos = new ObjectOutputStream(fos)) {
                oos.writeObject(settings);
            }
        } catch (IOException e) {
            e.printStackTrace();
        }
    }
```

```java
private ExternalizableProgramSettings loadSettings(String filename) {
    try {
        FileInputStream fis = new FileInputStream(filename);
        ObjectInputStream ois = new ObjectInputStream(fis);
        return (ExternalizableProgramSettings) ois.readObject();
    } catch (IOException | ClassNotFoundException e) {
        e.printStackTrace();
    }
    return null;

}

}
```

How It Works

The Java Serialization framework allows you to specify the implementation for serializing an object. It requires implementing the Externalizable interface instead of the Serializable interface. The Externalizable interface contains two methods: writeExternal(ObjectOutput out) and readExternal(ObjectInput in). By implementing these methods, you tell the framework how to encode/decode your object. You may choose to implement the Externalizable interface instead of the Serializable interface because Java's default serialization is very inefficient. Because the Java Serialization framework needs to ensure that every object (and dependent object) is serialized. It writes even objects with default values or that might be empty and/or null. Implementing the Externalizable interface also provides finer-grained control on how your class is being serialized. In our example, the Serializable version created a setting of 439 bytes, compared with the Externalizable version of only 103 bytes!

8-3. Serializing Java Objects as XML
Problem

Although you love the Serialization framework, you want to create something that is at least cross-language-compatible (or human-readable). You would like to save and load your objects using XML.

303

Solution

In this example, the XMLEncoder object encodes the Settings object, which contains program settings information, and writes it to the settings.xml file. The XMLDecoder object takes the settings.xml file and reads it as a stream, decoding the Settings object. FileSystem gains access to the machine's file system. FileOutputStream writes a file to the system. FileInputStream obtains input bytes from a file within the file system. In this example, these three file objects create new XML files reads them for processing.

```
public static void main(String[] args) {
    Ch_8_3_XMLExample example = new Ch_8_3_XMLExample();
    example.start();
}

private void start() {
    ProgramSettings settings = new ProgramSettings(new Point(10,10),new
    Dimension(300,200), Color.blue, "The title of the application" );
    try {
    //Encoding
    FileSystem fileSystem = FileSystems.getDefault();
    try (FileOutputStream fos = new FileOutputStream("settings.xml");
    XMLEncoder encoder =
            new XMLEncoder(fos)) {
        encoder.setExceptionListener((Exception e) -> {
            System.out.println("Exception! :"+e.toString());
        });
        encoder.writeObject(settings);
    }
    // Decoding
    try (FileInputStream fis = new FileInputStream("settings.xml");
    XMLDecoder decoder =
            new XMLDecoder(fis)) {
        ProgramSettings decodedSettings = (ProgramSettings) decoder.
        readObject();
        System.out.println("Is same? "+settings.
        equals(decodedSettings));
    }
```

```
    Path file= fileSystem.getPath("settings.xml");
    List<String> xmlLines = Files.readAllLines(file, Charset.
    defaultCharset());
    xmlLines.stream().forEach((line) -> {
        System.out.println(line);
    });
    } catch (IOException e) {
        e.printStackTrace();
    }
}
```

How It Works

XMLEncoder and XMLDecoder, like the Serialization framework, use reflection to determine which fields are to be written, but instead of writing the fields as binary, they are written as XML. Objects that are encoded do not need to be serializable, but they need to follow the JavaBeans specification.

JavaBeans is the name of any object that conforms to the following contract.

- The object contains a public empty (no-arg) constructor.

- The object contains public getters and setters for each protected/ private property that takes the name of get{Property}() and set{Property}().

XMLEncoder and XMLDecoder encode/decode only the properties of the bean that have public accessors (get{property}, set{property}), so any properties that are private and do not have accessors are not encoded/decoded.

Tip   It is a good idea to register an exception listener when encoding/decoding.

XMLEncoder creates a new instance of the class that is being serialized (remember that they need to be JavaBeans, so they must have an empty no-arg constructor), and then figures out which properties are accessible (via get{property}, set{property}). And if a property of the newly instantiated class contains the same value as the property of the original class (i.e., has the same default value), XMLEncoder doesn't write that property. In other words, if the default value of a property hasn't changed, XMLEncoder does not write it. This provides the flexibility of changing what a "default" value is between versions. For example, if the default value of a property is 2 when an object is encoded and later decoded after the default property changes from 2 to 4, the decoded object contains the new default property of 4 (which might not be correct).

XMLEncoder also keeps track of references. If an object appears more than once when being persisted in the object graph (for example, an object is inside a Map from the main class but is also as the DefaultValue property), then XMLEncoder only encodes it once and link up a reference by putting a link in the XML. The XMLEncoder/XMLDecoder class is much more forgiving than the Serialization framework. When decoding, if a property type is changed or deleted/added/moved/renamed, the decoding decodes "as much as it can" while skipping the properties that it couldn't decode.

The recommendation is to not persist your main classes (even though XMLEncoder is more forgiving) but to create special objects that are simple, hold the basic information, and do not perform many tasks by themselves.

8-4. Creating a Socket Connection and Sending Serializable Objects Across the Wire

Problem

You need to open a network connection to send/receive objects.

Solution

Use Java's New Input/Output API version 2 (NIO.2) to send and receive objects. The following solution utilizes the NIO.2 features of nonblocking sockets (using Future tasks).

```
public class Ch_8_4_AsyncChannel {
    private AsynchronousSocketChannel clientWorker;

    InetSocketAddress hostAddress;

    public Ch_8_4_AsyncChannel() {
    }
```

```java
private void start() throws IOException, ExecutionException,
TimeoutException, InterruptedException {
    hostAddress = new InetSocketAddress(InetAddress.
    getByName("127.0.0.1"), 2583);

    Thread serverThread = new Thread(() -> {

        serverStart();
    });

    serverThread.start();

    Thread clientThread = new Thread(() -> {
        clientStart();
    });
    clientThread.start();
}
private void clientStart() {
    try {
        try (AsynchronousSocketChannel clientSocketChannel =
        AsynchronousSocketChannel.open()) {
            Future<Void> connectFuture = clientSocketChannel.
            connect(hostAddress);
            connectFuture.get();               // Wait until connection
                                                  is done.
            OutputStream os = Channels.newOutputStream(clientSocke
            tChannel);
            try (ObjectOutputStream oos = new ObjectOutputStream(os)) {
                for (int i = 0; i < 5; i++) {
                    oos.writeObject("Look at me " + i);
                    Thread.sleep(1000);
                }
                oos.writeObject("EOF");
            }
        }
    } catch (IOException | InterruptedException |
    ExecutionException e) {
```

```java
            e.printStackTrace();
        }
    }

    private void serverStart() {
        try {
            AsynchronousServerSocketChannel serverSocketChannel =
            AsynchronousServerSocketChannel.open().bind(hostAddress);
            Future<AsynchronousSocketChannel> serverFuture =
            serverSocketChannel.accept();
            final AsynchronousSocketChannel clientSocket =
            serverFuture.get();
            System.out.println("Connected!");
            if ((clientSocket != null) && (clientSocket.isOpen())) {
                try (InputStream connectionInputStream = Channels.
                newInputStream(clientSocket)) {
                    ObjectInputStream ois = null;
                    ois = new ObjectInputStream(connectionInputStream);
                    while (true) {
                        Object object = ois.readObject();
                        if (object.equals("EOF")) {
                            clientSocket.close();
                            break;
                        }
                        System.out.println("Received :" + object);
                    }
                    ois.close();
                }
            }
        } catch (IOException | InterruptedException | ExecutionException |
        ClassNotFoundException e) {
            e.printStackTrace();
        }
    }
    public static void main(String[] args) throws IOException,
    ExecutionException, TimeoutException, InterruptedException {
```

```
        Ch_8_4_AsyncChannel example = new Ch_8_4_AsyncChannel();
        example.start();
    }
}
```

The output is:
Connected!
Received :Look at me 0
Received :Look at me 1
Received :Look at me 2
Received :Look at me 3
Received :Look at me 4

How It Works

At its basic level, sockets require a type, IP address, and port. While sockets literature has consumed whole books, the main idea is pretty straightforward. Like the post office, socket communication relies on addresses. These addresses deliver data. In this example, we picked the loopback (the same computer where the program is running) address (127.0.0.1) and chose a random port number (2583).

The advantage of the new NIO.2 is that it is asynchronous. By using asynchronous calls, you can scale your application without creating thousands of threads for each connection. In our example, we take the asynchronous calls and wait for a connection, effectively making it single-threaded for the sake of the example, but don't let that stop you from enhancing this example with more asynchronous calls. (Check the recipes on the multithreaded section of this book.)

For a client to connect, it requires a socket channel. The NIO.2 API allows the creation of asynchronous socket channels. Once a socket channel is created, it needs an address to connect to. The socketChannel.connect() operation does not block; instead, it returns a Future object (this is a different from traditional NIO, where calling socketChannel.connect() block until a connection is established). The Future object allows a Java program to continue what it is doing and simply query the status of the submitted task. To take the analogy further, instead of waiting at the front door for your mail to arrive, you do other stuff and check periodically to see whether the mail has arrived. Future objects have methods like isDone() and isCancelled() that let you know if the task is done or canceled. It also has the get() method, which allows you to wait for the task to finish. In our example, we use Future.get () to wait for the client connection to be established.

Once the connection is established, use Channels.newOutputStream() to create an output stream to send information. Using the decorator pattern, decorate outputStream with ObjectOutputStream to finally send objects through the socket.

The server code is a little more elaborate. Server socket connections allow more than one connection to occur. Thus they monitor or receive connections instead of initiating a connection. For this reason, the server is usually waiting for a connection asynchronously.

The server begins by establishing the address it listens to (127.0.0.1:2583) and accepting connections. The call to serverSocketChannel.accept() returns another Future object that gives you the flexibility to deal with incoming connections. In our example, the server connection simply calls future.get(), which blocks (stop the program's execution) until a connection is accepted.

After the server acquires a socket channel, it creates an inputStream by calling Channels.newInputStream(socket) and then wrapping that input stream with an ObjectInputStream. The server then proceeds to loop and read each object coming from the ObjectInputStream. If the object received's toString() method equals EOF, the server stops looping, and the connection is closed.

Note   Using ObjectOutputStream and ObjectInputStream to send and receive a lot of objects can lead to memory leaks. ObjectOutputStream keeps a copy of the sent object for efficiency. If you were to send the same object again, ObjectOutputStream and ObjectInputStream do not send the same object again, but instead, send a previously sent Object ID. This behavior or sending the Object ID instead of the whole object raises two issues.

The first issue is that objects that are changed in place (mutable) do not reflect the change in the receiving client when sent through the wire. The reason is that because the object was sent once, ObjectOutputStream believes that the object is already transmitted and only sends the ID, negating any changes to the object that have happened since it was sent. To avoid this, don't make changes to objects sent down the wire. This rule also applies to subobjects from the object graph.

The second issue is that because `ObjectOutputStream` maintains a list of sent objects and their Object IDs, if you send a lot of objects, the dictionary of sent objects to keys grows indefinitely, causing memory starvation on a long-running program. To alleviate this issue, you can call `ObjectOutputStream.reset()`, which clears the dictionary of sent objects. Alternatively, you can invoke `ObjectOutputStream.writeUnshared()` to not cache the object in the `ObjectOutputStream` dictionary.

8-5. Obtaining the Java Execution Path

Problem

You want to get the path where the Java program is running.

Solution

Invoke the `System` class's `getProperty` method. The following is an example.

```
String  path = System.getProperty("user.dir");
```

The main class is:

```
public class Ch_8_5_path {
    public static void main(String[] args) {
        String  path = System.getProperty("user.dir");
        System.out.println(path);
    }
}
```

And the output in a windows OS is:

```
C:\eclipse-workspace\java17Recipes
```

How It Works

When a Java program starts, the JRE updates the `user.dir` system property to record where the JRE was invoked. The solution example passes the `"user.dir"` property name to the `getProperty` method, which returns the value.

8-6. Copying a File
Problem

You need to copy a file from one folder to another.

Solution

From the default `java.nio.file.FileSystem` abstract class, you create the "to" and
"from" paths where the files/folders exist and then use the `Files.copy` static method
to copy files between the created paths.

```
public static void main (String[] args) {
    Ch_8_6_CopyFileExample exampleCh86 = new Ch_8_6_CopyFileExample();
    exampleCh86.copyFile();
}

private void copyFile() {
    FileSystem fileSystem = FileSystems.getDefault();
    Path sourcePath = fileSystem.getPath("file.log");
    Path targetPath = fileSystem.getPath("file2.log");
    System.out.println("Copy from "+sourcePath.toAbsolutePath().
    toString()+
    " to "+targetPath.toAbsolutePath().toString());
    try {
        Files.copy(sourcePath, targetPath, StandardCopyOption.REPLACE_
        EXISTING);
    } catch (IOException e) {
        e.printStackTrace();
    }
}
}
```

How It Works

In the new NIO.2 libraries, Java works with an abstraction level that allows for more direct
manipulation of file attributes belonging to the underlying operating system. `FileSystems.`
`getDefaults()` gets the usable abstract system on which you can do file operations.

After getting the default FileSystem object, you can query for file objects. In the NIO.2 file, folders and links are all called *paths*. Once you get a path, you can perform operations with it. In this example, Files.copy is called with the source and destination paths. The last parameter refers to the different copy options. The different copy options are file system dependent, so make sure that the one you choose is compatible with the operating system you intend to run the application in.

8-7. Moving a File

Problem

You need to move a file from one file system location to another.

Solution

You use the default java.nio.file.FileSystem abstract class to create the "to" and "from" paths, and invoke the Files.move() static method.

```
public static void main (String[] args) {
    Ch_8_7_MoveFileExample exampleCh87 = new Ch_8_7_MoveFileExample();
    exampleCh87.moveFile();
}

private void moveFile() {
    FileSystem fileSystem = FileSystems.getDefault();
    Path sourcePath = fileSystem.getPath("file.log");
    Path targetPath = fileSystem.getPath("file2.log");
    System.out.println("Copy from "+sourcePath.toAbsolutePath().
    toString()+ " to "+targetPath.toAbsolutePath().toString());
    try {
        Files.move(sourcePath, targetPath);
    } catch (IOException e) {
        e.printStackTrace();
    }
}
```

How It Works

In the same manner as copying a file, create the source and destination path. Then, Files.move moves the file from one location to another for you. Other methods provided by the Files object are the following.

- Delete (path): Deletes a file (or a folder, if it's empty).

- Exists (path): Checks whether a file/folder exists.

- isDirectory (path): Checks whether the path created points to a directory.

- isExecutable (path): Checks whether the file is an executable.

- isHidden (path): Checks whether the file is visible or hidden in the operating system.

You can work with the Delete and Exist methods with the following main method.

```java
public static void main (String[] args) {
    FileSystem fileSystem = FileSystems.getDefault();
    Path deletePath = fileSystem.getPath("deletePath");
    System.out.println("Path to delete:"+deletePath.
    toAbsolutePath().toString());
    System.out.println("Exist Path to delete? "+Files.
    exists(deletePath));
    try {
        Files.delete(deletePath);
    } catch (IOException e) {
        e.printStackTrace();
    }
}
```

The output is:
```
Path to delete:C:\eclipse-workspace\java17Recipes\deletePath
Exist Path to delete? true
```

8-8. Iterating Over Files in a Directory

Problem

You need to scan files from a directory. There are possibly subdirectories with more files. You want to include those in your scan.

Solution

Using the NIO.2, creates a java.nio.file.FileVisitor<T> interface object and performs the desired implementation within its visitFile method. Next, obtain the default FileSystem object and grab a reference to the path you'd like to scan via the getPath() method. Lastly, invoke the Files.walkFileTree() method, passing the Path and the FileVisitor<T> that you created. The following code demonstrates how to perform these tasks.

```
public class Ch_8_8_TraverseDirectory {
    private void start() {
        FileVisitor<Path> myFileVisitor = new SimpleFileVisitor<Path>() {
        @Override
        public FileVisitResult visitFile(Path file,
        BasicFileAttributes attrs)
                               throws IOException {
            System.out.println("Visited File: "+file.toString());
            return FileVisitResult.CONTINUE;
        }
    };
    FileSystem fileSystem = FileSystems.getDefault();
    Path directory= fileSystem.getPath(".");
    try {
        Files.walkFileTree(directory, myFileVisitor);
    } catch (IOException e) {
        e.printStackTrace();
    }
  }
```

```
public static void main (String args[]) {
    Ch_8_8_TraverseDirectory traverseDirectory = new Ch_8_8_
    TraverseDirectory();
    traverseDirectory.start();
}
```

How It Works

Before NIO.2, trying to traverse a directory tree involved recursion, and depending on the implementation, it could be very brittle. The calls to get files within a folder were synchronous. They required scanning the whole directory before returning, generating what would appear to be an unresponsive method call to an application user. With NIO.2, one can specify which folder to start traversing on, and the NIO.2 calls handle the recursion details. The only item you provide to the NIO.2 API is a class that tells it what to do when a file/folder is found (java.nio.file.SimpleFileVisitor<T> class implementation). NIO.2 uses a Visitor pattern, so it isn't required to prescan the entire folder but instead processes files as they are being iterated over.

The implementation of the SimpleFileVisitor<T> class as an anonymous inner class includes overriding the visitFile(Path file, BasicFileAttributesattrs() method. When you override this method, you can specify the tasks to perform when a file is encountered.

The visitFile method returns a FileVisitReturn enum. This enum then tells the FileVisitor<T> which action to take.

- CONTINUE continues with the traversing of the directory tree.

- TERMINATE stops the traversing.

- SKIP_SUBTREE stops going deeper from the current tree level (useful only if this enum is returned on the preVisitDirectory() method).

- SKIP_SIBLINGS skips the other directories at the same tree level as the current.

The SimpleFileVisitor<T> class, aside from the visitFile() method, also contains the following.

- preVisitDirectory is called before entering a directory to be traversed.

- postVisitDirectory is called after finished traversing a directory.

- visitFile is called as it visits the file, as in the example code.

- visitFileFailed is called if the file cannot be visited; for example, on an I/O error.

8-9. Querying (and Setting) File Metadata
Problem

You need to get information about a particular file, such as file size, whether it is a directory, and so on. Also, you might want to mark a file as *archived* in the Windows operating system or grant-specific POSIX file permissions in the *nix operating system.

Solution

Using Java NIO.2, you can obtain any file information by simply invoking methods on the java.nio.file.Files utility class, passing the path you'd like to obtain the metadata. You can obtain attribute information by calling the Files.getFileAttributeView() method, passing the specific implementation for the attribute view that you would like to use. The following code demonstrates these techniques for obtaining metadata.

```
public class Ch_8_09_MetadataInfo {
private void start() {
        Path path = FileSystems.getDefault().getPath("./file2.log");
        try {
            // General file attributes, supported by all Java systems
            System.out.println("File Size:"+Files.size(path));
            System.out.println("Is Directory:"+Files.isDirectory(path));
            System.out.println("Is Regular File:"+Files.
            isRegularFile(path));
            System.out.println("Is Symbolic Link:"+Files.
            isSymbolicLink(path));
            System.out.println("Is Hidden:"+Files.isHidden(path));
            System.out.println("Last Modified Time:"+Files.
            getLastModifiedTime(path));
            System.out.println("Owner:"+Files.getOwner(path));
```

```
            // Specific attribute views.
            DosFileAttributeView view = Files.getFileAttributeView(path,
                DosFileAttributeView.class);
            System.out.println("DOS File Attributes\n");
            System.out.println("------------------------------------\n");
            System.out.println("Archive  :"+view.readAttributes().
            isArchive());
            System.out.println("Hidden   :"+view.readAttributes().
            isHidden());
            System.out.println("Read-only:"+view.readAttributes().
            isReadOnly());
            System.out.println("System   :"+view.readAttributes().
            isSystem());

            view.setArchive(false);

        } catch (IOException e) {
            e.printStackTrace();
        }
    }
    public static void main(String[] args) {
        Ch_8_09_MetadataInfo info = new Ch_8_09_MetadataInfo();
        info.start();
    }
```

How It Works

Java NIO.2 allows much more flexibility in getting and setting file attributes than older I/O techniques. NIO.2 abstracts the different operating system attributes into both a "common" and an "OS-specific" set of attributes. The standard attributes are the following.

- isDirectory is true if it's a directory

- isRegularFile returns false if the file isn't considered a regular file, the file doesn't exist, or it can't be determined whether it's a regular file.

- isSymbolicLink is true if the link is symbolic (most prevalent in Unix systems).

- isHidden is true if the file is considered hidden in the operating system.

- LastModifiedTime is the time the file was last updated.

- Owner is the file's owner per the operating system.

Also, NIO.2 allows entering the specific attributes of the underlying operating system. To do so, you first need to get a view representing the operating system's file attributes (in this example, it is a DosFileAttributeView). Once you get the view, you can query and change the OS-specific attributes.

8-10. Monitoring a Directory for Content Changes
Problem

You need to keep track when a directory's content has changed (for example, a file was added, changed, or deleted) and act on those changes.

Solution

By using a java.nio.file.WatchService interface, you can subscribe to be notified about events occurring within a folder. In the following example, we subscribe for ENTRY_CREATE, ENTRY_MODIFY, and ENTRY_DELETE events.

```
public class Ch_8_10_MonitorFolder {
    private void start() {
        try {
            System.out.println("Watch Event, press q<Enter> to exit");
            FileSystem fileSystem = FileSystems.getDefault();
            WatchService service = fileSystem.newWatchService();
            Path path = fileSystem.getPath(".");
            System.out.println("Watching :"+path.toAbsolutePath());
```

```
        path.register(service, StandardWatchEventKinds.ENTRY_CREATE,
        StandardWatchEventKinds.ENTRY_DELETE, StandardWatchEventKinds.
        ENTRY_MODIFY);
        boolean shouldContinue = true;
        while(shouldContinue) {
            WatchKey key = service.poll(250, TimeUnit.MILLISECONDS);
            // Code to stop the program
            while (System.in.available() > 0) {
                int readChar = System.in.read();
                if ((readChar == 'q') || (readChar == 'Q')) {
                    shouldContinue = false;
                    break;
                }
            }
            if (key == null) continue;
            key.pollEvents().stream()
                    .filter((event) -> !(event.kind() ==
                    StandardWatchEventKinds.OVERFLOW))
                    .map((event) -> (WatchEvent<Path>)event).
                    forEach((ev) -> {
                Path filename = ev.context();
                System.out.println("Event detected :"+filename.
                toString()+" "+ev.kind());
            });
            boolean valid = key.reset();
            if (!valid) {
                break;
            }
        }
    } catch (IOException | InterruptedException e) {
        e.printStackTrace();
    }
}

public static void main (String[] args) {
    Ch_8_10_MonitorFolder monitorFolder = new Ch_8_10_MonitorFolder();
```

```
        monitorFolder.start();
    }
}
}
```

The output - if a document is created and then removed - is:
Watch Event, press q<Enter> to exit
Watching :C:\eclipse-workspace\java17Recipes\.
Event detected :test.txt ENTRY_CREATE
Event detected :test.txt ENTRY_DELETE

How It Works

NIO.2 includes a built-in polling mechanism to monitor for changes in the file system. Using a poll mechanism allows you to wait for events and poll for updates at a specified interval. Once an event occurs, you can process and consume it. A consumed event tells the NIO.2 framework that you are ready to handle a new event.

To start monitoring a folder, create a `WatchService` that you can use to poll for changes. After the `WatchService` has been created, register the `WatchService` with a path. A path symbolizes a folder in the file system. When the `WatchService` is registered with the path, you define the kinds of events you want to monitor (see Table 8-1). They are declared on the `java.nio.file` package's `StandardWatchEventKinds` class.

Table 8-1. *Types of watchEvents*

WatchEvent	Description
OVERFLOW	An event that has overflown (ignore)
ENTRY_CREATE	A directory or file was created
ENTRY_DELETE	A directory or file has been deleted
ENTRY_MODIFY	A directory or file has been modified

After registering the `WatchService` with the path, you can "poll" the `WatchService` for event occurrences. By calling the `watchService.poll()` method, you wait for a file/folder event to occur on that path. Using the `watchService.poll(int timeout, Timeunit timeUnit)` wait until the specified timeout is reached before continuing.

If the WatchService receives an event, or if the allowed time has passed, then it continues execution. If there were no events and the timeout was reached, the WatchKey object returned by the watchService.poll(int timeout) is null; otherwise, the WatchKey object returned contains the relevant information for the event that has occurred.

Because many events can occur at the same time (for example, moving an entire folder or pasting a bunch of files into a folder), the WatchKey object key might contain more than one event. You can use the key to obtain all the events associated with that object key by calling the key.pollEvents() method.

The watchKey.pollEvents() call returns a list of watchEvents that can be iterated. Each watchEvent contains information on the actual file or folder to which the event refers (for example, an entire subfolder could have been moved or deleted) and the event type (add, edit, delete). Only those events that were registered in WatchService are processed.

Once an event has been processed, it is important to call the EventKey.reset(). The reset returns a Boolean value determining whether the WatchKey is still valid. A WatchKey becomes invalid if it is canceled or if its originating WatchService is closed. If the eventKey returns false, you should break from the watch loop.

8-11. Reading Property Files
Problem

You want to establish some configurational settings for your application. You want to modify the settings manually or programmatically. Moreover, you want some configurations to be changed without recompiling and redeploying.

Solution

Create a properties file to store the application configurations. Using the Properties object, load properties stored within the properties file for application processing. Properties can also be updated and modified within the properties file. The following example demonstrates how to read a properties file named properties.conf, load the values for application use, and finally set a property and write it to the file.

```
public class Ch_8_11_PropertiesExample {
private void start() {
        File file = new File("properties.conf");
        Properties properties = null;
        try {
            if (!file.exists()) {
                file.createNewFile();
            }
            properties = new Properties();
            properties.load(new FileInputStream("properties.conf"));
        } catch (IOException e) {
            e.printStackTrace();
        }
        boolean shouldWakeUp = false;
        int startCounter = 100;
        String shouldWakeUpProperty = properties.
        getProperty("ShouldWakeup");
        shouldWakeUp = (shouldWakeUpProperty == null) ? false : Boolean.par
        seBoolean(shouldWakeUpProperty.trim());
        String startCounterProperty = properties.
        getProperty("StartCounter");
        try {
            startCounter = Integer.parseInt(startCounterProperty);
        } catch (Exception e) {
            System.out.println("Couldn't read startCounter, defaulting to "
            + startCounter);
        }
        String dateFormatStringProperty = properties.
        getProperty("DateFormatString", "MMM dd yy");
        System.out.println("Should Wake up? " + shouldWakeUp);
        System.out.println("Start Counter: " + startCounter);
        System.out.println("Date Format String:" +
        dateFormatStringProperty);
        //setting property
        properties.setProperty("StartCounter", "250");
```

```
        try {
        properties.store(new FileOutputStream("properties.conf"),
        "Properties Description");
        } catch (IOException e) {
            e.printStackTrace();
        }
        properties.list(System.out);
    }

    public static void main(String[] args) {
        Ch_8_11_PropertiesExample propertiesExample = new Ch_8_11_
        PropertiesExample();
        propertiesExample.start();
    }
}
```

An output is:
Should Wake up? false
Start Counter: 250
Date Format String:MMM dd yy
-- listing properties --
StartCounter=250

How It Works

The Java Properties class helps you manage program properties. It allows you to manage the properties either via external modification (someone editing a property file) or internally by using the Properties.store() method.

The Properties object can be instantiated either without a file or with a preloaded file. The files that the Properties object read are in the form of [name]=[value] and are textually represented. If you need to store values in other formats, you must write to and read from a string.

If you are expecting the files to be modified outside the program (the user directly opens a text editor and changes the values), be sure to sanitize the inputs, like trimming the values for extra spaces and ignoring the case if need be.

To query the different properties programmatically, you call the getProperty(String) method, passing the string-based name of the property whose value you want to retrieve. The method returns null if the property is not found. Alternatively, you can invoke the getProperty (String,String) method, on which if the property is not found in the Properties object, it returns the second parameter as its value. It is a good practice to specify default values if the file doesn't have an entry for a particular key.

Upon looking at a generated property file, you notice that the first two lines indicate the description of the file and the date when it was modified. These two lines start with #, which in Java property files is the equivalent of a comment. The Properties object skips any line starting with # when processing the file.

Note   If you allow users to modify your configuration files directly, it is important to have validation when retrieving properties from the Properties object. One of the most common issues encountered in the value of properties is leading and/ or trailing spaces. If specifying a Boolean or integer property, be sure that they can be parsed from a string. At a minimum, catch an exception when trying to parse to survive an unconventional value (and log the offending value).

8-12. Uncompressing Files
Problem

Your application has the requirement to decompress and extract files from a compressed .zip file.

Solution

Using the java.util.zip package, you can open a .zip file and iterate through its entries. While traversing the entries, directories can be created for directory entries. The following lines of code demonstrate how to perform the decompress and file iteration technique, as described.

```java
public class Ch_8_12_ZipExample {
    public static void
    main(String[] args) {
        Ch_8_12_ZipExample example = new Ch_8_12_ZipExample();
        example.start();
    }

    private void start() {
ZipFile file = null;
try {
    file = new ZipFile("file.zip");
    FileSystem fileSystem = FileSystems.getDefault();
    Enumeration<? extends ZipEntry> entries = file.entries();
    String uncompressedDirectory = "uncompressed/";
    Files.createDirectory(fileSystem.getPath(uncompressedDirectory));
    while (entries.hasMoreElements()) {
        ZipEntry entry = entries.nextElement();
        if (entry.isDirectory()) {
            System.out.println("Creating Directory:" +
            uncompressedDirectory + entry.getName());
            Files.createDirectories(fileSystem.
            getPath(uncompressedDirectory +
                                    entry.getName()));
        } else {
            InputStream is = file.getInputStream(entry);
            System.out.println("File :" + entry.getName());
            BufferedInputStream bis = new BufferedInputStream(is);

            String uncompressedFileName = uncompressedDirectory + entry.
            getName();
            Path uncompressedFilePath = fileSystem.
            getPath(uncompressedFileName);
            Files.createFile(uncompressedFilePath);
            try (FileOutputStream fileOutput = new FileOutputStream(uncompr
            essedFileName)) {
```

```
            while (bis.available() > 0) {
                fileOutput.write(bis.read());
            }
        }
        System.out.println("Written :" + entry.getName());
    }
}
} catch (IOException e) {
    e.printStackTrace();
}
}
```

How It Works

To work with the contents of a .zip archive, create a ZipFile object. A ZipFile object can be instantiated, passing the name of a .zip archive to the constructor. After creating the object, you access the specified .zip file information. Each ZipFile object contains entries representing the directories and files contained within the archive. By iterating through the entries, you can obtain information on each compressed file. Each ZipEntry instance has the compressed and uncompressed size, the name, and the input stream of the uncompressed bytes.

The uncompressed bytes can be read into a byte buffer by generating an InputStream, and later (in our case) written to a file. Using the FileStream, it is possible to determine how many bytes can be read without blocking the process. Once the determined number of bytes has been read, those bytes are written to the output file. This process continues until the total number of bytes has been read.

Note   Reading the entire file into memory may not be a good idea if the file is extremely large. If you need to work with a large file, it's best to first write it in an uncompressed format to disk (as in the example) and then open it and load it in chunks. If the file you are working on is not large (you can limit the size by checking the getSize() method), you can probably load it in memory.

8-13. Summary

This chapter demonstrated several examples for working with file and network I/O in Java. You learned how to serialize files to be stored to disk and how to manipulate a host's file system with the Java APIs. The chapter also covered how to read and write property files and perform file compression. Lastly, the chapter touched on the new features of the Process API added in Java 9.

CHAPTER 9

Exceptions and Logging

Exceptions are a way of describing exceptional circumstances within a program. They are an indicator that something unexpected (exceptional) has occurred. For that reason, exceptions are efficient at interrupting the current flow of the program and signaling that there is something that requires attention. As such, programs that utilize exceptions judiciously benefit from a better control flow and become more robust and informative for the user. Even so, using exceptions indiscriminately can cause performance degradation.

Within Java, exceptions can be *thrown* or *caught*. Throwing an exception involves indicating to the code that an exception has been encountered, using the throw keyword to signal the JVM to find any code capable of handling this exceptional circumstance within the current stack. Catching an exception involves telling the compiler which exceptions can be handled and which part of the code should be monitored for these exceptions to occur. This is denoted within the try/catch Java block (described in Recipe 9-1).

All exceptions inherit from the Throwable class and can be defined in the catch clause of a try/catch statement. The JVM primarily uses the Error classes to denote serious and/or fatal errors. According to the Java documentation, applications are not expected to catch Error exceptions since they are considered fatal (think of a computer being on fire). The bulk of exceptions within a Java program are inherited from the Exception class.

Within the JVM, there are two types of exceptions: checked and unchecked. Methods enforce checked exceptions. You can specify the exceptions a method can throw in the method signature. This requires any caller of the method to create a try/catch block, which handles the exceptions declared within the method signature. Unchecked exceptions do not require a stringent convention and are free to be thrown anywhere without implementing a try/catch block. Even so, unchecked exceptions (as described in Recipe 9-7) are usually discouraged because they can lead to threads unraveling (if nothing catches the exception) and poor visibility of problems. Exception

© Josh Juneau, Luciano Manelli 2022
J. Juneau and L. Manelli, *Java 17 Recipes*, https://doi.org/10.1007/978-1-4842-7963-2_9

classes that inherit from `RuntimeException` are considered unchecked exceptions, whereas exception classes that inherit directly from `Exception` are considered checked exceptions.

Be aware that the act of throwing exceptions is expensive (compared with other language construct alternatives), and as such, throwing exceptions makes a poor substitute for control flow. For example, you shouldn't throw an exception to indicate an expected result of a method call (e.g., a method like `isUsernameValid (String username)`). It is better to call the method and return a Boolean with the result than throwing `InvalidUsernameException` to indicate failure.

While exceptions play an essential role in solid software development, logging exceptions can be just as important. Logging within an application helps the developer understand what events occur without debugging the code. This is especially true in production environments where there isn't the opportunity for live debugging. In that sense, logging collects clues on what is occurring (most likely what went wrong) and helps you troubleshoot production problems. Many developers utilize a structured logging framework to provide more robust logging for an application. A solid logging framework with a solid methodology saves many late nights at work wondering, "what happened?"

Logging for Java is very mature. Many open source projects are widely accepted as the de facto standard for logging. In the recipes in this chapter, you use Java's Logback framework and the Simple Logging Facade for Java (SLF4J). Both of these projects together create a good-enough solution for most logging needs. For the recipes involving SLF4J and Log4j, download SLF4J (`www.slf4j.org`) and put it in your project's dependency path. This chapter also touches upon the lower-level JVM logging added in Java 9.

9-1. Catching Exceptions

Problem

You want to gracefully handle any exceptions generated from your code.

Solution

Use the built-in try/catch language construct to catch exceptions. Do so by wrapping any blocks of code that may throw an exception within a try/catch block. The following example generates a Boolean value to indicate whether a specified string is greater than five characters long. If the string passed as an argument is null, a NullPointerException (RuntimeException type) is thrown by the length() method and caught within the catch block.

```java
public class Recipe9_1 {
    public static void main(String[] args) {
        Recipe9_1 recipe = new Recipe9_1();
        recipe.start();
    }
private void start() {
    System.out.println("Is th string 1234 longer than 5 chars?:"+
            isStringShorterThanFiveCharacters("1234"));
    System.out.println("Is th string 12345 longer than 5 chars?:"+
            isStringShorterThanFiveCharacters("12345"));
    System.out.println("Is th string 123456 longer than 5 chars?:"+
            isStringShorterThanFiveCharacters("123456"));
    System.out.println("Is th string null longer than 5 chars?:"+
            isStringShorterThanFiveCharacters(null));
}
private boolean isStringShorterThanFiveCharacters(String aString) {
    try {
        return aString.length() > 5;
    } catch (NullPointerException e) {
        System.err.println("An Exception Occurred: " + e);
        return false;
    }
}
}
```

How It Works

The try keyword specifies that the enclosed code segment can raise an exception. The catch clause is placed at the end of the try clause. Each catch clause specifies which exception is being caught. The compiler generates an error if a catch clause is not provided for a checked exception. Two possible solutions are to add a catch clause or to include the exception in the throws clause of the enclosing method. Any checked exceptions that are thrown but not caught propagate up the call stack. If this method doesn't catch the exception, the thread that executed the code terminates. If the thread terminating is the only thread in the program, it terminates its execution.

If a try clause needs to catch more than one exception, more than one exception can be specified, separated by a bar character. For instance, the following try/catch block could be used for catching both NumberFormatException (a RuntimeException type) and NullPointerException.

```
try {
  // code here
} catch (NumberFormatException|NullPointerException ex) {
  // logging
}
```

Note   Be careful when throwing an exception. If the thrown exception is not caught, it propagates up the call stack; and if there isn't any catch clause capable of handling the exception, it causes the running thread to terminate (also known as *unraveling*). If your program has only one main thread, an uncaught exception terminates your program.

9-2. Guaranteeing a Block of Code Is Executed

Problem

You want to write code that executes when control leaves a code segment, even if control leaves due to an error being thrown or the segment ending abnormally. For example, you have acquired a lock and want to be sure that you are releasing it correctly. You want to release the lock in the event of an error or no error.

Solution

Use a try/catch/finally block to properly release locks and other resources that you acquire in a code segment. Place the code that you want to have executed regardless of exceptions into the finally clause. In the example, the finally keyword specifies a code block that always executes, regardless of whether an exception was thrown in the try block. Within the finally block, the lock is released by calling lock.unlock().

```
public class Recipe9_2 {
        Lock myLock = new ReentrantLock();
        Random random = new Random();

        public static void main(String[] args) {
            Recipe9_2 recipe = new Recipe9_2();
            recipe.start();
        }

        private void start() {
            for (int i = 0; i < 10; i++) {
                callFunctionThatHoldsLock();
            }
        }

    private void callFunctionThatHoldsLock() {
        myLock.lock();
        try {
            int number = random.nextInt(5);
            int result = 100 / number;
            System.out.println("A result is " + result);
            FileOutputStream file = new FileOutputStream("file.out");
            file.write(result);
            file.close();
        } catch (FileNotFoundException e) {
            e.printStackTrace();
        } catch (IOException e) {
            e.printStackTrace();
        } catch (Exception e) {
            e.printStackTrace();
```

```
        } finally {
            myLock.unlock();
        }
    }
}
```

How It Works

Code placed within the `finally` clause of a `try/catch/finally` block is always executed. In this example, acquiring the lock at the beginning of the function and releasing it in the `finally` block guarantees that it is released at the end of the function, regardless of whether an exception (checked or unchecked) is thrown. In all, acquired locks should always be released in a `finally` block. In the example, suppose that the `mylock.unlock()` function call was not in the `finally` block (but at the end of the `try` block); if an exception were to happen in this case, the call to `mylock.unlock()` would not happen because code execution would be interrupted in the location where the exception happened. In that case, the lock would be forever acquired and never released.

Caution   If you need to return a value on a method, avoid returning values in the `finally` block. A `return` statement in the `finally` block always executes, regardless of any other `return` statements that might have happened within the `try` block.

9-3. Throwing Exceptions
Problem

You want to abort the execution of the current code path by throwing an exception if a certain situation occurs within your application.

Solution

Use the `throw` keyword to throw a specified exception when the situation occurs. Using the `throw` keyword, you can signal the current thread to look for `try/catch` blocks (at the current level and up the stack), which can process the thrown exception. In the following example, the callSomeMethodThatMightThrow throws a NullPointerException (RuntimeException type) if the parameter passed in is null.

```
public class Recipe9_3 {
    public static void main(String[] args) {
        Recipe9_3 recipe = new Recipe9_3();
        recipe.start();
    }
private void start() {
    try {
        callSomeMethodThatMightThrow(null);
    } catch (IllegalArgumentException e) {
        System.err.println("There was an illegal argument exception!");
    }
}
}
private void callSomeFunctionThatMightThrow(Object o) {
    if (o == null) throw new NullPointerException("The object is null");
}
```

In this code example, the callSomeMethodThatMightThrow method checks to ensure that a valid argument was passed to it. If the argument is null, it then throws a NullPointerException (RuntimeException type), signaling that the caller of this method invoked it with the wrong parameters.

How It Works

The throw keyword allows you to explicitly generate an exceptional condition. When the current thread throws an exception, it doesn't execute anything beyond the throw statement and instead transfers control to the catch clause (if there are any) or terminates the thread.

Note   When throwing an exception, be sure that you intend to do so. If an exception is not caught as it propagates up the stack, it terminates the executing thread (also known as *unraveling*). If your program has only one main thread, an uncaught exception terminates your program.

9-4. Catching Multiple Exceptions

Problem

A block of code in your application has the possibility of throwing multiple exceptions. You want to catch each of the exceptions that may occur within a try block.

Solution 1

More than one catch clause can be specified when multiple exceptions may be encountered within the same block. Each catch clause can specify a different exception to handle so that each exception can be handled differently. In the following code, two catch clauses handle IOException and a ClassNotFoundException.

```
public static void main(String[] args) {
    Recipe9_4 recipe = new Recipe9_4();
    recipe.startClassic();
}

private void startClassic() {
    try {
        Class<?> stringClass = Class.forName("java.lang.String");
        FileInputStream in = new FileInputStream("myFile.log") ;
        // Can throw IOException
        in.read();

    } catch (IOException e) {
        System.err.println("There was an exception "+e);
    } catch (ClassNotFoundException e) {
        System.err.println("There was an exception "+e);
    }
}
```

Solution 2

If your application tends to throw multiple exceptions within a single block, then a vertical bar operator (|) can be utilized for handling each of the exceptions in the same manner. In the following example, the catch clause specifies multiple exception types separated with a vertical bar (|) to handle each exception in the same manner.

```
public static void main(String[] args) {
    Recipe9_4 recipe = new Recipe9_4();
    recipe.start();
}

private void start() {
    try {
            Class<?> stringClass = Class.forName("java.lang.String");
            FileInputStream in = new
            FileInputStream("myFile.log") ;
    // Can throw IOException
            in.read();

        } catch (IOException | ClassNotFoundException e) {
            System.out.println("An exception of type
            "+e.getClass()+" was thrown! "+e);
        }
}
```

How It Works

There are many different ways to handle situations where multiple exceptions may be thrown. You can specify separate catch clauses to handle each of the exceptions differently. To handle each exception in the same manner, you can utilize a single catch clause and specify each exception separated with a vertical bar operator.

> **Note**   If you're catching an exception in multiple `catch` blocks (solution 1), make sure that the `catch` blocks are defined from the most specific to the most general. Failure to follow this convention prevents an exception from handling the more specific blocks. This is most important when there are `catch (Exception e)` blocks, which catch almost all exceptions.

Having a catch (`Exception e`) block—called a *catch-all* or *Pokémon exception handler* (gotta catch them all)—is usually poor practice because such a block catches every exception type and treats them all the same. This becomes a problem because the block can catch other exceptions that may occur deeper within the call stack that you may not have intended the block to catch (`OutOfMemoryException`). It is best to specify each possible exception rather than specifying a catch-all exception handler to catch all exceptions.

9-5. Catching the Uncaught Exceptions

Problem

You want to know when a thread is terminated due to an uncaught exception such as `NullPointerException`.

Solution 1

When creating a Java thread, sometimes you need to ensure that any exception is caught and handled properly to help determine the reason for the thread termination. The following code demonstrates registering an exception handler on a per-thread basis.

```
public static void main(String[] args) {
    Recipe9_5 recipe = new Recipe9_5();
    recipe.start();
    recipe.startForCurrentThread();
}
```

```
private void start() {
    Thread.setDefaultUncaughtExceptionHandler((Thread t, Throwable e) -> {
        System.out.println("Woa! there was an exception thrown somewhere!
        "+t.getName()+": "+e);
    });
    final Random random = new Random();
    for (int j = 0; j < 10; j++) {
        int divisor = random.nextInt(4);
        System.out.println("200 / " + divisor + " Is " + (200 / divisor));
    }
}
```

The following is the output.

```
200 / 2 Is 100
Woa! there was an exception thrown somewhere! main:
java.lang.ArithmeticException: / by zero
```

The for loop in this thread executes properly until an exception is encountered, when DefaultUncaughtExceptionHandler is invoked. UncaughtExceptionHandler is a functional interface, so utilizing a lambda expression to implement the exception handler is possible.

Solution 2

It is possible to register UncaughtExceptionHandler in a specific thread. After doing so, any exception within the thread that has not been caught is handled by the uncaughtException() method. The following is an example.

```
private void startForCurrentThread() {
    Thread.currentThread().setUncaughtExceptionHandler((Thread t,
    Throwable e) -> {
        System.out.println("In this thread "+t.getName()+" an exception was
        thrown "+e);
    });
    Thread someThread = new Thread(() -> {
        System.out.println(200/0);
    });
```

```
    someThread.setName("Some Unlucky Thread");
    someThread.start();
    System.out.println("In the main thread "+ (200/0));
}
```

The following is the output.

```
In this thread main an exception was thrown java.lang.ArithmeticException:
/ by zero
```

In the previous code, UncaughtExceptionHandler is registered on currentThread. As in solution 1, UncaughtExceptionHandler is a functional interface, so utilizing a lambda expression to implement the exception handler is possible.

How It Works

Thread.defaultUncaughtExceptionHandler() is invoked for each unchecked exception that has not been caught. When UncaughtExceptionHandler() handles an exception, it means that there was no try/catch block in place to catch the exception. As such, the exception bubbled up the thread stack. This is the last code executed on that thread before it terminates. The thread terminates when an exception is caught on either the thread's or the default's UncaughtExceptionHandler(), which logs information on the exception to help pinpoint the reason for the exception.

In solution 2, UncaughtExceptionHandler() is set up specifically for the current thread. When the thread throws an exception that is not caught, it bubbles up to UncaughtExceptionHandler() in the thread. If this is not present, it bubbles up to defaultUncaughtExceptionHandler(). Again, in either situation, the thread originating the exception terminates.

Tip   When dealing with multiple threads, it is always good practice to explicitly name the threads. It makes life easier to know exactly which thread caused the exception, rather than having to trace down an unknown thread named like Thread-## (the default naming pattern of unnamed threads).

9-6. Managing Resources with try/catch Blocks

Problem

In the event of an exception, you need to ensure that any resources used within a try/catch block are released.

Solution

Use the Automatic Resource Management (ARM) feature, which can be specified with a try-with-resources statement. When using that statement, any resources specified within the try clause are automatically released when the block terminates. In the following code, the FileOutputStream, BufferedOutputStream, and DataOutputStream resources are automatically handled by the try-with-resources block.

```
public class Recipe9_6 {
    public static void main(String []args) {
        Recipe9_6 recipe = new Recipe9_6();
        recipe.start();
    }

    private void start() {
        try (
                FileOutputStream fos = new FileOutputStream("out.log");
                BufferedOutputStream bos = new BufferedOutputStream(fos);
                DataOutputStream dos = new DataOutputStream(bos)
        ) {
            dos.writeUTF("This is being written");
        } catch (Exception e) {
            System.out.println("Some bad exception happened ");
        }
    }
}
```

How It Works

In most cases, you want to cleanly close/dispose of resources acquired within a try/catch block after the block execution is complete. If a program does not close/dispose of its resources or does so improperly, the resources could be acquired indefinitely, causing issues such as memory leaks. Most resources are limited (file handles or database connections), and as such, cause performance degradation (and more exceptions to be thrown). To avoid these situations, Java provides a means of automatically releasing resources when an exception occurs within a try/catch block. By declaring a try-with-resources block, the resource on which the try block was checked is closed if an exception is thrown within the block. Most of the resources built into Java work properly within a try-with-resources statement (for a full list, see implementers of the java.lang.AutoCloseable interface). Also, third-party implementers can create resources that work with the try-with-resources statements by implementing the AutoCloseable interface.

The syntax for the try-with-resources statement involves the try keyword, followed by an opening parenthesis and then followed by all the resource declarations that you want to have released in the event of an exception or when the block completes and ending with a closing parenthesis. You receive a compiler error if you try to declare a resource/variable that doesn't implement the AutoCloseable interface. After the closing parenthesis, the syntax of the try/catch block is the same as a normal block.

The main advantage of the try-with-resources feature is that it allows a cleaner release of resources. Usually, when acquiring a resource, there are a lot of interdependencies (creating file handlers, which are wrapped in output streams, which are wrapped in buffered streams). Properly closing and disposing of these resources in exceptional conditions requires checking the status of each dependent resource and carefully disposing of it, and doing so requires that you write a lot of code. By contrast, the try-with-resources construct allows the JVM to properly dispose of resources, even in exceptional conditions.

Note A try-with-resources block always closes the defined resources, even if no exceptions were thrown.

9-7. Creating an Exception Class

Problem

You want to create a new type of exception that indicates a particular event.

Solution 1

Create a class that extends java.lang.RuntimeException to create an exception class that can be thrown at any time. In the following code, a class identified by IllegalChatServerException extends RuntimeException and accepts a string as an argument to the constructor. The exception is then thrown when a specified event occurs within the code.

```java
class IllegalChatServerException extends RuntimeException {
    IllegalChatServerException(String message) {
        super(message);
    }
}
private void disconnectChatServer(Object chatServer) {
    if (chatServer == null) throw new IllegalChatServerException("Chat
    server is empty");
}
```

Solution 2

Create a class that extends java.lang.Exception to generate a checked exception class. A checked exception is required to be caught or rethrown up the stack. In the following example, a class identified as ConnectionUnavailableException extends java.lang.Exception and accepts a string as an argument to the constructor. The checked exception is then thrown by a method in the code.

```java
class ConnectionUnavailableException extends Exception {
    ConnectionUnavailableException(String message) {
        super(message);
    }
}
```

```
private void sendChat(String chatMessage) throws
ConnectionUnavailableException {
    if (chatServer == null)
            throw new ConnectionUnavailableException("Can't find the
            chat server");
}
```

The main method is as follows.

```
Object chatServer = null;
```

```
public static void main (String[] args) {
    Recipe9_7 recipe = new Recipe9_7();
    recipe.start();
}
```

```
private void start() {
    try {
        sendChat("Hello, how are you?");
    } catch (ConnectionUnavailableException e) {
        System.out.println("Caught a connection unavailable Exception!");
    }

    disconnectChatServer(chatServer);
}
```

How It Works

Sometimes there is a requirement to create a custom exception, especially when creating an API. The usual recommendation is to use one of the available Exception classes provided by the JDK. For example, use IOException for I/O-related issues or IllegalArgumentException for illegal parameters. If there isn't a JDK exception that fits cleanly, you can always extend java.lang.Exception or java.lang.RuntimeException and implement its own family of exceptions.

Depending on the base class, creating an Exception class is fairly straightforward. Extending RuntimeException allows you to throw the resulting exception any time without requiring it to be caught up in the stack. This is advantageous in that RuntimeException is a more lax contract to work with, but throwing such an exception can lead to thread termination if the exception is not caught. Extending Exception instead allows you to force any code that throws the exception to handle it within a catch clause. The checked exception is then forced by contract to implement a catch handler, potentially avoiding a thread termination.

In practice, we discourage extending RuntimeException because it can lead to poor exception handling. Our rule of thumb is that if it's possible to recover from an exception, you should create the associated exception class by extending Exception. If a developer cannot reasonably recover from the exception (i.e., NullPointerException), extend RuntimeException.

9-8. Logging Events Within Your Application

Problem

You want to log events, debug messages, error conditions, and other events within your application.

Solution

Utilize the Java Logging API within your application to implement a logging solution. The following example first creates a logger object named recipeLogger. In this example, the Java Logger logs an informational message, a warning message, and an error message.

```
private void loadLoggingConfiguration() {
    FileInputStream ins = null;
    try {
        ins = new FileInputStream(new File("logging.properties"));
        LogManager.getLogManager().readConfiguration(ins);
    } catch (IOException e) {
        e.printStackTrace();
    }
}
private void start() {
    loadLoggingConfiguration();
    Logger logger = Logger.getLogger("recipeLogger");
    logger.info("Logging for the first Time!");
```

```
        logger.warn("A warning to be had");
        logger. severe ("This is an error!");
}
    public static void main (String[] args) {
        Recipe9_8 recipe = new Recipe9_8();
        recipe.start();
    }
```

The following output is defined in the `logging.properties` file.

```
dic 02, 2021 10:27:38 PM org.java17recipes.chapter09.recipe09_08
.Recipe9_8 start
INFO: Logging for the first Time!
dic 02, 2021 10:27:38 PM org.java17recipes.chapter09.recipe09_08
.Recipe9_8 start
WARNING: A warning to be had
dic 02, 2021 10:27:38 PM org.java17recipes.chapter09.recipe09_08
.Recipe9_8 start
SEVERE: This is an error!
```

Use the default properties file of the JDK in the conf folder and copy it in your project folder.

The following is the `logging.properties` file in the main folder of the project.

```
handlers = java.util.logging.FileHandler
recipeLogger.level=INFO
.level=ALL
java.util.logging.FileHandler.formatter=java.util.logging.SimpleFormatter
java.util.logging.FileHandler.pattern=LogApplication%g.log
java.util.logging.FileHandler.limit=50000
java.util.logging.FileHandler.count=4
```

How It Works

In the example, `loadLoggingConfiguration()` function opens a stream to the `logging.properties` file and passes it to `java.util.logging.LogManager()`. Doing so configures the `java.util.logging` framework to use the settings specified in the logging.properties file. Then, within the start method of the solution, the code acquires a logger object named recipeLogger. The example proceeds to log messages through recipeLogger.

Note   The java.util.logging framework is configured by the properties log file.

9-9. Rotating and Purging Logs
Problem

You have started to log information, but the information logged continues growing out of control. You would like to keep only the last 250 KB worth of log entries within your log files.

Solution

Use java.util.logging to configure rolling logs. In this example, a logger named recipeLogger logs many messages. The output produces rolled log files with the most recent logged information in the important Log0.log file.

```
public static void main (String[] args) throws IOException {
    Recipe9_9 recipe = new Recipe9_9();
    recipe.start();
}

private void start() {
        loadLoggingConfiguration();

            Logger logger = LoggerFactory.getLogger("recipeLogger");
            logger.info("Logging for the first Time!");
            logger.warn("A warning to be had");
            logger.severe("This is an error!");
```

```
                    Logger rollingLogger = Logger.getLogger("rollingLogger");
                    for (int i =0;i < 5000;i++) {
                            rollingLogger.info("Logging for an event with :"+i);
                    }
}

    private void loadLoggingConfiguration() {
        FileInputStream ins = null;
        try {
            ins = new FileInputStream(new File("logging.properties"));
            LogManager.getLogManager().readConfiguration(ins);
        } catch (IOException e) {
            e.printStackTrace();
        }
    }
```

The following is the logging.properties file in the main folder of the project.

```
handlers = java.util.logging.FileHandler

recipeLogger.level=INFO
.level=ALL

java.util.logging.FileHandler.formatter=java.util.logging.SimpleFormatter
java.util.logging.FileHandler.pattern=LogApplication%g.log
java.util.logging.FileHandler.limit=50000
java.util.logging.FileHandler.count=4
```

How It Works

To control the size of log files, configure the java.util.logging framework and specify rolling log files. Choosing the rolling log files option causes the latest information to be kept in LogApplication0.log. Progressively older information is in LogApplication1 .log, LogApplication2.log, and so forth. When LogApplication0.log fills to the limit you specify (50,000 bytes in this example), its name is rotated to LogApplicationLog1 .log, and the other files have their names similarly rotated downward. The number of log files to maintain is determined by the java.util.logging.FileHandler.count property, which is set to 4 in this recipe's example. The FileHandler configuration parameter to distinguish rotated logs is "%g" (a generation number). If it is not specified in the properties file, and the count is greater than 1 (4 in this recipe), the generation number is added to the end of the file name—after a dot.

The `logging.properties` file begins by defining the handlers that the `java.util.logging` framework use. Handlers are objects that take care of logging messages. `FileHandler` is specified in the recipe, which logs messages to files. Next, the logging levels are defined. Within a logging framework, there is the concept of separate `logger` objects. A logger can carry different configurations (for example, different logging levels) and be identified in the log file. The example configures the `recipeLogger`'s level to `info`. In contrast, the root `logger`'s level is ALL (root loggers in the `java.util.logging` framework are denoted by no prefix before the property). On the other side, OFF disables logging.

The next section of the `logging.properties` file defines the `FileHandler` configuration. The formatter indicates how the log information is written to disk. The `simpleFormatter` writes the information as plain text, with a line indicating the date and time, a line with the logging level, and the message to be logged. Following the formatter, the `FileHandler` pattern is defined. This specifies the file name and location of the log files (the %g is replaced by the rolling log number [0 ~ 3]). The `Limit` property defines how many bytes the log can have before rolling over (50,000 bytes ~ 50kb). The count defines the maximum index of log files to keep (in this recipe's case, 4).

9-10. Logging Exceptions

In the previous recipes, you learned how to catch exceptions and log information. This recipe put these two recipes together.

Problem

You want to record exceptions in your log file.

Solution

Configure your application to use SLF4J. Utilize `try/catch` blocks to log exceptions within the error log. In the following example, an SLF4J Logger logs messages from within an exception handler.

```java
    public static void main (String [] args) {
        Recipe9_10 recipe = new Recipe9_10();
        recipe.start();
    }
static Logger rootLogger = Logger.getLogger("");
private void start() {
    loadLoggingConfiguration();
    Thread.setDefaultUncaughtExceptionHandler((Thread t, Throwable e) -> {
        rootLogger.error("Error in thread "+t+" caused by "+e);
    });
    int c = 20/0;
}
private void loadLoggingConfiguration() {
    FileInputStream ins = null;
    try {
        ins = new FileInputStream(new File("logging.properties"));
        LogManager.getLogManager().readConfiguration(ins);
    } catch (IOException e) {
        e.printStackTrace();
    }
}
}
```

How It Works

The example demonstrates how to use UncaughtExceptionHandler to log exceptions
to a logging file. When logging an exception, it is good to include the stack trace
showing where the exception was thrown. In the example, a thread contains
UncaughtExceptionHandler, which utilizes a lambda expression containing a logger.
The logger writes any caught exceptions to a log file.

9-11. Summary

This chapter looked at one of the most important phases in application development,
exception handling. It discussed how to handle single and multiple exceptions and log
those exceptions.

CHAPTER 10

Concurrency

Concurrency is the ability of a program to execute different (or the same) instructions at the same time. A concurrent program can be split up and run on multiple CPUs. By making concurrent programs, you take advantage of today's multicore CPUs. You can even see the benefit on single-core CPUs that are I/O intensive. Concurrency is one of the toughest topics to handle in modern computer programming; understanding concurrency requires the capacity of thinking abstractly, and debugging concurrent problems is like trying to pilot an airplane by dead reckoning. Even so, with modern releases of Java, it has become easier (and more accessible) to write bug-free concurrent code.

This chapter presents the most common need for concurrency tasks—from running a background task to splitting a computation into work units. Throughout the chapter, you find the most up-to-date recipes for accomplishing concurrency in Java.

10-1. Starting a Background Task

Problem

You have a task that needs to run outside of your main thread.

Solution

Create a class implementation that includes the task that needs to be run in a different thread. Implement a `Runnable` functional interface in the task implementation class and start a new thread. In the following example, a counter simulates activity, as a separate task is run in the background.

© Josh Juneau, Luciano Manelli 2022
J. Juneau and L. Manelli, *Java 17 Recipes*, https://doi.org/10.1007/978-1-4842-7963-2_10

```java
public class Recipe10_1 {
    public static void main(String[] args) {
        Recipe10_1 recipe = new Recipe10_1();
        recipe.startProcess();
    }

    private void startProcess() {
        Thread backgroundThread = new Thread(new Runnable() {
            public void run() {
                doSomethingInBackground();
            }
        },"Background Thread");
        System.out.println("Start");
        backgroundThread.start();
        for (int i= 0;i < 10;i++) {
            System.out.println(Thread.currentThread().getName()+": is
            counting "+i);
        }
        System.out.println("Done");
    }

    private void doSomethingInBackground() {
        System.out.println(Thread.currentThread().getName()+
          ": is Running in the background");
    }
}
```

If the code is executed more than once, the output should be different from time to time. The background thread executes separately, so its message is printed differently across each run.

The same code for creating the background thread can be written as follows if you're using lambda expressions.

```java
Thread backgroundThread = new Thread(this::doSomethingInBackground,
"Background Thread");
```

The following is the output.

```
Start
main: is counting 0
main: is counting 1
main: is counting 2
main: is counting 3
main: is counting 4
main: is counting 5
main: is counting 6
main: is counting 7
main: is counting 8
main: is counting 9
Done
Background Thread: is Running in the background
```

How It Works

The Thread class allows executing code in a new thread (path of execution), distinct from the current thread. The Thread constructor requires as a parameter a class that implements the Runnable interface. The Runnable interface requires implementing only one method: public void run(). Hence, it is a functional interface, which facilitates the use of lambda expressions. When the Thread.start() method is invoked, it creates a new thread and invokes the run() method from the Runnable interface.

Within the JVM are two types of threads: User and Daemon. User threads keep executing until their run() method completes, whereas Daemon threads can be terminated if the application needs to exit. An application exits if there are only Daemon threads running in the JVM. When you start to create multithreaded applications, you must be aware of these differences and understand when to use each type of thread.

Usually, Daemon threads have a Runnable interface that doesn't complete; for example, a while (true) loop. This allows these threads to periodically check or perform a certain condition throughout the life of the program and be discarded when the program is finished executing. If you happen to have a program that is not closing and/or exiting when expected, you might want to check the threads that are actively running. To set a thread as a Daemon thread, use thread.setDaemon(true) before calling the thread.start() method.

10-2. Updating (and Iterating) a Map

Problem

You need to update a Map<K,V> object from multiple threads, and you want to make
sure that the update doesn't break the contents of the Map object and that the Map object
is always in a consistent state. You also want to traverse (look at) the content of the Map
object while other threads are updating the Map object.

Solution

Use ConcurrentMap<K,V> to update map entries. The following example creates 1,000
threads. Each thread then tries to modify the map at the same time. The main thread
waits for a second and proceeds to iterate through the map (even when the other threads
are still modifying the map).

```
public class Recipe10_2 {
    Set<Thread> updateThreads = new HashSet<>();
    public static void main(String[] args) {
        Recipe10_2 recipe = new Recipe10_2();
        recipe.startProcess();
    }
        private void startProcess() {
            ConcurrentMap<Integer,String> concurrentMap = new
            ConcurrentHashMap<>();
            for (int i =0;i < 1000;i++) {
                startUpdateThread(i, concurrentMap);
            }
            try {
                Thread.sleep(1000);
            } catch (InterruptedException e) {
                e.printStackTrace();
            }
            concurrentMap.entrySet().stream().forEach((entry) -> {
                System.out.println("Key :"+entry.getKey()+"
                Value:"+entry.getValue());
            });
```

```
        updateThreads.stream().forEach((thread) -> {
            thread.interrupt();
        });
    }

    Random random = new Random();
    private void startUpdateThread(int i, final ConcurrentMap<Integer,
    String> concurrentMap) {
        Thread thread = new Thread(() -> {
            while (!Thread.interrupted()) {
                int randomInt = random.nextInt(20);
                concurrentMap.put(randomInt,
                UUID.randomUUID().toString());
            }
        });
        thread.setName("Update Thread "+i);
        updateThreads.add(thread);
        thread.start();
    }
}
```

The following is the output.

```
Key :0 Value:d4476b69-a28f-44d6-b1ce-f47128ed5a59
Key :1 Value:1f47b9ee-5b01-4ea3-ac2a-b1a2231187ad
Key :2 Value:95322e14-73a5-449e-87e2-d7d0dafdbabd
...
```

How It Works

For performing work on a hash table in a concurrent manner, ConcurrentHashMap allows multiple threads to modify the hash table concurrently and safely. ConcurrentHashMap is a hash table supporting full concurrency for retrievals and adjustable expected concurrency for updates. In the example, 1,000 threads make modifications to the map over a short period of time. The ConcurrentHashMap iterator, as well as streams that are generated on a ConcurrentHashMap, allows safe iteration over its contents. When using the ConcurrentMap's iterator, you do not have to worry about locking the contents of the ConcurrentMap while iterating over it.

10-3. Inserting a Key into a Map Only If the Key Is Not Already Present

Problem

A map within your application is continuously updated, and you need to put a key/value pair into it if the key does not exist. Therefore, you need to check for the key's presence, and you need assurance that some other thread doesn't insert the same key in the meantime.

Solution

Using the ConcurrentMap.putIfAbsent() method, you can determine whether the map was modified atomically. For example, the following code uses this method to check and insert in a single step, thus avoiding the concurrency problem.

```java
public class Recipe10_3 {

    Set<Thread> updateThreads = new HashSet<>();
    Random random = new Random();

    public static void main(String[] args) {
        Recipe10_3 recipe = new Recipe10_3();
        recipe.startProcess();
    }

    private void startProcess() {
        ConcurrentMap<Integer, String> concurrentMap = new
        ConcurrentHashMap<>();
        for (int i = 0; i < 100; i++) {
            startUpdateThread(i, concurrentMap);
        }

        try {
            Thread.sleep(1000);
        } catch (InterruptedException e) {
            e.printStackTrace();
        }
```

```
        concurrentMap.entrySet().stream().forEach((entry) -> {
            System.out.println("Key :" + entry.getKey() + " Value:" +
            entry.getValue());
        });
    }

    private void startUpdateThread(final int i, final
ConcurrentMap<Integer, String> concurrentMap) {
        Thread thread = new Thread(() -> {
            int randomInt = random.nextInt(20);
            String previousEntry = concurrentMap.putIfAbsent(randomInt,
            "Thread # " + i + " has made it!");
            if (previousEntry != null) {
                System.out.println("Thread # " + i + " tried to update
                it but guess what, we're too late!");
            } else {
                System.out.println("Thread # " + i + " has made it!");
            }
        });
        thread.start();
    }
}
```

The following is the output.

```
Thread # 1 has made it!
Thread # 0 has made it!
Thread # 3 has made it!
Thread # 2 has made it!
Thread # 4 has made it!
Thread # 5 has made it!
Thread # 9 has made it!
Thread # 8 tried to update it but guess what, we're too late!
Thread # 10 tried to update it but guess what, we're too late!
Thread # 7 has made it!
Thread # 12 has made it!
```

```
Thread # 6 tried to update it but guess what, we're too late!
Thread # 13 tried to update it but guess what, we're too late!
Thread # 11 tried to update it but guess what, we're too late!
```

When running the program, some of the entries will be successfully inserted, while others will not because another thread has already inserted the key. Note that in the example, startUpdateThread() accepts a final int i argument. Marking a method argument as final ensures that the method cannot change the value of the i variable. If the value of i changes inside the method, it is not visible from outside the method.

How It Works

Concurrently updating a map is difficult because it involves two operations: a *check-then-act* type of operation. First, the map must be checked to see whether an entry already exists in it. If the entry doesn't exist, you can put the key and the value into the map. On the other hand, if the key exists, the value for the key is retrieved. To do so, we use the ConcurrentMap's putIfAbsent atomic operation. This ensures that the key was present, so the value is not overwritten, or the key was not present, so the value is set. For the JDK implementations of ConcurrentMap, the putIfAbsent() method returns null if there was no value for the key or returns the current value if the key has a value. By asserting that the putIfAbsent() method returns null, you are assured that the operation was successful and that a new entry in the map has been created.

There are cases when putIfAbsent() might not be efficient to execute. For example, if the result is a large database query, executing the database query all the time and then invoking putIfAbsent() will not be efficient. In this kind of scenario, you could first call the map's containsKey() method to ensure that the key is not present. If it's not present, call the putIfAbsent() with the expensive database query. There might be a chance that the putIfAbsent() didn't put the entry, but this type of check reduces the number of potentially expensive value creation.

Note the following code snippet.

```
keyPresent = concurrentMap.containsKey(randomInt);
        if (!keyPresent) {
            concurrentMap.putIfAbsent(randomInt, "Thread # " + i + " has
            made it!");
        }
```

In this code, the first operation is to check whether the key is already in the map. If it is, it doesn't execute the putIfAbsent() operation. If the key is not present, we can execute the putIfAbsent() operation.

If you are accessing the map's values from different threads, you should make sure that the values are thread-safe. This is most evident when using collections as values because they could be accessed from different threads. Ensuring that the main map is thread-safe prevent concurrent modifications to the map. However, once you gain access to the map's values, you must exercise good concurrency practices around the map's values.

10-4. Iterating Through a Changing Collection

Problem

You need to iterate over each element in a collection. However, other threads are constantly updating the collection.

Solution 1

By using CopyOnWriteArrayList<E>, you can safely iterate through the collection without worrying about concurrency. In the following solution, the startUpdatingThread() method creates a new thread, which actively changes the list passed to it. While startUpdatingThread() modifies the list, it is concurrently iterated using the stream forEach() function.

```
public class Recipe10_4 {
    public static void main(String[] args) {
        Recipe10_4 recipe = new Recipe10_4();
        recipe.start();
    }
    private void start() {
        System.out.println("Using CopyOnWrite");
        copyOnWriteSolution();
    }
```

```java
    private void stopUpdatingThread() {
        updatingThread.interrupt();
    }
    Random random = new Random();

    Thread updatingThread ;
    private void startUpdatingThread(final List<String> list) {
        updatingThread = new Thread(() -> {
            long counter =0;
            while (!Thread.interrupted()) {
                int size = list.size();
                if (random.nextBoolean()) {
                    if (size > 1) {
                        list.remove(random.nextInt(size - 1));
                    }
                } else {
                    if (size < 20) {
                        list.add("Random string "+counter);
                    }
                }
                counter ++;
            }
        });
        updatingThread.start();

        // let it warm up for a second
        try {
            Thread.sleep(100);
        } catch (InterruptedException e) {
            e.printStackTrace();
        }

    }
private void copyOnWriteSolution() {
    CopyOnWriteArrayList<String> list = new CopyOnWriteArrayList<String>();
    startUpdatingThread(list);
    list.stream().forEach((element) -> {
```

```
        System.out.println("Element :" + element);
    });
    stopUpdatingThread();
}

}
```

Solution 2

Using a synchronizedList() method allows you to atomically change the collection. It also provides a way to synchronize safely on the list while iterating through it (which is done in the stream). The following is an example.

```
public class Recipe10_4 {
    public static void main(String[] args) {
        Recipe10_4 recipe = new Recipe10_4();
        recipe.start();
    }
    private void start() {
        System.out.println("Using SynchronizedList");
        synchronizedListSolution();
    }
    private void stopUpdatingThread() {
        updatingThread.interrupt();
    }
    Random random = new Random();

    Thread updatingThread ;
    private void startUpdatingThread(final List<String> list) {
        updatingThread = new Thread(() -> {
            long counter =0;
            while (!Thread.interrupted()) {
                int size = list.size();
                if (random.nextBoolean()) {
                    if (size > 1) {
                        list.remove(random.nextInt(size - 1));
                    }
```

```
                } else {
                    if (size < 20) {
                        list.add("Random string "+counter);
                    }
                }
                counter ++;
            }
        });
        updatingThread.start();

        // let it warm up for a second
        try {
            Thread.sleep(100);
        } catch (InterruptedException e) {
            e.printStackTrace();
        }
    }
private void synchronizedListSolution() {
    final List<String> list = Collections.synchronizedList(new
    ArrayList<String>());
    startUpdatingThread(list);
    synchronized (list) {
        list.stream().forEach((element) -> {
            System.out.println("Element :" + element);
        });
    }
    stopUpdatingThread();
}
}
```

The following is the output.

```
Using CopyOnWrite
Element :Random string 731774
Using SynchronizedList
Element :Random string 1100164
Element :Random string 1100177
Element :Random string 1100180
```

How It Works

Java comes with many concurrent collection options. Which collection to use depends on how the read operations compare with the write operations within the context of your application. If writing occurs far and in-between compared with reads, using a CopyOnWriteArrayList<E> instance is most efficient because it doesn't *block* (stop) other threads from reading the list and is thread-safe to iterate over (no ConcurrentModificationException is thrown when iterating through it). If there are the same number of writes and reads, the SynchronizedList method from the Collections class is the preferred choice.

In solution 1, the CopyOnWriteArrayList<E> is being updated while you traverse the list. Because the recipe uses the CopyOnWriteArrayList instance, there is no need to worry about thread safety when iterating through the collection (as done in this recipe by using the stream). It is good to note that CopyOnWriteArrayList<E> offers a snapshot in time when iterating through it. If another thread modifies the list as you're iterating through it, the modified list is likely not visible when iterating.

Note   Locking properly depends on the type of collection being used. Any collections returned as a result of using Collections.synchronized can be locked via the collection itself (synchronized (collectionInstance)). However, some more efficient (newer) concurrent collections such as the ConcurrentMap cannot be used in this fashion because their internal implementations don't lock in the object itself.

Solution 2 creates a synchronized list, which is created by using the Collections helper class. The Collection.synchronizedList() method wraps a List object (it can be ArrayList<E>, LinkedList<E>, or another List<E> implementation) into a list that synchronizes the access to the list operations. Each time you need to iterate over a list (either by using the stream, a for loop, or an iterator), you must be aware of the concurrency implications for that list's iterator. CopyOnWriteArrayList<E> is safe to iterate over (as specified in the JavaDoc). But, the iterator of the SynchronizedList method from the Collections class must be synchronized manually (also specified in the JavaDoc Collections.synchronizedList iterator). In the solution, the list can safely be iterated while inside the synchronized(list) block. When synchronizing on the list, no read/updates/other iterations can occur until the synchronized(list) block is completed.

10-5. Coordinating Different Collections

Problem

You need to modify different but related collections at the same time, and you want to ensure that no other threads can see these modifications until they have been completed.

Solution 1

By synchronizing on the principal collection, you can guarantee that collection can be updated simultaneously. In the following example, the fulfillOrder method needs to check the inventory of the order to be fulfilled. If there is enough inventory to fulfill the order, it needs to add the order to the customerOrders list. The fulfillOrder() method synchronizes on the inventoryMap map and modifies both the inventoryMap and the customerOrders list before finishing the synchronized block.

```
Set<Thread> orderingThreads = new HashSet<>();
public static void main(String[] args) throws InterruptedException {
    Recipe10_5_1 recipe = new Recipe10_5_1();
    recipe.start();
}

final Map<String,Integer> inventoryMap = new LinkedHashMap<>();
List<CustomerOrder> customerOrders = new ArrayList<>();
Random random = new Random();
private void start() throws InterruptedException {
    loadLoggingConfiguration();
    // let's populate our inventory with items.
    // at most, we have 20 books
    for (int i =0;i < 100;i++) {
        inventoryMap.put("Apress Book #"+i,100);
    }

    // now, let's create ordering threads.
    for (int i= 0;i < 20;i++) {
        createOrderingThread();
    }
```

```
        //wait a little
        Thread.sleep(100);

        // Check on inventory right now
        checkInventoryLevels();

        // Wait little longer
        Thread.sleep(100);

        orderingThreads.stream().forEach((thread) -> {
            thread.interrupt();
        });

        Thread.sleep(1000);

        // Check inventory levels again
        checkInventoryLevels();
        // Print the orders.
        displayOrders();

    }

    Logger logger = Logger.getLogger("recipeLogger");

private void createOrderingThread() {
        Thread orderingThread = new Thread(() -> {
            while (!Thread.interrupted()) {
                createRandomOrder();
            }
        });
        orderingThread.start();
        orderingThreads.add(orderingThread);

    }

    private void createRandomOrder() {
        String itemOrdered = "Apress Book #"+random.nextInt(100);
        int quantityOrdered = random.nextInt(2)+1;
        String customerName = "Customer :"+UUID.randomUUID().toString();
        fulfillOrder(itemOrdered, quantityOrdered, customerName);
    }
```

```
class CustomerOrder {
    String itemOrdered;
    int quantityOrdered;
    String customerName;

    CustomerOrder(String itemOrdered, int quantityOrdered, String
    customerName) {
        this.itemOrdered = itemOrdered;
        this.quantityOrdered = quantityOrdered;
        this.customerName = customerName;
    }

    public String getItemOrdered() {
        return itemOrdered;
    }

    public int getQuantityOrdered() {
        return quantityOrdered;
    }

    public String getCustomerName() {
        return customerName;
    }
}
    private boolean fulfillOrder(String itemOrdered, int quantityOrdered,
    String customerName) {
        synchronized (inventoryMap) {
            int currentInventory  = 0;
            if (inventoryMap != null) {
                currentInventory = inventoryMap.get(itemOrdered);
            }
            if (currentInventory < quantityOrdered) {
                System.out.println("Couldn't fulfill order for
                "+customerName+" not enough "+itemOrdered+"
                ("+quantityOrdered+")");
                return false; // sorry, we sold out
            }
```

```
            inventoryMap.put(itemOrdered,currentInventory - quantityOrdered);
            CustomerOrder order = new CustomerOrder(itemOrdered,
            quantityOrdered, customerName);
            customerOrders.add(order);
            System.out.println("Order fulfilled for "+customerName+" of
            "+itemOrdered+" ("+quantityOrdered+")");
            return true;
        }
    }

    private void checkInventoryLevels() {
        synchronized (inventoryMap) {
            System.out.println("-------------------------------------");
            inventoryMap.entrySet().stream().forEach((inventoryEntry) -> {
                System.out.println("Inventory Level :"+inventoryEntry
                .getKey()+" "+inventoryEntry.getValue());
            });
            System.out.println("-------------------------------------");
        }
    }

    private void displayOrders() {
        synchronized (inventoryMap) {
            customerOrders.stream().forEach((order) -> {
                System.out.println(order.getQuantityOrdered()+"
                "+order.getItemOrdered()+" for "+order.getCustomerName());
            });
        }
    }
```

The output is similar to:

```
-----------------------------------
Inventory Level :Apress Book #0 100
Inventory Level :Apress Book #1 100
Inventory Level :Apress Book #2 100
Inventory Level :Apress Book #3 100
Inventory Level :Apress Book #4 100
```

```
Inventory Level :Apress Book #5 100
Inventory Level :Apress Book #6 100
Inventory Level :Apress Book #7 100
Inventory Level :Apress Book #8 100
Inventory Level :Apress Book #9 100
Inventory Level :Apress Book #10 100
Inventory Level :Apress Book #11 100
Inventory Level :Apress Book #12 100
Inventory Level :Apress Book #13 100
Inventory Level :Apress Book #14 100
Inventory Level :Apress Book #15 100
...

--------------------------------------
Order fulfilled for Customer :70a697d1-08d2-4ad7-b00c-17558930e0ab of
Apress Book #64 (2)
Order fulfilled for Customer :4db86e58-a895-4992-9090-84a52f9314f6 of
Apress Book #44 (2)
Order fulfilled for Customer :cc278024-0630-424f-99bb-091d4bb73d25 of
Apress Book #20 (1)
Order fulfilled for Customer :f43f9edd-17f3-403c-b3b6-b91521b9f970 of
Apress Book #24 (1)
Order fulfilled for Customer :a1c94246-3671-4373-bbbb-968d32fca100 of
Apress Book #53 (2)
Order fulfilled for Customer :110382cf-79ff-4042-9ad4-bb4316764281 of
Apress Book #31 (2)
Order fulfilled for Customer :e3255a74-dfdc-4ef4-b388-02745249c0a9 of
Apress Book #38 (1)
Order fulfilled for Customer :fd2fa1fd-b9b8-4bca-92a8-6023a1fbde3e of
Apress Book #40 (2)
Order fulfilled for Customer :5cead5b3-70bf-4f98-82c4-5ee34e90f02d of
Apress Book #53 (2)
Order fulfilled for Customer :c0e0b2d3-4d58-41ef-9127-8e3d5665d976 of
Apress Book #38 (1)
Order fulfilled for Customer :38f5ea73-d22b-4714-a319-7599d30a1b9a of
Apress Book #86 (1)
...
```

Solution 2

Using a reentrant lock, you can prevent multiple threads from accessing the same critical area of the code. In this solution, the inventoryLock is acquired by calling inventoryLock.lock(). Any other thread that tries to acquire the inventoryLock lock must wait until the inventoryLock lock is released. At the end of the fulfillOrder() method (in the finally block), the inventoryLock is released by calling the inventoryLock.unlock() method.

```java
Lock inventoryLock = new ReentrantLock();
private boolean fulfillOrder(String itemOrdered, int quantityOrdered,
String customerName) {
    try {
        inventoryLock.lock();
        int currentInventory = inventoryMap.get(itemOrdered);
        if (currentInventory < quantityOrdered) {
            System.out.println("Couldn't fulfill order for " +
            customerName +
                " not enough " + itemOrdered + " (" +
                quantityOrdered + ")");
            return false; // sorry, we sold out
        }
        inventoryMap.put(itemOrdered, currentInventory - quantityOrdered);
        CustomerOrder order = new CustomerOrder(itemOrdered,
        quantityOrdered, customerName);
        customerOrders.add(order);
        System.out.println("Order fulfilled for " + customerName + " of " +
        itemOrdered + " (" + quantityOrdered + ")");
        return true;
    } finally {
        inventoryLock.unlock();
    }
}
```

```
    private void checkInventoryLevels() {
        try {
            inventoryLock.lock();
            System.out.println("-------------------------------------");
            inventoryMap.entrySet().stream().forEach((inventoryEntry) -> {
                System.out.println("Inventory Level :" + inventoryEntry
                    .getKey() + " " + inventoryEntry.getValue());
            });
            System.out.println("-----------------------------------");
        } finally {
            inventoryLock.unlock();
        }
    }
    private void displayOrders() {
        try {
            inventoryLock.lock();
            customerOrders.stream().forEach((order) -> {
                System.out.println(order.getQuantityOrdered() + " " +
                    order.getItemOrdered() + " for " + order.getCustomerName());
            });
        } finally {
            inventoryLock.unlock();
        }
    }
```

How It Works

If you have different structures that are required to be modified at the same time, you need to make sure that these structures are updated atomically. An *atomic* operation refers to a set of instructions that can be executed as a whole or none at all. An atomic operation is visible to the rest of the program only when complete.

In solution 1 (atomically modifying both the inventoryMap map and the customerOrders list), you pick a "principal" collection on which you lock (inventoryMap). Locking on the principal collection guarantees that if another thread tries to lock on the same principal collection, it must wait until the currently executing thread releases the lock on the collection.

Solution 2 is more explicit, offering an independent lock that coordinates the atomic operations instead of picking a principal collection. *Locking* refers to the ability of the JVM to restrict certain code paths to be executed by only one thread. Threads try to obtain the lock (locks are provided, for example, by a ReentrantLock instance, as shown in the example), and the lock can be given to only one thread at a time. If other threads were trying to acquire the same lock, they are suspended (WAIT) until the lock becomes available. The lock becomes available when the thread that currently holds the lock releases it. When a lock is released, it can then be acquired by one (and only one) of the threads waiting for that lock.

Locks are not "fair" by default. In other words, the order of the threads that requested the lock is not kept; this allows for very fast locking/unlocking implementation in the JVM, and in most situations, it is generally okay to use unfair locks. On a very highly contended lock, if there is a requirement to evenly distribute the lock (make it fair), you do so by setting the setFair property on the lock.

In solution 2, calling the inventoryLock.lock() method, either acquires the lock and continues or suspends execution (WAIT) until the lock can be acquired. Once the lock is acquired, no other thread can execute within the locked block. At the end of the block, the lock is released by calling inventoryLock.unlock().

When working with Lock objects (ReentrantLock, ReadLock, and WriteLock), it is common practice to surround the use of these Lock objects by a try/finally clause. After opening the try block, the first instruction would be to call the lock.lock() method. This guarantees that the first instruction executed is the acquisition of the lock. The release of the lock (by calling lock.unlock()) is done in the matching finally block. In the event of RuntimeException occurring while you have acquired the lock, unlocking within the finally clause assures that one doesn't "keep" the lock and prevent other threads from acquiring it.

The use of the ReentrantLock object offers additional features that the synchronized statement doesn't offer. For example, ReentrantLock has the tryLock() function, which attempts to get the lock only if no other threads have it (the method doesn't make the invoking thread wait). If another thread holds the lock, the method returns false but continues executing. It is better to use the synchronized keyword for synchronization and use ReentrantLock only when its features are needed.

Tip   While this is only a recipe book and proper threading techniques span their own volumes, it is important to raise awareness of deadlocks. *Deadlocks* occur when two locks are involved (acquired in reverse order within another thread). The simplest way to avoid a deadlock is to avoid letting the lock "escape." This means that the lock, when acquired, should not execute code calling on other methods that could acquire a different lock. If that's not possible, release the lock before calling such a method.

Be careful: any operation that refers to one or both collections needs to be protected by the same lock. Operations that depend on the result of one collection to query the second collection need to be executed atomically; they need to be done as a unit in which neither collection can change until the operation is completed.

10-6. Splitting Work into Separate Threads
Problem

You have work that can be split into separate threads and want to maximize available CPU resources.

Solution

Use a ThreadpoolExecutor instance, which allows you to break the tasks into discrete units. In the following example, a BlockingQueue<E> interface is created, including a Runnable object. It then is passed to the ThreadPoolExecutor instance, which is then initialized and started by calling the prestartAllCoreThreads() method. Next, perform an orderly shutdown in which all previously submitted tasks are executed by calling the shutdown() method, followed by the awaitTermination() method.

```
private void start() throws InterruptedException {
    BlockingQueue<Runnable> queue = new LinkedBlockingQueue<>();
    for (int i =0;i < 10;i++) {
        final int localI = i;
        queue.add((Runnable) () -> {
```

```
            doExpensiveOperation(localI);
        });
    }
    ThreadPoolExecutor executor = new ThreadPoolExecutor(10,10,1000,
            TimeUnit.MILLISECONDS, queue);
    executor.prestartAllCoreThreads();
    executor.shutdown();
    executor.awaitTermination(100000,TimeUnit.SECONDS);
    System.out.println("Look ma! all operations were completed");
}

    public static void main (String [] args) throws InterruptedException {
        Recipe10_6 recipe = new Recipe10_6();
        recipe.start();
    }
    private void doExpensiveOperation(int index) {
        System.out.println("Starting expensive operation "+index);
        try {
            Thread.sleep(index * 1000);
        } catch (InterruptedException e) {
            e.printStackTrace();
        }
        System.out.println("Ending   expensive operation " + index);
    }
```

The following is the output.

```
Starting expensive operation 1
Starting expensive operation 3
Starting expensive operation 2
Starting expensive operation 0
Starting expensive operation 4
Ending   expensive operation 0
Starting expensive operation 6
Starting expensive operation 5
Starting expensive operation 7
Starting expensive operation 8
```

```
Starting expensive operation 9
Ending   expensive operation 1
Ending   expensive operation 2
Ending   expensive operation 3
Ending   expensive operation 4
Ending   expensive operation 5
Ending   expensive operation 6
Ending   expensive operation 7
Ending   expensive operation 8
Ending   expensive operation 9
Look ma! all operations were completed
```

How It Works

ThreadPoolExecutor consists of two components: Queue<E>, the tasks to be executed, and Executor, which tells how to execute the tasks. Queue<E> is filled with Runnable objects, on which the run() method contains the code to be executed.

The Queue<E> component used by ThreadPoolExecutor is an implementer of the BlockingQueue<E> interface, which denotes a queue in which the consumers of the queue wait (be suspended) if there are no elements within Queue<E>. This is necessary for ThreadPoolExecutor to work efficiently.

The first step is to fill Queue<E> with the tasks that need to be executed in parallel. This is done by calling Queue<E>'s add() method and passing a class that implements the Runnable interface. Once that's done, the executor is initialized.

After ThreadPoolExecutor is initialized, you call the prestartAllCoreThreads() method, which "warms up" ThreadPoolExecutor by creating the number of threads specified in CorePoolSize and actively starts consuming tasks from Queue<E> if it is not empty.

Call the shutdown() method from ThreadPoolExecutor to wait for all the tasks to complete. By calling this method, ThreadPoolExecutor is instructed to accept no new events from the queue (previously submitted events finish processing). This is the first step in the orderly termination of ThreadPoolExecutor. Call the awaitTermination() method to wait for all the tasks in ThreadPoolExecutor to be done. This method forces the main thread to wait until all Runnable objects in ThreadPoolExecutor's queue have completed executing. After all Runnable objects have been executed, the main thread wakes up and continues.

10-7. Coordinating Threads

Problem

Your application requires that two or more threads be coordinated to work in unison.

Solution 1

With wait/notify for thread synchronization, threads can be coordinated. In this solution, the main thread waits for the objectToSync object until the database-loading thread is finished executing. Once the database-loading thread is finished, it notifies the objectToSync that whoever is waiting on it can continue executing. The same process occurs when loading the orders into our system. The main thread waits on objectToSync until the orders-loading thread notifies objectToSync to continue by calling the objectToSync.notify() method. After ensuring that both the inventory and the orders are loaded, the main thread executes the processOrder() method to process all orders.

```
public static void main(String[] args) {
    Recipe10_7_1 recipe = new Recipe10_7_1();
    recipe.start();
}
private final Object objectToSync = new Object();
private void start() {
    loadItems();
    Thread inventoryThread = new Thread(() -> {
        System.out.println("Loading Inventory from Database...");
        loadInventory();
        synchronized (objectToSync) {
            objectToSync.notify();
        }
    });
    synchronized (objectToSync) {
        inventoryThread.start();
        try {
            objectToSync.wait();
        } catch (InterruptedException e) {
```

```
            e.printStackTrace();
        }
    }

    Thread ordersThread = new Thread(() -> {

        System.out.println("Loading Orders from XML Web service...");
        loadOrders();
        synchronized (objectToSync) {
            objectToSync.notify();

        }
    });
    synchronized (objectToSync) {
        ordersThread.start();
        try {
            objectToSync.wait();
        } catch (InterruptedException e) {
            e.printStackTrace();
        }
    }
    processOrders();
}

    private void processOrders() {
        orderList.stream().forEach((order) -> {
            boolean fulfillable = canFulfill(order);
            if (fulfillable) {
                doFulfill (order);
                System.out.println("Order # " + String.valueOf(order
                .getOrderId()) + " has been fulfilled");
            } else {
                System.out.println("Order # "+String.valueOf(order
                .getOrderId())+" CANNOT be fulfilled");
            }
        });
    }
```

The following is the output.

```
Loading Inventory from Database...
Loading Orders from XML Web service...
Order # 0 has been fulfilled
Order # 1 has been fulfilled
Order # 2 has been fulfilled
Order # 3 has been fulfilled
Order # 4 has been fulfilled
Order # 5 CANNOT be fulfilled
Order # 6 has been fulfilled
Order # 7 has been fulfilled
Order # 8 has been fulfilled
Order # 9 has been fulfilled
Order # 10 has been fulfilled
Order # 11 has been fulfilled
Order # 12 has been fulfilled
Order # 13 CANNOT be fulfilled
Order # 14 has been fulfilled
Order # 15 CANNOT be fulfilled
Order # 16 CANNOT be fulfilled
Order # 17 has been fulfilled
Order # 18 has been fulfilled
Order # 19 has been fulfilled
Order # 20 has been fulfilled
Order # 21 has been fulfilled
Order # 22 has been fulfilled
...
```

Solution 2

You can control when the main thread continues using a CountDownLatch object. In
the following code, a CountDownLatch with an initial value of 2 is created; then, the two
threads for loading the inventory and loading the order information are created and

started. As each of the two threads finishes executing, they call the CountDownLatch's countDown() method, which decrements the latch's value by one. The main thread waits until the CountDownLatch reaches 0, at which point it resumes execution.

```
public static void main(String[] args) {
    Recipe10_7_2 recipe = new Recipe10_7_2();
    recipe.start();
}
CountDownLatch latch = new CountDownLatch(2);
private void start() {
    loadItems();
    Thread inventoryThread = new Thread(() -> {
        System.out.println("Loading Inventory from Database...");
        loadInventory();
        latch.countDown();
    });
    inventoryThread.start();
    Thread ordersThread = new Thread(() -> {
        System.out.println("Loading Orders from XML Web service...");
        loadOrders();
        latch.countDown();
    });
    ordersThread.start();
    try {
        latch.await();
    } catch (InterruptedException e) {
        e.printStackTrace();
    }
    processOrders();
}
```

The following is the output.

```
Loading Inventory from Database...
Loading Orders from XML Web service...
Order # 0 has been fulfilled
Order # 1 has been fulfilled
```

Order # 2 has been fulfilled
Order # 3 has been fulfilled
Order # 4 has been fulfilled
Order # 5 has been fulfilled
Order # 6 has been fulfilled
Order # 7 has been fulfilled
Order # 8 has been fulfilled
Order # 9 has been fulfilled
Order # 10 has been fulfilled
Order # 11 has been fulfilled
Order # 12 has been fulfilled
Order # 13 has been fulfilled
...

Solution 3

Thread.join() allows you to wait for a thread to finish executing. The following example has a thread for loading the inventory and another thread for loading the orders. Once each thread is started, a call to inventoryThread.join() make the main thread wait for the inventoryThread to finish executing before continuing.

```java
public static void main(String[] args) {
    Recipe10_7_3 recipe = new Recipe10_7_3();
    recipe.start();
}
private void start() {
    loadItems();
    Thread inventoryThread = new Thread(() -> {
        System.out.println("Loading Inventory from Database...");
        loadInventory();
    });
    inventoryThread.start();
    try {
        inventoryThread.join();
    } catch (InterruptedException e) {
```

```
        e.printStackTrace();
    }
    Thread ordersThread = new Thread(() -> {
        System.out.println("Loading Orders from XML Web service...");
        loadOrders();
    });
    ordersThread.start();
    try {
        ordersThread.join();
    } catch (InterruptedException e) {
        e.printStackTrace();
    }
    processOrders();
}
```

The following is the output.

```
Loading Inventory from Database...
Loading Orders from XML Web service...
Order # 0 has been fulfilled
Order # 1 has been fulfilled
Order # 2 has been fulfilled
Order # 3 has been fulfilled
Order # 4 has been fulfilled
Order # 5 has been fulfilled
Order # 6 has been fulfilled
Order # 7 has been fulfilled
Order # 8 has been fulfilled
Order # 9 has been fulfilled
Order # 10 has been fulfilled
Order # 11 has been fulfilled
Order # 12 has been fulfilled
Order # 13 has been fulfilled
...
```

How It Works

There are many ways of coordinating threads in Java, and these coordination efforts rely on making a thread wait. When a thread waits, it suspends execution (it doesn't continue to the next instruction and is removed from the JVM's thread scheduler). If a thread is waiting, it can be awakened by notifying it. Within Java's concurrency lingo, the word *notify* implies that a thread resumes execution (the JVM adds the thread to the thread scheduler). So, in the natural course of thread coordination, the most common sequence of events is the main thread waiting and a secondary thread then notifying the main thread to continue (or wake up). Even so, there is the possibility of a waiting thread being interrupted by some other event. When a thread is interrupted, it doesn't continue to the next instruction. Instead, it throws InterruptedException, which is a way of signaling that even though the thread was waiting for something to happen, some other event happened that requires the thread's attention. This is better illustrated in the following example.

```
BlockingQueue queue = new LinkedBlockingQueue<>();
while (true) {
    synchronized (this) {
        Object itemToProcess = queue.take();
        processItem (itemToProcess);
    }
}
```

If you look at the previous code, the thread that executes it would never terminate because it loops forever and waits for an item to be processed. If there are no items in Queue<E>, the main thread waits until something is added to Queue<E> from another thread. You couldn't graciously shut down the previous code (especially if the thread running the loop is not a Daemon thread).

```
BlockingQueue<Object> queue = new LinkedBlockingQueue<>();
while (true) {
    synchronized (this) {
        Object itemToProcess = null;
        try {
            itemToProcess = queue.take();
```

381

```
        } catch (InterruptedException e) {
            return;
        }
        processItem (itemToProcess);
    }
}
```

The new code now can "escape" the infinite loop. You can call thread.interrupt() from another thread, which throws the InterruptedException that is then caught by the main thread's catch clause. The infinite loop can be exited within this clause.

InterruptedExceptions are a way of sending extra information to waiting (or sleeping) threads so that they may handle a different scenario (for example, an orderly program shutdown). For this reason, every operation that changes the state of the thread to sleep/wait must be surrounded by a try/catch block that can catch the InterruptedException. This is one of the cases in which the exception (InterruptedException) is not an error but more of a way of signaling between threads that something has occurred that requires attention.

Solution 1 demonstrates the most common (oldest) form of coordination. The solution requires making a thread wait and suspending execution until the thread gets notified (or awakened) by another thread.

For solution 1 to work, the originating thread needs to acquire a lock. This lock will then be the "phone number" on which another thread can notify the originating thread to wake up. After the originating thread acquires the lock (phone number), it proceeds to wait. As soon as the wait() method is called, the lock is released, allowing other threads to acquire the same lock. The secondary thread then proceeds to acquire the lock (the phone number) and notifies (which would be like dialing a wake-up call) the originating thread. After the notification, the originating thread resumes execution.

In the solution 1 code, the lock is a dummy object identified as objectToSync. In practice, the object on which locks are waiting and notifying could be any valid instance object in Java; for example, we could have used the this reference to make the main thread wait.

The main advantage of using this technique is the explicitness of controlling whom to wait and when to notify (and the ability to notify all threads waiting on the same object; see the following tip).

> **Tip**   Multiple threads can wait on the same lock (same phone number to be awakened). When a secondary thread calls the `notify()` method, it wakes up one of the "waiting" threads (there is no fairness about which is awakened). Sometimes you need to notify all the threads; you can call the `notifyAll()` method instead of the `notify()` method. This is mostly used when preparing many threads to take some work, but the work is not yet finished setting up.

Solution 2 uses a more modern approach to notification, as it involves a `CountDownLatch`. When setting up, specify the number of "counts" the latch will have. The main thread then waits (stop execution) by calling the `CountDownLatch`'s `await()` method until the latch counts down to 0. When the latch reaches 0, the main thread wakes up and continues execution. As the worker thread completes, call the `latch.countdown()` method, which decrements the latch's current count value. If the latch's current value reaches 0, the main thread waiting on the `CountDownLatch` wakes up and continues execution.

The main advantage of using `CountDownLatches` is that it is possible to spawn multiple tasks simultaneously and wait for all of them to complete. (In the solution example, we didn't need to wait until one or the other threads were completed before continuing; they all were started, and when the latch was 0, the main thread continued.)

Solution 3 lets you access to the thread you want to wait on. For the main thread, it's just a matter of calling the secondary thread's `join()` method. Then the main thread waits (stop executing) until the secondary thread completes.

The advantage of this method is that it doesn't require the secondary threads to know any synchronization mechanism. As long as the secondary thread terminates execution, the main thread can wait on them.

10-8. Creating Thread-Safe Objects

Problem

You need to create a thread-safe object that is accessed from multiple threads.

Solution 1

Use synchronized getters and setters and protect critical regions that change state.
In the following example, an object is created with getters and setters that are
synchronized for each internal variable. The critical regions are protected by using the
synchronized(this) lock.

```java
public class CustomerOrder {
    private String itemOrdered;
    private int quantityOrdered;
    private String customerName;
    public CustomerOrder() {
    }

    public double calculateOrderTotal (double price) {
        synchronized (this) {
            return getQuantityOrdered()*price;
        }
    }

    public synchronized String getItemOrdered() {
        return itemOrdered;
    }

    public synchronized int getQuantityOrdered() {
        return quantityOrdered;
    }

    public synchronized String getCustomerName() {
        return customerName;
    }

    public synchronized void setItemOrdered(String itemOrdered) {
        this.itemOrdered = itemOrdered;
    }

    public synchronized void setQuantityOrdered(int quantityOrdered) {
        this.quantityOrdered = quantityOrdered;
    }
```

```
public synchronized void setCustomerName(String customerName) {
    this.customerName = customerName;
}
}
```

Solution 2

Create an immutable object (an object that, once created, doesn't change its internal state). In the following code, the object's internal variables are declared final and are assigned at construction. By doing so, it is guaranteed that the object is immutable.

```
public class ImmutableCustomerOrder {
    final private String itemOrdered;
    final private int quantityOrdered;
    final private String customerName;

    ImmutableCustomerOrder(String itemOrdered, int quantityOrdered,
    String customerName) {
        this.itemOrdered = itemOrdered;
        this.quantityOrdered = quantityOrdered;
        this.customerName = customerName;
    }

    public String getItemOrdered() {
        return itemOrdered;
    }

    public int getQuantityOrdered() {
        return quantityOrdered;
    }

    public String getCustomerName() {
        return customerName;
    }

    public double calculateOrderTotal (double price) {
        return getQuantityOrdered()*price;
    }
}
```

How It Works

Solution 1 relies on the principle that a lock protects any change done to the object. Using the synchronized keyword is a shortcut to writing the expression synchronized (this). By synchronizing your getters and setters (and any other operation that alters the internal state of your object), you guarantee that the object is consistent. Also, any operations that should occur as a unit (e.g., something that modifies two collections at the same time) must be done within a method of the object and are protected by using the synchronized keyword.

For instance, if an object offers a getSize() method and getItemNumber(int index), it would be unsafe to write the following object.getItemNumber (object .getSize()-1). Even though it looks that the statement is concise, another thread can alter the object's contents between getting the size and getting the item number. Instead, it is safer to create a object.getLastElement() method, which atomically figures out the size and the last element.

Solution 2 relies on the property of immutable objects. Immutable objects cannot change their internal state, and objects that cannot change their internal state (are *immutable*) are thread-safe. If you need to modify the immutable object due to an event, create a new object with the changed properties instead of explicitly changing its property. This new object then takes the place of the old object, and on future requests for the object, the new immutable object is returned. This is the easiest (albeit lengthy) method for creating thread-safe code.

10-9. Implementing Thread-Safe Counters

Problem

You need a thread-safe counter so that it can be incremented from within different execution threads.

Solution

Using the inherently thread-safe objects makes it possible to create a counter that guarantees thread safety and has an optimized synchronization strategy. In the following code, an Order object is created, and it requires a unique order ID that is generated using the AtomicLong incrementAndGet() method.

```java
AtomicLong orderIdGenerator = new AtomicLong(0);
        for (int i =0;i < 10;i++) {
            Thread orderCreationThread = new Thread(() -> {
                for (int i1 = 0; i1 < 10; i1++) {
                    createOrder(Thread.currentThread().getName());
                }
            });
            orderCreationThread.setName("Order Creation Thread "+i);
            orderCreationThread.start();
        }
    private void createOrder(String name) {
        long orderId = orderIdGenerator.incrementAndGet();
        Order order = new Order(name, orderId);
        orders.add(order);
    }

  public  class Order {
        String orderName;
        long orderId;

        Order(String orderName, long orderId) {
            this.orderName = orderName;
            this.orderId = orderId;
        }

        public String getOrderName() {
            return orderName;
        }

        public long getOrderId() {
            return orderId;
        }
    }
```

The following is the output.

```
Order id:9
Order id:2
Order id:8
Order id:11
Order id:12
Order id:13
Order id:14
Order id:15
Order id:16
Order id:18
Order id:19
Order id:21
Order id:22
Order id:7
Order id:23
Order id:24
...
```

How It Works

AtomicLong (and its cousin AtomicInteger) are built to be used safely in concurrent environments. They have methods to atomically increment (and get) the changed value. Even if hundreds of threads call the AtomicLong increment() method, the returned value is unique.

If you need to make decisions and update the variables, always use the atomic operations that AtomicLong offers; for example, compareAndSet. If not, your code is not thread-safe (as any check-then-act operation needs to be atomic) unless you externally protect the atomic reference by using your own locks.

Changing a long value may be done in two memory write operations (as allowed by the Java Memory Model). Thus two threads could end up overlapping those two operations in what might appear to be thread-safe code. The result would be a completely unexpected (and likely wrong) long value.

```
long counter = 0;
public long incrementCounter() {
  return counter++;
}
```

Even though it looks like there is only one operation to increment the counter, in reality, there are two operations that occur at the machine-language level (a retrieve of the variable and then an increment). Two or more threads could obtain the same value since they both retrieve the variable but haven't incremented it yet. Then all the threads increment the counter to the same number.

10-10. Updating a Common Value Across Multiple Threads

Problem

Your application needs to safely maintain a single summed value across multiple threads.

Solution

Utilize DoubleAdder or LongAdder to contain the value that is being summed across multiple threads to ensure safe handling. In the following example, two threads are adding values to DoubleAdder at the same time. In the end, the value is summed and displayed.

```
public static void main(String[] args) {
    Recipe10_10 recipe10_10 = new Recipe10_10();
    recipe10_10.start();
}
DoubleAdder da = new DoubleAdder();
private void start() {
    Thread thread1 = new Thread(() -> {
        for (int i1 = 0; i1 < 10; i1++) {
```

```
                da.add(i1);
                System.out.println("Adding " + i1);
            }
        });
        Thread thread2 = new Thread(() -> {
            for (int i1 = 0; i1 < 10; i1++) {
                da.add(i1);
                System.out.println("Adding " + i1);
            }
        });
        thread1.start();
        thread2.start();
        try {
            System.out.println("Sleep while summing....");
            Thread.sleep(10000);
        } catch (InterruptedException e) {
            e.printStackTrace();
        }
        System.out.println("The sum is: " + da.doubleValue());
    }
}
```

The following are the results.

```
Adding 0
Adding 1
Adding 2
Adding 3
Adding 4
Adding 5
Adding 6
Adding 7
Adding 0
Adding 8
Adding 9
Adding 1
```

```
Adding 2
Adding 3
Adding 4
Adding 5
Adding 6
Adding 7
Adding 8
Adding 9
The sum is: 90.0
```

How It Works

Prior to Java 8, it was important to utilize atomic numbers when working with values across multiple threads. Atomic variables prevent thread interference without obstructing the way that synchronized access may cause in some cases. Java 8 introduced a new line of atomic variables that provide faster throughput than standard atomic variables. The java.util.concurrent.atomic.DoubleAdder and java.util .concurrent.atomic.LongAdder classes are preferable to AtomicDouble and AtomicLong in most cases when the values may be accessed and updated across multiple threads. Both DoubleAdder and LongAdder extend numbers, and they are useful when summing values across threads, especially under high contention.

In the solution, DoubleAdder sums numbers across two different threads. Using the add() method, various numbers are "added" to the DoubleAdder value. After the threads have had ample time to perform their work, the doubleValue() method is called on to return the sum of all values as a double.

Both the DoubleAdder and LongAdder classes contain similar methods, although the LongAdder does contain a couple of additional helper methods for incrementing and decrementing the value of the adder.

10-11. Executing Multiple Tasks Asynchronously

Problem

Your application requires multiple tasks to be performed simultaneously in an asynchronous manner, such that none of the tasks block one another.

391

Solution

Utilize CompletableFuture<T> objects to represent the state of each task that is currently being performed. Each CompletableFuture object runs on a designated or application-determined background thread, issuing a callback to the original calling method once completed.

In the following solution, two long-running tasks are invoked by a calling method, and they each utilize the CompletableFuture to report status once the task has been completed.

```java
public class Recipe10_11 {
    public static void main(String[] args) {
        try {
            CompletableFuture tasks = performWork()
                    .thenApply(work -> {
                        String newTask = work + " Second task complete!";
                        System.out.println(newTask);
                        return newTask;
                    }).thenApply(finalTask -> finalTask + " Final Task
                    Complete!");
            CompletableFuture future = performSecondWork("Java 9 is
            Great! ");
            while(!tasks.isDone()){
                System.out.println(future.get());
            }
            System.out.println(tasks.get());
        } catch (ExecutionException | InterruptedException ex) {
        }
    }
    /**
     * Returns a CompleableFuture object.
     * @return
     */
    public static CompletableFuture performWork() {
        CompletableFuture resultingWork = CompletableFuture.supplyAsync(
                () -> {
```

```
                String taskMessage = "First task complete!";
                try {
                    Thread.sleep(1000);
                } catch (InterruptedException ex) {
                    System.out.println(ex);
                }
                System.out.println(taskMessage);
                return taskMessage;
            });
        return resultingWork;
    }
    /**
     * Accepts a String and returns a CompletableFuture.
     * @param message
     * @return
     */
    public static CompletableFuture performSecondWork(String message) {
        CompletableFuture resultingWork = CompletableFuture.supplyAsync(
            () -> {
                String taskMessage = message + " Another task complete!";
                try {
                    Thread.sleep(1000);
                } catch (InterruptedException ex) {
                    System.out.println(ex);
                }
                return taskMessage;
            });
        return resultingWork;
    }
}
```

The following are the results.

```
First task complete!
First task complete! Second task complete!
Java 9 is Great! Another task complete!
First task complete! Second task complete! Final Task Complete!
```

How It Works

CompletableFuture<T> was added in Java 8 to support asynchronous tasks.
CompletableFuture<T> is an extension of Future<T>, which adds many methods to
promote asynchronous, event-driven programming models, and also allows for values to
be set at any time. The latter functionality means that a CompletableFuture object can
be created before it is required if an application needs to use it in the future.

There are a couple of options for creating a CompletableFuture object, either
manually or via factory methods. Manual creation can be done without binding to
any thread. Such a tactic is useful when an application requires a placeholder for
an event that occurs in the future. The following code demonstrates how to create a
CompletableFuture object manually.

```
final <CompletableFutureString> completableFuture = new
CompletableFuture<>();
```

One would utilize a factory to generate a CompletableFuture to return an object
geared toward a specific task or outcome. There are several different factory methods
to call on to return such an object. Some of the factory methods accept arguments, and
others do not. For instance, the CompletableFuture.runAsync(Runnable) method
returns a CompletableFuture that first executes the provided Runnable and then
asynchronously completes it by a task running in the ForkJoinPool.commonPool().
Another variation of the runAsync() method accepts both Runnable and Executor,
which first executes the provided Runnable, then asynchronously completes by a task
within the given Executor.

The CompletableFuture object also contains several methods similar to that
of the standard Future<T> object. For instance, the isDone(), cancel(), and
isCompletedExceptionally() methods each return boolean to indicate a status on the
object. It is also possible to stack asynchronous tasks with a CompletableFuture object
by calling on the thenApply() method, which accepts lambda expressions and method
references. The solution to this recipe demonstrates how to utilize the thenApply()
method to invoke an asynchronous task from another. First, a CompletableFuture object
named performWork() is executed, then a lambda expression is executed, creating a
concatenated string based on the string generated within performWork(). Once the
second task has been completed, another task is invoked to append more text to the string.
The future.get() method is then called within a loop to see the string being transformed
by the application over time. Lastly, the outcome of the fully completed task is printed.

10-12. Summary

It is important to understand the fundamentals of concurrency when developing applications. There is nothing worse than testing an application successfully and then having it fail with a deadlock once it is released into production. This chapter started with the basics, demonstrating how to spawn a background task.

CHAPTER 11

Unicode, Internationalization, and Currency Codes

The Java platform provides a rich set of internationalization features to help you create applications that can be used across the world. The platform provides the means to localize your applications, format dates, and numbers in a variety of culturally appropriate formats and display characters used in dozens of writing systems. This chapter describes only some of the most frequent and common tasks that programmers must perform when developing internationalized applications.

11-1. Converting Unicode Characters to Digits

Problem

You want to convert a Unicode digit character to its respective integer value. For example, you have a string containing the Thai digit for the value 8, and you want to generate an integer with that value.

Solution

The `java.lang.Character` final class has several static methods to convert characters to integer digit values.

- `public static intdigit(char ch, int radix)`
- `public static intdigit(intch, int radix)`

© Josh Juneau, Luciano Manelli 2022
J. Juneau and L. Manelli, *Java 17 Recipes*, https://doi.org/10.1007/978-1-4842-7963-2_11

The following code snippet iterates through the entire range of Unicode code points from 0x0000 through 0x10FFFF. Each code point that is also a digit displays the character and its digit value 0 through 9. You can find this example in the org.java17recipes.chapter11.recipe11_01.Recipe11_1 class.

```java
public static void main(String[] args) {
    Recipe11_1 example = new Recipe11_1();
    example.run();
}

public void run() {
    int x = 0;
    for (int c=0; c <= 0x10FFFF; c++) {
        if (Character.isDigit(c)) {
            ++x;
            System.out.printf("Codepoint: 0x%04X\tCharacter: %c\tDigit:
            %d\tName: %s\n", c, c,
                Character.digit(c, 10), Character.getName(c));
        }
    }
    System.out.printf("Total digits: %d\n", x);
}
}
```

The following is some of the output.

```
Codepoint: 0x0030    Character: 0    Digit: 0    Name: DIGIT ZERO
Codepoint: 0x0031    Character: 1    Digit: 1    Name: DIGIT ONE
Codepoint: 0x0032    Character: 2    Digit: 2    Name: DIGIT TWO
Codepoint: 0x0033    Character: 3    Digit: 3    Name: DIGIT THREE
Codepoint: 0x0034    Character: 4    Digit: 4    Name: DIGIT FOUR
Codepoint: 0x0035    Character: 5    Digit: 5    Name: DIGIT FIVE
Codepoint: 0x0036    Character: 6    Digit: 6    Name: DIGIT SIX
Codepoint: 0x0037    Character: 7    Digit: 7    Name: DIGIT SEVEN
Codepoint: 0x0038    Character: 8    Digit: 8    Name: DIGIT EIGHT
```

```
Codepoint: 0x0039      Character: 9      Digit: 9      Name: DIGIT NINE
Codepoint: 0x0660      Character: ٠      Digit: 0      Name: ARABIC-INDIC
                                                             DIGIT ZERO
Codepoint: 0x0661      Character: ١      Digit: 1      Name: ARABIC-INDIC
                                                             DIGIT ONE
Codepoint: 0x0662      Character: ٢      Digit: 2      Name: ARABIC-INDIC
                                                             DIGIT TWO
Codepoint: 0x0663      Character: ٣      Digit: 3      Name: ARABIC-INDIC
                                                             DIGIT THREE
Codepoint: 0x0664      Character: ٤      Digit: 4      Name: ARABIC-INDIC
                                                             DIGIT FOUR
Codepoint: 0x0665      Character: ٥      Digit: 5      Name: ARABIC-INDIC
                                                             DIGIT FIVE
Codepoint: 0x0666      Character: ٦      Digit: 6      Name: ARABIC-INDIC
                                                             DIGIT SIX
Codepoint: 0x0667      Character: ٧      Digit: 7      Name: ARABIC-INDIC
                                                             DIGIT SEVEN
Codepoint: 0x0668      Character: ٨      Digit: 8      Name: ARABIC-INDIC
                                                             DIGIT EIGHT
Codepoint: 0x0669      Character: ٩      Digit: 9      Name: ARABIC-INDIC
                                                             DIGIT NINE
...
Codepoint: 0x0E50      Character: ๐      Digit: 0      Name: THAI DIGIT ZERO
Codepoint: 0x0E51      Character: ๑      Digit: 1      Name: THAI DIGIT ONE
Codepoint: 0x0E52      Character: ๒      Digit: 2      Name: THAI DIGIT TWO
Codepoint: 0x0E53      Character: ๓      Digit: 3      Name: THAI DIGIT THREE
Codepoint: 0x0E54      Character: ๔      Digit: 4      Name: THAI DIGIT FOUR
Codepoint: 0x0E55      Character: ๕      Digit: 5      Name: THAI DIGIT FIVE
Codepoint: 0x0E56      Character: ๖      Digit: 6      Name: THAI DIGIT SIX
Codepoint: 0x0E57      Character: ๗      Digit: 7      Name: THAI DIGIT SEVEN
Codepoint: 0x0E58      Character: ๘      Digit: 8      Name: THAI DIGIT EIGHT
Codepoint: 0x0E59      Character: ๙      Digit: 9      Name: THAI DIGIT NINE
...
```

Note   The sample code prints to the console. Your console may not print all the character glyphs shown in this example because of font or platform differences. However, the characters are correctly converted to integers.

How It Works

The Unicode character set contains more than a million unique code points with integer values ranging from 0x0000 through 0x10FFFF. Each character value has a set of properties. One of the properties is isDigit. If this property is true, the character represents a numeric digit from 0 through 9. For example, the characters with code point values 0x30 through 0x39 have the character glyphs 0, 1, 2, 3, 4, 5, 6, 7, 8, and 9. If you simply convert these code values to their corresponding integer values, you get the hexadecimal values 0x30 through 0x39. The corresponding decimal values are 48 through 57. However, these characters also represent numeric digits. When using them in calculations, these characters represent the values 0 through 9.

When a character has the digit property, use the Character.digit() static method to convert it to its corresponding integer digit value. Note that the digit() method is overloaded to accept either char or int arguments. Additionally, the method requires a radix. Common values for the radix are 2, 10, and 16. Interestingly, although the characters a–f and A–F do not have the digit property, they can be used as digits using radix 16. For these characters, the digit() method returns the expected integer values 10 through 15.

A complete understanding of the Unicode character set and Java's implementation requires familiarity with several new terms: character, code point, char, encoding, serialization encoding, UTF-8, and UTF-16. These terms are beyond the scope of this recipe, but you can learn more about these and other Unicode concepts from the Unicode website at http://unicode.org or the Character class Java API documentation.

11-2. Creating and Working with Locales

Problem

You want to display numbers, dates, and time in a user-friendly way that conforms to your customers' language and cultural expectations.

Solution

The display format for numbers, dates, and time varies across the world and depends on your user's language and cultural region. Additionally, text collation rules vary by language. The java.util.Locale final class represents a specific language and region of the world. By determining and using your customer's locale, you can apply that locale to a variety of format classes, which can create user-visible data in expected forms. Classes that use Locale instances to modify their behavior for a particular language or region are called *locale-sensitive* classes. You can learn more about locale-sensitive classes in Chapter 4. That chapter shows you how to use Locale instances in the NumberFormat and DateFormat classes. In this recipe, however, you learn different options for creating these Locale instances.

You can create a Locale instance in any of the following ways.

- Use the Locale.Builder class to configure and build a Locale object.

- Use the static Locale.forLanguageTag() method.

- Use the Locale constructors to create an object.

- Use preconfigured static Locale objects.

The Java Locale.Builder class has setter methods to create locales that can be transformed into well-formed Best Common Practices (BCP) 47 language tags. The "How It Works" section describes the BCP 47 standard in more detail. For now, you should simply understand that a Builder creates Locale instances that comply with that standard.

The following code snippet from the org.java17recipes.chapter11.recipe11_02 .Recipe11_2 class demonstrates how to create Builder and Locale instances. You create locales in locale-sensitive classes to produce culturally correct display formats.

```
private static final long number = 123456789L;
private static final Date now = new Date();

    public static void main(String[] args) {
        Recipe11_2 app = new Recipe11_2();
        app.run();
    }

    public void run() {
        createFromBuilder();
        createFromLanguageTag();
        createFromConstructor();
        createFromStatics();
    }
private void createFromBuilder() {
    System.out.printf("Creating from Builder...\n\n");
    String[][] langRegions = {{"fr", "FR"}, {"ja", "JP"}, {"en", "US"}};
    Builder builder = new Builder();
    Locale l = null;
    NumberFormat nf = null;
    DateFormat df = null;
    for (String[] lr: langRegions) {
        builder.clear();
        builder.setLanguage(lr[0]).setRegion(lr[1]);
        l = builder.build();
        nf = NumberFormat.getInstance(l);
        df = DateFormat.getDateTimeInstance(DateFormat.LONG, DateFormat.
        LONG, l);
        System.out.printf("Locale: %s\nNumber: %s\nDate: %s\n\n",
            l.getDisplayName(),
            nf.format(number),
            df.format(now));
    }
```

The previous code prints the following to the standard console.

```
Creating from Builder...

Locale: French (France)
Number: 123 456 789
Date: 14 septembre 2016 00:08:06 PDT

Locale: Japanese (Japan)
Number: 123,456,789
Date: 2016/09/14 0:08:06 PDT

Locale: English (United States)
Number: 123,456,789
Date: September 14, 2016 12:08:06 AM PDT
```

Another way to create `Locale` instances is by using the static `Locale.forLanguageTag()` method. This method allows you to use BCP 47 language tag arguments. The following code uses the `forLanguageTag()` method to create three locales from their corresponding language tags.

```
...
System.out.printf("Creating from BCP 47 language tags \n\n");
String[] bcp47LangTags= {"fr-FR", "ja-JP", "en-US"};
Locale l = null;
NumberFormat nf = null;
DateFormat df = null;
for (String langTag: bcp47LangTags) {
    l = Locale.forLanguageTag(langTag);
    nf = NumberFormat.getInstance(l);
    df = DateFormat.getDateTimeInstance(DateFormat.LONG, DateFormat.LONG, l);
    System.out.printf("Locale: %s\nNumber: %s\nDate: %s\n\n",
        l.getDisplayName(),
        nf.format(number),
        df.format(now));
}
...
```

The output is similar to the results created from the `Builder`-generated `Locale` instance.

```
Creating from BCP 47 language tags...
Locale: French (France)
Number: 123 456 789
Date: 14 septembre 2016 01:07:22 PDT
...
```

You can also use constructors to create instances. The following code shows how to do this.

```
Locale l = new Locale("fr", "FR");
```

Other constructors allow you to pass fewer or more arguments. The argument parameters can include language, region, and optional variant codes.

Finally, the `Locale` class has many predefined static instances for some commonly used cases. Because the instances are predefined, your code needs to reference only the static instances. For example, the following example shows how to reference existing static instances representing `fr-FR`, `ja-JP`, and `en-US` locales.

```
Locale frenchInFrance = Locale.FRANCE;
Locale japaneseInJapan = Locale.JAPAN;
Locale englishInUS = Locale.US;
```

How It Works

The `Locale` class gives locale-sensitive classes the context to perform culturally appropriate data formatting and parsing. Some of the locale-sensitive classes include the following.

- `java.text.NumberFormat`

- `java.text.DateFormat`

- `java.util.Calendar`

A `Locale` instance identifies a specific language and can be finely tuned to identify languages written in a particular script or spoken in a specific world region. It is an important and necessary element for creating anything that depends on language or regional influences.

The Java `Locale` class is always being enhanced to support modern BCP 47 language tags. BCP 47 defines the best common practices for using ISO standards for language, region, script, and variant identifiers. Although the existing `Locale` constructors continue to be compatible with prior versions of the Java platform, the constructors do not support the additional script tags. For example, only the more recently added `Locale.Builder` class and `Locale.forLanguageTag()` method support the newer functionality that identifies scripts. Because the `Locale` constructors do not enforce strict BCP 47 compliance, you should avoid the constructors in any new code. Instead, developers should use the `Builder` class and the `forLanguageTag()` method.

A `Locale.Builder` instance has a variety of setter methods that help you configure it to create a valid, BCP 47–compliant `Locale` instance.

- `public Locale.BuildersetLanguage(String language)`

- `public Locale.BuildersetRegion(String region)`

- `public Locale.BuildersetScript(String script)`

Each of these methods throws a `java.util.IllFormedLocaleException` if its argument is not a well-formed element of the BCP 47 standard. The language parameter must be a valid two- or three-letter ISO 639 language identifier. The region parameter must be a valid two-letter ISO 3166 region code or a three-digit M.49 United Nations "area" code. Finally, the script parameter must be a valid four-letter ISO 15924 script code.

The `Builder` lets you configure it to create a specific BCP 47–compliant locale. Once you set all the configurations, the `build()` method creates and returns a `Locale` instance. Notice that all the setters can be chained together for a single statement. The `Builder` pattern works by having each configuration method return a reference to the current instance, on which further configuration methods may be called.

```
Locale aLocale = new Builder().setLanguage("fr").setRegion("FR").build();
```

The BCP 47 document and the standards that comprise it can be found at the following locations.

- ISO 3166 (region identifiers): `www.iso.org/iso-3166-country-codes.html`

- ISO 15924 (script identifiers): `https://unicode.org/iso15924/`

- United Nations M.49 (area identifiers): `https://unstats.un.org/unsd/methods/m49/m49.htm`

11-3. Matching and Filtering Locales

Problem

You want to match against or filter a list of locales and return only those that meet the specified criteria.

Solution

Make use of the new locale matching and filtering methods that have been introduced in the java.util.Locale class in Java 8. If you're given a comma-separated list of locales in string format, you can apply a filter or "priority list" to that string to return only those locales within the string that meet the filter. In the following example, a list of language tags is filtered using the java.util.Locale filterTag method, returning the matching tags in string format.

```
public static void main(String[] args) {
    filterTags();
    localeMatching();
}

public static void filterTags(){
    List<Locale.LanguageRange> list1 = Locale.LanguageRange.parse
    ("ja-JP, en-US");
    list1.stream().forEach((range) -> {
        System.out.println("Range:" + range.getRange());
    });
    ArrayList localeList = new ArrayList();
    localeList.add("en-US");
    localeList.add("en-JP");

    List<String> tags1 = Locale.filterTags(list1, localeList);
    System.out.println("The following is the filtered list of
    locales:");
    tags1.stream().forEach((tag) -> {
        System.out.println(tag);
    });
}
```

406

These are the results.

```
Range:ja-jp
Range:en-us
The following is the filtered list of Locales:
en-us
```

The filter() method of the Locale classes allows you to return a list of matching Locale instances. In the following example, a list of locale language tags filters Locale classes out of a list of locales.

```
public static void localeMatching(){
        String localeTags = Locale.ENGLISH.toLanguageTag() + "," +
                            Locale.CANADA.toLanguageTag();
        List<Locale.LanguageRange> list1 = Locale.LanguageRange.
        parse(localeTags);
        list1.stream().forEach((range) -> {
            System.out.println("Range:" + range.getRange());
        });
        ArrayList<Locale> localeList = new ArrayList();
        localeList.add(new Locale("en"));
        localeList.add(new Locale("en-JP"));

        List<Locale> tags1 = Locale.filter(list1, localeList);
        System.out.println("The following is the matching list of Locales:");
        tags1.stream().forEach((tag) -> {
            System.out.println(tag);
        });
}
```

Here are the results.

```
Range:en
Range:en-ca
The following is the matching list of locales:
en
```

How It Works

In Java 8, methods were added to the `java.util.Locale` class to filter `Locale` instances or language tags based on a supplied priority list in `List<Locale.LanguageRange>` format. The following list contains a short summary of these filtering methods.

- `filter(List<Locale.LanguageRange>, Collection<Locale>)`

  `filter(List<Locale.LanguageRange>, Collection<Locale>, Locale.FilteringMode)`

  (Returns matching list of `Locale` instances)

- `filterTags(List<Locale.LanguageRange>, Collection<String>)`

  `filterTags(List<Locale.LanguageRange>, Collection<String>, Locale.FilteringMode)`

  (Returns matching list of language tags)

To work with each method, a sorted priority order should be sent as the first parameter. This priority order is a list of `Locale.LanguageRange` objects should be sorted in descending order, based on priority or weight. The second argument in the `filter()` methods is a collection of locales. This collection contains the locales that will be filtered. The optional third argument contains a `Locale.FilteringMode`.

11-4. Searching Unicode with Regular Expressions

Problem

You want to find or match Unicode characters in a string. You want to do that using regular expression syntax.

Solution 1

The easiest way to find or match characters is to use the `String` class. `String` instances store Unicode character sequences and provide relatively simple operations for finding, replacing, and tokenizing characters using regular expressions.

To determine whether a string matches a regular expression, use the matches()
method. The matches() method returns true if the entire string matches the regular
expression exactly.

The following code from the org.java17recipes.chapter11.recipe11_04.Recipe11_4
class uses two different expressions with two strings. The regular expression matches
simply confirm that the strings match a particular pattern as defined in the enRegEx and
jaRegEx variables.

```java
private String enText = "The fat cat sat on the mat with a brown rat.";
private String jaText = "Fight 文字化け!";
String enRegEx = "^The \\w+ cat.*";
String jaRegEx = ".*文字.*";
String jaRegExEscaped = ".*\u6587\u5B57.*";

    public static void main(String[] args) {
        Recipe11_4 app = new Recipe11_4();
        app.run();
    }

    public void run() {
        demoStringMatch();
        demoStringReplace();
        demoStringSplit();
        demoSimple();
        demoComplex();
    }

public void demoStringMatch() {
        boolean found = false;
        found = enText.matches(enRegEx);
        if (found) {
            System.out.printf("Matches %s.\n", enRegEx);
        }
        found = jaText.matches(jaRegEx);
        if (found) {
            System.out.printf("Matches %s.\n", jaRegEx);
        }
```

```
        found = jaText.matches(jaRegExEscaped);
        if (found) {
            System.out.printf("Matches %s.\n", jaRegExEscaped);
        }
}
```

This code prints the following.

```
Matches ^The \w+ cat.*.
Matches .*文字.*.
Matches .*文字.*.
```

Use the `replaceFirst()` method to create a new `String` instance in which the first occurrence of the regular expression in the target text is replaced with the replacement text. The code demonstrates how to use this method.

```
String replaced = jaText.replaceFirst("文字化け", "mojibake");
System.out.printf("Replaced: %s\n", replaced);
```

The replacement text is shown in the output.

```
Replaced: Fight mojibake!
```

The `replaceAll()` method replaces all occurrences of the expression with the replacement text.

Finally, the `split()` method creates a `String[]` that contains text separated by the matched expression. In other words, it returns text that is delimited by the expression. Optionally, you can provide a `limit` argument that constrains the number of times the delimiter is applied in the source text. The following code demonstrates the `split()` method splitting on space characters.

```
String[] matches = enText.split("\\s", 3);
for(String match: matches) {
    System.out.printf("Split: %s\n",match);
}
```

The code's output is as follows.

```
Split: The
Split: fat
Split: cat sat on the mat with a brown rat.
```

Solution 2

When the simple String methods aren't sufficient, you can use the more powerful
java.util.regex package to work with regular expressions. Create a regular expression
using the Pattern class. A Matcher works on a String instance using the pattern.
All Matcher operations perform their functions using Pattern and String instances.

The following code demonstrates how to search for ASCII and non-ASCII text in two
separate strings. See the org.java17recipes.chapter11.recipe11_04.Recipe11_4 class
for the complete source code. The demoSimple() method finds text with any character
followed by ".at". The demoComplex() method finds two Japanese symbols in a string.

```java
public void demoSimple() {
Pattern p = Pattern.compile(".at");
    Matcher m = p.matcher(enText);
    while(m.find()) {
        System.out.printf("%s\n", m.group());
    }
}
public void demoComplex() {
    Pattern p = Pattern.compile("文字");
    Matcher m = p.matcher(jaText);
    if (m.find()) {
        System.out.println(m.group());
    }
}
```

Running these two methods on the previously defined English and Japanese text
shows the following.

```
fat
cat
sat
mat
rat
文字
```

How It Works

The String methods that work with regular expressions are the following.

- `public boolean matches(String regex)`

- `public String replaceFirst(String regex, String replacement)`

- `public String replaceAll(String regex, String replacement)`

- `public String[] split(String regex, int limit)`

- `public String[] split(String regex)`

The String methods are limited and relatively simple wrappers around the more powerful functionality of the `java.util.regex` classes.

- `java.util.regex.Pattern`

- `java.util.regex.Matcher`

- `java.util.regex.PatternSyntaxException`

The Java regular expressions are similar to those used in the Perl language. Although there is a lot to learn about Java regular expressions, the most important points to understand from this recipe are the following.

- Your regular expressions can contain non-ASCII characters from the full range of Unicode characters.

- Because of a peculiarity of how the Java language compiler understands the backslash character, you must use two backslashes in your code instead of one for the predefined character class expressions.

The most convenient and readable way to use non-ASCII characters in regular expressions is to type them directly into your source files using your keyboard input methods. Operating systems and editors differ in how they allow you to enter complex text outside of ASCII. Regardless of the operating system, you should save the file in the UTF-8 encoding if your editor allows it. As an alternate but more difficult way to use non-ASCII regular expressions, you can encode characters using the \uXXXX notation. Using this notation, instead of directly typing the character using your keyboard, you enter \u or \U, followed by the hexadecimal representation of the Unicode code point.

This recipe's code sample uses the Japanese word "文字" (pronounced *mo-ji*). As the example shows, you can use the actual characters in the regular expression or look up the Unicode code point values. For this particular Japanese word, the encoding is \u6587\u5B57.

The Java language's regular expression support includes special character classes. For example, \d and \w are shortcut notations for the regular expressions [0-9] and [a-zA-Z_0-9], respectively. However, because of the Java compiler's special handling of the backslash character, you must use an extra backslash when using predefined character classes such as \d (digits), \w (word characters), and \s (space characters). To use them in source code, for example, you enter **d**, **w**, and **s**, respectively. The sample code used the double backslash in Solution 1 to represent the \w character class.

```
String enRegEx = "^The \\w+ cat.*";
```

11-5. Overriding the Default Currency
Problem

You want to display a number value using a currency not associated with the default locale.

Solution

Take control of which currency is printed with a formatted currency value by explicitly setting the currency used in a NumberFormat instance. The following example assumes that the default locale is Locale.JAPAN. It changes the currency by calling the setCurrency(Currency c) method of its NumberFormat instance. This example comes from the org.java17recipes.chapter11.recipe11_05.Recipe11_5 class.

```
public static void main(String[] args) {
    Recipe11_5 app  = new Recipe11_5();
    app.run();
}
public void run() {
        BigDecimal value = new BigDecimal(12345);
        System.out.printf("Default locale: %s\n", Locale.getDefault()
        .getDisplayName());
```

413

```
        NumberFormat nf = NumberFormat.getCurrencyInstance();
        String formattedCurrency = nf.format(value);
        System.out.printf("%s\n", formattedCurrency);
        Currency c = Currency.getInstance(Locale.US);
        nf.setCurrency(c);
        formattedCurrency = nf.format(value);
        System.out.printf("%s\n\n", formattedCurrency);
}
```

The previous code prints out the following.

```
Default locale: 日本語 (日本)
¥12,345
USD12,345
```

How It Works

You use a NumberFormat instance to format currency values. You should explicitly call the getCurrencyInstance() method to create a formatter for currencies.

```
NumberFormat nf = NumberFormat.getCurrencyInstance();
```

The previous formatter uses your default locale's preferences for formatting numbers as currency values. Also, it uses a currency symbol associated with the locale's region. However, one common use case involves formatting a value for a different region's currency.

Use the setCurrency() method to explicitly set the currency in the number formatter.

```
nf.setCurrency(aCurrencyInstance); // requires a Currency instance
```

Note that the java.util.Currency final class is a factory. It allows you to create currency objects in two ways.

- Currency.getInstance(Locale locale)

- Currency.getInstance(String currencyCode)

The first getInstance call uses a Locale instance to retrieve a currency object. The Java platform associates a default currency with the locale's region. In this case, the default currency currently associated with the United States is the US dollar.

```
Currency c1 = Currency.getInstance(Locale.US);
```

The second getInstance call uses a valid ISO 4217 currency code. The currency code for the US dollar is USD.

```
Currency c2 = Currency.getInstance("USD");
```

Once you have a currency instance, you simply have to use that instance in your formatter.

```
nf.setCurrency(c2);
```

This formatter is configured to use the default locale's number format symbols and patterns to format the number value, but it displays the targeted currency code as part of the displayable text. This allows you to mix the default number format patterns with other currency codes.

11-6. Converting Byte Arrays to and from Strings
Problem

You need to convert characters in a byte array from a legacy character set encoding to a Unicode string.

Solution

Convert legacy character encodings from a byte array to a Unicode string using the String class. The following code snippet from the org.java17recipes.chapter11 .recipe11_06.Recipe11_6 class demonstrates how to convert a legacy Shift-JIS encoded byte array to a string. Later in this same example, the code demonstrates how to convert Unicode back to the Shift-JIS byte array.

```
    public static void main(String[] args) {
        Recipe11_6 app = new Recipe11_6();
        app.run();
    }
    public void run() {
        byte[] legacySJIS = {(byte)0x82,(byte)0xB1,(byte)0x82,(byte)0xF1,
         (byte)0x82,(byte)0xC9,(byte)0x82,(byte)0xBF,
         (byte)0x82,(byte)0xCD,(byte)0x81,(byte)0x41,
         (byte)0x90,(byte)0xA2,(byte)0x8A,(byte)0x45,
         (byte)0x81,(byte)0x49};

        // Convert a byte[] to a String
        Charset cs =Charset.forName("SJIS");
        String greeting = new String(legacySJIS, cs);
        System.out.printf("Greeting: %s\n", greeting);
```

This code prints out the converted text, which is "Hello, world!" in Japanese.

```
Greeting: こんにちは、世界!
```

Use the getBytes() method to convert characters from a string to a byte array. Building on the previous code, convert back to the original encoding with the following code and compare the results.

```
// Convert a String to a byte[]
byte[] toSJIS = greeting.getBytes(cs);

// Confirm that the original array and newly converted array are same
Boolean same = false;
if (legacySJIS.length == toSJIS.length) {
    for (int x=0; x< legacySJIS.length; x++) {
        if(legacySJIS[x] != toSJIS[x]) break;
    }
    same = true;
}
System.out.printf("Same: %s\n", same.toString());
```

As expected, the output indicates that the round-trip conversion back to the legacy encoding was successful. The original byte array and the converted byte array contain the same bytes.

Same: true

How It Works

The Java platform provides conversion support for many legacy character set encodings. When you create a String instance from a byte array, you must provide a charset argument to the String constructor so that the platform knows how to perform the mapping from the legacy encoding to Unicode. All Java strings use Unicode as their native encoding.

The number of bytes in the original array does not usually equal the number of characters in the result string. In this recipe's example, the original array contains 18 bytes. The Shift-JIS encoding needs the 18 bytes to represent the Japanese text. However, after conversion, the result string contains nine characters. There is not a 1:1 relationship between bytes and characters. Each character requires two bytes in the original Shift-JIS encoding in this example.

There are hundreds of different charset encodings. The number of encodings is dependent on your Java platform implementation. However, you are guaranteed support of several of the most common encodings, and your platform most likely contains many more than this minimal set.

- US-ASCII

- ISO-8859-1

- UTF-8

- UTF-16BE

- UTF-16LE

- UTF-16

When constructing a charset, you should be prepared to handle the possible exceptions when the character set is not supported.

- java.nio.charset.IllegalCharsetNameException, thrown when the charset name is illegal

- `java.lang.IllegalArgumentException`, thrown when the `charset` name is `null`

- `java.nio.charset.UnsupportedCharsetException`, thrown when your JVM doesn't support the targeted `charset`

11-7. Converting Character Streams and Buffers

Problem

You need to convert large blocks of Unicode character text to and from an arbitrary byte-oriented encoding. Large blocks of text may come from streams or files.

Solution 1

Use `java.io.InputStreamReader` to decode a byte stream to Unicode characters. Use `java.io.OutputStreamWriter` to encode Unicode characters to a byte stream.

The following code uses `InputStreamReader` to read and convert a potentially large block of text bytes from a file in the classpath. The `org.java17recipes.chapter11 .recipe11_07.StreamConversion` class provides the complete code for this example.

```
public static void main(String[] args) {
    StreamConversion app = new StreamConversion();
    app.run();
}
public void run() {
    try {
        String input = readStream();
        System.out.printf("Input stream: %s\n", input);
        writeStream(input);
    } catch (IOException ex) {
        Logger.getLogger(StreamConversion.class.getName()).log(Level.
        SEVERE, null, ex);
    }
}
```

```java
public String readStream() throws IOException {
    InputStream is = getClass().getResourceAsStream("/resources/helloworld.
    sjis.txt");
    StringBuilder sb = new StringBuilder();
    if (is != null) {
        try (InputStreamReader reader =
                new InputStreamReader(is, Charset.forName("SJIS"))) {
            int ch = reader.read();
            while (ch != -1) {
                sb.append((char) ch);
                ch = reader.read();
            }
        }
    }
    return sb.toString();
}
```

Similarly, you can use an `OutputStreamWriter` to write text to a byte stream. The following code writes a string to a UTF-8 encoded byte stream.

```java
public void writeStream(String text) throws IOException {
    FileOutputStream fos = new FileOutputStream("helloworld.utf8.txt");
    try (OutputStreamWriter writer
            = new OutputStreamWriter(fos, Charset.forName("UTF-8"))) {
        writer.write(text);
    }
}
```

Solution 2

Use `java.nio.charset.CharsetEncoder` and `java.nio.charset.CharsetDecoder` to convert Unicode character buffers to and from byte buffers. Retrieve an encoder or decoder from a `charset` instance with the `newEncoder()` or `newDecoder()` method. Then use the encoder's `encode()` method to create byte buffers. Use the decoder's `decode()` method to create character buffers. The following code from the `org.java17recipes.chapter11.recipe11_07.BufferConversion` class encodes and decodes character sets from buffers.

```java
    public static void main(String[] args) {
        BufferConversion app = new BufferConversion();
        app.run();
    }
    public void run() {
        try {
            System.out.printf("Original string: %s\n", unicodeString);
            CharBuffer srcBuffer = CharBuffer.wrap(unicodeString);
            ByteBuffer targetBytes = encodeBuffer("UTF8", srcBuffer);
            printBytes(targetBytes);
            CharBuffer roundtripBuffer = decodeBuffer("UTF8", targetBytes);
            printCharBuffer(roundtripBuffer);

        } catch (CharacterCodingException ex) {
            Logger.getLogger(BufferConversion.class.getName()).log(Level.
            SEVERE, null, ex);
        }
    }
    public ByteBuffer encodeBuffer(String charsetName, CharBuffer charBuffer)
            throws CharacterCodingException {
        Charset charset = Charset.forName(charsetName);
CharsetEncoder encoder = charset.newEncoder();
        ByteBuffer targetBuffer = encoder.encode(charBuffer);
return targetBuffer;

    }
    public CharBuffer decodeBuffer(String charsetName, ByteBuffer srcBuffer)
            throws CharacterCodingException {
        Charset charset = Charset.forName(charsetName);
        CharsetDecoder decoder = charset.newDecoder();
        CharBuffer charBuffer = decoder.decode(srcBuffer);
        return charBuffer;
    }
```

How It Works

The `java.io` and `java.nio.charset` packages contain several classes that can help you perform encoding conversions on large text streams or buffers. Streams are convenient abstractions that can assist you in converting text using a variety of sources and targets. A stream can represent incoming or outgoing text in an HTTP connection or even a file.

If you use an `InputStream` to represent the underlying source text, you wrap that stream in an `InputStreamReader` to perform conversions from a byte stream. The reader instance performs the conversion from bytes to Unicode characters.

Using an `OutputStream` instance to represent the target text, wrap the stream in an `OutputStreamWriter`. A writer converts your Unicode text to a byte-oriented encoding in the target stream.

To effectively use either an `OutputStreamWriter` or an `InputStreamReader`, you must know the character encoding of your target or source text. When you use an `OutputStreamWriter`, the source text is always Unicode, and you must supply a `charset` argument to tell the writer how to convert to the target byte-oriented text encoding. When you use an `InputStreamReader`, the target encoding is always Unicode. You must supply the source text encoding as an argument so that the reader understands how to convert the text.

Note   The Java platform's `String` represents characters in the UTF-16 encoding of Unicode. Unicode can have several encodings, including UTF-16, UTF-8, and even UTF-32. Converting to Unicode in this discussion always means converting to UTF-16. Converting to a byte-oriented encoding usually means a legacy non–Unicode `charset` encoding. However, a common byte-oriented encoding is UTF-8, and it is entirely reasonable to convert Java's "native" UTF-16 Unicode characters to or from UTF-8 using the `InputStreamReader` or `OutputStreamWriter` class.

Yet another way to perform encoding conversions is to use the `CharsetEncoder` and `CharsetDecoder` classes. `CharsetEncoder` encodes your Unicode `CharBuffer` instances to `ByteBuffer` instances. `CharsetDecoder` decodes `ByteBuffer` instances into `CharBuffer` instances. In either case, you must provide a `charset` argument.

11-8. Summary

Internationalization is a key to developing culturally responsive applications. It allows application text to be changed to adhere to the culture and language in which the application is being used. This chapter provided some examples of how to use internationalization techniques to overcome the nuances of cross-culture development.

CHAPTER 12

Working with Databases

Almost any nontrivial application contains a database of some sort. Some applications use an in-memory database, while others use a traditional relational database management system (RDBMS). Whatever the case, it is essential that every Java developer have some skills working with databases. Over the years, the Java Database Connectivity (JDBC) API has evolved quite a bit, and over the past couple of releases, there have been some major advancements.

This chapter covers the basics of using JDBC for working with databases. You learn how to perform all the standard database operations and some advanced techniques for manipulating data.

12-1. Installing MySQL

Problem

You want to install a database on your personal computer.

Solution

Install MySQL. Select the manual installation because it offers some benefits and more control. You can back up or move databases in seconds, and you can install and reinstall MySQL anywhere (including a USB drive).

To install MySQL, do the following.

1. Go to `https://dev.mysql.com/downloads/mysql/` (the MySQL Community Server web page) and agree to the privacy policy.

2. Ensure that the selected platform is your OS (we used Windows OS) and click the Download button. For Windows, select the version without the installer —Windows (x86, 64-bit), ZIP Archive—under the Other Downloads section.

© Josh Juneau, Luciano Manelli 2022
J. Juneau and L. Manelli, *Java 17 Recipes*, https://doi.org/10.1007/978-1-4842-7963-2_12

3. Log in as a user, or register, or, if you want, you can skip this step.

4. Download the version without the installer. (The latest version when we downloaded was `mysql-8.0.27-winx64.zip`; it had a dimension of 209 MB.) This package contains the MySQL database server.

5. Extract the zip file into your root folder drive. Rename the folder from `mysql-8.0.27-winx64` to `mysql`.

6. Create the "data" folder. I chose in the same `mysql` folder, even if we recommend always placing the data folder on another drive. This prevents loss of data and allows easy reinstallation.

7. Initialize the data directory manually before MySQL can be started. Open a command window and type the following under the bin folder.

```
C:\mysql\bin>mysqld --console --initialize
```

The `--console` option enables writing the diagnostic output to console (if you omit this option, the server writes output to the error log in the data folder).

Listing 12-1 is the result shown on the console.

Listing 12-1. Log of Database Initialization

```
2021-10-31T19:30:01.391296Z 0 [System] [MY-013169] [Server] C:\mysql\
bin\mysqld.exe (mysqld 8.0.27) initializing of server in progress as
process 3816
2021-10-31T19:30:01.599643Z 1 [System] [MY-013576] [InnoDB] InnoDB
initialization has started.
2021-10-31T19:30:19.281112Z 1 [System] [MY-013577] [InnoDB] InnoDB
initialization has ended.
2021-10-31T19:30:49.726138Z 6 [Note] [MY-010454] [Server] A temporary
password is generated for root@localhost: )r%Crfs1reOS
```

The string highlighted in bold is the generated password for the root user (the default administrative account in the MySQL grant system) displayed in the stream during the initialization. Now, you are ready to work with your database.

Open two console windows. In the first, start the database with the following command.

```
C:\mysql\bin>mysqld.exe --console
```

Listing 12-2 shows the starting up of the server. The --console command lets you see the start-up logs being printed.

Listing 12-2. Log of Database Starting Up

```
C:\mysql\bin>mysqld.exe --console
2021-10-31T19:39:25.558678Z 0 [System] [MY-010116] [Server]
C:\mysql\bin\mysqld.exe (mysqld 8.0.27) starting as process 5500
2021-10-31T19:39:25.597447Z 1 [System] [MY-013576] [InnoDB] InnoDB
initialization has started.
2021-10-31T19:39:29.188084Z 1 [System] [MY-013577] [InnoDB] InnoDB
initialization has ended.
2021-10-31T19:39:31.625112Z 0 [Warning] [MY-010068] [Server] CA certificate
ca.pem is self signed.
2021-10-31T19:39:31.842513Z 0 [System] [MY-011323] [Server] X Plugin ready
for connections. Bind-address: '::' port: 33060
2021-10-31T19:39:31.842945Z 0 [System] [MY-010931] [Server] C:\mysql\bin\
mysqld.exe: ready for connections. Version: '8.0.27'  socket: ''  port:
3306  MySQL Community Server - GPL.
```

In the second console window, connect to the database with user and password and start the MySQL console with the following command.

```
C:\mysql\bin>mysql -u root -p
```

After typing the password when prompted (Enter password: ************), you see the welcome message on the console, as you can see in Listing 12-3.

Listing 12-3. Log of Database Connection

```
C:\mysql\bin>mysql -u root -p
Enter password: ************
Enter password: ************
Welcome to the MySQL monitor.  Commands end with ; or \g.
```

```
Your MySQL connection id is 8
Server version: 8.0.27
Copyright (c) 2000, 2021, Oracle and/or its affiliates.
Oracle is a registered trademark of Oracle Corporation and/or its
affiliates. Other names may be trademarks of their respective
owners.
Type 'help;' or '\h' for help. Type '\c' to clear the current input
statement. mysql>
```

Now the *command-line interface* (CLI) is activated, note the change in the highlighted prompt command.

We recommend changing the password with the following command.

```
mysql> ALTER USER 'root'@'localhost' IDENTIFIED BY 'root';
```

The string highlighted in bold is the new password.

Then, run the following command.

```
mysql> FLUSH PRIVILEGES;
```

It tells the server to reload the grant tables, which puts your new changes into effect.

Finally, if you want to stop the database enter exit in the prompt to stop the command-line client and then type the following.

```
C:\mysql\bin>mysqladmin.exe -u root -p shutdown
Enter password: ****
```

The mysqladmin command invokes the administrative utility to connect to MySQL server as root user and tell it to shut down.

Listing 12-4 is the message shown on the console.

Listing 12-4. Log of Server Shutdown

```
2021-10-31T19:46:01.347489Z 8 [System] [MY-013172] [Server] Received
SHUTDOWN from user root. Shutting down mysqld (Version: 8.0.27).
2021-10-31T19:46:01.347680Z 0 [System] [MY-013105] [Server]
C:\mysql\bin\mysqld.exe: Normal shutdown.
2021-10-31T19:46:01.970912Z 0 [System] [MY-010910] [Server]
C:\mysql\bin\mysqld.exe: Shutdown complete (mysqld 8.0.27)
  MySQL Community Server - GPL.
```

Now you can create and populate your database and follow along with the examples in this chapter. Run the ApressBookDatabase_create.sql script to create a database user schema and populate it.

We suggest you work with the database we created in MySQL, even if you are able to develop Java applications that work with Oracle database, PostgreSQL, and all traditional RDBMSs.

First, define a simple database called apressBooks with recipes and publications tables. The logic design of the database is shown in Table 12-1 and Table 12-2, characterized by name, length, type of data, and constraints (i.e., a field is a primary key and another must be not null).

Table 12-1. *Recipes*

Field Name	Length	Type	Constraints
id	-	INT	Primary Key Not null
recipe_number	10	VARCHAR	Not Null
recipe_name	100	VARCHAR	Not Null
description	500	VARCHAR	Default Null

Table 12-2. *Publications*

Field Name	Length	Type	Constraints
id	-	INT	Primary Key Not null
book_title	500	VARCHAR	Not Null
publish_date	-	DATE	Default Null
publish_co	100	VARCHAR	Default Null

Listing 12-5 shows the SQL script for the creation of the apressBooks database.

Listing 12-5. ApressBookDatabase_create.sql

```
01 DROP DATABASE IF EXISTS `apressBooks`;
02 CREATE DATABASE `apressBooks`;
03 CREATE TABLE `apressBooks`.`recipes` (
04  `id` int NOT NULL AUTO_INCREMENT,
05  `recipe_number` varchar(10) NOT NULL,
06  `recipe_name` varchar(100) NOT NULL,
07  `description` varchar(500) DEFAULT NULL,
08  PRIMARY KEY (`id`)
09 ) ;
10 insert into apressBooks.recipes values(1,
11 '12-1',
12 'Installing MySQL',
13 'Downloading and installation of a MySQL Database');
14 insert into apressBooks.recipes values(2,
15 '12-2',
16 'Connecting to a Database',
17 'DriverManager and DataSource Implementations');
18 insert into apressBooks.recipes values(3,
19 '12-3',
20 'Handling SQL Exceptions',
21 'Using SQLException');
22 insert into apressBooks.recipes values(4,
23 '12-4',
24 'Querying a Database and Retrieving Results',
25 'Obtaining and using data from a DBMS');
26 CREATE TABLE `apressBooks`.`publication` (
27   `id` int NOT NULL AUTO_INCREMENT,
28   `book_title` varchar(500) NOT NULL,
29  `publish_date` date DEFAULT NULL,
30  `publish_co` varchar(100) DEFAULT NULL,
31  PRIMARY KEY (`id`)
32 );
33 insert into apressBooks.publication values (
34 1,
```

```
35 'Java EE 17 Recipes',
36 date('2021-12-01'),
37 'APRESS');
38 insert into apressBooks.publication values (
39 2,
40 'Beginning Jakarta EE Web Development',
41 date('2020-04-03'),
42 'APRESS');
```

Line 01 removes the database. The IF EXISTS option allows you to delete it only if it already exists. This option prevents the reported error when you use the creation script the first time if the database does not exist. The DROP statement deletes the database and the physical disk files, so you should have a backup of the database if you want to restore it in the future.

Line 02 creates a blank database named apressBooks.

Lines 03 to 09 create a table to store recipes named *recipes*.

Lines 10 to 25 populate the *recipes* table.

Lines 26 to 32 create a table named *publication*.

Lines 33 to 42 populate the *publication* table.

To execute the SQL script, you can use the command-line client you have just seen. You find the script in the software package for this chapter. Open the command-line client. Open `ApressBookDatabase_create.sql` with a text editor, copy everything and paste it onto the command-line client to create and populate the tables.

How It Works

A database consists of organized data; that is, the data itself and a schema that provides data structures. Nowadays, most databases are organized in tables consisting of rows and columns. This is a natural way of organizing data, and you're probably familiar with it through the use of spreadsheets. You can define the table characteristics independently of the actual data you're going to store into it. A field is an individual data item within a table corresponding to the intersection of a row and a column. One or more columns can be specified as unique keys to identify each employee. For this purpose, you could use either one of the columns mentioned previously or the combination of first name, last name, and date of birth. The unique key used in preference over the others is called the primary key of a table.

A database management system (DBMS), such as MySQL, is a software package that lets you create, read, update, and delete (CRUD) both items of data and elements of the schema.

Therefore, when talking about a database, you need to distinguish between three aspects.

- The data it contains.

- The structure you impose on the data to CRUD it efficiently.

- The software that allows you to manipulate both the data itself and the database structure (the DBMS).

Working with a database means that you're interacting with its DBMS. You can do that through a CLI, graphical user interfaces (GUIs) provided by the DBMS vendor and third parties, or programmatically through an API.

The DBMS can build an *index* for each key to retrieve the data more quickly. This slows down insertion and deletion of rows (i.e., new records) because the DBMS have to spend time updating the indexes. Most databases are more frequently interrogated than modified. Therefore, it usually pays to define indexes, at least those that can speed up the most common queries.

Structured Query Language (SQL) is the most widely used language to interact with DBMSs. Most DBMSs don't support the whole SQL standard. Moreover, vendors sometimes add nonstandard elements that, in practice, prevent full portability across DBMSs. In general, regardless of whether we're talking about database organization, table structure, or actual data, you'll need to perform four CRUD operations. The corresponding SQL statements begin with a keyword that identifies the operation (e.g., INSERT, SELECT, UPDATE, or DELETE), followed when necessary by a keyword specifying on what type of entity the operation is to be performed (e.g., DATABASE, TABLE, or INDEX) and by additional elements. You use the SELECT statement for retrieving information.

You can create databases, tables, and indexes with the CREATE statement, update them with ALTER and delete them with DROP. Similarly, you can create and delete views with CREATE and DROP, but you cannot update them once you've created them. You use INSERT to create new rows within a table, and you use DELETE to delete them. The UPDATE statement lets you modify entire rows or one or more individual fields within them.

The statements that let you modify the structures are collectively referred to as Data Definition Language (DDL). Those that let you modify the content are called Data Manipulation Language (DML).

In many applications, the structure of databases, tables, indexes, and views, once initially defined, remains unchanged. Therefore, you'll often need only the statements operating on rows and fields within your applications. In any case, you'll certainly need SELECT, which you use to interrogate databases both in terms of their structure and the data they contain. Finally, to complete the list of statements you're likely to need when developing applications, there are START TRANSACTION, COMMIT, and ROLLBACK, which you need to use transactions.

When you want to retrieve, update, or delete rows, you must identify them. You do this with the WHERE keyword followed by a `<where_condition>`.

In this chapter's examples, we used *MySQL* as the DBMS of choice because, first, it's available for free, and second, it's the most widely used of the freely available DBMSs. As such, it has been proven to work reliably in all sorts of environments. However, in the end, you can develop Java applications that work with other traditional RDBMSs, such as Oracle Database or PostgreSQL.

12-2. Connecting to a Database
Problem

You want to connect to a database from within a desktop Java application.

Solution

Use a JDBC `Connection` object to obtain the connection. Do this by creating a new connection object, and then load the driver that you need to use for your particular database vendor. Once the connection object is ready, call its `getConnection()` method. The following code demonstrates how to obtain a connection to a MySQL database: in general, the connection depends on the specified driver.

```
package org.java17recipes.chapter12.recipe12_02;

import java.sql.Connection;
import java.sql.DriverManager;
```

```java
import java.sql.SQLException;
import java.util.Properties;

public class CreateConnection {

        static Properties props = new Properties();

        String hostname = "localhost";
        String port = "3306";
        String database = "apressbooks";
        String username = "root";
        String password = "root";

        public Connection getConnection() throws SQLException {
                Connection conn = null;
                String jdbcUrl;
                jdbcUrl = "jdbc:mysql://" + this.hostname + ":" +
                                    this.port  + "/" + this.database;
                System.out.println(jdbcUrl);
                conn = DriverManager.getConnection(jdbcUrl, this.username,
                this.password);
                System.out.println("Successfully connected");
                return conn;
        }

        public static void main(String[] args) {
                CreateConnection createConnection = new CreateConnection();
                try {
                        createConnection.getConnection();
                } catch (SQLException e){
                        e.printStackTrace();
                }
        }
}
```

The method portrayed in this example returns a Connection object that is ready to be used for database access.

How It Works

Creating a JDBC connection involves a few steps. First, you need to determine which database driver you need. After you've determined which driver you need, you download the JAR file containing that driver and place it into your classpath. Each database vendor provides different JDBC drivers packaged in JAR files with different names; consult the documentation for your database for more information. For this recipe, you can download the connector at `https://dev.mysql.com/downloads/connector/j/`. Ensure that the selected platform is "Platform Independent": this is important for distributing the software on different systems. Next, use a JDBC `DriverManager` class to obtain a connection to the database.

To obtain a connection to your database using the `DriverManager` class, you need to pass a string containing the JDBC URL to it. The JDBC URL consists of the database vendor name, along with the name of the server that hosts the database, the name of the database, the database port number, and a valid database username and password that has access to the schema or database objects that you want to work with. The values to create the JDBC URL are often obtained from a `Properties` file so that they can be easily changed if needed. The code that creates the MySQL database JDBC URL for solution 1 looks like the following.

```
String jdbcUrl = "jdbc:mysql:thin:@" + this.hostname + ":" +
                 this.port  + ":" + this.database;
```

Once all the variables have been substituted into the string, it looks like the following.

```
jdbc:mysql://localhost:3306/apressbooks
```

Once the JDBC URL has been created, it can be passed to the `DriverManager` `.getConnection()` method to obtain a `java.sql.Connection` object. If incorrect information has been passed to the `getConnection()` method, `java.sql.SQLException` is thrown; otherwise, a valid `Connection` object is returned.

12-3. Handling Connection and SQL Exceptions

Problem

A database activity in your application has thrown an exception. You need to handle the
SQL exception so that your application does not crash.

Solution

Use a `try-catch` block to capture and handle any SQL exceptions thrown by your JDBC
connection or SQL queries. The following code demonstrates how to implement a `try-`
`catch` block to capture SQL exceptions.

```
try {
    // perform database tasks
} catch (java.sql.SQLException){
    // perform exception handling
}
```

How It Works

A standard `try-catch` block can catch `java.sql.SQLException` exceptions. Your code
will not compile if these exceptions are not handled. It is a good idea to handle them
properly to prevent your application from crashing if one of these exceptions is thrown.
Almost any work that is performed against a `java.sql.Connection` object needs to
contain error handling to ensure that database exceptions are handled correctly. Nested
`try-catch` blocks are often required to handle all the possible exceptions. You need to
ensure that connections are closed once work has been performed and the `Connection`
object is no longer used. Similarly, it is a good idea to close `java.sql.Statement` objects
for memory allocation cleanup as well.

Because `Statement` and `Connection` objects need to be closed, it is common to see
`try-catch-finally` blocks ensure that all resources have been tended to as needed. It is
likely that you see older JDBC code that resembles the following style.

```
try {
    // perform database tasks
} catch (java.sql.SQLException ex) {
```

```
        // perform exception handling
} finally {
    try {
        // close Connection and Statement objects
    } catch (java.sql.SQLException ex){
        // perform exception handling
    }
}
```

Newer code should be written to take advantage of the try-with-resources statement, which allows one to offload resource management to Java, rather than performing manual closes. The following code demonstrates how to use try-with-resources to open a connection, create a statement, and then close both the connection and statement when finished.

```
try (Connection conn = createConn.getConnection();
        Statement stmt = conn.createStatement();) {
    ResultSet rs = stmt.executeQuery(qry);
    while (rs.next()) {
        // PERFORM SOME WORK
    }
} catch (SQLException e) {
    e.printStackTrace();
}
```

As seen in the previous pseudocode, nested try-catch blocks are often required to clean unused resources. Proper exception handling sometimes makes JDBC code rather laborious to write, but it also ensures that an application requiring database access does not fail, causing data to be lost.

12-4. Querying a Database and Retrieving Results

Problem

A process in your application needs to query a database table for data.

Solution

Obtain a JDBC connection, and then use the `java.sql.Connection` object to create a Statement object. A `java.sql.Statement` object contains the executeQuery() method, which parses a string of text and uses it to query a database. Once you've executed the query, you can retrieve the results in a ResultSet object. The following example queries a database table named RECIPES and prints the results.

```java
public class QueryDatabase {
    private static CreateConnection createConn;
    public static void main(String[] args) {
        createConn = new CreateConnection();
        queryDatabase();
    }
    public static void queryDatabase() {
        String qry = "select recipe_num, recipe_name, description
        from recipes";
        try (Connection conn = createConn.getConnection();
                Statement stmt = conn.createStatement();) {
            ResultSet rs = stmt.executeQuery(qry);
            while (rs.next()) {
                String recipe = rs.getString("RECIPE_NUM");
                String name = rs.getString("RECIPE_NAME");
                String desc = rs.getString("DESCRIPTION");
                System.out.println(recipe + "\t" + name + "\t"
                + desc);
            }
        } catch (SQLException e) {
    e.printStackTrace();
        }
    }
}
```

If you execute this code using the database script included with Chapter 12, you receive the following results.

How It Works

One of the most commonly performed operations against a database is a query. Performing database queries using JDBC is quite easy, although there is a bit of boilerplate code that needs to be used each time a query is executed. First, you need to obtain a Connection object for the database and schema that you want to run the query against. Next, you need to form a query and store it in string format. The Connection object then creates a Statement object. Your query string is passed to the Statement object's executeQuery() method to query the database. Here, you can see what this looks like without try-with-resources for resource management.

```
String qry = "select recipe_num, recipe_name, description from recipes";
Connection conn;
Statement stmt = null;
try {
    conn = createConn.getConnection()
    stmt = conn.createStatement();
    ResultSet rs = stmt.executeQuery(qry);
...
```

The same code can be more efficiently written as follows.

```
try (Connection conn = createConn.getConnection();
        Statement stmt = conn.createStatement();) {
    ResultSet rs = stmt.executeQuery(qry);
...
```

As you can see, the Statement object's executeQuery() method accepts a string and returns a ResultSet object. The ResultSet object makes it easy to work with the query results to obtain the information you need in any order. If you look at the next line of code in the example, a while loop is created on the ResultSet object. This loop continues to call the ResultSet object's next() method, obtaining the next row returned from the query with each iteration. In this case, the ResultSet object is named rs. So while rs.next() returns true, the loop continues to be processed. Once all the returned rows have been processed, rs.next() return a false to indicate that there are no more rows to be processed.

Within the while loop, each returned row is processed. The ResultSet object is parsed to obtain the values of the given column names with each pass. Notice that if the column is expected to return a string, you must call the ResultSet getString() method, passing the column name in string format. Similarly, if the column is expected to return an int, you'd call the ResultSet getInt() method, passing the column name in string format. The same holds true for the other data types. These methods return the corresponding column values. In the example in the solution to this recipe, those values are stored into local variables.

```
String recipe = rs.getString("RECIPE_NUM");
String name = rs.getString("RECIPE_NAME");
String desc = rs.getString("DESCRIPTION");
```

Once the column value has been obtained, you can do what you want with the values you have stored within local variables. In this case, they are printed out using the System.out() method.

```
System.out.println(recipe + "\t" + name + "\t" + desc);
```

java.sql.SQLException could be thrown when attempting to query a database (for instance, if the Connection object has not been properly obtained or if the database tables that you are trying to query do not exist). You must provide exception handling to handle errors in these situations. Therefore, all database-processing code should be placed within a try block. The catch block then handles SQLException; so if thrown, the exception is handled using the code within the catch block. Sounds easy enough, right? It is, but you must do it each time you perform a database query—lots of boilerplate code.

It is always a good idea to close statements and connections if they are open. Using the try-with-resources construct is the most efficient solution to resource management. Closing resources when finished helps ensure that the system can reallocate resources as needed, and act respectfully on the database. It is important to close connections as soon as possible so that other processes can use them.

12-5. Performing CRUD Operations
Problem

You need to have the ability to perform standard database operations within your application. That is, you need the ability to CRUD database records.

Solution

Create a Connection object and obtain a database connection, then perform the CRUD operation using a java.sql.Statement object that is obtained from the java. sql.Connection object. The database table that is used for these operations has the following format.

```
RECIPES (
    id                int not null,
    recipe_number     varchar(10) not null,
    recipe_name       varchar(100) not null,
    description       varchar(500),
    constraint recipes_pk primary key (id) enable
);
```

The following code excerpts demonstrate how to perform each of the CRUD operations using JDBC.

```java
import java.sql.Connection;
import java.sql.ResultSet;
import java.sql.SQLException;
import java.sql.Statement;
import org.java17recipes.chapter12.recipe12_01.CreateConnection;

public class CrudOperations {

    static CreateConnection createConn;
    public static void main(String[] args) {

            createConn = new CreateConnection();
            performCreate();
            performRead();
```

```java
            performUpdate();
            performDelete();
            System.out.println("-- Final State --");
            performRead();
    }

    private static void performCreate(){
        String sql = "INSERT INTO RECIPES VALUES(" +
                    "NULL, " +
                    "'12-5', " +
                    "'Performing CRUD Operations', " +
                    "'How to perform create, read, update, delete
                    functions')";

        try (Connection conn = createConn.getConnection();
                Statement stmt = conn.createStatement();) {
            // Returns row-count or 0 if not successful
            int result = stmt.executeUpdate(sql);
            if (result == 1{
                System.out.println("-- Record created --");
            } else {
                System.err.println("!! Record NOT Created !!");
            }
        } catch (SQLException e) {
            e.printStackTrace();
        }
    }

    private static void performRead(){
        String qry = "select recipe_number, recipe_name, description from
        recipes";

        try (Connection conn = createConn.getConnection();
                Statement stmt = conn.createStatement();) {
            ResultSet rs = stmt.executeQuery(qry);
            while (rs.next()) {
                String recipe = rs.getString("RECIPE_NUMBER");
```

```
                String name = rs.getString("RECIPE_NAME");
                String desc = rs.getString("DESCRIPTION");
                System.out.println(recipe + "\t" + name + "\t" + desc);
            }
        } catch (SQLException e) {
            e.printStackTrace();
        }
    }
    private static void performUpdate(){
        String sql = "UPDATE RECIPES " +
                     "SET RECIPE_NUMBER = '12-5' " +
                     "WHERE RECIPE_NUMBER = '12-4'";
        try (Connection conn = createConn.getConnection();
             Statement stmt = conn.createStatement();) {
            int result = stmt.executeUpdate(sql);
            if (result == 1){
                System.out.println("-- Record Updated --");
            } else {
                System.out.println("!! Record NOT Updated !!");
            }
        } catch (SQLException e) {
            e.printStackTrace();
        }
    }

    private static void performDelete(){
        String sql = "DELETE FROM RECIPES WHERE RECIPE_NUMBER = '12-5'";

        try (Connection conn = createConn.getConnection();
             Statement stmt = conn.createStatement();) {
            int result = stmt.executeUpdate(sql);
            if (result > 0){
                System.out.println("-- Record Deleted --");
            } else {
                System.out.println("!! Record NOT Deleted!!");
            }
        }
```

```
      } catch (SQLException e) {
          e.printStackTrace();
      }
    }
}
```

Here is the result of running the code.

```
-- Record created -

12-1 Installing MySQL Downloading and installation of a MySQL Database
12-2 Connecting to a Database DriverManager and DataSource Implementations
12-3 Handling SQL Exceptions Using SQLException
12-4 Querying a Database and Retrieving Results Obtaining and using data
     from a DBMS
12-5 Performing CRUD Operations How to perform create, read, update, delete
     functions

-- Record Updated --

-- Record Deleted -

-- Final State --
12-1 Installing MySQL  Downloading and installation of a MySQL Database
12-2 Connecting to a Database DriverManager and DataSource Implementations
12-3 Handling SQL Exceptions Using SQLException
```

How It Works

The same basic code format is used for performing just about every database task. The format is as follows.

1. Obtain a connection to the database.

2. Create a statement from the connection.

3. Perform a database task with the statement.

4. Do something with the results of the database task.

5. Close the statement (and database connection if you're finished using it).

The main difference between performing a query using JDBC and DML is that you call different methods on the Statement object, depending on which operation you want to perform. To perform a query, you need to call the Statement executeQuery() method. To perform DML tasks such as insert, update, and delete, call the executeUpdate() method.

The performCreate() method in the solution to this recipe demonstrates inserting a record into a database. To insert a record in the database, construct a SQL INSERT statement in string format. To perform the insert, pass the SQL string to the Statement object's executeUpdate() method. If the INSERT is performed, an int value is returned that specifies the number of rows that have been inserted. If the INSERT operation is not performed successfully, either a zero is returned, or SQLException is thrown, indicating a problem with the statement or database connection.

The performRead() method in the solution to this recipe demonstrates querying the database. To execute a query, call the Statement object's executeQuery() method, passing a SQL statement in string format. The result is a ResultSet object, which can then work with the returned data. For more information on performing queries, see Recipe 12-4.

The performUpdate() method in the solution to this recipe demonstrates updating records within a database table. First, construct a SQL UPDATE statement in string format. Next, to perform the update operation, pass the SQL string to the Statement object's executeUpdate() method. If the UPDATE is successfully performed, an int value is returned, which specifies the number of updated records. If the UPDATE operation is not performed successfully, either a zero is returned, or SQLException is thrown, indicating a problem with the statement or database connection.

The last database operation that needs to be covered is the DELETE operation. The performDelete() method in the solution to this recipe demonstrates deleting records from the database. First, construct a SQL DELETE statement in string format. Next, to execute the deletion, pass the SQL string to the Statement object's executeUpdate() method. If the deletion is successful, an int value specifying the number of rows deleted is returned. Otherwise, if the deletion fails, a zero is returned, or SQLException is thrown, indicating a problem with the statement or database connection.

Almost every database application uses at least one of the CRUD operations at some point. This is foundational JDBC that needs to be known if you are working with databases within Java applications. Even if you do not work directly with the JDBC API, it is good to know these foundational basics.

12-6. Simplifying Connection Management

Problem

Your application requires the use of a database, and to work with the database, you need to open a connection for each interaction. Rather than code the logic to open a database connection every time you need to access the database, you want to use a single class to perform that task.

Solution

Write a class to handle all the connection management within your application. Doing so allows you to call that class to obtain a connection, rather than setting up a new Connection object each time you need access to the database. Perform the following steps to set up a connection management environment for your JDBC application.

1. Create a class named CreateConnection.java that encapsulates your application's connection logic.

2. Create a Properties file to store your connection information. Place the file somewhere on your classpath so that the CreateConnection class can load it.

3. Use the CreateConnection class to obtain your database connections.

The following code of the CreateConnection class can be used for centralized connection management.

```java
import java.io.File;
import java.io.IOException;
import java.io.InputStream;
import java.nio.file.FileSystems;
import java.nio.file.Files;
import java.sql.Connection;
import java.sql.DriverManager;
import java.sql.SQLException;
import java.util.Properties;
```

```java
public class CreateConnection {

        static Properties props = new Properties();

        String hostname = null;
        String port = null;
        String database = null;
        String username = null;
        String password = null;

        public CreateConnection(){

                try (InputStream in = Files.newInputStream(FileSystems
                .getDefault().
                                getPath(System.getProperty("user.dir") +
                                        File.separator + "db_props
                                        .properties")); ) {

                        props.load(in);
                        in.close();
                } catch (IOException ex) {
                        ex.printStackTrace();

                }
                loadProperties();
        }

        public final void loadProperties(){
                this.hostname = props.getProperty("host_name");
                port = props.getProperty("port_number");
                database = props.getProperty("db_name");
                username = props.getProperty("username");
                password = props.getProperty("password");
        }

        public Connection getConnection() throws SQLException {
                Connection conn = null;
                String jdbcUrl;
                jdbcUrl = "jdbc:mysql://" + this.hostname + ":" +
                                this.port  + "/" + this.database;
```

```
            System.out.println(jdbcUrl);
            conn = DriverManager.getConnection(jdbcUrl, this.username,
            this.password);
            System.out.println("Successfully connected");
            return conn;
    }

    public static void main(String[] args) {
        CreateConnection createConnection = new CreateConnection();
        try {
            Connection conn = createConnection.getConnection();
            if (conn != null) {
                System.out.println("Closing
                Connection...");
                conn.close();
            }
        } catch (SQLException e){
            e.printStackTrace();
        }
    }
}
```

The following is the output.

```
jdbc:mysql://localhost:3306/apressbooks
Successfully connected
Closing Connection...
```

Next, the following lines of text are an example of what should be contained in the properties file that is used for obtaining a connection to the database. For this example, the properties file is named db_props.properties.

```
host_name=your_db_server_name
db_name=your_db_name
username=db_username
password=db_username_password
port_number=db_port_number
```

Finally, use the CreateConnection class to obtain connections for your application. The following code demonstrates this concept.

```
CreateConnection createConn = new CreateConnection();
try(Connection conn = createConn.getConnection()) {
    performDbTask();
} catch (java.sql.SQLException ex) {
    ex.printStackTrace();
}
```

This code uses try-with-resources to automatically close the connection after performing the database task.

How It Works

Obtaining a connection within a database application can be code-intensive. Moreover, the process can be prone to error if you retype the code each time you obtain a connection. By encapsulating database connection logic within a single class, you can reuse the same connection code when you require a connection to the database. This increases your productivity, reduces the chances of typing errors, and enhances manageability. If you have to make a change, it can occur in one place rather than in several different locations.

Creating a strategic connection methodology is beneficial to you and others who might need to maintain your code in the future. Although data sources are the preferred technique for managing database connections when using an application server, the solution to this recipe demonstrates the use of standard JDBC DriverManager connections. One of the security implications of using DriverManager is that you need to store the database credentials somewhere for use by the application. It is not safe to store those credentials in plain text anywhere, and it is also not safe to embed them in application code, which might be decompiled at some point in the future. As seen in the solution, a properties file that on disk stores the database credentials. Assume that this properties file is encrypted at some point before deployment to a server and that the application can handle decryption.

As seen in the solution, the code reads the database credentials, hostname, database name, and port number from the properties file. That information is then pieced together to form a JDBC URL that DriverManager can use to obtain a connection to the database. Once obtained, that connection can be used anywhere and then closed.

You could develop a JDBC application so that the code used to obtain a connection needs to be hard-coded throughout. Instead, this solution enables all the code for obtaining a connection to be encapsulated by a single class so that the developer does not need to worry about it. Such a technique also allows the code to become more maintainable. For instance, if the application were originally deployed using DriverManager, but then later had the ability to use DataSource, very little code would need to be changed.

12-7. Guarding Against SQL Injection

Problem

Your application performs database tasks. To reduce the chances of a SQL injection attack, you need to ensure that no unfiltered strings of text are being appended to SQL statements and executed against the database.

Tip   Although prepared statements are the solution to this recipe, they can be used more than protecting against SQL injection. They also provide a way to centralize and better control the SQL used in an application. Instead of creating multiple, possibly different, versions of the same query, for example, you can create the query once as a prepared statement and invoke it from many different places throughout your code. Any change to the query logic needs to happen only when you prepare the statement.

Solution

Use PreparedStatement objects for performing the database tasks. They send a precompiled SQL statement to the DBMS rather than a string. The following code demonstrates how to perform a database query and a database update using a java.sql.PreparedStatement object.

In the following code example, PreparedStatement queries a database for a given record. Assume that the a String[] of recipe numbers is passed to this code as a variable.

```
private static void queryDbRecipe(String[] recipeNumbers) {
    String sql = "SELECT ID, RECIPE_NUMBER, RECIPE_NAME, DESCRIPTION "
            + "FROM RECIPES "
            + "WHERE RECIPE_NUMBER = ?";

    try (PreparedStatement pstmt = conn.prepareStatement(sql)) {
        for (String recipeNumber : recipeNumbers) {
            pstmt.setString(1, recipeNumber);
            ResultSet rs = pstmt.executeQuery();
            while (rs.next()) {
                System.out.println(rs.getString(2) + ": " + rs.getString(3)
                        + " - " + rs.getString(4));
            }
        }
    } catch (SQLException ex) {
        ex.printStackTrace();
    }
}
```

The next example demonstrates a PreparedStatement object that inserts a record into the database. Assume that the recipe number, title, and description are passed to this code as variables. The ID column is declared NOT NULL and AUTO-INCREMENT, so it is also possible to assign NULL to the column to generate sequence numbers.

```
private static void insertRecord(String recipeNumber,
        String title,
        String description) {
    String sql = "INSERT INTO RECIPES VALUES(" +
                "null, ?,?,?)";
    try(PreparedStatement pstmt = conn.prepareStatement(sql);) {
        pstmt.setString(1, recipeNumber);
        pstmt.setString(2, title);
        pstmt.setString(3, description);
        pstmt.executeUpdate();
        System.out.println("Record successfully inserted.");
```

```
        } catch (SQLException ex){
            ex.printStackTrace();
        }
}
```

In this last example, a `PreparedStatement` object deletes a record from the database. Again, assume that the `recipeNumber` string is passed to this code as a variable.

```
private static void deleteRecord(String recipeNumber) {
        String sql = "DELETE FROM RECIPES WHERE " +
                    "RECIPE_NUMBER = ?";
        try(PreparedStatement pstmt = conn.prepareStatement(sql);) {
            pstmt.setString(1, recipeNumber);
            pstmt.executeUpdate();
            System.out.println("Recipe " + recipeNumber + " successfully
            deleted.");
        } catch (SQLException ex){
            ex.printStackTrace();
        }
}
```

The main method is:

```
        public static void main(String[] args) {
            try {
                CreateConnection createConn = new CreateConnection();
                conn = createConn.getConnection();
                String[] recipeArr = new String[1];
                recipeArr[0] ="12-1";
                queryDbRecipe(recipeArr);
                insertRecord(
                    "12-6",
                    "Simplifying and Adding Security with Prepared
                    Statements",
                    "Working with Prepared Statements");
                recipeArr[0] ="12-6";
                queryDbRecipe(recipeArr);
                deleteRecord("12-6");
```

```
            } catch (java.sql.SQLException ex) {
                System.out.println(ex);
            } finally {
                if (conn != null) {
                    try {
                        conn.close();
                    } catch (SQLException ex) {
                        ex.printStackTrace();
                    }
                }
            }
        }
    }
```

The following is the output.

12-1: Installing MySQL - Downloading and installation of a MySQL Database
    Record successfully inserted.
12-6: Simplifying and Adding Security with Prepared Statements - Working
    with Prepared Statements
Recipe 12-6 successfully deleted.

As you can see, a `PreparedStatement` object is very much the same as a standard JDBC statement object, but instead, it sends precompiled SQL to the DBMS rather than strings of text.

How It Works

While standard JDBC statements get the job done, the harsh reality is that they can sometimes be insecure and cumbersome to work with. For instance, bad things can occur if a dynamic SQL statement queries a database. A user-accepted string is assigned to a variable and concatenated with the intended SQL string. In most ordinary cases, the user-accepted string would be concatenated, and the SQL string would query the database as expected. However, an attacker could decide to place malicious code inside the string (a.k.a. SQL injection), which would then be inadvertently sent to the database using a standard `Statement` object.

The use of PreparedStatements prevents such malicious strings from being concatenated into a SQL string and passed to the DBMS because they use a different approach. PreparedStatements use substitution variables rather than concatenation to make SQL strings dynamic. They are also precompiled, which means that a valid SQL string is formed prior to the SQL being sent to the DBMS. Moreover, PreparedStatements can help your application perform better because if the same SQL must be run more than once, it must be compiled only once. After that, the substitution variables are interchangeable, but the overall SQL can be executed by PreparedStatement very quickly.

Let's look at how a PreparedStatement object works in practice. If you look at the first example in the solution to this recipe, you can see that the database table RECIPES is being queried, passing a RECIPE_NUMBER and retrieving the results for the matching record. The SQL string looks like the following.

```
String sql = "SELECT ID, RECIPE_NUMBER, RECIPE_NAME, DESCRIPTION " +
             "FROM RECIPES " +
             "WHERE RECIPE_NUM = ?";
```

Everything looks standard with the SQL text except for the question mark (?) at the end of the string. Placing a question mark in a string of SQL signifies that a substitute variable is used in place of that question mark when the SQL is executed. The next step for using a PreparedStatement object is to declare a variable of type PreparedStatement. This can be seen with the following line of code.

```
PreparedStatement pstmt = null;
```

PreparedStatement implements AutoCloseable, and therefore it can be utilized within the context of a try-with-resources block. Once PreparedStatement has been declared, it can be put to use. However, the use of PreparedStatement might not cause an exception to be thrown. Therefore, if try-with-resources is not used, PreparedStatement should occur within a try-catch block so that any exceptions can be handled gracefully. For instance, exceptions can occur if the database connection is unavailable for some reason or if the SQL string is invalid. Rather than crashing an application due to such issues, it is best to handle the exceptions wisely within a catch block. The following try-catch block includes the code necessary to send the SQL string to the database and retrieve results.

```java
try(PreparedStatement pstmt = conn.prepareStatement(sql);) {
    pstmt.setString(1, recipeNumber);
    ResultSet rs = pstmt.executeQuery();
    while(rs.next()){
        System.out.println(rs.getString(2) + ": " + rs.getString(3) +
                        " - " + rs.getString(4));
    }
} catch (SQLException ex) {
    ex.printStackTrace();
}
```

First, you can see that the `Connection` object instantiates a `PreparedStatement` object. The SQL string is passed to the `PreparedStatement` object's constructor on creation. Since `PreparedStatement` is instantiated within the `try-with-resources` construct, it is automatically closed when it is no longer in use. Next, the `PreparedStatement` object sets values for any substitution variables that have been placed into the SQL string. As you can see, the `PreparedStatement` `setString()` method is used in the example to set the substitution variable at position 1 equal to the contents of the `recipeNumber` variable. The positioning of the substitution variable is associated with the placement of the question mark (?) within the SQL string. The first question mark within the string is assigned to the first position, the second one is assigned to the second position, and so forth. If more than one substitution variable were assigned, there would be more than one call against the `PreparedStatement` object, assigning each of the variables until each one has been accounted for. `PreparedStatement` objects can accept substitution variables of many different data types. For instance, if an int value were assigned to a substitution variable, a call to the `setInt(position, variable)` method would be in order. See the online documentation or your IDE's code completion for a complete set of methods that can be used for assigning substitution variables using `PreparedStatement` objects.

Once all the variables have been assigned, the SQL string can be executed. The `PreparedStatement` object contains an `executeQuery()` method that executes a SQL string that represents a query. The `executeQuery()` method returns a `ResultSet` object, which contains the results fetched from the database for the particular SQL query. Next, `ResultSet` can be traversed to obtain the values retrieved from the database. Again, positional assignments retrieve the results by calling the `ResultSet` object's corresponding getter methods and passing the position of the column value that you want to obtain. The position is determined by the order in which the column names appear within the SQL string. In the example, the first position corresponds to the RECIPE_NUMBER column, the second corresponds to the RECIPE_NAME column, and so forth. If the recipeNumber string variable was equal to 12-1, the results of executing the query in the example would look like the following.

12-1: Installing MySQL - downloading and installation of a MySQL Database

Of course, if the substitution variable is not set correctly or if there is an issue with the SQL string, an exception is thrown. This would cause the code contained within the catch block to be executed. You should also be sure to clean up after using PreparedStatements by closing the statement when you are finished using it. If you're not using a try-with-resources construct, it is a good practice to put all the cleanup code within a finally block to be sure that the PreparedStatement object is closed properly, even if an exception is thrown. In the example, the finally block looks like the following.

```
finally {
    if (pstmt != null){
        try {
            pstmt.close();
        } catch (SQLException ex) {
            ex.printStackTrace();
        }
    }
}
```

You can see that the PreparedStatement object that was instantiated, pstmt, is checked to see whether it is NULL. If not, it is closed by calling the close() method.

Working through the code in the solution to this recipe, you can see that similar code processes database INSERT, UPDATE, and DELETE statements. The only difference in those cases is that the PreparedStatement executeUpdate() method is called rather than the executeQuery() method. The executeUpdate() method returns an int value representing the number of rows affected by the SQL statement.

The use of PreparedStatement objects is preferred over JDBC Statement objects. This is because they are more secure and perform better. They can also make your code easier to follow and maintain.

12-8. Performing Transactions

Problem

The way in which your application is structured requires sequential processing of tasks. One task depends on another, and each process performs a different database action. If one of the tasks along the way fails, the database processing that has already occurred needs to be reversed.

Solution

Set your `Connection` object autocommit to false and perform the transactions you want to complete. Once you've successfully performed each of the transactions, manually commit the `Connection` object; otherwise, roll back each of the transactions that have taken place. The following code example demonstrates transaction management. If you look at the `main()` method of the `TransactionExample` class, you see that the `Connection` object's `autoCommit()` preference has been set to false so that database statements are grouped together to form one transaction. If all the statements within the transaction are successful, the `Connection` object is manually committed by calling the `commit()` method; otherwise, all the statements are rolled back by calling the `rollback()` method. By default, autoCommit is set to true, which automatically treats every statement as a single transaction.

```
import java.sql.Connection;
import java.sql.PreparedStatement;
import java.sql.ResultSet;
import java.sql.SQLException;
import org.java17recipes.chapter12.recipe12_01.CreateConnection;
public class TransactionExample {

    public static Connection conn = null;
    public static void main(String[] args) {
        boolean successFlag = false;
        try {
            CreateConnection createConn = new CreateConnection();
            conn = createConn.getConnection();
            conn.setAutoCommit(false);
```

455

```
        queryDbRecipes();
        successFlag = insertRecord(
                "12-6",
                "Simplifying and Adding Security with Prepared
                Statements",
                "Working with Prepared Statements");

        if (successFlag == true){

            successFlag = insertRecord(
                    null,
                    "Simplifying and Adding Security with Prepared
                    Statements",
                    "Working with Prepared Statements");
        }
        // Commit Transactions
        if (successFlag == true)
            conn.commit();
        else
            conn.rollback();
        conn.setAutoCommit(true);
        queryDbRecipes();
    } catch (java.sql.SQLException ex) {
        System.out.println(ex);
    } finally {
        if (conn != null) {
            try {
                conn.close();
            } catch (SQLException ex) {
                ex.printStackTrace();
            }
        }
    }
}
```

```java
private static void queryDbRecipes(){
    String sql = "SELECT ID, RECIPE_NUMBER, RECIPE_NAME, DESCRIPTION " +
    "FROM RECIPES";
    try(PreparedStatement pstmt = conn.prepareStatement(sql);) {
        ResultSet rs = pstmt.executeQuery();
        while(rs.next()){
            System.out.println(rs.getString(2) + ": " +
            rs.getString(3) + " - " + rs.getString(4));
        }
    } catch (SQLException ex) {
        ex.printStackTrace();
    }
}
private static boolean insertRecord(String recipeNumber,
                        String title,
                        String description){
    String sql = "INSERT INTO RECIPES VALUES(" +
                "NULL, ?,?,?)";
    boolean success = false;
    try(PreparedStatement pstmt = conn.prepareStatement(sql);) {
        pstmt.setString(1, recipeNumber);
        pstmt.setString(2, title);
        pstmt.setString(3, description);
        pstmt.executeUpdate();
        System.out.println("Record successfully inserted.");
        success = true;
    } catch (SQLException ex){
        success = false;
        ex.printStackTrace();
    }
    return success;
}
}
```

The following is the output.

```
12-2: Connecting to a Database - DriverManager and DataSource Implementations
12-3: Handling SQL Exceptions - Using SQLException
Record successfully inserted.
java.sql.SQLIntegrityConstraintViolationException: Column 'recipe_number'
cannot be null
        at mysql.connector.java@8.0.27/com.mysql.cj.jdbc.exceptions
        .SQLError.createSQLException(SQLError.java:117)
        at mysql.connector.java@8.0.27/com.mysql.cj.jdbc.exceptions
        .SQLExceptionsMapping.translateException(SQLExceptionsMapping
        .java:122)
        at mysql.connector.java@8.0.27/com.mysql.cj.jdbc
        .ClientPreparedStatement.executeInternal(ClientPreparedStatement
        .java:953)
        at mysql.connector.java@8.0.27/com.mysql.cj.jdbc
        .ClientPreparedStatement.executeUpdateInternal(ClientPrepared
        Statement.java:1098)
        at mysql.connector.java@8.0.27/com.mysql.cj.jdbc
        .ClientPreparedStatement.executeUpdateInternal(ClientPrepared
        Statement.java:1046)
        at mysql.connector.java@8.0.27/com.mysql.cj.jdbc
        .ClientPreparedStatement.executeLargeUpdate(ClientPrepared
        Statement.java:1371)
        at mysql.connector.java@8.0.27/com.mysql.cj.jdbc
        .ClientPreparedStatement.executeUpdate(ClientPreparedStatement
        .java:1031)
        at org.java17recipes.chapter12.recipe12_08.Transaction
        Example.insertRecord(TransactionExample.java:83)
        at org.java17recipes.chapter12.recipe12_08.TransactionExample
        .main(TransactionExample.java:29)
12-1: Installing MySQL - Downloading and installation of a MySQL Database
12-2: Connecting to a Database - DriverManager and DataSource Implementations
12-3: Handling SQL Exceptions - Using SQLException
```

In the end, if any of the statements fails, all transactions are rolled back. However, if all the statements execute properly, everything is committed.

How It Works

Transaction management can play an important role in an application. This holds true especially for applications that perform different tasks that depend on each other. In many cases, if one of the tasks performed within a transaction fails, it is preferable for the entire transaction to fail rather than having it only partially complete. For instance, imagine that you were adding database user records to your application database. Now let's say that adding a user for your application required a couple of different database tables to be modified, maybe a table for roles, and so on. What would happen if your first table was modified correctly and the second table modification failed? You would be left with a partially complete application user addition, and your user would most likely not be able to access the application as expected. In such a situation, it would be nicer to roll back all the already-completed database modifications if one of the updates failed so that the database was left in a clean state and the transaction could be attempted once again.

By default, a Connection object is set up so that autocommit is turned on. That means that each database INSERT, UPDATE, or DELETE statement is committed right away. Usually, this is the way that you want your applications to function. However, when you have many database statements that rely on one another, it is important to turn off autocommit so that all the statements can be committed at once. To do so, call the Connection object's setAutoCommit() method and pass a false value. As you can see in the solution to this recipe, the setAutoCommit() method is called passing a false value, the database statements are executed. Doing so cause all the database statement changes to be temporary until the Connection object's commit() method is called. This allows you to ensure that all the statements execute properly before issuing commit(). Take a look at this transaction management code contained within the main() method of the TransactionExample class within the solution to this recipe.

```
boolean successFlag = false;
...
CreateConnection createConn = new CreateConnection();
conn = createConn.getConnection();
conn.setAutoCommit(false);
queryDbRecipes();
```

```
successFlag = insertRecord(
                "12-6",
                "Simplifying and Adding Security with Prepared
                Statements",
                "Working with Prepared Statements);
if (successFlag == true){
    successFlag = insertRecord(
        null,
        "Simplifying and Adding Security with Prepared Statements",
        "Working with Prepared Statements);
}
// Commit Transactions
if (successFlag == true)
    conn.commit();
else
    conn.rollback();
conn.setAutoCommit(true);
```

Note that the commit() method is called only if all transaction statements were processed successfully. If any of them fail, the successFlag is equal to false, which would cause the rollback() method to be called instead. In the solution to this recipe, the second call to insertRecord() attempts to insert a NULL value into the RECIPE_NUMBER column, which is not allowed. Therefore, that insert fails, and everything, including the previous insert, gets rolled back.

12-9. Creating a Scrollable ResultSet

Problem

You have queried the database and obtained some results. You want to store those results in an object that allows you to traverse forward and backward through the results, updating values as needed.

Solution

Create a scrollable ResultSet object, and then you can read the next, first, last, and previous record. Using a scrollable ResultSet object allows the query results to be fetched in any direction so that the data can be retrieved as needed. The following example method demonstrates the creation of a scrollable ResultSet object.

```
private static void queryDbRecipes(){
    String sql = "SELECT ID, RECIPE_NUMBER, RECIPE_NAME, DESCRIPTION " +
                "FROM RECIPES";

    try(PreparedStatement pstmt =conn.prepareStatement(sql,
            ResultSet.TYPE_SCROLL_INSENSITIVE, ResultSet.CONCUR_READ_ONLY);
        ResultSet rs = pstmt.executeQuery()) {

        rs.first();
        System.out.println(rs.getString(2) + ": " + rs.getString(3) +
                    " - " + rs.getString(4));

        rs.next();
        System.out.println(rs.getString(2) + ": " + rs.getString(3) +
                    " - " + rs.getString(4));

        rs.previous();
        System.out.println(rs.getString(2) + ": " + rs.getString(3) +
                    " - " + rs.getString(4));

        rs.last();
        System.out.println(rs.getString(2) + ": " + rs.getString(3) +
                    " - " + rs.getString(4));
    } catch (SQLException ex) {
        ex.printStackTrace();
    }
}
```

The main method is:
```
public static void main(String[] args) {
        boolean successFlag = false;
        try {
```

```
            CreateConnection createConn = new CreateConnection();
            conn = createConn.getConnection();
            // Perform Scrollable Query
            queryDbRecipes();
        } catch (java.sql.SQLException ex) {
            System.out.println(ex);
        } finally {
            if (conn != null) {
                try {
                    conn.close();
                } catch (SQLException ex) {
                    ex.printStackTrace();
                }
            }
        }

    }
```

Executing this method results in the following output using the originally loaded data for this chapter.

```
Successfully connected
12-1: Connecting to a Database - DriverManager and DataSource
      Implementations - More to Come
12-2: Querying a Database and Retrieving Results - Obtaining and Using Data
      from a DBMS
12-1: Connecting to a Database - DriverManager and DataSource
      Implementations - More to Come
12-3: Handling SQL Exceptions - Using SQLException
```

How It Works

Ordinary ResultSet objects allow results to be fetched in a forward direction. An application can process a default ResultSet object from the first record retrieved forward to the last. Sometimes an application requires more functionality when it comes to traversing a ResultSet object. For instance, let's say you want to write an application that allows someone to display the first or last record retrieved, or perhaps page forward or backward through results. You could not do this very easily using a standard ResultSet. However, by creating a scrollable ResultSet, you can easily move backward and forward through the results.

To create a scrollable ResultSet object, you must first create an instance of Statement or PreparedStatement that can create a scrollable ResultSet. When creating the Statement, you must pass the ResultSet scroll type constant value to the Connection object's createStatement() method. Likewise, you must pass the scroll type constant value to the Connection object's prepareStatement() method when using PreparedStatement.

You must also pass a ResultSet concurrency constant to advise whether ResultSet is intended to be updatable. The default is ResultSet.CONCUR_READ_ONLY, which means that the ResultSet object is not updatable. The other concurrency type is ResultSet .CONCUR_UPDATABLE, which signifies an updatable ResultSet object.

In the solution to this recipe, a PreparedStatement object is used. Creating a PreparedStatement object that can generate a scrollable ResultSet looks like the following line.

```
pstmt = conn.prepareStatement(sql, ResultSet.TYPE_SCROLL_INSENSITIVE,
                            ResultSet.CONCUR_READ_ONLY);
```

Once the PreparedStatement object has been created, a scrollable ResultSet is returned. You can traverse in several directions using a scrollable ResultSet by calling the ResultSet methods indicating the direction you want to move or the placement that you want to be. The following line of code retrieves the first record within the ResultSet.

```
ResultSet rs = pstmt.executeQuery();
rs.first();
```

The solution to this recipe demonstrates a few different scroll directions. Specifically, you can see that the ResultSet first(), next(), last(), and previous() methods are called to move to different positions within the ResultSet.

Scrollable ResultSet objects have a niche in application development. They are one of those niceties that are there when you need them, but they are also something that you might not need very often.

12-10. Creating an Updatable ResultSet

Problem

An application task has queried the database and obtained results. You have stored those results into a ResultSet object, and you want to update some of those values in ResultSet and commit them back to the database.

Solution

Make your ResultSet object updatable, and then update the rows as needed while iterating through the results. The following example method demonstrates how to make ResultSet updatable and then how to update content within that ResultSet, eventually persisting it in the database.

```
private static void queryAndUpdateDbRecipes(String recipeNumber){
        String sql = "SELECT ID, RECIPE_NUMBER, RECIPE_NAME, DESCRIPTION " +
                    "FROM RECIPES " +
                    "WHERE RECIPE_NUMBER = ?";
        ResultSet rs = null;
        try (PreparedStatement pstmt =
            conn.prepareStatement(sql, ResultSet.TYPE_SCROLL_SENSITIVE,
            ResultSet.CONCUR_UPDATABLE);){
        pstmt.setString(1, recipeNumber);
        rs = pstmt.executeQuery();
        while(rs.next()){
            String desc = rs.getString(4);
            System.out.println("Updating row" + desc);
            rs.updateString(4, desc + " -- More to come");
            rs.updateRow();
        }
    } catch (SQLException ex) {
        ex.printStackTrace();
    } finally {
        if (rs != null){
            try {
```

```
                    rs.close();
                } catch (SQLException ex) {
                    ex.printStackTrace();
                }
            }
        }
```

The main method method is:

```
public class UpdateResultSetExample {
    public static Connection conn = null;

    public static void main(String[] args) {
        boolean successFlag = false;
        try {
            CreateConnection createConn = new CreateConnection();
            conn = createConn.getConnection();

            // Perform Initial Query
            queryDbRecipes();

            // Update Resultset Row
            queryAndUpdateDbRecipes("12-1");

            // Query to see final results
            queryDbRecipes();
        } catch (java.sql.SQLException ex) {
            System.out.println(ex);
        } finally {
            if (conn != null) {
                try {
                    conn.close();
                } catch (SQLException ex) {
                    ex.printStackTrace();
                }
            }
        }
    }
```

This method could be called passing a string value containing a recipe number. Suppose that the recipe number "12-1" was passed to this method; the following output would be the result.

```
Successfully connected
12-1: Installing MySQL - Downloading and installation of a MySQL Database
12-2: Connecting to a Database - DriverManager and DataSource
       Implementations
12-3: Handling SQL Exceptions - Using SQLException
12-4: Querying a Database and Retrieving Results - Obtaining and using data
       from a DBMS
Updating row:Downloading and installation of a MySQL Database
12-1: Installing MySQL - Downloading and installation of a MySQL
       Database -- More to come
12-2: Connecting to a Database - DriverManager and DataSource
       Implementations
12-3: Handling SQL Exceptions - Using SQLException
12-4: Querying a Database and Retrieving Results - Obtaining and using data
       from a DBMS
```

How It Works

Sometimes you need to update data as you are parsing it. Usually, this technique involves testing the values returned from the database and updating them after comparison with another value. The easiest way is to make the ResultSet object updatable by passing the ResultSet.CONCUR_UPDATABLE constant to the Connection object's createStatement() or prepareStatement() method. Doing so causes the Statement or PreparedStatement to produce an updatable ResultSet.

Note   Some database JDBC drivers do not support updatable ResultSets. See the documentation of your JDBC driver for more information. This code was run using Oracle's ojdbc6.jar JDBC driver on Oracle database 11.2 release.

The format for creating a `Statement` object that produces an `updatable ResultSet` is to pass the `ResultSet` type as the first argument and the `ResultSet` concurrency as the second argument. The scroll type must be `TYPE_SCROLL_SENSITIVE` to ensure that `ResultSet` is sensitive to any updates. The following code demonstrates this technique by creating a `Statement` object that produces a scrollable and updatable `ResultSet` object.

```
Statement stmt = conn.createStatement(ResultSet.TYPE_SCROLL_SENSITIVE,
ResultSet.CONCUR_UPDATABLE);
```

The format for creating a `PreparedStatement` object that produces an updatable `ResultSet` is to pass the SQL string as the first argument, the `ResultSet` type as the second argument, and the `ResultSet` concurrency as the third argument. The solution to this recipe demonstrates this technique using the following line of code.

```
pstmt = conn.prepareStatement(sql, ResultSet.TYPE_SCROLL_SENSITIVE,
ResultSet.CONCUR_UPDATABLE);
```

Both lines of code discussed in this section produce scrollable and updatable `ResultSet` objects. Once you have obtained an updatable `ResultSet`, you can use it just like an ordinary `ResultSet` for fetching values retrieved from the database. In addition, you can call one of the `ResultSet` object's `updateXXX()` methods to update any value within the `ResultSet`. In the solution to this recipe, the `updateString()` method is called, passing the position of the value from the query as the first argument and the updated text as the second argument. In this case, the fourth element column listed in the SQL query is updated.

```
rs.updateString(4, desc + " -- More to come");
```

Finally, to persist the values that you have changed, call the `ResultSet updateRow()` method, as seen in the solution to this recipe.

```
rs.updateRow();
```

Creating an updatable `ResultSet` is not something that you need to do every day. In fact, you might never need to create an updatable `ResultSet`. However, for the cases in which such a strategy is needed, this technique can come in very handy.

12-11. Caching Data for Use When Disconnected

Problem

You want to work with data from a DBMS when you are in a disconnected state. That is, you are working on a device that is not connected to the database, and you still want to have the ability to work with a set of data as though you are connected. For instance, you are working with data on a portable device, and you are away from the office without a connection. You want to have the ability to query, insert, update, and delete data, even though there is no connection. Once a connection becomes available, you want to have your device synchronize any database changes that have been made while you were disconnected.

Solution

Use a CachedRowSet object to store the data that you want to work with while offline. This allows your application to work with data as though it were connected to a database. Once your connection is restored, or you connect back to the database, synchronize the data changed within the CachedRowSet with the database repository. The following example class demonstrates the use of a CachedRowSet. In this scenario, the main() method executes the example. Suppose that there was no main() method, though, and that another application on a portable device was to invoke the methods of this class. Follow the code in the example and consider working with the results stored within the CachedRowSet while not connected to the database. For instance, suppose that you began some work in the office while connected to the network and are now outside of the office, where the network is spotty, and you cannot maintain a constant connection to the database.

```
package org.java17recipes.chapter12.recipe12_10;
import java.sql.Connection;
import java.sql.SQLException;
import javax.sql.rowset.CachedRowSet;
import javax.sql.rowset.RowSetFactory;
import javax.sql.rowset.RowSetProvider;
import javax.sql.rowset.spi.SyncProviderException;
import org.java17recipes.chapter12.recipe12_01.CreateConnection;
```

```java
public class CachedRowSetExample {

    public static Connection conn = null;
    public static CreateConnection createConn;
    public static CachedRowSet crs = null;
    public static void main(String[] args) {
        boolean successFlag = false;
        try {
            createConn = new CreateConnection();
            conn = createConn.getConnection();
            // Perform Scrollable Query
            queryWithRowSet();
            // Update the CachedRowSet
            updateData();
            // Synchronize changes
            syncWithDatabase();
        } catch (java.sql.SQLException ex) {
            System.out.println(ex);
        } finally {
            if (conn != null) {
                try {
                    conn.close();
                } catch (SQLException ex) {
                    ex.printStackTrace();
                }
            }
        }
    }
    /**
     * Call this method to synchronize the data that has been used in the
     * CachedRowSet with the database
     */
    public static void syncWithDatabase() {
        try {
            crs.acceptChanges(conn);
        } catch (SyncProviderException ex) {
```

```
            // If there is a conflict while synchronizing, this exception
            // will be thrown.
            ex.printStackTrace();
        } finally {
            // Clean up resources by closing CachedRowSet
            if (crs != null) {
                try {
                    crs.close();
                } catch (SQLException ex) {
                    ex.printStackTrace();
                }
            }
        }
    }
    public static void queryWithRowSet() {
        RowSetFactory factory;
        try {
            // Create a new RowSetFactory
            factory = RowSetProvider.newFactory();
            // Create a CachedRowSet object using the factory
            crs = factory.createCachedRowSet();
            // Alternatively populate the CachedRowSet connection settings
            // crs.setUsername(createConn.getUsername());
            // crs.setPassword(createConn.getPassword());
            // crs.setUrl(createConn.getJdbcUrl());
            // Populate a query that will obtain the data that will be used
            crs.setCommand("select id, recipe_number, recipe_name,
            description from recipes");
            // Set key columns
            int[] keys = {1};
            crs.setKeyColumns(keys);
            crs.execute(conn);
            // You can now work with the object contents in a
            disconnected state
            while (crs.next()) {
```

```java
                System.out.println(crs.getString(2) + ": " + crs.
                getString(3) + " - " + crs.getString(4));
            }
        } catch (SQLException ex) {
            ex.printStackTrace();
        }
    }
    public static boolean updateData() {
        boolean returnValue = false;
        try {
            // Move to the position before the first row in the result set
            crs.beforeFirst();
            // traverse result set
            while (crs.next()) {
                // If the recipe_num equals 11-2 then update
                if (crs.getString("RECIPE_NUMBER").equals("12-2")) {
                    System.out.println("updating recipe 12-2");
                    crs.updateString("description", "Subject to change");
                    crs.updateRow();
                }
            }
        returnValue = true;
        // Move to the position before the first row in the result set
            crs.beforeFirst();
            // traverse result set to see changes
            while (crs.next()) {
                    System.out.println(crs.getString(2) + ":
                    " + crs.getString(3) + " - " + crs.getString(4));
            }
        } catch (SQLException ex) {
            returnValue = false;
            ex.printStackTrace();
        }
        return returnValue;
    }
}
```

Running this example code display output that looks similar to the following code, although the text might vary depending on the values in the database. Notice that the database record for Recipe 12-2 has a changed description after the update of the CachedRowSet.

```
Successfully connected
12-1: Installing MySQL - Downloading and installation of a MySQL
      Database -- More to come
12-2: Connecting to a Database - DriverManager and DataSource
      Implementations
12-3: Handling SQL Exceptions - Using SQLException
12-4: Querying a Database and Retrieving Results - Obtaining and using data
      from a DBMS
updating recipe 12-2
12-1: Installing MySQL - Downloading and installation of a MySQL
      Database -- More to come
12-2: Connecting to a Database - Subject to change
12-3: Handling SQL Exceptions - Using SQLException
12-4: Querying a Database and Retrieving Results - Obtaining and using data
      from a DBMS
```

How It Works

It is not possible to remain connected to the Internet all the time if you are working on a mobile device and traveling. Nowadays, some devices allow you to perform substantial work while on the go, even when you are not connected directly to a database. In such cases, solutions like the CachedRowSet object can come into play. The CachedRowSet is the same as a regular ResultSet object, except it does not have to maintain a connection to a database to remain usable. You can query the database, obtain the results, and place them into a CachedRowSet object; and then work with them while not connected to the database. If changes are made to the data at any point, those changes can be synchronized with the database later.

There are a couple of ways to create a CachedRowSet. The solution to this recipe uses a RowSetFactory to instantiate a CachedRowSet. However, you can also use the CachedRowSet default constructor to create a new instance. Doing so would look like the following line of code.

```
CachedRowSet crs = new CachedRowSetImpl();
```

Once instantiated, you need to set up a connection to the database. There are also a couple of ways to do this. Properties could be set for the connection used, and the solution to this recipe demonstrates this technique within comments. The following excerpt from the solution sets the connection properties using the `CachedRowSet` object's `setUsername()`, `setPassword()`, and `setUrl()` methods. Each of them accepts a string value, and in the example, that string is obtained from the `CreateConnection` class.

```
// Alternatively populate the CachedRowSet connection settings
// crs.setUsername(createConn.getUsername());
// crs.setPassword(createConn.getPassword());
// crs.setUrl(createConn.getJdbcUrl());
```

Another way to set up the connection is to wait until the query is executed and pass a `Connection` object to the `executeQuery()` method. This is the technique that is used in the solution to this recipe. But before you can execute the query, it must be set using the `setCommand()` method, which accepts a string value. In this case, the string is the SQL query that you need to execute.

```
crs.setCommand("select id, recipe_number, recipe_name, description from
recipes");
```

Next, if a `CachedRowSet` is used for updates, the primary key values should be noted using the `setKeys()` method. This method accepts an int array that includes the positional indices of the key columns. These keys identify unique columns. In this case, the first column listed in the query, ID, is the primary key.

```
int[] keys = {1};
crs.setKeyColumns(keys);
```

Finally, execute the query and populate the `CachedRowSet` using the `execute()` method. As mentioned previously, the `execute()` method optionally accepts a `Connection` object, which allows the `CachedRowSet` to obtain a database connection.

```
crs.execute(conn);
```

Once the query has been executed, and `CachedRowSet` has been populated, it can be used just like any other `ResultSet`. You can use it to fetch records forward and backward or by specifying the absolute position of the row you'd like to retrieve.

It is possible to insert and update rows within a CachedRowSet. To insert rows, use the moveToInsertRow() method to move to a new row position. Then populate a row by using the various methods (CachedRowSet, updateString(), updateInt(), and so on) that correspond to the data type of the column you are populating within the row. Once you have populated each of the required columns within the row, call the insertRow() method, followed by the moveToCurrentRow() method. The following lines of code demonstrate inserting a record into the RECIPES table.

```
crs.moveToInsertRow();
crs.updateInt(1, sequenceValue); // obtain current sequence values with a
                                 prior query
crs.updateString(2, "12-x");
crs.updateString(3, "This is a new recipe title");
crs.insertRow();
crs.moveToCurrentRow();
```

Updating rows is similar to using an updatable ResultSet. Simply update the values using the CachedRowSet object's methods [updateString(), updateInt(), and so on] that correspond to the data type of the column that you are updating within the row. Once you have updated the column or columns within the row, call the updateRow() method. This technique is demonstrated in the solution to this recipe.

```
crs.updateString("description", "Subject to change");
crs.updateRow();
```

To propagate any updates or inserts to the database, the acceptChanges() method must be called. This method can accept an optional Connection argument to connect to the database. Once called, all changes are flushed to the database. Unfortunately, there could be conflicts because time might have elapsed since the data was last retrieved for CachedRowSet. If such a conflict arises, SyncProviderException is thrown. You can catch these exceptions and handle the conflicts manually using a SyncResolver object. However, resolving conflicts is out of the scope of this recipe.

For more information, see the documentation at http://download.oracle.com/javase/tutorial/jdbc/basics/cachedrowset.html.

CachedRowSet objects provide great flexibility for working with data, especially when you are using a device that is not always connected to the database. However, they can also be overkill in situations where you can simply use a standard ResultSet or even a scrollable ResultSet.

12-12. Obtaining Dates for Database Use

Problem

You want to convert a LocalDate object properly to insert it into a database record.

Solution

Utilize the static java.sql.Date.valueOf(LocalDate) method to convert a LocalDate object to a java.sql.Date object, which can be utilized by JDBC for insertion or querying of the database. In the following example, the current date is inserted into a database column of type Date.

```java
public class DatesTimes {

    static CreateConnection createConn = new CreateConnection();

    public static void main(String[] args) {
        insertRecord(
                "Java 17 Recipes",
                "APRESS");
    }

    private static void insertRecord(
            String title,
            String publisher) {
        String sql = "INSERT INTO PUBLICATION VALUES("
                + "null, ?,?,?)";
        LocalDate pubDate = LocalDate.now();
        try (Connection conn = createConn.getConnection();
                PreparedStatement pstmt = conn.prepareStatement(sql);) {
            pstmt.setString(1, title);
            pstmt.setDate(2,  java.sql.Date.valueOf(pubDate));
            pstmt.setString(3, publisher);
            pstmt.executeUpdate();
            System.out.println("Record successfully inserted.");
```

```
    } catch (SQLException ex) {
        ex.printStackTrace();
    }
  }
}
```

How It Works

In Java 8, the new Date-Time API (Chapter 4) is the preferred API for working with dates and times. Therefore, when working with date values and databases, the JDBC API must convert between SQL dates and new Date-Time LocalDate objects. The solution to this recipe demonstrates that to obtain an instance of java.sql.Date from a LocalDate object, you simply invoke the static java.sql.Date.valueOf() method, passing the pertinent LocalDate object.

12-13. Closing Resources Automatically
Problem

Rather than manually opening and closing resources with each database call, you would prefer to have the application handle such boilerplate code for you.

Solution

Use the try-with-resources syntax to automatically close the resources that you open. The following block of code uses this tactic to automatically close the Connection, Statement, and ResultSet resources when it is finished using them.

```
public class TryWithResourcesExample {
    public static CreateConnection createConn;
    public static void main(String[] args) {
        createConn = new CreateConnection();
        queryDatabase();
    }
```

```
public static void queryDatabase() {
        String qry = "select recipe_number, recipe_name,
        description from recipes";

        try (Connection conn = createConn.getConnection();
                    Statement stmt = conn.createStatement();
                    ResultSet rs = stmt.executeQuery(qry);) {
            while (rs.next()) {
                    String recipe = rs.getString(
                    "RECIPE_NUMBER");
                    String name = rs.getString("RECIPE_NAME");
                    String desc = rs.getString("DESCRIPTION");
                    System.out.println(recipe + "\t" + name +
                    "\t" + desc);              }

        } catch (SQLException e) {
                e.printStackTrace();
        }
    }
}
```

The resulting output from running this code should look similar to the following.

```
Successfully connected
12-1 Connecting to a Database DriverManager and DataSource
     Implementations - More to Come
12-2 Querying a Database and Retrieving Results Subject to Change
12-3 Handling SQL Exceptions Using SQLException
```

How It Works

Java 7 introduced automatic resource management using try-with-resources. Through this technique, the developer no longer needs to close each resource manually, which is a change that can cut down on many lines of code.

To use this technique, you must instantiate all the resources you want to have automatic handling enabled within a set of parentheses after a try clause. In the solution to this recipe, the declared resources are Connection, Statement, and ResultSet.

```
try (Connection conn = createConn.getConnection();
    Statement stmt = conn.createStatement();
    ResultSet rs = stmt.executeQuery(qry);) {
```

Once those resources are out of scope, they are automatically closed. This means there is no longer a requirement to code a `finally` block to ensure that resources are closed. The automatic resource handling is available to database work and any resource that complies with the new `java.lang.Autocloseable` API. Other operations such as file I/O adhere to the new API as well. There is a single `close()` method within `java.lang.Autoclosable` that manages the closing of the resource. Classes that implement the `java.io.Closeable` interface can adhere to the API.

12-14. Summary

In many applications, databases have become essential for storing important information. It is important to have a good understanding of how to utilize databases for use within applications. This chapter started from the beginning, covering recipes on getting started with database access. It then covered important topics such as securely accessing and modifying data, transaction management, and data access when not connected to a network. You should now have a sound understanding of some techniques for working with data for your Java solutions. Keep in mind that there are many data access solutions, and the recipes in this chapter cover only some of the ways to tackle the beast of information management.

CHAPTER 13

Java Web Applications

Java development is not done on the desktop alone. Nowadays, web applications and apps can be considered the cornerstone of modern technology in private and government organizations. In fact, by interacting with a remote server, it is possible to find the needed information or purchase something online and, in general, use many services for your job or personal life. Thousands of enterprise applications are written using Java, enabling the development of sophisticated, robust, and secure applications.

This chapter introduces the Java servlet based on Jakarta EE (a Java class that runs on an application server) and JSP (a file that builds web pages dynamically). It shows how they work together within Tomcat to generate dynamic web pages.

Since web application development contains several interconnected processes, it is recommended to utilize an integrated development environment such as Eclipse EE (`www.eclipse.org/downloads/packages`) to more easily organize web projects. This chapter demonstrates some solutions to the recipes utilizing Eclipse. However, you can apply these same basic concepts to projects using any number of Java IDEs.

13-1. Installing Tomcat
Problem

You want to download and configure the main components for creating and configuring a simple Java web application project.

Solution

To run the examples in this chapter, you need to install the following components.

- Tomcat web server
- Eclipse development environment EE

Let's install Tomcat. It is the Java web server of Apache's Tomcat service, which is the servlet container that allows you to run JSP and in which Java code can run (Tomcat 10 is the latest version). It is easier and safer to download a compressed version and run the relevant scripts for the respective operating system.

Tomcat listens to three main communication ports of your PC (8005, 8009, and 8080). Before installing Tomcat, you should check whether any of your other applications already listen to one or more of those ports. To do so, use the `netstat` command that displays information about your computer's network communications. In Windows, you can open a terminal window and type the `netstat /a` command. It displays a list of active connections in tabular form. The second column of the table looks like the following.

```
Local Address
0.0.0.0:135
0.0.0.0:445
0.0.0.0:3306
```

The port numbers are the numbers after the colon. After installation, if you see one or more of the ports Tomcat uses, you must change the ports it listens to.

Here's how to install Tomcat 10 correctly.

1. Go to `https://tomcat.apache.org/download-10.cgi`. Below Quick Navigation, you see four links: KEYS, 10.0.13, Browse, and Archives.

2. Click **10.0.13** to take you toward the bottom of the same page to a heading with the same version number. Below the version heading, you see the Core subheading. Below that, you see the link for the zip download, arranged as follows: zip (pgp, sha512) apache-tomcat-10.0.13.zip. Click the zip link to download the apache-tomcat-10.0.13.zip (12.2 MB) file.

3. Unzip the downloaded file in the root. At this point, you should have the `C:\apache-tomcat-10.0.13` folder. We prefer to maintain the default folder name, in this case, to use different server versions without confusion. A business situation includes different environments (such as development, test, and delivery), so remember to maintain consistency between the server versions to prevent bugs or different behaviors.

4. Configure the server in the `setenv.bat` file in the `C:\ apache-tomcat-10.0.13\bin` folder with the following code.

    ```
    set "JRE_HOME=C:\jdk-17"
    set "JAVA_HOME=C:\jdk-17"
    exit /b 0
    ```

Note   Tomcat 10.0 requires Java 8 or later.

Now the server is ready to start. Go to `C:\apache-tomcat-10.0.13\bin` and double-click the startup.bat file. Or, open a command window, go to the bin folder, and type **startup.bat**. A second window is generated with the log of our applications.

To check that Tomcat is working properly, open a browser and type **localhost:8080**. You should see the page shown in Figure 13-1.

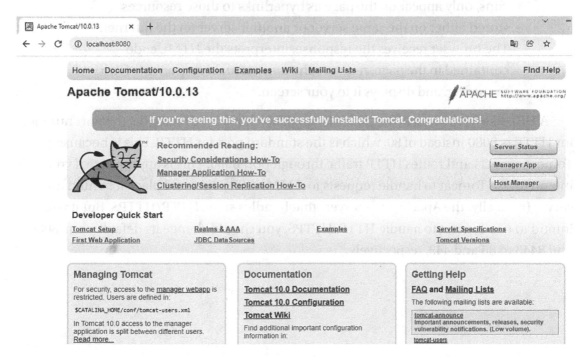

Figure 13-1. *The localhost home page*

How It Works

The following steps show what happens when you request your browser to view a web page (e.g., `http://localhost:8080/`) on your browser.

1. When you type an address such as `www.website.com` into the address field, your browser resolves into the corresponding Internet Protocol (IP) address, usually by asking the Domain Name System provided by your Internet Service Provider (ISP). Then your browser sends an HTTP (HyperText Transfer Protocol) request to the newly found IP address to receive the content required.

2. In reply, the web server sends an HTTP response containing a plain-text HTML (HyperText Markup Language) page. Images and other non-textual components, such as sound and video clips, only appear on the page as hyperlinks to those resources stored either on the same server or another server on the internet. The browser receives the response, interprets the HTML code contained in the page, requests the non-textual components from the server, and displays it to your screen.

A URL like `http://localhost:8080/` specifies that on the host side, the port number for HTTP is 8080 instead of 80, which is the standard port for HTTP. This is because Tomcat expects and routes HTTP traffic through port 8080. This is appropriate if you intend to use Tomcat to handle requests for HTML/JSP pages and place it behind a server (typically, the Apache web server) that handles static HTTP/HTTPS. But if you intend to use Tomcat to handle HTTP/HTTPS, you should change its default ports 8080 and 8443 to 80 and 443, respectively.

MVC (MODEL-VIEW-CONTROLLER)

The most widely used pattern in application development is MVC (Model-View-Controller). This pattern was described by Xerox, for the first time, in several publications in the late eighties. The most important aspect is the separation into three distinct components.

- Model is related to the application logic and persistence of data manipulation.

- View is related to the presentation, that is, the interface with the end user.

- Controller is related to the processing of requests.

This level of separation is important both for reasons of stability and security of the application. In this chapter, the development of Java web applications is based on the following main components.

- MySQL is a powerful relational database (RDBMS) for creating and managing databases for web applications: in fact, any non-trivial web application is likely to need handling data.

- JavaServer Pages (JSP) is a technology that helps you create such dynamically generated pages by converting script files into executable Java modules.

- Tomcat is a server application that can execute your code and act as a web server for your dynamic pages.

13-2. Creating an HTML Page

Problem

You want to create a simple HTML page.

Solution

HTML documents are organized as a hierarchy of elements that normally consist of content enclosed between a pair of start and end tags.

The following is the schema.

```
<TAG attributes>contents</TAG>
```

You can nest HTML elements inside each other. In fact, without nesting, no HTML page would be possible. The tag can be organized in the following way (with indentation).

```
<TAG1 attributes >
      <TAG2 attributes >
            content 2
      </TAG2>
</TAG1>
```

For example, the `<html>` and `</html>` tags delimit the whole HTML document. However, some elements are empty, in which case you can usually replace the end tag with a slash immediately before the closing bracket of the start tag, as in `<img src="mypict.gif"/>`.

You can insert comments in the following way.

```
<!-- comments -->
```

Each tag can have attributes with values.

```
<tag1 attribute1= "value1" attribute2= "value2">
```

The HTML document presents two sections.

```
<head>...</head>
<body>...</body>
```

The following are the definitions.

- Bold characters: `<b>`

- Underline characters: `<u>`

- Italic characters: `<i>`

- Newline: `<br>`

- Paragraph: `<p>`

- Heading: from `<h1>` to `<h6>`

The title tag defines a title for the HTML document.

The style tag defines style information for the HTML document. It can be inline for a section of the page or general (in this case, it is defined in the head tag of the HTML page).

Listing 13-1 shows the simplest possible HTML page. Copy the code in a text document and then change the extension in HTML. Double-click the file, and the HTML page opens in the predefined browser.

Listing 13-1. basic.html

```html
<html>
        <head><title>Page title</title></head>
                <style type="text/css">
                    body {background-color:gray; font-size=10pt;}
                </style>
        <body>
                <b>Bold characters</b>
                <u>Underline characters</u>
                <i>Italic characters</i>
                A newline<br>
                <p>A paragraph</p>
                <h1>A heading</h1>
        </body>
</html>
```

You can directly open a page or insert it in the `apache-tomcat-10.0.13\webapps\examples` folder (see Figure 13-2) that shows the outcome of Listing 13-2.

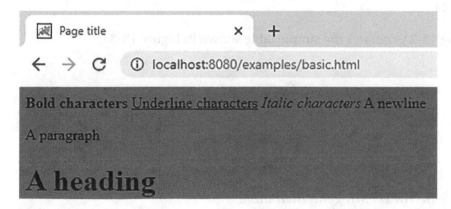

Figure 13-2. *A basic HTML page*

Essentially, an HTML document consists of text, images, audio and video clips, active components such as scripts and executables, and hyperlinks. A browser then interprets and renders the components in sequence, mostly without inserting any empty space or newline between them.

The following are the defining tables.

- `<table>...</table>` opens/closes a table

- `<tr>...</tr>` (table row) creates a row

- `<td>...</td>` (table data) creates a cell

A table consists of rows and columns containing text, images, and other components. In almost every chapter of this book, you'll find examples of tables. Tables are an easy way to present components in an organized fashion.

Listing 13-2 is an example.

Listing 13-2. table.html

```
<table border="1">
    <tr>
        <td> content 1</td>
        <td> content 2</td>
    </tr>
    <tr>
        <td> content 3</td>
        <td> content 4</td>
    </tr>
</table>
```

Listing 13-2 generates the simple table shown in Figure 13-3.

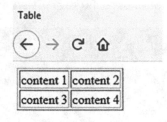

Figure 13-3. *An HTML-generated table*

To turn your web pages into an interactive experience, you must give users the ability to make choices and type or upload information (i.e., when you create a new email, you type data in an online form). To achieve this, you use the form element, which accepts data from the user and sends it to the server.

This book is full of examples of input forms. In Figure 13-4, the browser is Firefox.

Figure 13-4. *An HTML form with examples of all input elements*

The various types of input elements let the user enter a string of text or a password, check one or more check boxes, choose one of several radio buttons, submit a form or reset a form's fields. The textarea element lets the user enter several lines of text, while the fieldset element lets you group several input fields under one or more headings. To present multiple choices, you use the select element, which contains one option element for each alternative. Listing 13-3 is the source code for Figure 13-4.

Listing 13-3. form.html

```
<html>
<head>
  <title>Example of input form</title>
  <style type="text/css">
    td.h {font-size: 120%; font-weight: bold}
    </style>
  </head>
<body>
<form name="nameForm" action="" method="GET">
  <input type="hidden" name="agent" value="007"/>
  <table  cellpadding="5" border="1" rules="all">
    <tr>
      <td class="h">Element</td><td class="h">Attribute</td>
      <td class="h">Result</td></tr>
    <tr>
      <td>input</td><td>type="text"</td>
      <td><input type="text" name="t"/></td>
      </tr>
    <tr>
      <td>input</td><td>type="password"</td>
      <td><input type="password" name="p"/></td>
      </tr>
    <tr>
      <td>input</td><td>type="checkbox"</td>
      <td>
        <input type="checkbox" value="a" name="abc">A</input>
        <input type="checkbox" value="b" name="abc">B</input>
```

```
        <input type="checkbox" value="c" name="abc">C</input>
        </td>
    </tr>
<tr>
    <td>input</td><td>type="radio"</td>
    <td>
        <input type="radio" name="yn" value="y">yes</input>
        <input type="radio" name="yn" value="n">no</input>
        </td>
    </tr>
<tr>
    <td>input</td><td>type="submit"</td>
    <td><input type="submit"/></td>
    </tr>
<tr>
    <td>input</td><td>type="reset"</td>
    <td><input type="reset"/></td>
    </tr>
<tr>
    <td>input</td><td>type="button"</td>
    <td><input type="button" value="click me" name="b"/></td>
    </tr>
<tr>
    <td>textarea</td><td></td>
    <td><textarea name="ta">Default text</textarea></td>
    </tr>
<tr>
    <td>fieldset</td><td></td>
    <td><fieldset>
      <legend>Dimensions:</legend>
      Width <input type="text" size="3" name="w"/>
      Height <input type="text" size="3" name="h"/>
      </fieldset></td>
    </tr>
```

```
  <tr>
    <td>select / option</td><td></td>
    <td><select name="food">
      <option value="pizza" selected >Pizza</option>
      <option value="spaghetti">Spaghetti</option>
      </select></td>
    </tr>
  </table>
</form>
</body>
</html>
```

we've highlighted two lines. The first line, which contains the form element, shows that the action attribute is set to the empty string. The action attribute defines the URL of the page that must handle the request form. An empty string means that the same page displaying the form also handles it. The second highlighted line shows how you can use the input element to set parameters without the user being aware of it (unless he or she peeks at the source, that is).

If you fill in the form shown in Figure 13-4 and click the Submit button (or hit the Enter key), you'll see in the address field of your browser that the following string appears at the end of the URL (we've inserted newlines for readability).

```
?agent=007
&t=bla+bla+bla
&p=abc
&abc=a
&abc=c
&yn=n
&ta=ciao!
&w=1
&h=2
&food=pizza
```

The browser has translated each `input` element into a `parameter-name=parameter-value` string. Notice that each space in the text fields has been replaced by a plus sign, including the spaces within the password. Also, notice that the `abc` parameter appears twice because two of the three available check boxes are checked. To avoid seeing all the parameters in the browser, use in the `form` element the attribute `method="POST"`. Moreover, the POST method is more secure because data are stored in the HTTP request body, and it has no restrictions on data length.

For more information, you can simply go to `www.w3schools.com`, one of the more important and complete sites for web development.

How It Works

Several web sites explain HTML and components like CSS and JavaScript. Therefore, instead of covering everything there is to know about them, a few key concepts are introduced here for anyone beginning the study of web development. HyperText Markup Language (HTML) is the standard "tag" markup language used for creating HTML pages (with an `.htm` or `.html` extension). Therefore, it is the base for JSP pages. The browser interprets the HTML code contained in the page and requests the non-textual components from the server to display everything, such as images and video clips, to the user window.

13-3. Creating a JSP Page
Problem

You want to create and configure a simple dynamic web page.

Solution

JSP is a technology that lets you add dynamic content to web pages.

Listing 13-4 is a plain HTML page that displays "Hello World!" in your browser's window.

Listing 13-4. hello.html

```
<html>
        <head>
                <title>Hello World static HTML</title>
        </head>
        <body>
                Hello World!
        </body>
</html>
```

Create the %CATALINA_HOME%\webapps\ROOT\tests\ folder and store in it hello. html. Then type the following URL in your browser to see the web page.

http://localhost:8080/tests/hello.html

Normally, to ask your browser to check that the syntax of the page conforms to the XHTML standard of the World Wide Web Consortium (W3C), you would have to start the page with the following lines.

```
<?xml version="1.0" encoding="UTF-8"?>
<!DOCTYPE html PUBLIC "-//W3C//DTD XHTML 1.0 Strict//EN"
  "http://www.w3.org/TR/xhtml1/DTD/xhtml1-strict.dtd">
```

You'd also have to replace

```
<html>
```

with

```
<html xmlns="http://www.w3.org/1999/xhtml">
```

However, for this simple example, let's keep the code to what's essential. Figure 13-5 shows how this page appears in a browser.

Figure 13-5. *"Hello World!" in plain HTML*

If you direct your browser to show the page source, not surprisingly, you'll see what's shown in Listing 13-4. To obtain the same result with a JSP page, you only need to insert a JSP directive before the first line, as shown in Listing 13-5, and change the file extension from .html to .jsp.

Listing 13-5. "Hello World!" in a Boring JSP Page

```
<%@page language="java" contentType="text/html"%>
<html>
        <head>
                <title>Hello World dynamic HTML</title>
        </head>
        <body>
                Hello World!
        </body>
</html>
```

As with hello.html, you can view hello.jsp by placing it in Tomcat's ROOT\tests folder. Type the following URL in your browser to see the web page (see Figure 13-6).

http://localhost:8080/tests/hello.jsp

Hello World!

Figure 13-6. *"Hello World!" in JSP*

There isn't much point in using JSP for such a simple page. It only pays to use JSP if you include dynamic content. Check out Listing 13-6 for something juicier.

Listing 13-6. hello.jsp

```
<%@page language="java" contentType="text/html"%>
<html>
        <head>
                <title>Hello World dynamic HTML</title>
        </head>
        <body>
                Hello World!
                <%
                String userAgent = request.getHeader("user-agent");
                out.println("<br/>user-agent " + userAgent);
                %>
        </body>
</html>
```

The code within the `<% ... %>` pair is a scriptlet written in Java. When Tomcat's JSP engine interprets this module, it creates a Java servlet like that shown in Listing 13-7 (with some indentation and empty lines removed).

Listing 13-7. Java Code from the "Hello World!" JSP Page

```
out.write("\r\n");
out.write("<html>\r\n");
out.write("<head><title>Hello World dynamic
 HTML </title></head>\r\n");
out.write("<body>\r\n");
String userAgent = request.getHeader("user-agent");
out.println("<br/>User-agent: " + userAgent);
out.write("\r\n");
out.write("Hello World!\r\n");
out.write("</body>\r\n");
out.write("</html>\r\n");
```

How It Works

In absence of JSP, to update the appearance or the content of plain static HTML pages, you must always do it by hand. Even if all you want to do is change a date or a picture, you must edit the HTML file and type in your modifications. Nobody is going to do it for you, whereas with JSP, you can make the content dependent on many factors, including the time of the day, the information provided by the user, the user's history of interaction with your web site, and even the user's browser type. This capability is essential to provide online services in which you can tailor each response to the viewer who made the request, depending on the viewer's preferences and requirements.

The following steps explain how the web server creates the web page.

1. Your browser sends an HTTP request to the web server. This doesn't change with JSP, although the URL probably ends in `.jsp` instead of `.html` or `.htm`.

2. The web server is a Java server, with the extensions necessary to identify and handle Java servlets. The web server recognizes that the HTTP request is for a JSP page and forwards it to a JSP engine.

3. The JSP engine loads the JSP page from the disk and converts it into a Java servlet. From this point on, this servlet is indistinguishable from any other servlet developed directly in Java rather than JSP. However, the automatically generated Java code of a JSP servlet is not always easy to read, and you should never modify it by hand.

4. The JSP engine compiles the servlet into an executable class and forwards the original request to another part of the web server called the *servlet engine*. Note that the JSP engine only converts the JSP page to Java and recompiles the servlet if it finds that the JSP page has changed since the last request.

5. The servlet engine loads the servlet class and executes it. During execution, the servlet produces an output in HTML format, which the servlet engine passes to the web server inside an HTTP response.

6. The web server forwards the HTTP response to your browser.

7. Your web browser handles the dynamically generated HTML page inside the HTTP response exactly as if it were a static page. In fact, static and dynamic web pages are in the same format.

What reaches your browser is the output generated by the servlet (the converted and compiled JSP page), not the JSP page itself. The same servlet produces different outputs depending on the parameters of the HTTP request and other factors. For example, suppose you're browsing the products offered by an online shop. When you click the product's image, your browser generates an HTTP request with the product code as a parameter. As a result, the servlet generates an HTML page with that product's description. The server doesn't need to recompile the servlet for each product code. The servlet queries a database containing the details of all the products, obtains the description of the product you're interested in, and formats an HTML page with that data. This is what dynamic HTML is all about! Plain HTML is not capable of interrogating a database, but Java is, and JSP gives you the means of including snippets of Java inside an HTML page.

An evolution of JSP is the JavaServer Faces (JSF) API for creating component-based UIs for Java web applications. Within the MVC application architecture, JSF takes e place of the controller, thereby mediating every interaction between JSP (the view) and the model, which encapsulates the application data. JSF makes the development of web applications easier by letting you create user interfaces from a set of standard UI components wired to server-side objects and making available four custom tag libraries to handle those UI components. JSF transparently saves state information of the UI components and repopulates forms when they redisplay. This is possible because the states of the components live beyond the lifespan of HTTP requests. JSF operates by providing a controller servlet and a component model that includes event handling, server-side validation, data conversion, and component rendering.

JSF doesn't change the basic page life cycle that you already know from JSP: the client makes an HTTP request, and the server replies with a dynamically generated HTML page. Be warned that JSF isn't very easy to use, and it requires a non-negligible initial effort to get it going.

For more information on comprehensive Java web application development and how JSP and JSF are key technologies in the Jakarta EE platform with Eclipse, check out *Beginning Jakarta EE Web Development* by Luciano Manelli and Giulio Zambon (Apress, 2020).

13-4. Listing the HTML-Request Parameters

Problem

You want to list the parameters of an HTML request on a JSP page.

Solution

With JSP, you can generate dynamic web pages. That's settled. But the utility of dynamic pages goes well beyond recognizing what browser the viewer is using or displaying different information on different days. Adapting the content of a web page based on who the viewer is and what the viewer wants is what matters.

Each HTML request includes a series of parameters, which are usually the results of what the viewer enters in a form before hitting the Submit button. Additional parameters can also be part of the URL itself. For example, pages in multilingual websites sometimes have URLs ending with "?lang=en" to tell the server to format the requested page in English.

Listing 13-8 shows a simple JSP page that lists all the HTML-request parameters. It is a useful little tool to easily check what your HTML pages send to the server.

Listing 13-8. req_params.jsp

```
<%@page language="java" contentType="text/html"%>
<%@page import="java.util.*, java.io.*"%>
<%
  Map       map = request.getParameterMap();
  Object[] keys = map.keySet().toArray();
  %>
<html><head><title>Request Parameters</title></head><body>
  Map size = <%=map.size()%>
  <table border="1">
    <tr><td>Map element</td><td>Par name</td><td>Par value[s]</td></tr>
<%
    for (int k = 0; k < keys.length; k++) {
      String[] pars = request.getParameterValues((String)keys[k]);
      out.print("<tr><td>" + k + "</td><td>'" + keys[k] + "'</td><td>");
```

```
      for (int j = 0; j < pars.length; j++) {
        if (j > 0) out.print(", ");
        out.print("'" + pars[j] + "'");
        }
      out.println("</td></tr>");
      }
  %>
    </table>
</body></html>
```

How It Works

The interesting bits are in the lines are highlighted in bold. The first one tells you that the parameters are stored in an object of type Map and shows you how to retrieve the list of the parameter names.

The second highlighted line shows you how to insert the value of a Java variable directly into the output (i.e., into the HTML page) by enclosing it between the pair <%= and %>. This is different from using a scriptlet—in which you can use JSP to build dynamicity into a web page.

The third highlighted line shows how to request the values of each parameter you know the name of. The word *values* is used instead of *value* because each parameter can appear more than once within the same request. For example, save the JSP in the folder test created in \apache-tomcat-10.0.13\webapps\. Enter the following URL to get what is shown in Figure 13-7.

```
http://localhost:8080/test/req_params.jsp?a=b&c=d&a=zzz&empty=&empty=&1=22
```

Request Parameters   ✕   +

← → C ⌂   🛈 localhost:8080/test/req_params.jsp?a=b&c=d&a=zzz&empty=&empty=&1=22

Map size = 4

Map element	Par name	Par value[s]
0	'a'	'b', 'zzz'
1	'c'	'd'
2	'empty'	'', ''
3	'1'	'22'

Figure 13-7. *Output of req_params.jsp*

Notice that the parameter aptly named `empty` appears twice in the query string, which results in two empty strings in the parameter map. Also, looking at the `a` parameter, you'll notice that the values are returned in the same order in which they appear in the query string.

13-5. Creating and Configuring a Web Project

Problem

You want to create and configure a simple Java web application project that utilizes JSP.

Solution

There are a number of different project formats for creating a web application. Eclipse is an extremely powerful and extensible IDE, also well suited for web application development.

Note   You need to download the Eclipse IDE for Enterprise Java and web developers from `www.eclipse.org/downloads/packages/` and select your OS version, as explained in Chapter 1.

Once created, the new `eclipseEE` folder starts the IDE.

Once you see the Workbench screen, select the Servers tab, and click the new server wizard link, as shown in Figure 13-8.

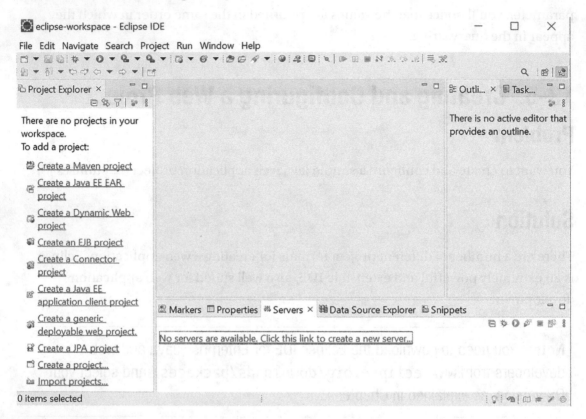

Figure 13-8. *Eclipse–the Workbench screen*

The screen that comes up is where you tell Eclipse to use Tomcat 10, as shown in Figure 13-9.

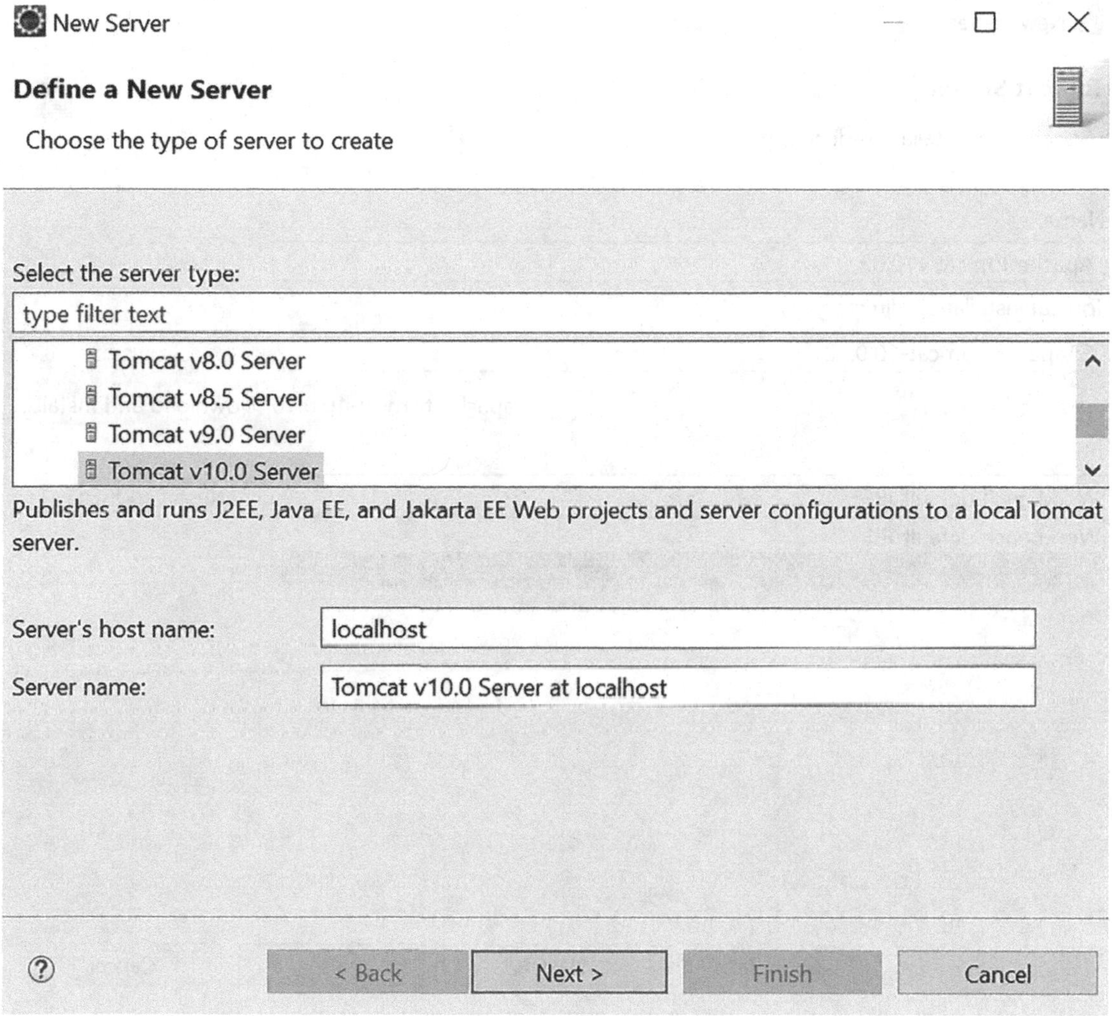

Figure 13-9. Eclipse—choosing Tomcat 10 as localhost

Next (and last), you need to tell Eclipse where to find Tomcat 9 and which version of the newly installed JDK 17 to use, as shown in Figure 13-10.

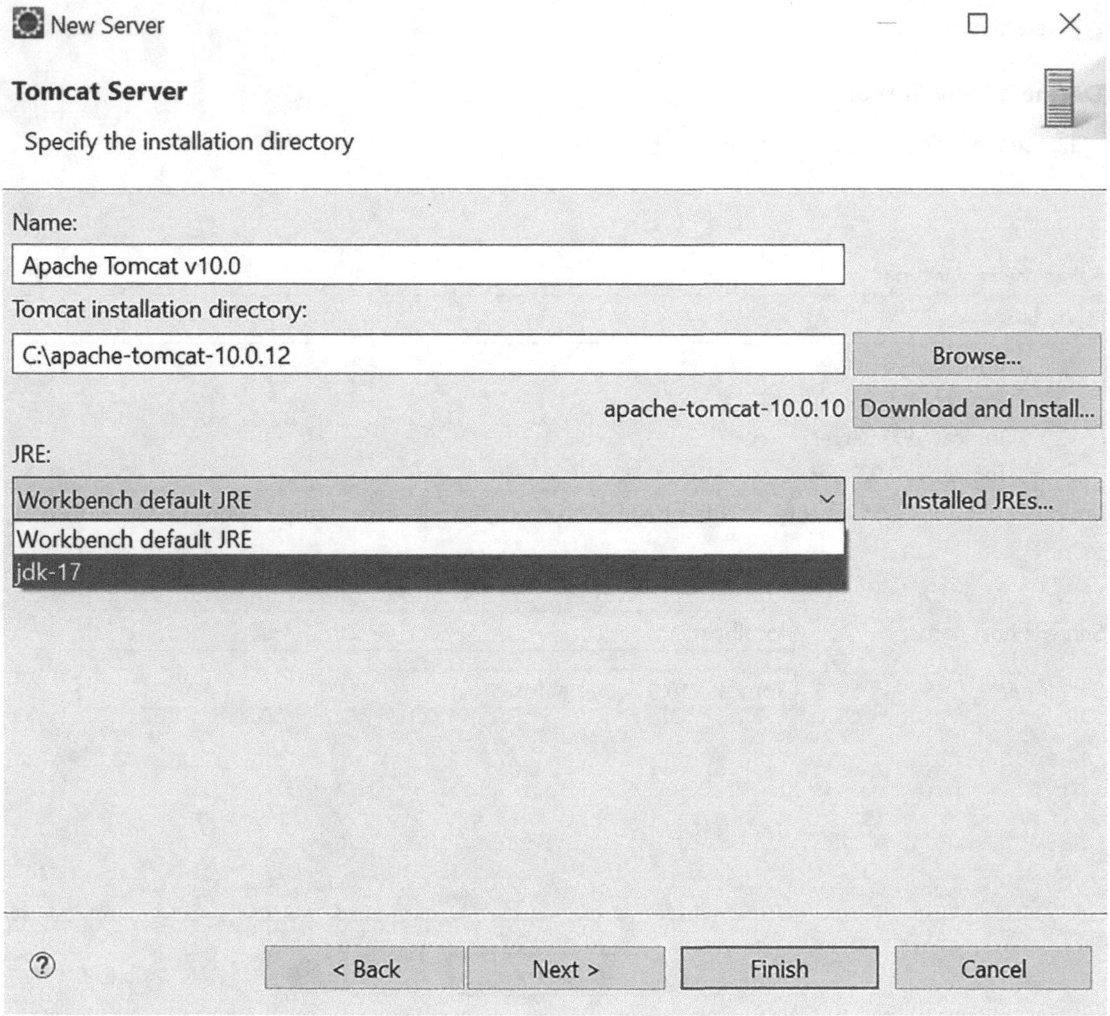

Figure 13-10. *Eclipse—completing the Tomcat configuration*

If you have done everything correctly, Tomcat 10 should appear under the Servers tab in Eclipse (see Figure 13-11).

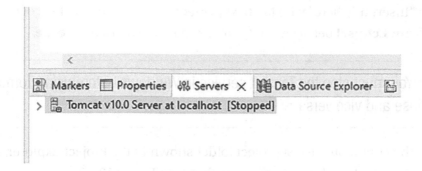

Figure 13-11. *Servers tab in Eclipse*

This configuration procedure is explained because Eclipse is a very complex application, and it is easy to get lost among the many options.

In the menu bar of the Workbench, select File ➤ New ➤ Dynamic Web Project, type a project name (e.g., `java17recipe`), and click the Next button. In the new screen, named Java, click the Next button. On the Web Module screen, click the Finish button.

The new project appears in the Project Explorer pane of Workbench.

Next, right-click the Web Content folder and select New ➤ JSP File. In the new JSP screen that appears, replace the default `NewFile.jsp` name with `index.jsp` and click the Finish button.

Eclipse shows the newly created file in the Project Explorer pane and opens it in Workbench's central pane for you to edit. Listing 13-9 shows the content.

Listing 13-9. java17recipe Project index.jsp

```
<%@ page language="java" contentType="text/html; charset=ISO-8859-1"
pageEncoding="ISO-8859-1"%>
<!DOCTYPE html>
<html>
      <head>
            <meta charset=ISO-8859-1">
            <title>Insert title here</title>
      </head>
      <body>

      </body>
</html>
```

Replace "Insert title here" with **My first project** (or whatever you like, of course), and type **Hello from Eclipse!** between <body> and </body>. Then save the file.

Caution   You must stop the Tomcat service in Windows before using Tomcat from within Eclipse and vice versa.

Position the cursor on the test project folder shown in the Project Explorer, right-click, and select Run As ➤ Run on Server, as shown in Figure 13-12.

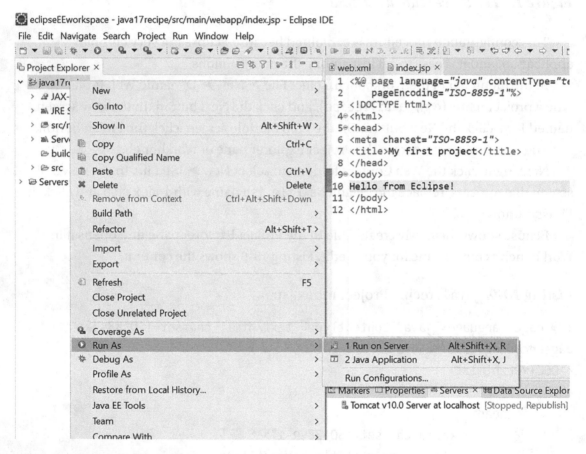

Figure 13-12.   *Eclipse—the run on Tomcat of the first project*

When a screen comes up, click Finish. You are rewarded with what is shown in Figure 13-13.

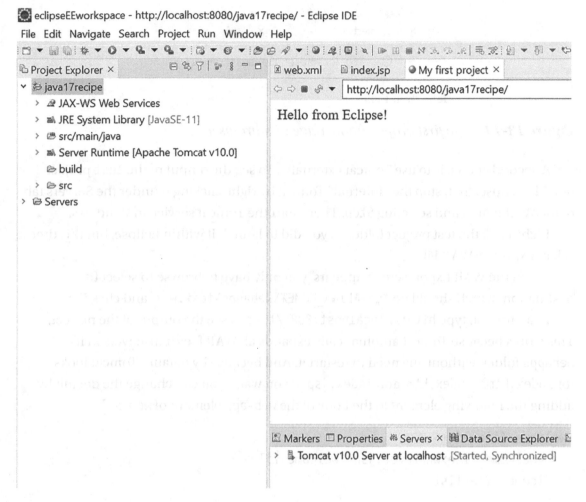

Figure 13-13. *Eclipse—the output of the first project*

It might seem very convenient that Eclipse can launch Tomcat and show the output within the Workbench. In practice, though, it has a couple of drawbacks. First, the space available in the central pane is limited because of the side and bottom panes. As a result, most web pages are "too squeezed" to display correctly.

You can maximize the web panel by double-clicking on the title bar, but there is also a more important reason: Eclipse doesn't always display everything. It should copy all files from the project folder to a Tomcat work directory, but it doesn't! It tends to "lose" CSS files and images. This means that, except for a quick check of simple features, you might also want to use Tomcat in Eclipse with an external browser.

Open a browser and type `localhost:8080/test`. You should see the same result on a browser page, as shown in Figure 13-14 (Chrome in the example).

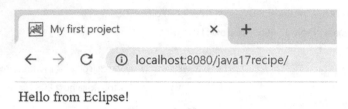

Hello from Eclipse!

Figure 13-14.   *The first project home page in a browser*

A second choice is to use Tomcat externally. To see the output of the `test` project outside Eclipse, first, stop the "internal" Tomcat by right-clicking it under the Servers tab of the Workbench and selecting `Stop`. Then, start the Tomcat service in Windows.

Right-click the test project folder as you did to launch it within Eclipse, but this time select Export ➤ WAR File.

When the WAR Export screen appears, you only have to browse to select the destination, which should be `%CATALINA_HOME%\webapps\test.war`, and click Finish.

In a browser, type `http://localhost:8080/test` to see the output of the project. This works because Tomcat automatically expands all WAR files it discovers in its `webapps` folder, without any need to restart it. And because by default, Tomcat looks for `index.html`, `index.htm`, and `index.jsp`. If you want, you can change the default by adding the following element to the body of the `web-app` element of `web.xml`.

```
<welcome-file-list>
    <welcome-file>whatever.jsp</welcome-file>
</welcome-file-list>
```

How It Works

The development of web applications requires the orchestration of several different files. While it is possible to develop a Java EE web application without using an IDE, using a development environment makes it almost a trivial task. In this recipe, the Eclipse EE IDE configures web applications.

13-6. Creating a Servlet

Problem

You want to create a controller for a web application project.

Solution

Create a Java servlet at File ➤ New ➤ Servlet. Define `FirstServlet` in the `org.java17recipes.chapter13` package (conventionally, class and servlet names are capitalized). It is important to check the `init` and `destroy` methods in a servlet.

The following shows the Java code of the newly created servlet.

```java
package org.java17recipes.chapter13;

import java.io.IOException;
import jakarta.servlet.ServletConfig;
import jakarta.servlet.ServletException;
import jakarta.servlet.annotation.WebServlet;
import jakarta.servlet.http.HttpServlet;
import jakarta.servlet.http.HttpServletRequest;
import jakarta.servlet.http.HttpServletResponse;

/**
 * Servlet implementation class FirstServlet
 */
public class FirstServlet extends HttpServlet {
        private static final long serialVersionUID = 1L;

    /**
     * Default constructor.
     */
    public FirstServlet() {
        // TODO Auto-generated constructor stub
    }
        /**
         * @see Servlet#init(ServletConfig)
         */
```

```java
    public void init(ServletConfig config) throws ServletException {
        // TODO Auto-generated method stub
    }

    /**
     * @see Servlet#destroy()
     */
    public void destroy() {
        // TODO Auto-generated method stub
    }

    /**
     * @see HttpServlet#doGet(HttpServletRequest request,
     HttpServletResponse response)
     */
    protected void doGet(HttpServletRequest request, HttpServlet
    Response response) throws ServletException, IOException {
    // TODO Auto-generated method stub
    response.getWriter().append("Served at: ").append(request.get
    ContextPath());
    }

    /**
     * @see HttpServlet#doPost(HttpServletRequest request,
     HttpServletResponse response)
     */
    protected void doPost(HttpServletRequest request, HttpServlet
    Response response) throws ServletException, IOException {
        // TODO Auto-generated method stub
        doGet(request, response);
    }

}
```

The output is shown in Figure 13-15, where you can see the bold line.

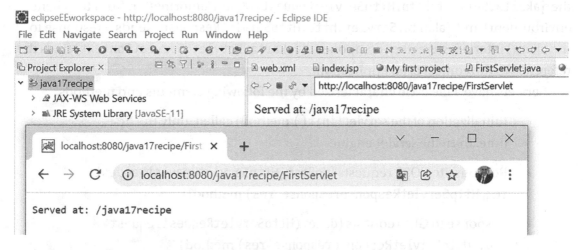

Figure 13-15. *The first servlet browser output*

Note   If you have worked with the javax.* package, it has been renamed to jakarta.* package. If you're targeting the Servlet API version 5.0 or newer (part of Jakarta EE 9 used in Tomcat 10), you need to replace the package to get it to compile. Otherwise, you might risk facing the "superclass "javax.servlet.http. HttpServlet" was not found on the Java Build Path" error.

How It Works

Servlets are Java classes, which run in a *servlet container* (e.g., Tomcat, TomEE 9, WildFly, GlassFish) and are exposed as standard web resources. These classes process data from the HTML form and handle requests and responses for one or more clients. The latest version is Jakarta Servlet 5.0, released in 2020. A servlet corresponds to the controller in the MVC architecture, and it implements many complex functionalities. We can use a single servlet to handle different behaviors or many servlets for each behavior.

Briefly, a client sends a request to a servlet (in a web application server). The servlet is instantiated (only the first time), starts a thread to handle the communication, and builds the response forwarded to the client. If the servlet has already loaded, it creates an additional thread associated to the new client. The servlet usually has no algorithmic code inside, but it is delegated to other classes. Request and response are managed by the jakarta.Servlet.http.HttpServletRequest (obtains information from the client environment) and jakarta.Servlet.http.HttpServletResponse (sends a response to the client) interfaces. Another component (jakarta.Servlet.ServletContext) finds the reference to the context of an application.

Servlets have a life cycle characterized by the following elements and methods.

- Initialization of the servlet (init() method) called, only the first time, from the servlet engine

- Response to POST requests (doPost(HttpServletRequestrequest req, HttpServletResponseresponse res) method))

- Response to GET requests (doGet(HttpServletRequestrequest req, HttpServletResponseresponse res) method)

- Destruction of the servlet context (destroy() method)

Let's create a single servlet with different behaviors according to the parameters from data entry forms. The actions are consequences of method calls (doGet method or doPost method).

A deployment descriptor must be used to invoke different web application objects (listeners, servlets, and filters). The deployment descriptor is the web.xml file. In this case, it is the following.

```
<servlet>
  <description></description>
  <display-name>FirstServlet</display-name>
  <servlet-name>FirstServlet</servlet-name>
  <servlet-class>org.java17recipes.chapter13.FirstServlet</servlet-class>
</servlet>
<servlet-mapping>
  <servlet-name>FirstServlet</servlet-name>
  <url-pattern>/FirstServlet</url-pattern>
</servlet-mapping>
```

The bold <url-pattern> tag is the string displayed in the browser.

For more information on Jakarta Servlet 5.0, see the specifications at https://jakarta.ee/specifications/servlet/5.0/.

13-7. Using a Servlet for Representing Values

Problem

You want to use a servlet and JSP to process data of a form in a web application.

Solution

Create the JSP page with a form. Go to the File ➤ New ➤ JSP files. Name the file formExample.jsp.

Listing 13-10 is the Java code.

Listing 13-10. The Java Code

```
<%@ page language="java" contentType="text/html; charset=ISO-8859-1"
    pageEncoding="ISO-8859-1"%>
<!DOCTYPE html>
<html>
<head>
<meta charset="ISO-8859-1">
<title>Form Example</title>
</head>
<body>
        <form action="/java17recipe/FirstServlet" method="post">
                first name:<input type="text" value="" name="firstname"/>
                <input type = "submit" value="POST SUBMIT">
        </form>
        <form action="/java17recipe/FirstServlet" method="get">
                last name:<input type="text" value="" name="lastname"/>
                <input type = "submit" value="GET SUBMIT">
        </form>
</body>
</html>
```

There are two forms, characterized by two methods (POST and GET), two different input fields, and two Submit buttons.

The output of the JSP is shown in Figure 13-16.

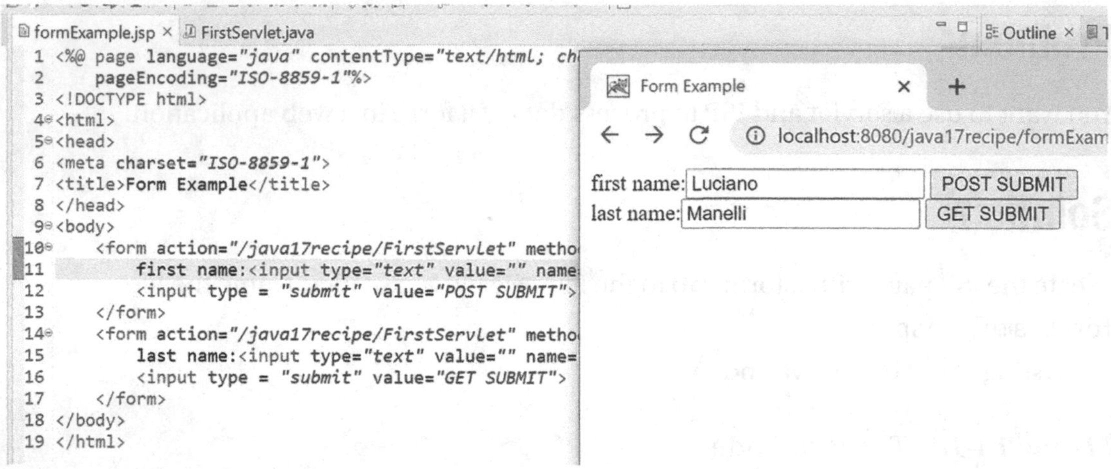

Figure 13-16. Output form

The following is the FirstServlet.java code.

```
protected void doGet(HttpServletRequest request, HttpServlet
Response response) throws ServletException, IOException {
        // TODO Auto-generated method stub
        System.out.println("GET");
        String lastname = request.getParameter("lastname");
        System.out.println("lastname (GET):"+lastname);

        PrintWriter out = response.getWriter();
        java.util.Date today = new java.util.Date();
        out.println("<html><body>" + today  +
                    " GET parameter: " + lastname +
                    "</body></html>");
        response.getWriter().append("Served at: ").append
        (request.getContextPath());
}

protected void doPost(HttpServletRequest request, HttpServlet
Response response) throws ServletException, IOException {
        // TODO Auto-generated method stub
```

```
            //doGet(request, response);
            System.out.println("POST");
            String firstname = request.getParameter("firstname");
            System.out.println("firstname (POST):"+firstname);

            PrintWriter out = response.getWriter();
            java.util.Date today = new java.util.Date();
            out.println("<html><body>" + today +
                        " POST parameter: " + firstname+
                        "</body></html>");
    }
```

If you click the GET SUBMIT button, which sends a GET message to the servlet, you get the result shown in Figure 13-17 in the browser.

Sun Nov 14 18:14:02 CET 2021 GET parameter: Manelli Served at: /java17recipe

Figure 13-17. *Output GET*

Click the POST SUBMIT button, which sends a POST message to the servlet, to get the result shown in Figure 13-18 in the browser.

Sun Nov 14 18:15:01 CET 2021 POST parameter: Luciano

Figure 13-18. *Output POST*

How It Works

The servlet works with two methods: doGet and doPost, which manage messages coming from the request (HttpServletRequest), using the request. getParameter("firstname") method. If you want to see the data successfully processed by the servlet, simply use the System.out.println command, which allows you to view data on the Eclipse console. In the following example, it is also used as a response. getWriter() method to display the sent parameters on the browser.

13-8. Summary

In this chapter, you learned how to install Java, Tomcat, and check that they work correctly. You then learned how to install the Eclipse EE IDE, configure it to use the latest versions of Java and Tomcat, and create JSP and servlets from scratch. You learned how to use JSP to display the HTTP-request parameters and use a servlet to manage POST and GET requests.

CHAPTER 14

Email

Email notification is an integral part of today's enterprise systems. Java enables email notification by offering JavaMail API. Using this API, you can send email communications in response to an event (e.g., a completed form or a finalized script). You can also use the JavaMail API to check an IMAP or POP3 mailbox.

To follow along with the recipes in this chapter, make sure that you have set up your firewall to allow email communication. Most of the time, firewalls allow outbound communications to email servers without an issue. But, if you are running your own local SMTP (email) server, you may need to configure your firewall to allow the email server to operate correctly.

14-1. Installing JavaMail

Problem

You want to install JavaMail for use by your application in sending email notifications.

Solution

Download JavaMail from Oracle's JavaMail website. The download you need is at `https://javaee.github.io/javamail/`. Once you download it, unzip it and add the JavaMail.jar files as dependencies for your project. You also need to download the JavaBeans Activation Framework from `https://eclipse-ee4j.github.io/jaf/` as dependencies for your project: it is used by JavaMail for data content handling. It lets you determine the type of data, access data as streams or objects, identify the MIME type of the data, and instantiate the appropriate bean to perform the needed and required operations.

© Josh Juneau, Luciano Manelli 2022
J. Juneau and L. Manelli, *Java 17 Recipes*, https://doi.org/10.1007/978-1-4842-7963-2_14

How It Works

By downloading and adding the dependencies, you access the robust email API that allows you to send and receive emails.

14-2. Sending an Email

Problem

You need your application to send an email.

Solution

Using the Transport() methods, you can send an email to specific recipients. In this solution, an email message is constructed and sent through the smtp.somewhere.com server.

```
private void start() {
    Properties properties = new Properties();
    properties.put("mail.smtp.host", "smtp.somewhere.com");
    properties.put("mail.smtp.auth", "true");
    properties.put("mail.smtp.port", "465");
    properties.put("mail.smtp.ssl.enable", "true")
  Session session = Session.getInstance(properties, new javax.mail.
  Authenticator() {
      protected PasswordAuthentication getPasswordAuthentication() {
          return new PasswordAuthentication("username", "password");
                }
            });

session.setDebug(true);

    Message message = new MimeMessage(session);
    try {
        message.setFrom(new InternetAddress("someone@somewhere.com"));
        message.setRecipient(Message.RecipientType.TO, new InternetAddress
        ("someone@somewhere.com"));
```

```
        message.setSubject("Subject");
        message.setContent("This is a test message", "text/plain");
        Transport.send(message);
    } catch (MessagingException e) {
        e.printStackTrace();
    }
}
```

The main is:

```
        public static void main(String[] args) {
            Recipe14_2 recipe = new Recipe14_2();
            recipe.start();
        }
```

In the next examples I used smtp.gmail.com and a gmail user and password.

How It Works

To utilize the JavaMail API, start by creating a Properties object that works as a standard Map object (in fact, it inherits from it). You put the different properties that the JavaMail service might need. The hostname is set using the mail.smtp.host property, and if the host requires authentication, you must set the mail.smtp.auth property to true. The port is 465 for a mail submission agent. For negotiation of TLS/SSL at connection setup, set the SSL property to true. After the properties object is configured, fetch a javax.mail. Session to hold the connection information for the email message.

When creating a session, you can specify the login information if the service requires authentication. This might be necessary when connecting to an SMTP service outside of your local area network. To specify the login information, you must create an Authenticator object, which contains the getPasswordAuthentication() method. By making the getPasswordAuthentication() method return a PasswordAuthentication object, you can specify the username/password used for the SMTP service. You can use Session.setDebug(true) to debug SMTP issues.

The Message object (javax.mail package) represents an actual email message and exposes email properties such as From/To/Subject and content. After setting these properties, you call the Transport.send() static method to send the email message.

14-3. Attaching Files to an Email Message

Problem

You need to attach one or more files to an email message.

Solution

Creating a message that contains different parts (called a *multipart message*) allows you to send attachments such as files and images. You can specify the body of the email message and an attachment. Messages containing different parts are called Multipurpose Internet Mail Extensions (MIME) messages. They are represented in the javax.mail API by the MimeMessage class. The following code creates such a message.

```
public static void main(String[] args) {
    Recipe14_3 recipe = new Recipe14_3();
    recipe.start();
}

private void start() {
    String host = "smtp.somewhere.com";
    String username = "username";
    String password = "password";
    String from = "someone@somewhere.com";
    String to = "anotherone@somewhere.com";

    Properties properties = new Properties();
    properties.put("mail.smtp.host", host);
    properties.put("mail.smtp.port", "465");
            properties.put("mail.smtp.ssl.enable", "true");
            properties.put("mail.smtp.auth", "true");

            Session session = Session.getInstance(properties, new
            javax.mail.Authenticator() {
                    protected PasswordAuthentication getPassword
                    Authentication() {
                            return new PasswordAuthentication
                            (username, password);
```

```
                    }
            });

                session.setDebug(true);

        try {
        Message message = new MimeMessage(session);
        message.setFrom(new InternetAddress(from));
        message.setRecipient(Message.RecipientType.TO, new
        InternetAddress(to));
        message.setSubject("Subject");
        // Create Mime "Message" part
        MimeBodyPart messageBodyPart = new MimeBodyPart();
        messageBodyPart.setContent("This is a test message", "text/plain");

        // Create Mime "File" part
        MimeBodyPart fileBodyPart = new MimeBodyPart();
        fileBodyPart.attachFile(System.getProperty("user.dir")+ File.
        separator + "attach.txt");

        MimeBodyPart fileBodyPart2 = new MimeBodyPart();
        fileBodyPart2.attachFile(System.getProperty("user.dir")+ File.
        separator + "attach2.txt");

        // Piece the body parts together
        Multipart multipart = new MimeMultipart();
        multipart.addBodyPart(messageBodyPart);
        multipart.addBodyPart(fileBodyPart);
        //add another body part to supply another attachment
        multipart.addBodyPart(fileBodyPart2);

        // Set the content of the message to be the MultiPart
        message.setContent(multipart);
        Transport.send(message);
                System.out.println("Sent message successfully....");
        } catch (MessagingException | IOException e) {
            e.printStackTrace();
        }

    }
```

How It Works

Within the JavaMail API you can create a MIME email. This type of message allows it to contain different body parts. In the example, a plain text body part is generated (which contains the text that the email displays), and then two attachment body parts containing the attachments you are trying to send are created. Depending on the type of attachment, the Java API automatically chooses an appropriate encoding for the attachment body part.

After each body part is created, they are combined by creating a `MultiPart` object and adding each part (the plain text and the attachments). Once the `MultiPart` object has been assembled to contain all the parts, it is assigned the content of `MimeMessage` and sent (like in Recipe 14-2).

14-4. Sending an HTML Email

Problem

You want to send an email that contains HTML.

Solution

You specify the content type of the email as `text/html` and send a string of HTML as the message body. In the following example, an email is constructed using HTML content, and then sent.

```
public static void main(String[] args) {
        Recipe14_4 recipe = new Recipe14_4();
        recipe.start();
}

private void start() {
        String host = "smtp.gmail.com";
        String username = "mymailusername";
        String password = "mygmailpassword";
        String from = "mygmailusername@gmail.com";
        String to = "someuser@somewhere.com";
```

```java
Properties properties = new Properties();
properties.put("mail.smtp.host", host);
properties.put("mail.smtp.port", "465");
properties.put("mail.smtp.auth", "true");
properties.put("mail.smtp.ssl.enable", "true");

Session session = Session.getInstance(properties, new
javax.mail.Authenticator() {
        protected PasswordAuthentication
        getPasswordAuthentication() {
            return new PasswordAuthentication(username,
                password);
        }
});

session.setDebug(true);
try {
        MimeMessage message = new MimeMessage(session);

        message.setFrom(new InternetAddress(from));
        message.setRecipient(Message.RecipientType.TO,
        new InternetAddress(to));
        message.setSubject("Subject Test");

        // Create Mime Content
        MimeBodyPart messageBodyPart = new
        MimeBodyPart();
        String html = "<H1>Important Message</H1>" +
                    "<b>This is an important
                    message...</b>"+
                    "<br/><br/>" +
                    "<i>Be sure to code your Java
                    today!</i>" +
                    "<H2>It is the right thing to
                    do!</H2>";
        messageBodyPart.setContent(html, "text/html;
        charset=utf-8");
```

```
                    MimeBodyPart fileBodyPart = new MimeBodyPart();
                    fileBodyPart.attachFile("/path-to/attach.txt");
                    MimeBodyPart fileBodyPart2 = new
                    MimeBodyPart();
                    fileBodyPart2.attachFile("/path-to/
                    attach2.txt");

                    Multipart multipart = new MimeMultipart();
                    multipart.addBodyPart(messageBodyPart);
                    multipart.addBodyPart(fileBodyPart);
                    //add another body part to supply another
                    attachment
                    multipart.addBodyPart(fileBodyPart2);
                    message.setContent(multipart);
                    Transport.send(message);
        } catch (MessagingException | IOException e) {
            e.printStackTrace();
        }
}
```

How It Works

Sending an email message that contains HTML content is nearly the same as sending
an email with standard text—the only difference is the content type. In the message
body part of the email, set the content to text/HTML so that it is treated as HTML. There
are various ways to construct the HTML content, including links, photos, or any other
valid HTML markup. A few basic HTML tags have been embedded into a string in this
example.

Although the example code may not be very useful in real-life systems, it is easy
to generate dynamic HTML content for inclusion within an email. At its most basic
form, dynamically generated HTML can be strings of text concatenated to formulate
the HTML.

14-5. Sending Email to a Group of Recipients
Problem

You want to send the same email to multiple recipients.

Solution

Use the setRecipients() method from the JavaMail API to send email to multiple recipients. The setRecipients() method allows you to specify more than one recipient at a time. The following is an example.

```java
public static void main(String[] args) {
            Recipe14_5 recipe = new Recipe14_5();
            recipe.start();
    }

    private void start() {
            List<String> emails = getEmails();

            String host = "smtp.gmail.com";
            String username = "mymailusername";
            String password = "mygmailpassword";
            String from = "mygmailusername@gmail.com";

            Properties properties = new Properties();
            properties.put("mail.smtp.host", host);
            properties.put("mail.smtp.port", "465");
            properties.put("mail.smtp.auth", "true");
            properties.put("mail.smtp.ssl.enable", "true");

            Session session = Session.getInstance(properties, new
            javax.mail.Authenticator() {
                    protected PasswordAuthentication getPassword
                    Authentication() {
                            return new PasswordAuthentication(username,
                            password);
                    }
```

```
        });

        session.setDebug(true);

        try {
                MimeMessage message = new MimeMessage(session);
                message.setFrom(new InternetAddress(from));
                message.setRecipients(Message.RecipientType.BCC,
                getRecipients(emails));
                message.setSubject("Subject");
                message.setContent("This is a test message",
                "text/plain");
                Transport.send(message);
        } catch (MessagingException e) {
                e.printStackTrace();
        }
    }

    private Address[] getRecipients(List<String> emails) throws
    AddressException {
        Address[] addresses = new Address[emails.size()];
        for (int i =0;i < emails.size();i++) {
            addresses[i] = new InternetAddress(emails.get(i));
        }
        return addresses;
    }

    public List<String> getEmails() {
        ArrayList<String> emails = new ArrayList<>();
        emails.add("jack@hill.com");
        emails.add("jill@hill.com");
        emails.add("water@hill.com");
        return emails;
    }
}
```

How It Works

By using the setRecipients() method of the Message object, you can specify multiple recipients on the same message. The setRecipients() method accepts an array of Address objects. In this recipe, because you have a collection of strings, you create the array as the size of the collection and create InternetAddress objects to fill the array. Sending emails using multiple email addresses (as opposed to individual emails) is much more efficient because only one message is sent from your client to the target mail servers. Each target mail server then delivers to all recipients that it has mailboxes for. For example, if you're sending to five different Yahoo.com accounts, the Yahoo.com mail server needs to receive only one copy of the message. It delivers the message to all the yahoo.com recipients specified in the message.

Tip If you want to send bulk messages, you might want to specify the recipient type as BCC so that the email received doesn't show everyone else getting the email. To do so, specify Message.RecipientType.BCC in the setRecipients() method.

14-6. Checking Email

Problem

You need to check if a new email has arrived for a specified email account.

Solution

You can use javax.mail.Store to connect, query, and retrieve messages from an Internet Message Access Protocol (IMAP) email account. For example, the following code connects to an IMAP account, retrieves the last five messages from that IMAP account, and marks the messages as read.

```
public static void main(String[] args) {
        Recipe14_6 recipe = new Recipe14_6();
        recipe.start();
}
```

```java
private void start() {
        String username = "username";
        String password = "password";
        String folder = "Inbox";
        String host = "imap.host.com";

        Properties properties = new Properties();
        properties.put("mail.imap.host", host);
        properties.put("mail.imap.ssl.enable", "true");
        properties.put("mail.imap.auth", "true");

        try {
                Session session = Session.getInstance(properties,
                new javax.mail.Authenticator() {
                        protected PasswordAuthentication
                        getPasswordAuthentication() {
                                return new PasswordAuthentication
                                (username, password);
                        }
                });
                session.setDebug(true);
                Store store = session.getStore("imap");
                store.connect(host,username,password);
                System.out.println(store);
                Folder inbox = store.getFolder(folder);
                inbox.open(Folder.READ_WRITE);
                int messageCount = inbox.getMessageCount();
                int startMessage = messageCount - 10;
                if (startMessage< 1) startMessage =1;
                Message messages[]  = inbox.getMessages
                (startMessage, messageCount);
                for (Message message : messages) {
                        boolean hasBeenRead = false;
                        for (Flags.Flag flag : message.getFlags().
                        getSystemFlags()) {
```

```
                            if (flag == Flags.Flag.SEEN) {
                                    hasBeenRead = true;
                                    break;
                            }
                        }
                        message.setFlag(Flags.Flag.SEEN, false);
                        System.out.println(message.getSubject() +
                        " "+ (hasBeenRead? "(read)" : "") +
                        message.getContent());

                }
                inbox.close(true);
        } catch (MessagingException | IOException e) {
                e.printStackTrace();
        }
    }
}
```

How It Works

A Store objcct allows you to access email mailbox information. By creating a Store and then requesting the Inbox folder, you gain access to the messages in the main mailbox of your IMAP account. With the folder object, you can request to download the messages from the inbox using the getMessages(start, end) method. The inbox also provides a getMessageCount() method, which allows you to know how many emails are in the inbox. Keep in mind that the messages start at index 1.

Each message has a set of flags that can tell whether the message has been read (Flags.Flag.SEEN) or whether the message has been replied to (Flags.Flag.ANSWERED). By parsing the SEEN flag, you can process messages that haven't been read before.

To set a message as being read (or answered), call the message.setFlag() method. This method allows you to set (or reset) email flags. If you're setting message flags, you need to open the folder as READ_WRITE, allowing you to change email flags. You also need to call inbox.close(true) at the end of your code to tell the JavaMail API to flush the changes to the IMAP store.

14-7. Summary

Email plays an important role in many systems that we use today. The Java language includes the JavaMail API, which enables developers to include robust email functionality within their Java applications. The recipes in this chapter covered the JavaMail API from installation through advanced usage.

JSON and XML Processing

JSON is one of the most widely used forms of media for sending communications between two or more machines. In expanded form, it stands for JavaScript Object Notation. It is very easy to work with JSON data by simply including the JSON library, which is included in Java EE. XML APIs have always been available to the Java developer, usually supplied as third-party libraries that could be added to the runtime classpath. The most fundamental XML processing tasks that you will encounter involve only a few use cases: writing and reading XML documents, validating those documents and using JAXB to assist in marshaling/unmarshaling Java objects.

This chapter provides recipes for performing XML and JSON tasks. The JSON recipes require the inclusion of the JSON API, which can be done by adding the dependencies to a maven application. In this chapter, you learn how to create JSON and write it to disk and perform the parsing.

15-1. Writing an XML File

Problem

You want to create an XML document to store application data.

Solution

To write an XML document, use the `javax.xml.stream.XMLStreamWriter` interface. The following code iterates over an array of `Patient` objects and writes the data to an `.xml` file. To use this Java class, you need JAXB libraries that give an efficient and

© Josh Juneau, Luciano Manelli 2022
J. Juneau and L. Manelli, *Java 17 Recipes*, https://doi.org/10.1007/978-1-4842-7963-2_15

standard way of mapping between XML and Java code. Go to `https://eclipse-ee4j.` `github.io/jaxb-ri/`, download the `jakarta.xml.bind-api.jar` 3.0.0 library, and copy it into your `lib` project folder or onto your server.

This sample code comes from the `org.java17recipes.chapter15.recipe15_1.` DocWriter example.

```java
import javax.xml.stream.XMLOutputFactory;
import javax.xml.stream.XMLStreamException;
import javax.xml.stream.XMLStreamWriter;
...
public void run(String outputFile) throws FileNotFoundException,
XMLStreamException,
        IOException {
    List<Patient> patients = new ArrayList<>();
    Patient p1 = new Patient();
    Patient p2 = new Patient();
    Patient p3 = new Patient();
    p1.setId(BigInteger.valueOf(1));
    p1.setName("John Smith");
    p1.setDiagnosis("Common Cold");
    p2.setId(BigInteger.valueOf(2));
    p2.setName("Jane Doe");
    p2.setDiagnosis("Broken Ankle");
    p3.setId(BigInteger.valueOf(3));
    p3.setName("Jack Brown");
    p3.setDiagnosis("Food Allergy");
    patients.add(p1);
    patients.add(p2);
    patients.add(p3);
    XMLOutputFactory factory = XMLOutputFactory.newFactory();
    try (FileOutputStream fos = new FileOutputStream(outputFile)) {
        XMLStreamWriter writer = factory.createXMLStreamWriter(fos, "UTF-8");
        writer.writeStartDocument();
        writer.writeCharacters("\n");
        writer.writeStartElement("patients");
        writer.writeCharacters("\n");
```

```java
        for (Patient p : patients) {
            writer.writeCharacters("\t");
            writer.writeStartElement("patient");
            writer.writeAttribute("id", String.valueOf(p.getId()));
            writer.writeCharacters("\n\t\t");
            writer.writeStartElement("name");
            writer.writeCharacters(p.getName());
            writer.writeEndElement();
            writer.writeCharacters("\n\t\t");
            writer.writeStartElement("diagnosis");
            writer.writeCharacters(p.getDiagnosis());
            writer.writeEndElement();
            writer.writeCharacters("\n\t");
            writer.writeEndElement();
            writer.writeCharacters("\n");
        }
        writer.writeEndElement();
        writer.writeEndDocument();
        writer.close();
    }
}

    public static void main(String[] args) {
            String fileName = null;
            if (args.length != 1) {
                    System.out.printf("Usage: java org.java17recipes
                    .chapter15.recipe15_01.DocWriter <outputXmlFile>\n");
                    fileName = "patients.xml";
            } else {
                    fileName = args[0];
            }
            DocWriter app = new DocWriter();
            try {
                    app.run(fileName);
            } catch (FileNotFoundException|XMLStreamException ex) {
                    Logger.getLogger(DocWriter.class.getName()).
                    log(Level.SEVERE, null, ex);
```

```
            } catch (IOException ex) {
                    Logger.getLogger(DocWriter.class.getName()).
                    log(Level.SEVERE, null, ex);
            }
      }
```

The code of Patient class is:
```
import jakarta.xml.bind.annotation.*;

public class Patient {
    @XmlElement(required = true)
    protected String name;
    @XmlElement(required = true)
    protected String diagnosis;
    @XmlAttribute(name = "id", required = true)
    protected BigInteger id;

    public String getName() {
        return name;
    }
    public void setName(String value) {
        this.name = value;
    }
    public String getDiagnosis() {
        return diagnosis;
    }
    public void setDiagnosis(String value) {
        this.diagnosis = value;
    }
    public BigInteger getId() {
        return id;
    }
    public void setId(BigInteger value) {
        this.id = value;
    }
}
```

The previous code writes the following file contents.

```xml
<?xml version="1.0" ?>
<patients>
    <patient id="1">
        <name>John Smith</name>
        <diagnosis>Common Cold</diagnosis>
    </patient>
    <patient id="2">
        <name>Jane Doe</name>
        <diagnosis>Broken ankle</diagnosis>
    </patient>
    <patient id="3">
        <name>Jack Brown</name>
<diagnosis>Food allergy</diagnosis>
</patient>
</patients>
```

How It Works

The Java standard library provides several ways to write XML documents. This recipe uses StAX defined in the `javax.xml.stream` package. Writing an XML document takes five steps.

1. Create a file output stream.

2. Create an XML output factory and an XML output stream writer.

3. Wrap the file stream in the XML stream writer.

4. Use the XML stream writer's write methods to create the document and write the XML elements.

5. Close the output streams.

Create a file output stream using the `java.io.FileOutputStream` class. You can use a `try-block` to open and close this stream.

The `javax.xml.stream.XMLOutputFactory` provides a static method that creates an output factory. Use the factory to create a `javax.xml.stream.XMLStreamWriter`.

Once you have the writer, wrap the file stream object in the XML writer instance. You use the various write methods to create the XML document elements and attributes. Finally, you simply close the writer when you finish writing to the file. Some of the more useful methods of the `XMLStreamWriter` instance are these.

- `writeStartDocument()`

- `writeStartElement()`

- `writeEndElement()`

- `writeEndDocument()`

- `writeAttribute()`

After creating the file and `XMLStreamWriter`, you should always begin the document by calling the `writeStartDocumentMethod()` method. Follow this by writing individual elements using the `writeStartElement()` and `writeEndElement()` methods in combination. Of course, elements can have nested elements. You are responsible for calling these in the proper sequence to create well-formed documents. Use the `writeAttribute()` method to place an attribute name and value into the current element. You should call `writeAttribute()` immediately after calling the `writeStartElement()` method. Finally, signal the end of the document with the `writeEndDocument()` method and close the `Writer` instance.

One interesting point of using the `XMLStreamWriter` is that it does not format the document output. Unless you specifically use the `writeCharacters()` method to output space and newline characters, the output stream to a single unformatted line. Of course, this doesn't invalidate the resulting XML file, but it does make it inconvenient and difficult for humans to read. Therefore, you should consider using the `writeCharacters()` method to output spacing and newline characters as needed to create a human-readable document. You can safely ignore this method of writing additional whitespace and line breaks if you do not need a document for human readability. Regardless of the format, the XML document will be well-formed because it adheres to correct XML syntax.

The following is the command-line usage pattern for this example code.

```
java org.java17recipes.chapter15.recipe15_1.DocWriter <outputXmlFile>
```

Invoke this application to create a file named `patients.xml` in the following way.

```
java org.java17recipes.chapter15.recipe15_1.DocWriter patients.xml
```

15-2. Reading an XML File

Problem

You need to parse an XML document, retrieving known elements and attributes.

Solution 1

Use the javax.xml.stream.XMLStreamReader interface to read documents. Using this API, your code pulls XML elements using a cursor-like interface similar to that in SQL to process each element in turn. The following code snippet from org.java17recipes. DocReader demonstrates how to read the patients.xml file that was generated in the previous recipe.

```
public void cursorReader(String xmlFile)
throws FileNotFoundException, IOException, XMLStreamException {
    XMLInputFactory factory = XMLInputFactory.newFactory();
    try (FileInputStream fis = new FileInputStream(xmlFile)) {
        XMLStreamReader reader = factory.createXMLStreamReader(fis);
        boolean inName = false;
        boolean inDiagnosis = false;
        String id = null;
        String name = null;
        String diagnosis = null;
        while (reader.hasNext()) {
            int event = reader.next();
            switch (event) {
                case XMLStreamConstants.START_ELEMENT:
                    String elementName = reader.getLocalName();
                    switch (elementName) {
                        case "patient":
                            id = reader.getAttributeValue(0);
                            break;
                        case "name":
                            inName = true;
                            break;
```

```java
                        case "diagnosis":
                            inDiagnosis = true;
                            break;
                        default:
                            break;
                    }
                    break;
                case XMLStreamConstants.END_ELEMENT:
                    String elementname = reader.getLocalName();
                    if (elementname.equals("patient")) {
                        System.out.printf("Patient: %s\nName:
                        %s\nDiagnosis: %s\n\n",id, name,
                        diagnosis);
                        id = name = diagnosis = null;
                        inName = inDiagnosis = false;
                    }
                    break;
                case XMLStreamConstants.CHARACTERS:
                    if (inName) {
                        name = reader.getText();
                        inName = false;
                    } else if (inDiagnosis) {
                        diagnosis = reader.getText();
                        inDiagnosis = false;
                    }
                    break;
                default:
                    break;
            }
        }
    reader.close();
    }
}
```

Solution 2

Use the XMLEventReader to read and process events using an event-oriented interface. This API is called an *iterator-oriented* API as well. The following code is much like the code in solution 1, except it uses the event-oriented API instead of the cursor-oriented API. This code snippet is available from the same org.java17recipes.chapter15. recipe15_1.DocReader class used in solution 1.

```java
public void eventReader(String xmlFile)
        throws FileNotFoundException, IOException, XMLStreamException {
    XMLInputFactory factory = XMLInputFactory.newFactory();
    XMLEventReader reader = null;
    try(FileInputStream fis = new FileInputStream(xmlFile)) {
        reader = factory.createXMLEventReader(fis);
        boolean inName = false;
        boolean inDiagnosis = false;
        String id = null;
        String name = null;
        String diagnosis = null;
        while(reader.hasNext()) {
            XMLEvent event = reader.nextEvent();
            String elementName = null;
            switch(event.getEventType()) {
                case XMLEvent.START_ELEMENT:
                    StartElement startElement = event.asStartElement();
                    elementName = startElement.getName().getLocalPart();
                    switch(elementName) {
                        case "patient":
                            id = startElement.getAttributeByName(QName.
                            valueOf("id")).getValue();
                            break;
                        case "name":
                            inName = true;
                            break;
```

```
                    case "diagnosis":
                        inDiagnosis = true;
                        break;
                    default:
                        break;
                }
                break;
            case XMLEvent.END_ELEMENT:
                EndElement endElement = event.asEndElement();
                elementName = endElement.getName().getLocalPart();
                if (elementName.equals("patient")) {
                    System.out.printf("Patient: %s\nName:
                    %s\nDiagnosis: %s\n\n",id, name, diagnosis);
                    id = name = diagnosis = null;
                    inName = inDiagnosis = false;
                }
                break;
            case XMLEvent.CHARACTERS:
                String value = event.asCharacters().getData();
                if (inName) {
                    name = value;
                    inName = false;
                } else if (inDiagnosis) {
                    diagnosis = value;
                    inDiagnosis = false;
                }
                break;
            }
        }
    }
    if(reader != null) {
        reader.close();
    }
}
```

The main method is:

```java
public static void main(String[] args) {
    String fileName = null;
    if (args.length != 1) {
        System.out.printf("Usage: java org.java8recipes.
        chapter20.recipe20_2.DocReader <xmlFile>\n");
        fileName = "patients.xml";
    } else {
        fileName = args[0];
    }
    DocReader app = new DocReader();
    try {
        app.run(fileName);
    } catch (FileNotFoundException ex) {
        ex.printStackTrace();
    } catch (IOException | XMLStreamException ioex) {
        ioex.printStackTrace();
    }

}
public void run(String xmlFile) throws FileNotFoundException,
IOException, XMLStreamException {
    cursorReader(xmlFile);
    eventReader(xmlFile);
}
```

The XML file is:

```xml
<?xml version="1.0" ?>
<patients>
    <patient id="1">
        <name>John Smith</name>
        <diagnosis>Common Cold</diagnosis>
    </patient>
    <patient id="2">
        <name>Jane Doe</name>
        <diagnosis>Broken Ankle</diagnosis>
    </patient>
```

539

```
        <patient id="3">
                <name>Jack Brown</name>
                <diagnosis>Food Allergy</diagnosis>
        </patient>
</patients>
```

The output is:

```
Patient: 1
Name: John Smith
Diagnosis: Common Cold

Patient: 2
Name: Jane Doe
Diagnosis: Broken Ankle

Patient: 3
Name: Jack Brown
Diagnosis: Food Allergy
```

How It Works

Java provides several ways to read XML documents. One way is to use StAX, a streaming model. It is better than the older SAX API because it allows you to read and write XML documents. Although StAX is not quite as powerful as a DOM API, it is an excellent and efficient API that is less taxing on memory resources.

StAX provides two methods for reading XML documents: a cursor API and an iterator API. The cursor-oriented API utilizes a cursor that can walk an XML document from start to finish, pointing to one element at a time, and always moving forward. The iterator API represents an XML document stream as a set of discrete event objects, provided in the order that they are read in the source XML. The event-oriented iterator API is preferred over the cursor API because it provides XMLEvent objects with the following benefits.

- The XMLEvent objects are immutable and can persist even though the StAX parser has moved on to subsequent events. You can pass these XMLEvent objects to other processes or store them in lists, arrays, and maps.

- You can subclass XMLEvent, creating your specialized events as needed.

- You can modify the incoming event stream by adding or removing events, which is more flexible than the cursor API.

To use StAX to read documents, create an XML event reader on your file input stream. Check that events are still available with the hasNext() method and read each event using the nextEvent() method. The nextEvent() method returns a specific type of XMLEvent that corresponds to the start and stop elements, attributes, and value data in the XML file. Remember to close your readers and file streams when you're finished with those objects.

15-3. Transforming XML
Problem

You want to convert an XML document to another format, such as HTML.

Solution

Use the javax.xml.transform package to transform an XML document to another document format.

The following code demonstrates how to read a source document, apply an Extensible Stylesheet Language (XSL) transform file, and produce the transformed, new document. Use the sample code from the org.java17recipes.chapter15.recipe15_3. TransformXml class to read the patients.xml file and create a patients.html file. The following snippet shows the important pieces of this class.

```
import javax.xml.transform.TransformerConfigurationException;
import javax.xml.transform.TransformerException;
import javax.xml.transform.TransformerFactory;
import javax.xml.transform.Transformer;
import javax.xml.transform.Source;
import javax.xml.transform.stream.StreamResult;
import javax.xml.transform.stream.StreamSource;
...
```

```java
public void run(String xmlFile, String xslFile, String outputFile)
        throws FileNotFoundException, TransformerConfigurationException,
        TransformerException {
    InputStream xslInputStream = new FileInputStream(xslFile);
    Source xslSource = new StreamSource(xslInputStream);
    TransformerFactory factory = TransformerFactory.newInstance();
    Transformer transformer = factory.newTransformer(xslSource);
    InputStream xmlInputStream = new FileInputStream(xmlFile);
    StreamSource in = new StreamSource(xmlInputStream);
    StreamResult out = new StreamResult(outputFile);
    transformer.transform(in, out);
}
    public static void main(String[] args) {
        String fileName = null;
        String fileName2 = null;
        String fileName3 = null;
        if (args.length != 3) {
            System.out.printf("Usage: java org.java17recipes.chapter15.
            recipe15_03.TransformXml <xmlFile> <xslFile> <outputFile>\n");
            fileName = "patients.xml";
            fileName2 = "patients.xsl";
            fileName3 = "patients.html";
        } else {
            fileName = args[0];
            fileName2 = args[1];
            fileName3 = args[2];
        }
        TransformXml app = new TransformXml();
        try {
            app.run(fileName, fileName2, fileName3);
        } catch (FileNotFoundException ex) {
            ex.printStackTrace();
        } catch (TransformerConfigurationException ex) {
            ex.printStackTrace();
```

```
        } catch (TransformerException ex) {
            ex.printStackTrace();
        }
    }
}
```

The output is the patients.html file.

How It Works

The javax.xml.transform package contains all the classes you need to transform an XML document into any other document type. The most common use case is to convert data-oriented XML documents into user-readable HTML documents.

Transforming from one document type to another requires three files.

- An XML source document

- An XSL transformation document that maps XML elements to the new document elements

- A target output file

The XML source document is, of course, your source data file. It most often contains data-oriented content that is easy to parse programmatically. However, people don't easily read XML files, especially complex, data-rich files. Instead, people are much more comfortable reading properly rendered HTML documents.

The XSL transformation document specifies how an XML document should be transformed into a different format. An XSL file usually contains an HTML template that specifies dynamic fields that hold the extracted contents of a source XML file.

In this example's source code, you'll find two source documents.

- chapter15/recipe15_3/patients.xml

- chapter15/recipe15_3/patients.xsl

The patients.xml file is short and contains the following data.

```
<?xml version="1.0" encoding="UTF-8"?>
<patients>
    <patient id="1">
        <name>John Smith</name>
        <diagnosis>Common Cold</diagnosis>
    </patient>
```

```
    <patient id="2">
        <name>Jane Doe</name>
        <diagnosis>Broken ankle</diagnosis>
    </patient>
    <patient id="3">
        <name>Jack Brown</name>
        <diagnosis>Food allergy</diagnosis>
    </patient>
</patients>
```

The patients.xml file defines a root element called patients. It has three nested patient elements. The patient elements contain three pieces of data.

- The patient identifier provided as the id attribute of the patient element

- The patient name provided as the name subelement

- The patient diagnosis provided as the diagnosis subelement

The transformation XSL document (patients.xsl) is quite small as well, and it simply maps the patient data to a more user-readable HTML format using XSL.

```
<?xml version="1.0" encoding="UTF-8"?>
<xsl:stylesheet xmlns:xsl="http://www.w3.org/1999/XSL/Transform"
version="1.0">
<xsl:output method="html"/>
<xsl:template match="/">
<html>
<head>
    <title>Patients</title>
</head>
<body>
    <table border="1">
        <tr>
            <th>Id</th>
            <th>Name</th>
            <th>Diagnosis</th>
        </tr>
```

```
        <xsl:for-each select="patients/patient">
        <tr>
            <td>
        <xsl:value-of select="@id"/>
            </td>
            <td>
        <xsl:value-of select="name"/>
            </td>
            <td>
        <xsl:value-of select="diagnosis"/>
            </td>
            </tr>
        </xsl:for-each>
    </table>
</body>
</html>
        </xsl:template>
        </xsl:stylesheet>
```

Using this style sheet, the sample code transforms the XML into an HTML table containing all the patients and their data. Rendered in a browser, the HTML table should look like Figure 15-1.

Id	Name	Diagnosis
1	John Smith	Common Cold
2	Jane Doe	Broken ankle
3	Jack Brown	Food allergy

Figure 15-1. *A common rendering of an HTML table*

The process for using this XSL file to convert the XML to an HTML file is straightforward, but every step can be enhanced with additional error checking and processing. For this example, refer to the previous code in the solution section.

The following are the most basic transformation steps.

1. Read the XSL document into your Java application as a
    `Source` object.

2. Create a `Transformer` instance and provide your XSL `Source`
    instance to use during its operation.

3. Create a `SourceStream` that represents the source XML contents.

4. Create a `StreamResult` instance for your output document, which
    is an HTML file in this case.

5. Use the `Transformer` object's `transform()` method to perform the
    conversion.

6. Close all the relevant streams and file instances, as needed.

If you choose to execute the sample code, you should invoke it in the following way,
using `patients.xml`, `patients.xsl`, and `patients.html` as arguments.

```
java org.java17recipes.chapter15.recipe15_3.TransformXml <xmlFile><xslFile>
<outputFile>
```

15-4. Validating XML

Problem

You want to confirm that your XML is valid—that it conforms to a known document
definition or schema.

Solution

Validate that your XML conforms to a specific schema by using the `javax.xml.`
`validation` package. The following code snippet from `org.java17recipes.chapter15.`
`recipe15_4.ValidateXml` demonstrates how to validate against an XML schema file.

```
import java.io.File;
import java.io.IOException;
import javax.xml.XMLConstants;
import javax.xml.transform.Source;
```

```java
import javax.xml.transform.stream.StreamSource;
import javax.xml.validation.Schema;
import javax.xml.validation.SchemaFactory;
import javax.xml.validation.Validator;
import org.xml.sax.SAXException;
...
public void run(String xmlFile, String validationFile) {
    boolean valid = true;
    SchemaFactory sFactory =
            SchemaFactory.newInstance(XMLConstants.W3C_XML_SCHEMA_NS_URI);
    try {
        Schema schema = sFactory.newSchema(new File(validationFile));
        Validator validator = schema.newValidator();
        Source source = new StreamSource(new File(xmlFile));
        validator.validate(source);
    } catch (SAXException | IOException | IllegalArgumentException ex) {
        valid = false;
    }
    System.out.printf("XML file is %s.\n", valid ? "valid" : "invalid");
}

        public static void main(String[] args) {
                if (args.length != 2) {
                        System.out.println("Usage: java org.java17recipes.
                        chapter15.recipe15_04.ValidateXml <xmlFile>
                        <validationFile>");
                        System.exit(1);
                }
                ValidateXml app = new ValidateXml();
                app.run(args[0], args[1]);
        }
```

How It Works

When utilizing XML, it is important to validate it to ensure that the correct syntax
is in place and that an XML document is an instance of the specified XML schema.
The validation process involves comparing the schema and the XML document to

find any discrepancies. The `javax.xml.validation` package provides all the classes needed to reliably validate an XML file against a variety of schemas. The most common schemas that you use for XML validation are defined as constant URIs within the `XMLConstants` class.

- `XMLConstants.W3C_XML_SCHEMA_NS_URI`

- `XMLConstants.RELAXNG_NS_URI`

Begin by creating a `SchemaFactory` for a specific type of schema definition. A `SchemaFactory` knows how to parse a particular schema type and prepares it for validation. Use the `SchemaFactory` instance to create a `Schema` object. The `Schema` object is an in-memory representation of the schema definition grammar. You can use the `Schema` instance to retrieve a `Validator` instance that understands this grammar. Finally, use the `validate()` method to check your XML. The method call generates several exceptions if anything goes wrong during the validation. Otherwise, the `validate()` method returns quietly, and you can continue to use the XML file.

Note   The XML Schema was the first to receive "Recommendation" status from the World Wide Web consortium (W3C) in 2001. Competing schemas have since become available. One competing schema is the Regular Language for XML Next Generation (RELAX NG) schema. RELAX NG may be a simpler schema and its specification also defines a non-XML, compact syntax. This recipe's example uses the XML schema.

Run the example code using the following command-line syntax, preferably with the sample `.xml` file and validation files provided as `resources/patients.xml` and `patients.xsl`, where the XSL is as follows.

```
<xsl:template match="/">
    <html>
        <head>
            <title>Patients</title>
        </head>
        <body>
            <table border="1">
                <tr>
                    <th>Id</th>
```

```
                    <th>Name</th>
                    <th>Diagnosis</th>
                </tr>
                <xsl:for-each select="patients/patient">
                    <tr>
                        <td>
                            <xsl:value-of select="@id"/>
                        </td>
                        <td>
                            <xsl:value-of select="name"/>
                        </td>
                        <td>
                            <xsl:value-of select="diagnosis"/>
                        </td>
                    </tr>
                </xsl:for-each>

            </table>


        </body>
    </html>
</xsl:template>
```

15-5. Working with JSON

Problem

You are interested in working with JSON in your Java application.

Solution

JSON is a free and independent data format derived from JavaScript. It is regularly used to read data from a web server and display the data on a web page, simply because its format is only text. There are different libraries to manage JSON in your Java project. Download the org.json library from https://github.com/stleary/JSON-java and add it as a dependency to your Java application.

How It Works

The org.JSON package implements encoders and decoders to parse JSON documents into Java objects and generate JSON documents from the Java classes and also includes the capability to convert between JSON and XML. It is also easy to include the API by adding the downloaded JAR files to the CLASSPATH. There are many JSON packages in Java (for example, GSON at https://github.com/google/gson), but the Java community has not standardized one yet.

15-6. Building a JSON Object

Problem

You want to build a JSON object within your Java application.

Solution

Utilize the JSON API to build a JSON object. In the following code, a JSON object pertaining to a book is built.

```java
public class BuildingJSONObject {
        public static void main(String[] args) {
                        JSONObject json = new JSONObject();
                json.put("title", "Java 17 Recipes");
                JSONObject authorName = new JSONObject();
                        authorName.put("firstName","Luciano");
                        authorName.put("lastName","Manelli");
                json.put("author", authorName);
                JSONObject editor1 = new JSONObject();
                        editor1.put("firstName", "Steve");
                        editor1.put("lastName", "Anglin");
                JSONObject editor2 = new JSONObject();
                        editor2.put("firstName","Matthew");
                        editor2.put("lastName","Moodie");
```

```
JSONArray editors = new JSONArray();
        editors.put(editor1);
        editors.put(editor2);
    json.put("editor", editors);
    System.out.println(json.toString());
  }
}
```

The following is the output.

```
{"editor":[{"firstName":"Steve","lastName":"Anglin"},{"firstName":"Matthew",
"lastName":"Moodie"}],"author":{"firstName":"Luciano","lastName":"Manelli"},
"title":"Java 17 Recipes"}
```

How It Works

The JSON API creates JSON objects using the builder pattern. Using the JSON object, JSON objects can be built using a series of put method calls, each building upon each other. Once the JSON object has been built, it is ready to be used or printed as a string.

In this recipe's example, you construct a JSON object that provides details regarding a book. The put method adds more name/value properties (much like Map's). Therefore, the following line adds a property named title with "Java 9 Recipes" value.

```
.put("title", "Java 17 Recipes")
```

Objects can be embedded inside each other, creating a hierarchy of subsections within one JSON object. For example, after the first call to put(), another object can be embedded inside the initial JSON object by calling a new JSON object as the value to a put() operation and passing the name of the embedded object. Embedded objects can also contain properties (authorName), so to add properties to the embedded object, call the put() method within the embedded object. JSON objects can embody as many embedded objects as needed. It is also possible that a JSON object may have an array of related subobjects. To add an array of subobjects, call the JSONArray() method, passing the name of the array as an argument. Arrays can consist of objects and hierarchies of objects, arrays, and so forth.

Once a JSON object has been created, it can be used and passed to a client.

15-7. Writing a JSON Object to File

Problem

You've generated or parsed a JSON object, and you want to store it on disk in file format.

Solution

Utilize the JSON API to build a JSON object, and then store it to the file system. The class, working with the `java.io.Writer` package, makes it possible to create a file on disk, and then write the JSON to that file. In the following example, the JSON object that was generated in Recipe 15-6 is written to disk using this technique.

```java
public class BuildingJSONObject {
        public static void main(String[] args) {
                JSONObject json = new JSONObject();
                json.put("title", "Java 17 Recipes");
                JSONObject authorName = new JSONObject();
                authorName.put("firstName","Luciano");
                authorName.put("lastName","Manelli");
                json.put("author", authorName);
                JSONObject editor1 = new JSONObject();
                editor1.put("firstName", "Steve");
                editor1.put("lastName", "Anglin");
                JSONObject editor2 = new JSONObject();
                editor2.put("firstName","Matthew");
                editor2.put("lastName","Moodie");
                JSONArray editors = new JSONArray();
                editors.put(editor1);
                editors.put(editor2);
                json.put("editor", editors);
        try {
                        Writer jsonWriter = json.write(new
                        FileWriter("Book.json")) ;
                        jsonWriter.flush();
```

```
        } catch (IOException ex) {
                System.out.println(ex);
        }
    }
}
```

The output is the Book.json file:

```
{"editor":[{"firstName":"Steve","lastName":"Anglin"},{"firstName":"Matthew",
"lastName":"Moodie"}],"author":{"firstName":"Luciano","lastName":"Manelli"},
"title":"Java 17 Recipes"}
```

How It Works

The .write method can be utilized to write a JSON object to a Java writer object. It is instantiated by passing a Writer object as an argument to the Json.write() method. After that jsonWriter has been created, the flush method can be invoked to write the JSON file.

15-8. Parsing a JSON Object
Problem

The application you've created requires the ability to read a JSON object and parse it accordingly. Use the following JSON script.

```
{
"title":"Java 17 Recipes",
"author":{"firstName":"Luciano","lastName":"Manelli"},
"projectCoordinator":{"firstName":"Mark","lastName":"Powers"},
"editor":[{"firstName":"Welmoed","lastName":"Spahr"},{"firstName":"Steve","
lastName":"Anglin"},{"firstName":"Matthew","lastName":"Moodie"}],
"technicalReviewer":[{"firstName":"Manuel","lastName":"Jordan"}]
}
```

Solution

Utilize a JSONObject class to convert the JSON string into a JSON object, read a JSON object, and then use the getJSONObject and getJSONArray methods to perform actions against the JSON data. The following example demonstrates how to parse a JSON string to display some content.

```
public void parseObject() {
    String json = "{\"title\":\"Java EE 17 Recipes\",\"author\":{\"first
    Name\":\"Luciano\",\"lastName\":\"Manelli\"},\"projectCoordinator\":
    {\"firstName\":\"Mark\",\"lastName\":\"Powers\"},\"editor\":[{\"first
    Name\":\"Welmoed\",\"lastName\":\"Spahr\"},{\"firstName\":\"Steve\",
    \"lastName\":\"Anglin\"},{\"firstName\":\"Matthew\",\"lastName\":
    \"Moodie\"}],\"technicalReviewer\":[{\"firstName\":\"Manuel\",\"last
    Name\":\"Jordan\"}]}";
        System.out.println(json);
            JSONObject parserJson = new JSONObject(json);
            String author = parserJson.getJSONObject("author").
            getString("lastName");
            System.out.println("Author:"+author);
            JSONArray arr = parserJson.getJSONArray("editor");
            for (int i = 0; i < arr.length(); i++) {
                String editor = arr.getJSONObject(i).
                getString("lastName");
                System.out.println(editor);
            }
}
```

In the example, the JSON string is parsed. The following output is the result.

```
Author:Manelli
editor:Spahr
editor:Anglin
editor:Moodie
```

How It Works

The JSON method produces a JSON object. To perform some tasks, a JSON object must be parsed to find only the desired and useful content for the current task. Utilizing a JSON parser can make jobs such as these easier, as a parser can break the object down into pieces so that each different piece can be examined as needed to produce the desired result.

In this case, we used a `getJSONArray` to `scroll an array of objects and a` `getJSONObject to parse an object.`

15-9. Summary

XML is commonly used to transfer data between disparate applications or store data of some kind to a file. Therefore, it is important to understand the fundamentals for working with XML in your application development platform. This chapter provided an overview of performing some key tasks for working with XML using Java. This chapter began with the basics of writing and reading XML. The chapter also worked with JSON demonstrating how to generate, write, and parse JSON data.

CHAPTER 16

Networking

Today, writing an application that does not communicate over the Internet in some fashion is rare. From sending data to another machine to scraping information off remote web pages, networking plays an integral part in today's computing world. Java makes it easy to communicate over a network using the new I/O (NIO) and many I/O features for the Java platform (NIO.2) APIs. This chapter does not attempt to cover every networking feature that is part of the Java language, as the topic is quite large. However, it does provide a handful of recipes that are the most useful to a broad base of developers. You learn about a few of the standard networking concepts, such as sockets, and some newer concepts introduced with the latest release of the Java language. If you find this chapter interesting and want to learn more about Java networking, you can find lots of resources online.

16-1. Listening for Connections on the Server
Problem

You want to create a server application that listens for connections from a remote client.

Solution

Set up a server-side application that uses `java.net.ServerSocket` to listen for requests on a specified port. The following Java class is representative of one that would be deployed onto a server, and it listens for incoming requests on port 1234. When a request is received, the incoming message is printed to the command line, and a response is sent back to the client.

```java
import java.io.BufferedReader;
import java.io.IOException;
```

557

© Josh Juneau, Luciano Manelli 2022
J. Juneau and L. Manelli, *Java 17 Recipes*, https://doi.org/10.1007/978-1-4842-7963-2_16

```java
import java.io.InputStreamReader;
import java.io.PrintWriter;
import java.net.ServerSocket;
import java.net.Socket;
public class SocketServer {
public static void main(String a[]) {
        final int httpd = 1234;
        ServerSocket ssock = null;
        try {
            ssock = new ServerSocket(httpd);
            System.out.println("have opened port 1234 locally");
            Socket sock = ssock.accept();
            System.out.println("client has made socket connection");
    communicateWithClient(sock);
System.out.println("closing socket");
} catch (Exception e) {
System.out.println(e);
} finally {
try{
ssock.close();
} catch (IOException ex) {
System.out.println(ex);
}
}
}
    public static void communicateWithClient(Socket socket) {
        BufferedReader in = null;
        PrintWriter out = null;
        try {
            in = new BufferedReader(
                    new InputStreamReader(socket.getInputStream()));
            out = new PrintWriter(
                    socket.getOutputStream(), true);
            String s = null;
            out.println("Server received communication!");
```

```
        while ((s = in.readLine()) != null) {
            System.out.println("received from client: " + s);
            out.flush();
            break;
        }
    } catch (Exception e) {
        e.printStackTrace();
    } finally {
        try {
            in.close();
            out.close();
        } catch (IOException ex) {
            ex.printStackTrace();
        }
    }
    }
}
```

This recipe works in concert with Recipe 16-2. This example initiates the server, and executing this program simply prints "have opened port 1234 locally." But executing it along with the client built in Recipe 16-2 results in the following output from the SocketServer.

```
have opened port 1234 locally
client has made socket connection
received from client: Here is a test.
closing socket
```

Note   To run the two recipes so that they work with each other, first start the SocketServer program (open a command window and type **java SocketServer**) so that the client can create a socket using the port opened in the server program. After the SocketServer starts, initiate the SocketClient (open another command window and type **java SocketClient**) program to see the two work together.

Caution   This SocketServer program opens a port on your machine (1234). Be sure that you have a firewall set running on your machine; otherwise, you open port 1234 to everyone. This could result in your machine being attacked. Open ports create vulnerabilities for attackers to break into machines, kind of like leaving a door in your house open. Note that the example in this recipe has a minimal attack profile because the server is run through only one pass and prints only a single message from the client before the session is closed.

How It Works

Server applications can enable work to be performed via direct communication from one or more client applications. Client applications normally communicate to the server application, send messages or data to the server for processing, and then disconnect. The server application typically listens for client applications and then performs processing against a client request once a connection is received and accepted. For a client application to connect to a server application, the server application must be listening for connections and then processing the connection data somehow. You cannot simply run a client against any given host and port number combination because doing so would likely result in a refused connection error. The server-side application must do three things: open a port, accept and establish client connections, and then communicate with the client connection in some way. In the solution to this recipe, the SocketServer class does all three.

Starting with the main() method, the class opens a new socket on port 1234. This is done by creating a new instance of ServerSocket and passing a port number to it. The port number must not conflict with any other port currently in use on the server. It is important to note that ports below 1024 are usually reserved for operating system use, so choose a port number above that range. If you attempt to open a port already in use, the server socket will not be successfully created, and the program will fail. Next, the ServerSocket object's accept() method is called, returning a new Socket object. Calling the accept() method does nothing until a client attempts to connect to the server program on the port that has been set up. The accept() method waits idly until a connection is requested, and then it returns the new Socket object bound to the port set up on the server socket. This socket also contains the remote port and hostname of the client attempting the connection. It contains the information on two endpoints and uniquely identifies the Transmission Control Protocol (TCP) connection.

At this point, the server program can communicate with the client program, and it does so using the `PrintWriter` and `BufferedReader` objects. In the solution to this recipe, the `communicateWithClient()` method contains all the code necessary to accept messages from the client program, sends messages back to the client, and returns control to the `main()` method that closes the server socket. A new `BufferedReader` object can be created by generating a new `InputStreamReader` instance using the socket's input stream. Similarly, a new `PrintWriter` object can be created using the socket's output stream. Notice that this code must be wrapped in a `try-catch` block if these objects are not successfully created.

```
in = new BufferedReader(
                    new InputStreamReader(socket.getInputStream()));
out = new PrintWriter(
                    socket.getOutputStream(), true);
```

Once these objects have been successfully created, the server can communicate with the client. It uses a loop to do so, reading from the `BufferedReader` object (the client input stream) and sending messages back to the client using the `PrintWriter` object. In the solution to this recipe, the server closes the connection by issuing a `break`, which causes the loop to end. Control then returns to the `main()` method.

```
out.println("Server received communication!");
while ((s = in.readLine()) != null) {
    System.out.println("received from client: " + s);
    out.flush();
    break;
}
```

In a real-life server program, the server would most likely listen endlessly without using a break to end communication. Each client connection would spawn a separate thread to handle communication to handle multiple concurrent clients. The server would do something useful with the client communication as well. In an HTML server, it would send back an HTML message to the client. On an SMTP server, the client would send an email message to the server, and the server would then process the email and send it. Socket communication is used for just about any TCP transmission, and both the client and servers create new sockets to perform a successful communication.

16-2. Defining a Network Connection to a Server

Problem

You need to establish a connection to a remote server.

Solution

Create a socket connection to the remote server using its name and port number to listen for incoming client requests. The following example class creates a socket connection to a remote server. The code then sends a textual message to the server and receives a response. In the example, the server that the client is attempting to contact is named server-name, and the port number is 1234.

Tip   To create a connection to a local program running on the client machine, set the server name to 127.0.0.1. This is done within the source listing for this recipe. Usually, local connections such as this are used for testing purposes only.

```
public class SocketClient {
    public static Socket socket = null;
    public static PrintWriter out;
    public static BufferedReader in;
    public static void main(String[] args) {
        createConnection("127.0.0.1", 1234);
    }
    public static void createConnection(String host, int port) {
        try {
            //Create socket connection
            socket = new Socket(host, port);
            // Obtain a handle on the socket output
            out = new PrintWriter(socket.getOutputStream(),
                    true);
```

```java
        // Obtain a handle on the socket input
        in = new BufferedReader(new InputStreamReader(
                socket.getInputStream()));
        testConnection();
        System.out.println("Closing the connection...");
        out.flush();
        out.close();
        in.close();
        socket.close();
        System.exit(0);
        } catch (UnknownHostException e) {
        System.out.println(e);
        System.exit(1);
        } catch (IOException e) {
        System.out.println(e);
        System.exit(1);
        }
    }
}

public static void testConnection() {
    String serverResponse = null;
    if (socket != null && in != null && out != null) {
        System.out.println("Successfully connected, now testing...");
        try {
            // Send data to server
            out.println("Here is a test.");
            // Receive data from server
            while((serverResponse = in.readLine()) != null)
            System.out.println(serverResponse);
            } catch (IOException e) {
            System.out.println(e);
            System.exit(1);
        }
    }
}
}
```

If you're testing this client against a server that successfully accepts the request, you see the following result.

```
Successfully connected, now testing...
Server received communication!
Closing the connection...
```

Note   This program does nothing on its own. To create a server-side socket application that accepts this connection for a complete test, see Recipe 16-1. If you attempt to run this class without specifying a server host listening on the provided port, you receive this exception: `java.net.ConnectException: Connection refused.`

How It Works

Every client/server connection occurs via a *socket*, which is an endpoint in a communication link between two different programs. Sockets have port numbers assigned to them, which act as an identifier for the TCP/IP layer to use when attempting a connection. A server program that accepts requests from client machines typically listens for new connections on a specified port number. When a client wants to make a request to the server, it creates a new socket utilizing the hostname of the server and the port on which the server is listening and attempts to establish a connection with that socket. If the server accepts the socket, then the connection is successful.

This recipe discusses the client side of the socket connection, so we do not go into the details of what occurs on the server side. However, more information regarding the server side of a connection is covered in Recipe 16-1. The example class in the solution to this recipe represents how a client-side program attempts and establishes connections to a server-side program. In this recipe, the `createConnection()` method performs the actual connection. It accepts a server hostname and port number, which creates the socket. Within the `createConnection()` method, the server hostname and port number are passed to the `Socket` class constructor, creating a new `Socket` object. Next, a `PrintWriter` object is created using the `Socket` object's output stream, and a `BufferedReader` object is created using the `Socket` object's input stream.

```
//Create socket connection
socket = new Socket(host, port);
// Obtain a handle on the socket output
out = new PrintWriter(socket.getOutputStream(),
                                    true);
// Obtain a handle on the socket input
in = new BufferedReader(new InputStreamReader(
            socket.getInputStream()));
```

After creating the socket and obtaining the socket's output stream and input stream, the client can write to the `PrintWriter` to send data to the server. Similarly, to receive a response from the server, the client reads from the `BufferedReader` object. The `testConnection()` method simulates a conversation between the client and the server program using the newly created socket. To do this, the `socket`, `in`, and `out` variables are checked to ensure that they are not equal to `null`. If they are not equal to `null`, the client attempts to send a message to the server by sending a message to the output stream using `out.println("Here is a test.")`. A loop is then created to listen for a response from the server by calling the `in.readLine()` method until nothing else is received. It then prints the messages that are received.

```
if (socket != null && in != null && out != null) {
    System.out.println("Successfully connected, now testing...");
    try {
        // Send data to server
        out.println("Here is a test.");
        // Receive data from server
        while((serverResponse = in.readLine()) != null)
            System.out.println(serverResponse);
    } catch (IOException e) {
        System.out.println(e);
        System.exit(1);
    }
}
```

The java.net.Socket class is true to the nature of the Java programming language. It enables developers to code against a platform-independent API to communicate with network protocols that are specific to different platforms. It abstracts the details of each platform from the developer and provides a straightforward and consistent implementation for enabling client/server communications.

16-3. Broadcasting to a Group of Recipients

Problem

You want to broadcast datagrams to zero or more hosts identified by a single address.

Solution

Use datagram multicasting using the DatagramChannel class. The DatagramChannel class enables more than one client to connect to a group and listen for datagrams that have been broadcasted from a server. The following sets of code demonstrate this technique using a client/server approach. The class demonstrates a multicast client.

```
package org.java17recipes.chapter16.recipe16_4;
import java.io.IOException;
import java.net.InetAddress;
import java.net.InetSocketAddress;
import java.net.NetworkInterface;
import java.net.StandardProtocolFamily;
import java.net.StandardSocketOptions;
import java.nio.ByteBuffer;
import java.nio.channels.DatagramChannel;
import java.nio.channels.MembershipKey;
public class MulticastClient {
    public MulticastClient() {
    }
    public static void main(String[] args) {
        try {
            // Obtain Supported network Interface
            NetworkInterface networkInterface = null;
```

```
java.util.Enumeration<NetworkInterface> enumNI =
NetworkInterface.getNetworkInterfaces();
java.util.Enumeration<InetAddress> enumIA;
NetworkInterface ni;
InetAddress ia;
ILOOP:
while (enumNI.hasMoreElements()) {
    ni = enumNI.nextElement();
    enumIA = ni.getInetAddresses();
    while (enumIA.hasMoreElements()) {
        ia = enumIA.nextElement();
        if (ni.isUp() && ni.supportsMulticast()
                && !ni.isVirtual() && !ni.isLoopback()
                && !ia.isSiteLocalAddress()) {
            networkInterface = ni;
            break ILOOP;
        }
    }
}
// Address within range
int port = 5239;
InetAddress group = InetAddress.getByName("226.18.84.25");
final DatagramChannel client = DatagramChannel.
open(StandardProtocolFamily.INET);
client.setOption(StandardSocketOptions.SO_REUSEADDR, true);
client.bind(new InetSocketAddress(port));
client.setOption(StandardSocketOptions.IP_MULTICAST_IF,
networkInterface);

System.out.println("Joining group: " + group + " with network
interface " + networkInterface);
// Multicasting join
MembershipKey key = client.join(group, networkInterface);
client.open();
```

```
            // receive message as a client
            final ByteBuffer buffer = ByteBuffer.allocateDirect(4096);
            buffer.clear();
            System.out.println("Waiting to receive message");
            // Configure client to be passive and non.blocking
            // client.configureBlocking(false);
            client.receive(buffer);
            System.out.println("Client Received Message:");
            buffer.flip();
            byte[] arr = new byte[buffer.remaining()];
            buffer.get(arr, 0, arr.length);

            System.out.println(new String(arr));
            System.out.println("Disconnecting...performing a single test
            pass only");
            client.disconnect();
        } catch (IOException ex) {
            ex.printStackTrace();
        }
    }
}
```

Next, a server class broadcasts datagrams to the address that multicast clients are connected to. The following code demonstrates a multicast server.

```
package org.java17recipes.chapter16.recipe16_4;
import java.io.IOException;
import java.net.InetAddress;
import java.net.InetSocketAddress;
import java.nio.ByteBuffer;
import java.nio.channels.DatagramChannel;

public class MulticastServer extends Thread {

    protected ByteBuffer message = null;
    public MulticastServer() {
    }
```

```java
public static void main(String[] args) {
    MulticastServer server = new MulticastServer();
    server.start();
}

@Override
public void run() {
    try {
        // send the response to the client at "address" and "port"
        InetAddress address = InetAddress.getByName("226.18.84.25");
        int port = 5239;
        DatagramChannel server = DatagramChannel.open().bind(null);
        System.out.println("Sending datagram packet to group " +
        address + " on port " + port);
        message = ByteBuffer.wrap("Hello to all listeners".getBytes());
        server.send(message, new InetSocketAddress(address, port));
        server.disconnect();
    } catch (IOException e) {
        e.printStackTrace();
    }
}
}
```

The server can broadcast a message to each client that is a member of the group. Once the server is started, it broadcasts the message, and the client receives it.

In this recipe, two classes—MulticastServer and MulticastClient—work in concert, so when MulticastClient is executed, it results in the following output.

```
Joining group: /226.18.84.25 with network interface name: networkName
Waiting to receive message
```

After the MulticastClient program starts, you can execute the MulticastServer program to see the two works together. The following is the MulticastServer output.

```
Sending datagram packet to group /226.18.84.25 on port 5239
```

The MulticastClient output is updated.

```
Client Received Message:
Hello to all listeners
```

How It Works

Multicasting is the ability to broadcast a message to a group of listeners in a single transmission. A good analogy of multicasting is radio. Thousands of people can tune in to a single broadcast event and listen to the same message. Computers can do similar things when sending messages to listeners. A group of client machines can tune in to the same address and port number to receive a message that a server broadcasts to that address and port. The Java language provides multicasting functionality via datagram messaging. Datagrams are independent, nonguaranteed messages that can be delivered over the network to clients. (Being *nonguaranteed* means that the arrival, arrival time, and content are not predictable.) Unlike messages sent over TCP, sending a datagram is a nonblocking event, and the sender is not notified of the receipt of the message. Datagrams are sent using the User Datagram Protocol (UDP) rather than TCP. The ability to send multicast messages via UDP is one benefit over TCP, if the ordering, reliability, and data integrity of the message are not mission-critical.

Java facilitates multicast messaging via the `MulticastChannel` interface. Classes that implement the `MulticastChannel` interface have multicasting enabled and can therefore broadcast to groups and receive group broadcasts. One such class is the `DatagramChannel`, which is a selectable channel for datagram-oriented sockets. In the solution to this recipe, both a client and a server program communicate via multicast messaging. The `DatagramChannel` class is used on both sides of the communication. A `DatagramChannel` must be configured in a specific way to be used for accepting multicast messages. Specifically, some options need to be set on the open `DatagramChannel` client. We discuss those options shortly. The following steps are required for creating a client that receives multicast messages.

1. Open a datagram channel.

2. Set the datagram channel options that are required to multicast.

3. Join the client to a multicast group and return a `MembershipKey` object.

4. Open the client.

In the solution to this recipe, the client application begins by obtaining a reference to the network interface that receives the broadcast messages. Setting up a NetworkInterface is required for multicasting. Next, a port number and a multicasting IP address are chosen. The group or registered listeners use the IP address to listen for broadcasts. The port number must not be in use; otherwise, an exception is thrown. For IPv4 multicasting, the IP address must range from 224.0.0.0 to 239.255.255.255, inclusive. This port and IP address is the same one used by a server to broadcast the message. Next, a new datagram channel is opened using StandardProtocolFamily. INET. The choices for opening a datagram channel are StandardProtocolFamily.INET or StandardProtocolFamily.INET6, corresponding to IPv4 and IPv6, respectively. The first option that is set on the datagram channel is StandardSocketOptions. SO_REUSEADDR, and it is set to true. This indicates that multiple clients can "reuse" the address or use it simultaneously. This needs to be set for a multicast to occur. The client is then bound to the port using a new InetSocketAddress instance. Last, the StandardSocketOptions.IP_MULTICAST_IF option is set to the network interface that is used. This option represents the outgoing interface for multicast datagrams sent by the datagram-oriented socket.

```
client.setOption(StandardSocketOptions.SO_REUSEADDR, true);
client.bind(new InetSocketAddress(port));
client.setOption(StandardSocketOptions.IP_MULTICAST_IF, networkInterface);
```

Once these options have been set and the port has been bound to the datagram channel, it is ready to join the group of listeners. This can be done by calling the Datagr amChanneljoin(InetAddress, NetworkInterface) method, passing the group address and network interface that are used by the client. As a result, a java.nio.channels. MembershipKey object is produced. It is a token that represents the membership of an IP multicast group. Last, the DatagramChannelopen() method is called, which opens the channel to listen for broadcasts. At this point, the client is ready to receive multicast messages, and it waits for a message to be received.

```
MembershipKey key = client.join(group, networkInterface);
client.open();
```

The next lines of code in the client take care of receiving messages from the server. To receive a broadcasted message, a byte buffer is created and then eventually passed to the DatagramChannel class's receive() method. Once the receive() method is called, the client pauses until a message is received. You can disable this feature by calling the

DatagramChannel configureBlocking(boolean) method and passing a false value. Next, the ByteBuffer is converted to a string value and printed out by repositioning the buffer index at 0 using the flip() method and then pulling the text starting at index 0 to the last index into a byte[]. Finally, be sure to disconnect the client when you're finished. That wraps up the client code portion.

```
// Configure client to be passive and non.blocking
// client.configureBlocking(false);
client.receive(buffer);
// client pauses until a message is received... in this case
System.out.println("Client Received Message:");
buffer.flip();
byte[] arr = new byte[buffer.remaining()];
buffer.get(arr, 0, arr.length);
System.out.println(new String(arr));
System.out.println("Disconnecting...performing a single test pass only");
client.disconnect();
```

Note   In the example to this recipe, a single pass is performed, and the client is disconnected. For extended listening, you need a loop with a timeout and provide tests for an ending state.

The server code is fairly basic. You can see that the MulticastServer class extends Thread. This means that this server application could run in a thread separate from other code within an application. If another class initiated the MulticastServer class's run() method, it would run in a thread separate from the class that initiated it. The run() method must exist in any class that extends Thread.

The bulk of the server code resides in the run() method. A new InetAddress object is created using the same IP address that the client registered with to join the multicast group. The same port number is also declared in the server code. These two objects are used later in the code block to send the message. A new datagram channel is opened and bound to null. The null value is important because by setting SocketAddress equal to null, the socket is bound to an address that is assigned automatically. Next, a byte buffer is created that contains a message that broadcasts to any listeners. The message is then sent using the DatagramChannel class's send(ByteBuffer, InetSocketAddress) method. The send() method in the solution accepts the message as a ByteBuffer object and a new InetSocketAddress instance created by using the address and port, which was declared at the beginning of the block. We told you we'd get back to those!

```
server.send(message, new InetSocketAddress(address, port));
```

At this point, the client would receive the message sent by the server. As for the client demonstrated in the solution to this recipe, it would then disconnect. A different class would likely initiate the server in a real-world scenario. Its run() method would contain a loop that would continue to execute until all messages have been broadcast or the loop was told to stop. The client would probably not disconnect until after a user initiated a shutdown.

Note   If your laptop or server uses a different network protocol other than standard IPv4, then results may vary. Please be sure to do a sufficient amount of testing before sending your code to a production environment.

16-4. Generating and Reading from URLs
Problem

You want to generate URLs programmatically in your application. Once the URLs have been created, you'd like to read data from them for use in your application.

Solution

Use the java.net.URL class to create a URL. There are a few different ways to generate a URL depending on the address you are attempting to work with. This solution demonstrates some of these options for creating URL objects and comments indicating the differences. Once the URL objects have been created, one of the URLs is read into BufferedReader and printed to the command line.

```
import java.io.BufferedReader;
import java.io.IOException;
import java.io.InputStreamReader;
import java.net.MalformedURLException;
```

```java
import java.net.URL;
public class GenerateAndReadUrl {
    public static void main(String[] args) {
        try {
            // Generate absolute URL
            URL url1 = new URL("https://openjdk.java.net");
            System.out.println(url1.toString());
            // Generate URL for pages with a common base
            URL url2 = new URL(url1, " projects/jdk/17");
            // Generate URL from different pieces of data
            URL url3 = new URL("http", "openjdk.java.net", "projects/jdk/17");
            readFromUrl(url1);
        } catch (MalformedURLException ex) {
            ex.printStackTrace();
        }
    }
    /**
     * Open URL stream as an input stream and print contents to command line.
     *
     * @param url
     */
    public static void readFromUrl(URL url) {
        try {
            BufferedReader in = new BufferedReader(
                    new InputStreamReader(
                    url.openStream()));
            String inputLine;
            while ((inputLine = in.readLine()) != null) {
                System.out.println(inputLine);
            }
            in.close();
        } catch (IOException ex) {
            ex.printStackTrace();
        }
    }
}
```

Running this program results in the HTML from the URL resource identified as `url1` being printed to the command line, as seen in the console shown in Figure 16-1.

```
Problems  @ Javadoc  Declaration  Search  Console ×
<terminated> GenerateAndReadUrl [Java Application] C:\jdk-17\bin\javaw.exe  (3 dic 2021, 14:07:35 – 14:07:37)
https://openjdk.java.net
<!DOCTYPE html PUBLIC "-//W3C//DTD XHTML 1.0 Strict//EN" "http://www.w3.org/TR/xhtml1/DTD/xhtml1-strict.dtd"><
/**/
        #openjdk-sidebar-logo IMG { display: none; }
        TABLE.main { border-collapse:  collapse; margin-top: 1.5ex; margin-right: 5em; }
        .main TD { padding-top: 4.5ex; padding-left: 2em; vertical-align: top; }
        .main TD:first-child + TD { padding-top: 5ex; }

        #announcements, #blogs { margin-right: 3em; }
        #announcements { padding-top: 10ex; }
        #blogs { padding-top: 6ex; }

        .head .leader { height: 1px; background: black; }
        .head .text { position: relative;
                      top: -1.3ex; margin-bottom: -1.3ex; }
        .head .text SPAN { background: white; }
        .head .text .title { font-weight: bold; padding-right: 1em; }
        .head .note { float: right; background: white; padding: 0pt 1em;
                      margin-right: 2em; }

        TABLE.ann { border-collapse: collapse; margin-top: 1ex; }
        .ann TD { vertical-align: top; }
```

Figure 16-1. *Output of Recipe 16-4*

How It Works

Creating URLs in Java code is fairly straightforward, thanks to the `java.net.URL` class, which does all the heavy lifting. A URL is a character string that points to a resource on the Internet. Sometimes it is useful to create URLs in Java code to read content from, or push content to, the Internet resource that the URL is pointing to. In the solution to this recipe, a few different URL objects are created, demonstrating the different constructors available for use.

The easiest route to use for creating a URL is to pass the standard readable URL string for a resource located on the Internet to the java.net.URL class to create a new URL instance. In the solution, an absolute URL is passed to the constructor to create the `url1` object.

```
URL url1 = new URL("https://openjdk.java.net ");
```

Another useful way to create a URL is to pass two arguments to the URL constructor and create a relative URL. It is useful to base relative URLs on the location of another URL.

For instance, if a particular site has several different pages, you could create a URL pointing to one of the subpages relative to the URL of the main site. Such is the case with the url2 object in the solution to this recipe.

```
URL url2 = new URL(url1, "projects/jdk/17");
```

As you can see, the path search/node/jdk8 is relative to the URL known as url1. In the end, the human-readable format of the url2 object is represented as http://www.java.net/search/node/jdk8. There are a couple more constructors for creating URL objects that take more than two arguments. Those constructors are as follows.

```
new URL (String protocol, String host, String port, String path);
new URL (String protocol, String host, String path);
```

In the solution, the second of the two constructors is demonstrated. The protocol, hostname, and path of the resource are passed to the constructor to create the url3 object. These last two constructors are usually most useful when you're dynamically generating a URL.

16-5. Parsing a URL
Problem

You want to programmatically gather information from a URL for your application.

Solution

Parse the URL using the built-in URL class methods. In the following example class named ParseUrl, a URL object is created and then parsed using the built-in URL class methods to gather information regarding the URL. After the information has been retrieved from the URL, it prints to the command line and creates another URL.

```
import java.net.MalformedURLException;
import java.net.URL;
public static void main(String[] args) {
URL url1 = null;
```

```
try {
        // Generate absolute URL
        url1 = new URL("https://link.springer.com/
        search?query=Manelli+Java");
        String host = url1.getHost();
        String path = url1.getPath();
        String query = url1.getQuery();
        String protocol = url1.getProtocol();
        String authority = url1.getAuthority();
        String ref = url1.getRef();
        System.out.println("The URL " + url1.toString() + " parses to
        the following:\n");
        System.out.println("Host: " + host + "\n");
        System.out.println("Path: " + path + "\n");
        System.out.println("Query: " + query + "\n");
        System.out.println("Protocol: " + protocol + "\n");
        System.out.println("Authority: " + authority + "\n");
        System.out.println("Reference: " + ref + "\n");
    } catch (IOException ex) {
        ex.printStackTrace();
    }
}
```

When this code is executed, the following lines are displayed.

The URL https://link.springer.com/search?query=Manelli+Java parses to the following:

Host: link.springer.com

Path: /search

Query: query=Manelli+Java

Protocol: https

Authority: link.springer.com

Reference: null

How It Works

When constructing and working with URLs in an application, it is sometimes beneficial to extract information pertaining to a URL. This can be easily done using the URL built-in class methods, which can call a given URL and return strings of information. Table 16-1 explains the accessor methods available in the URL class for obtaining information.

Table 16-1. *Accessor Methods for Querying URLs*

Method	URL Information Returned
getAuthority()	Authority component
getFile()	File name component
getHost()	Hostname component
getPath()	Path component
getProtocol()	Protocol identifier component
getRef()	Reference component
getQuery()	Query component

Each of these accessor methods returns a string value that can be used for informational purposes or for constructing other URLs dynamically, as was done in the example. If you look at the results from the solution to this recipe, you can see the information obtained regarding the URL via the accessor methods listed in Table 16-1. Most of the accessors are self-explanatory. However, a couple of them could use further explanation. The getFile() method returns the file name of the URL. The file name is the same as concatenating the value returned from getPath() with the value returned from getQuery(). The getRef() method may not be very straightforward. The reference component returned by calling the getRef() method refers to the "fragment" that may be appended to the end of a URL. For instance, a fragment is indicated using the pound character (#), followed by a string that usually corresponds to a subsection on a particular web page. Given the URL such as the following, recipe16_6 would be returned using the getRef() method.

```
http://www.java17recipes.org/chapters/chapter16#recipe16_6
```

Although it's not always needed, the ability to parse a URL to obtain information can come in very handy at times. Because the Java language has helper methods built into the `java.net.URL` class, it makes gathering information on URLs a piece of cake.

16-6. Summary

This chapter covered a few basic networking features of the Java language that are robust and easy to use, from using socket connections and URLs to broadcasting messages via the `DatagramChannel` class.

Index

A, B

Automatic Resource Management (ARM), 341, 477

C

Catching exceptions, 331–333
Collection types, 239
    alertListLegacy() method, 287
    arrays, 254–260
    concrete parameterized type, 263
    diamond operator, 267
    dynamic arrays, 268–272
    enum type, 239
    equals() method, 243
    external iteration, 280
    FieldType enum type, 244
    fixed set constants, 239–243
    generics, 261
    GradeAnalyzer class, 254–258
    intelligent constants, 243–248
    intermediate operation, 281
    internal iteration, 280
    isValidSwitchType() method, 253
    iteration, 277–282
    iterator() method, 272
    map classes (HashMap/
        TreeMap), 282–288
    objects iterable, 272–277
    object types/methods, 260–268
    ordinal() method, 242
    parallel execution, 288–290
    programmatic looping, 280
    raw types, 264
    RockPaperScissors class, 248–250
    singular expression, 248–254
    static and final modifiers, 241
    Stock objects, 277
    StockPortfolio class, 272–274, 276, 277
    StockScreener main() method, 271
    summary() method, 287
    switch expression, 251
    SwitchTypeChecker, 253
    terminal operation, 281
    type erasure/parameter, 263
    unbounded wildcard, 267
    values() and valueOf(String)
        methods, 243
    wildcard, 265, 266
Command-line interface (CLI), 426, 430
Compact strings, 79
Concurrency
    asynchronous, 391–394
    awaitTermination() method, 372–374
    background tasks, 351–353
    collection, 359–363
    CompletableFuture object, 392–394
    fulfillOrder() method, 364
    inventoryLock.unlock() method, 369
    inventoryMap/customerOrders
        methods, 364–366, 368
    learning tasks, 351
    locking, 371
    modifications, 364–372

© Josh Juneau, Luciano Manelli 2022
J. Juneau and L. Manelli, *Java 17 Recipes*, https://doi.org/10.1007/978-1-4842-7963-2

S

Printed in the United States
by Baker & Taylor Publisher Services